A History of the Artists Rifles

A History of the Artists Rifles
1859 – 1947

by

Barry Gregory

Pen & Sword
MILITARY

First published in Great Britain in 2006 by
Pen & Sword Military
an imprint of
Pen & Sword Books Ltd
47 Church Street
Barnsley
South Yorkshire
S70 2AS

Copyright © Barry Gregory and The Artists Rifles Association 2006
ISBN 978-1-84415-503-3

The right of Barry Gregory to be identified as Author of this Work has been asserted by him in accordance with the Copyright, Designs and Patents Act 1988.

A CIP catalogue record for this book is
available from the British Library
All rights reserved. No part of this book may be reproduced or transmitted in any form or by any means, electronic or mechanical including photocopying, recording or by any information storage and retrieval system, without permission from the Publisher in writing.

Typeset in 10/12 Sabon by
Lamorna Publishing Services

Printed and bound in England by Biddles Ltd.

For a complete list of Pen & Sword titles please contact
PEN & SWORD BOOKS LIMITED
47 Church Street, Barnsley, South Yorkshire, S70 2AS, England
E-mail: enquiries@pen-and-sword.co.uk
Website: www.pen-and-sword.co.uk

Contents

Foreword . . . . *vii*
Acknowledgements . . . .*xi*
Introduction . . . .*xiii*

1. Cum Marte Minerva, The Grey Black and Silver,
   1859-1882 1
2. The Royal Academy and the Artists Rifles,
   1768-1947 17
3. Frederick Leighton, The Royal Academy
   and the Artists Rifles, 1830-1896 39
4. Sir Robert W. Edis KBE, CB, VD, JP, FSA,
   1839-1927 48
5. The Boer War and the Artists Rifles,
   1899-1902 75
6. Walter C. Horsley, CB, VD, TD, JP, 1855-1934 88
7. H.A.R. May CB, VD, 1863-1930 102
8. The Artists at War, 1914 112
9. The Artists at War. The Duke's Road Depot,
   The Regiment Expands and Gidea Park, 1914-1915 122
10. The Artists at War.
    With the 1st Battalion in France, 1915 139
11. The Artists at War. On Two Fronts.
    The 1st and 2nd Battalions at Work, 1916 154
12. The Artists at War, Passchendaele. 'Over the Top', 1917 167
13. The Artists at War, The Year of Victory, 1918 177
14. The Great War, 1914-1918 188
15. Between the Wars, 1919-1929 212

16. Between the Wars, 1930-1935 230
17. Between the Wars, Crisis at Duke's Road, 1936-1938 248
18. The Second World War, 1939-1945 270
19. Postscript, 1945-1947 292
    Epilogue 300

Appendix I   Art in the Artists 302
Appendix II   Eight Artists Rifles VCs
                in the Great War and Why 313
Appendix III The Artists Rifles Conditions of
                Service and Notes (1920) 317
Appendix IV 'Cum Marte Minerva' 322
Appendix V   The Elfin Oak 323

    Bibliography......................................325
    Index 326

Foreword

by

Air Chief Marshal Sir John Barraclough KCB CBE DFC AFC FRAeS

The honour and compliment of being asked to write this foreword brings with it also the little difficulty of realizing that it is no less than seventy-one years since I joined the Artists Rifles at 17 Duke's Road, London in 1935. However my personal memories are as vivid as if of yesterday: the Royal Academy Guard, the Easter and Summer camps and the great State ceremonies of King George V's funeral and the Coronation of King George VI. All of which, amidst our routine training, was typical of the pattern of our Regiment and those whose dedication made it so unique. As with other Artists who ventured into different fields, that background was a foundation for our new military careers, whether from the echoing Drill Hall at Duke's Road or the challenge of the Bisley ranges.

The Artists were a prolific source of young officers for all three Services from the time that 'the First Fifty' were commissioned in the field in the Great War at the express request of the Commander-in-Chief of the Expeditionary Force – Sir John French. Armed with just a two hour talk from the commanding officer and a copy of the *Field Service Pocket Book*, they put up their first 'pips' and set forth to their new regiments. The Commander of the 7th Division, when commenting on how successful they were, asked, 'Have you any more like them?' Indeed we had, and between 1914 and 1918 no less than 10,256 officers were to be provided by the Artists to the Royal Marines, the Royal Flying Corps and of course the Army.

It was in the main from their new units, that the Artists set such a shining record of valour in the field with no fewer than eight Victoria Crosses, fifty-two Distinguished Service Orders and nearly a thousand other awards for gallantry in the face of the enemy. When that group of young painters, actors, poets, musicians and architects first proposed setting up a corps of Artists in 1859 they could not have dreamt that more than 15,000 would pass through its ranks in the next sixty years of whom, alas, over 2,500 were to make the ultimate sacrifice and be reported killed or missing in action.

Eminent men from the professions in the ranks of the Artists – largely but not solely from the arts – made up a galaxy of stars which have shone brightly throughout the history of the Regiment, to be especially well depicted by the author. To mention the merest few, they ranged from Lord Leighton, a President of the Royal Academy with others, from the Pre-Raphaelites to Wilfred Owen the poet and war artists like the brothers Paul and John Nash. Of later times, Corporal Barnes Wallis was yet to achieve his fame as an aircraft designer and inventor of the dam-busting bomb. While it was a regimental contemporary and fellow airman Squadron Leader Kenneth Doran, who was awarded the first Distinguished Flying Cross in the Second World War.

As things turned out, the rather surprising combination of the professions of arms and arts fitted quite easily into the ways of the Regiment and is well symbolized in the cap badge by Mars and Minerva, the Roman deities of War and Wisdom. This association was to be given an enduring and endearing currency by the wit of the painter James Whistler when describing the then, Sir Frederick Leighton, the commanding officer, as the 'Colonel of the Royal Academy and the President of the Artists Rifles – aye, and he paints a little!'

After the post-war demise of the Regiment in 1947 the War Office decision to re-establish the Special Air Service within the Territorial Army by merging the very different military traditions of the SAS and the Artists as the 21st SAS Regiment (Artists) TA, perhaps owed more to inspiration than to logic. But through mutual respect, we like to think the two traditions have bonded into the SAS of today – a regiment that is an unfailing source of pride and interest to us Old Artists. But that is another splendid story which happily can be picked up from the Epilogue to this volume, most appropriately subscribed by the present commanding officer of 21 SAS Regiment (Artists) (Reserve).

I know I speak for the Regiment at large, and many others besides, in thanking and congratulating Barry Gregory, a former 21st SAS officer, for taking on this daunting and lengthy task of research and authorship so admirably and eloquently. All who value the importance of our military history are much in his debt. With that, must also go a record of appreciation to the Artists Rifles Association for commissioning this long overdue account of one of the elite London Volunteer regiments.

J B
May 2006

Acknowledgements

I should especially like to thank Roy Fielder, as chairman of the Steering Group, for his support and encouragement throughout the six years it has taken me to research and write this book. My thanks also to the following members of the Steering Group for their useful comments: Bill Heath, (the late) John Gavin, Tony Poucher and Ian Dunning. I am most grateful to Graham Phimister for photographing sites of particular importance to the Artists Rifles, and I am also greatly indebted both to Oliver and Heather Sims, who incorporated the illustrations and much more, and to Derek Newton who read the manuscript. I should also like to thank my editor, Tom Hartman, John Mitchell, who drew the map, and Mrs Cath Warner who typed the manuscript.

I am most grateful to the following 'Old Artists' serving in the Regiment in the 1920s and 1930s for their letters which I found most interesting.

The late C.J.W. Bean, the late Stuart Bowles, Roddy Clube, Brian Collins, the late John D. Foxall, Douglas Garner, A.C. Goodger, Mrs K.J. Habersham (on behalf of P.M. Torrance), R.H.E. Heath, Peter Jamieson, the late Horace Lashbrook, Bernard Lush, Rex Lamming, Trevor Parnacott, the late Miles Partridge, Les Plowright, Jeff Powell, John Riggs, the late Ralph Robotham, the late Dr. J.M. Roderick, Henry Seaborne, Bill Scott, J.T. Stevenson, J.P. Stiles, Roderick Thomson (on behalf of D.J. and R.A. Thomson), E.H. Van Maurik, Louis Vanderpump, the late Bill Ward, Harold Warren, J.K. Yerbury and the late J.L. Young.

Barry Gregory, 2006

Introduction

Traditionally Britain – right up until the Second World War of 1939-45 – has relied on command of the sea as the main line of defence against invasion, itself a constant theme in English and British history, and in consequence the existence of a large standing Regular Army was distrusted on the grounds that it was both unnecessary and might promote military despotism, a lingering fear which actually pre-dated the creation of such a standing army in the seventeenth century. There was a distinct preference for amateur or temporary soldiers – the auxiliary forces brought into existence as needs dictated for defence against invasion – and as a means of preserving domestic order in the event of civil disturbances. Sometimes referred to as the 'old constitutional force', the oldest of the auxiliary forces was the Militia, which had its origins in the military obligations of the Anglo-Saxon fyrd.

The early Middle Ages saw the emergence of a quasi-professional military aristocracy which performed military service as required by the Sovereign in return for the right to control land and service. These rights were usually granted to noblemen or gentlemen of high estate who recruited the military force from the so-called free men or peasants who worked their land, which in turn provided the free men and their families with sustenance. A certain continuity derived from this obligation requiring service in the fyrd which was transmitted through medieval legislation such as the Assize of Arms in 1181 and the Statute of Westminster in 1285, which was enshrined in the first actual militia statutes of 1558 abolishing the fyrd. Thereafter the Militia had a formal statutory existence until 1604, from 1648 to 1735, from 1757 to 1831, and from 1852 to 1908.

Legally, units of the Militia could not be required to serve overseas but only as individual volunteers. The Militia and Lords Lieutenant from their inception in Tudor times provided the organization of recruitment. The Crown ordered the Lords Lieutenant and Commissioners of Musters to provide so many men from their county. For the expedition to Normandy in 1591, for example, a total of 3,400 men were demanded from twenty counties graded according to size, from 500 from Yorkshire to 50 from Surrey. In five months in Normandy sickness reduced the 3,400 men to 800 effectives. The ordinary male people of England and Wales, except during the period in the 1580s when the country was threatened with invasion by Catholic Spain, did not spring to volunteer, especially when the requirement rose to 5,000 men a year.

The actual basis of the service varied considerably but essentially the obligation was one imposed on property until 1757 and then as a tax upon manpower with the force raised by compulsory ballot until 1831, although a voluntary system was then applied from 1852 until 1908. The term 'trained bands' was used from 1573 to 1663 to describe the better-trained portion of the Militia, and continued to be used in respect of the Militia of London until 1793.

While Militia service had always implied an element of compulsion, it was only in 1757 that England and Wales followed the lead of the continental states by introducing the compulsory ballot. To create a force of 32,000 men serving a three-year term of service each county was required to submit an annual return of eligible men aged between 18 and 50, the numerous exceptions including clergy, teachers and those men with large families. A county quota could then be apportioned so that each theoretically contributed the same proportion of its ablebodied manpower, although in reality quotas fixed in 1757 remained unchanged until 1796, irrespective of intervening population change. A general lieutenancy meeting would order Chief Constables to produce hundredal lists – a task effected in turn by parish constables – and then proportionally fix hundredal quotas. A series of subdivision meetings would fix parish quotas and ballot to fill them. After the ballot there was a chance to claim exemption by substitution or by payment of a £10 fine, any deficiencies then being made up.

There were a variety of means by which the Militiaman could cheat the system. One way when the balloon went up was for the man picked by the ballot to pay another man to take his place. Agencies sprung up throughout the country to recruit the substitutes and take a cut of the payment offered by the reluctant Militiaman to dodge the service. This was unsatisfactory so far as the Army was concerned as the substitutes were unlikely to have had any military training. A Militiaman could also become a 'professional volunteer' accepting the bounty for signing on in one county before proceeding to another or more counties to sign on in the muster roll in each of them, thus profiting from a rich harvest of bounties.

Parliament often had reason to doubt the wisdom of arming civilians. Militiamen sometimes forgot their mission of 'cleansing and scouring the King's enemies', and in an edict issued in 1541 we find that:

> ...divers malicious and evil-disposed myandes and purposes have wilfully and shamefully committed divers detestable and shameful murthers, robberies, felonies, riots and routs, with crossbowes, little short hand guns, and little hagbuts, to the great pill and contynuall fear and damage of the Kynge's most loving subjects ... and now of late the said evil-disposed persons, and doe yet daylie use to ride and goe in the Kynge's highways .. with little hand guns, ready furnished with quarrell gunpowder, fyer and touche, to the great pill ... It is therefore enacted that these fire-arms shall be of a certain fixed length, 'provided always ... that it shall be lawfull for all gentlemen, yeomen, serving men, demyhake or hagbut, or any butt or bank of earth onlye, in place convenient for same' ... wherebye they may be better aydo and assist in the defence of the Realme when nede shall require.

It would appear from this edict that highway robbery was permissible provided the robbers observed certain rules!

In contrast to the Militia as an institution of the State, supposedly self-sufficient Volunteer forces existed under an often confusing variety of terms of service at other times or simultaneously with the Militia such as during the 1650s, 1660s, 1715, 1745, and from 1778 to 1782 when the first specific volunteer legislation was enacted; volunteers were principally created, however, during the French Revolutionary and Napoleonic Wars (1793-1802/1803-15), being raised as both Voluntary infantry and artillery, but also as the so-called Militia in 1808 but this was suspended in 1816, although the legislation remained on the statute book until 1921. Other Volunteer bodies survived post-war reductions but had virtually all disappeared by the 1840s to be revived in 1859.

In Elizabethan England the trained bands turned out on average ten days, spread throughout the year. Restoration Militiamen trained perhaps on twelve days per annum but, from 1762 onwards, the annual training for the Militia was a continuous twenty-eight days in midsummer. At times of emergency, too, the Militia would be embodied for permanent service, as from 1759-62, 1779-83, 1793-1802, 1803-16 and 1854-6. Volunteer infantry and mounted Yeomanry conditions of service were liable to vary, but after 1815, Yeomanry, largely raised from farmers, attended a minimum of eight drills per annum and Volunteer infantry nine drills, both being subjected to an annual inspection. Non-Militiamen were not paid but the officers, who were sons of the nobility and gentry awaiting their inheritances, as well as the non-commissioned officers and troopers, were eager for the excitement and swagger associated with an impending campaign. Officers belonging to the Volunteer movement further enjoyed an enhanced social status within their shires.

The Yeomanry had a considerable role to play in aid of the civil power after 1815, extending from the industrial disturbances of the 1820s to the Swing riots of 1830-31 and the Chartist disturbances of the 1840s. The military role in aid of the civil power was, of course, an especially difficult one for troops whether Yeomanry or Regulars, and the most enduring image of the Yeomanry, or Fencibles – the branch of the Yeomanry arm that was confined to home service only – is that of a class-bound instrument riding down the working-class population. Above all, perhaps, is the issue of nine men, two women dead with some 400 wounded attributed to forty horsemen of the Manchester and Salford Cavalry in dispersing a crowd estimated at 50-60,000, who had gathered at St Peter's Field, Manchester, to hear an orator named Hunt speak on parliamentary reform. The 'massacre' of Peterloo (a play on St. Peter's Field and Waterloo) took place on 16 August, 1819.

Napoleon's defeat at Waterloo (1815) was naturally greeted by the British in a triumphal mood, but the ghost of Napoleon lived on in even those with a limited sense of imagination and as the century progressed there were renewed fears of an invasion by France. Political lobbying and government decisions were caused by three panics.

The first panic was brought about in January 1847 when a letter from the Duke of Wellington to Field Marshal Sir John Burgoyne was published in which the Duke voiced his concern at the paucity of Britain's southern coastal defences. The Militia Ballot had been suspended in 1816 and there had been cutbacks in the Yeomanry in 1827. There was talk in Parliament of reviving the Militia Ballot in 1843 and again in 1848, but in the latter year the likely expense of Lord John Russell's 'Local Militia Plan', an increase in income tax from seven pence to one shilling in the pound, effectively disposed of the proposal.

The second panic occurred in 1851 on the *coup d'état* in France by Napoleon III. Lord Derby's Militia Bill was successful in 1852 and there followed a Militia Ballot to raise 80,000 men. Such action was positively encouraged by the comparisons drawn by Sir Francis Head in 1850 between the French standing army of 400,000 men and the British Army of 120,000 of which only 37,000 were stationed in Britain at the time. Although the French were allies at the juncture, patriotic spirit was undoubtedly boosted by the Crimean War of 1853-6. Among the things demonstrated by this war was the effect of modern shells on wooden ships. In 1855 the French announced a massive programme for an armoured navy.

The third panic arose on 14 January 1858 when Orsini, an Italian refugee, made an attempt on the life of Napoleon III. His bomb was allegedly made in Birmingham and he had links with compatriots in London. The strain which this attempted assassination placed on relations between France and Britain contributed to the atmosphere of tension at the time. The Queen and her consort, Prince Albert, noted new fortifications upon visiting Cherbourg in August 1858 and Napoleon III's foreign policy generally was a cause for concern. Britain as a defensive measure fortified ports in southern England.

Napoleon III, Emperor of the French, was born Charles Louis Napoleon Bonaparte in Paris on 20 April 1808. His father, Louis Bonaparte, was King of Holland, a younger brother of Napoleon I. His mother, Hortense de Beauharnais, was the daughter of Empress Josephine, Napoleon I's first wife, by her earlier marriage. Desperate as a young man to re-establish a Napoleon on the throne of France, Charles Louis participated in several revolts and in 1840 he was sentenced to life imprisonment in the castle of Ham after a failed bid to lead a mass rising to seize power. He escaped from the prison and returned to England where he had previously made a temporary home. The revolution of 1848 in France gave him a chance. The French masses now had the vote and to them the name of Napoleon was irresistible. In June 1848 four departments elected him to the Assembly, and in December the nation chose him as President. A year later a plebiscite made him Napoleon III, Emperor of France.

With his marriage in 1853 to Eugénie de Montigo, a Spanish lady of great beauty, Napoleon III made the French court once more famous for its splendour and extravagance. The reign, above all, became one of material and economic prosperity on a scale hitherto unknown by ordinary French people. He had grandiose ideas about redrawing the map of Europe on a national basis, aiding oppressed people, with France enjoying the power of hegemony, thus winning the glory which befitted his name and nation. Fears in Britain that Napoleon III planned to land an army in England were exacerbated when in 1859, in alliance with the Kingdom of Sardinia, he declared war on Austria, in order to liberate northern Italy from the Austrian invader. But he soon found events going further than he wished and he made peace.

In 1862-66 he tried to make good this setback when he decided to invade Mexico to establish a large chunk of empire under the Hapsburg Archduke Maximilian. This venture turned into a complete fiasco, and Maximilian was executed by Mexican Government captors. His downfall came when the French public clamoured against the rising power and conquests of Prussia under its leader, the Chancellor of the First Reich, Otto von Bismarck, and Napoleon III was unwise enough to declare war on Prussia on 19 July 1870. Within six weeks the French

Army had suffered a humiliating defeat at the hands of the Prussian Army and the Emperor was compelled to surrender at Sedan on 2 September 1870; two days later he was deposed by a revolution in Paris. Although Britain in 1859 may have had cause to doubt it, Napoleon III was an Anglophile and he returned once again to live in England with his wife and son where the family was welcomed by the court of Queen Victoria. He died in 1873. His son, the Prince Imperial Louis Napoleon, gained a commission in the British Army and served in the Zulu War of 1878-9 during which he was killed by a Zulu warrior.

Whether or not Napoleon III really did intend to invade Britain is doubtful but he did at least succeed in putting the wind up the perfidious Albion. The origin of the Rifle Volunteer Movement can be traced to a cold evening on 16 April 1859 and to a public meeting of the National and Constitutional Defence Association at St Martin's Hall, Long Acre, in London, convened by the Secretary Alfred Richards, later to be referred to as the 'Long Acre Indignation Meeting'. The hall was only one-third full and the main speaker of the evening, Admiral Sir Charles Napier, MP, arrived one hour late. Resolutions were passed to press for defence measures including the enrolment of volunteers. This brought to a peak the calls in the press, which had been led for some time by the editorial and correspondence columns of *The Times*, for defence measures generally, including the raising of volunteers. Within a month Lord Derby's government was to be persuaded to take measures to permit the raising of an armed Volunteer corps.

The volunteers were by no means the undisputed answer to invasion fears. Neither Wellington nor Burgoyne had been sympathetic to the idea of volunteers and the venerable Duke of Cambridge, Commander-in-Chief of the Army from 1855 to 1895, is quoted as regarding volunteers to be a 'very dangerous rabble' and 'unmanageable bodies that would ruin our Army'. A political view expressed by Lord Palmerston in 1855 held volunteers to be 'too costly, of no real military value and unfitted by habit, occupation and constitution to meet the hardship of campaigns'. Even a Royal Commission on Militia, whose brief was not even to consider the volunteer question, provided an opportunity for some effective criticism by Regular Army witnesses. However, by the time the report was published in 1860 the movement was well under way.

The poet laureate, Alfred Lord Tennyson, wrote a poem entitled *The War*, which was published in *The Times* on 9 May 1859. The poem both encapsulated the concern of the time, and in a manner akin to that adopted by Lord Kitchener's call for a volunteer army just over fifty years later, contained a direct appeal to the reader:

> There is a sound of thunder afar
> Storm in the south that darkens the day
> Storm of battle and thunder of war!
> Well, if it do not roll away,
> Storm, Storm, Riflemen form!
> Ready, be ready against the storm!
> Riflemen, riflemen, riflemen form!

The War was signed 'T' and was at first erroneously attributed to Martin Tupper, poet and a bit of a wag at the time and an active propagandist for the cause, who had sought, and failed, to raise a Corps in Surrey in 1852 and again in 1854. The title of one of Tupper's poems *Defence not Defiance* became recognized as the motto adopted by the volunteer force. Three days after *The War* was published the Government acceded to pressure, despite the military objections, and issued a circular, authorizing county Lords Lieutenant to raise volunteer corps under the 'Yeomanry and Volunteer Consolidation Act of 1804.'

A volunteer would take an oath of allegiance and be liable to serve on actual or contemplated invasion. He would be exempted from the Militia Ballot and required to participate in at least eight drills in four months or twenty-four in a year. Out of time of emergency he could resign on fourteen days' notice and was subject to military law only when under arms. Lords Lieutenants were responsible for administration including commissioning of officers and supervising uniforms. All arms, equipment, ammunition and other expenses were to be met privately and premises were to be vested in the commanding officers. Subscriptions and fines pursuant to the unit's rules were subject to the jurisdiction of the magistrates. It can thus be seen that, financially, this was a most economical concession to public opinion by the Government of the day. The absence of any definition of the objectives of the units to be raised further tends to suggest that the Government was prepared to suffer but not to support the volunteer movement.

Albert, the Prince Consort, initiated the second circular issued on 25 May 1859 out of concern to ensure that the efforts of all those involved in the movement's founding were expended for an enduring benefit. By this circular the object of the movement was defined, namely 'to induce those classes to come forward as volunteers who do not, under our present system, enter either the Army or the Militia'. The main purpose of the volunteer corps was to teach the use of the rifle in order to prepare the units to operate in open country in their local areas for the purpose as skirmishers of harassing the flanks and rear lines of communication of any invading army. Although the Government changed its mind and was now prepared to supply ammunition at cost, it remained reluctant to provide rifles! On 10 June 1859 Lord Derby's Tory Government fell to a Liberal coalition led by Lord Palmerston. On 1 July the new Government announced that it would issue twenty-five Long Enfield rifles per 100 volunteers.

Conditions for this concession were stipulated and confirmed in a circular of 13 July. This third circular required the Corps to provide each unit with a safe 200-yard range, secure custody for the weapons, an approved set of rules and a uniform approved by the Lord-Lieutenant. Provision was made for Militia instructors to be provided at the expense of the Corps, for musketry courses at Hythe (on payment of a fee), and for a recommended manual, namely *Drill and Rifle Instruction for Volunteer Rifle Corps* by Colonel D. Lyson, otherwise known as *The Green Book*, priced 6d. This circular also fixed the numerical strength ('the establishment') of a Corps. A company could have no less than sixty, no more than 100 effectives and would have one captain, one lieutenant and one ensign. Several companies raised in the same locality could be formed into a battalion of not less than eight companies or 500 men. This could have a lieutenant colonel, a major and the services of an adjutant provided by the Regular Army. It was recorded that an average of 7,000 recruits per month were enlisted from May 1859 to May 1861.

Within two years of the first circular, a considerable number of volunteer rifle corps had been raised. In Middlesex, for example, there were numbered some fifty Corps, in Kent forty-five, in Devon twenty-eight, in Hampshire twenty-five and in Surrey twenty-seven. There was an immediate need for organization and over a period of time there was to be an increase in standards of competence and efficiency and progressive assimilation in the Regular Army. The first issue of twenty-five government rifles per hundred men on 1 July 1859 was followed by a further issue of twenty-five on 14 October 1859, and an issue of the remaining fifty on 20 December 1859. On 8 February 1860 Regular drill instructors were made available for three-month periods for two shillings and sixpence a day with lodgings to be provided by the Corps. On 29 February the Corps was granted permission to appoint adjutants from ex-Regular officers of at least four years' experience in order to provide testimonials and certificates of fitness.

There occurred signs of acceptance by the Regular Army when on 10 August 1860 Regular guards were ordered to salute officers and volunteers under arms. In November 1861 permission was given to volunteers to brigade at Easter and summer camps with Regulars at Aldershot and Shorncliffe. On 24 March 1860 authority was given by circular for 'consolidated' and 'administrative' battalions. A consolidated battalion was an urban concept whereby several corps would be amalgamated in order to form a battalion. The administrative battalion was a more rural device enabling several corps to cooperate for the purposes of sharing the expenses of adjutants and instructors, and for the purpose of securing uniformity of drill, inspections and returns. The component corps of an administrative battalion remained anonymous for financial and internal purposes, and battalion parades could only be performed by consent. The authority of the administrative battalion's commanding officer thus tended to be limited to discipline at parades and to advisory roles. The system nevertheless proved not impractical due to a broad measure of goodwill.

Largely at the behest of the volunteers a Royal Commission was set up in May 1862 whose report gave rise to the Volunteer Act of 1863. After the first few years the flush of patriotism and enthusiasm was waning and many corps found difficulty in funding. The Volunteer Act introduced the Capitation Grant of twenty shillings for each effective, being a member who had attended nine drills (three battalion and six company drills and the annual inspection). A further ten shillings was available for firing sixty rounds in target practice. The Capitation Grant was intended to meet the necessary expenses of the corps which the Act defined; the recruits forfeiting these payments principally in exchange for their uniforms, and other items of personal equipment. Volunteer pressure for an increase in the grant was successfully resisted by the government. In 1869, Edward Cardwell, who is principally remembered as Gladstone's Secretary of State for War (1868-74) for the introduction of the short service principle as the basis for enlistment in the Regular army, supported by a newly created reserve, the introduction of the two-battalion regimental system, the reform of army administration and the abolition of the purchase of commissions, secured the amalgamation in the case of the volunteers of the basic and further grant and, but for the resistance encountered, would have introduced measures for further musketry and financial efficiency including consolidation of administrative battalions. In July 1870 he did, however, succeed in introducing a new Certificate of Proficiency in return for an increase in the grant from thirty shillings to thirty-five shillings.

The *Auxiliary and Reserve Forces Circular* of 28 May 1879 which further tightened efficiency regulations and provided for replacement of volunteer adjutants by Regular officers on five-year attachments, in no way enhanced the government's popularity with the volunteers, neither had the 'Regulation of the Forces Act' of 1871 which further tended to place the force into the hands of Regular officers. Responsibility for commissions was removed from the Lords Lieutenant and these were henceforth to be issued by the Crown. In addition Volunteers were made subject to the Mutiny Act when brigaded with Regulars and

Militia. In 1880 those administrative battalions which had not already done so were required to consolidate. The original individual corps became companies of the new battalion.

On 1 July 1881 full territorialization was introduced under Cardwell's Reforms and each battalion of volunteers became a volunteer battalion of a Regular regiment. This achieved maximum use of the brigade depot and it was hoped that local recruitment would be enhanced. Many individual corps resisted this change, choosing to retain their original descriptions and green or grey uniforms, but a restriction on any change of uniform except to scarlet nevertheless brought about a steady change of uniformity.

Of combined military and social nature were the field days and Easter Reviews. For the purpose of the latter large numbers of volunteers would travel by train to a town such as Brighton from whence they would march to the Downs for manoeuvres. These activities attracted substantial crowds (in one case providing useful cover for a flanking manoeuvre) and were considered valuable for recruiting. They also provided the participants with the opportunity to enjoy local hospitality to the occasional detriment of the appearance of discipline. Earl de Grey was obliged to issue a circular in August 1861 condemning the firing of rifles out of railway carriage windows after reviews. The first serious recorded casualty of the 19th Surrey Rifles was a clergyman who in 1864 was struck and killed at a review by a ramrod accidentally discharged from a rifle. In this manner the military value of reviews came into doubt. The Brighton review was abandoned in 1873 with the introduction of the Bank Holiday Act and the abolition of cheap rail fares for volunteers.

Of strict military necessity were the minimum drill nights and occasional parades, and the musketry 'that interesting healthful and manly exercise' which the Rifle Movement is supposed to supply, and which is calculated, perhaps more than anything else to keep alive the enthusiasm of the volunteers: a typical corps might provide regular class firings at evenings and weekends with recurrent spoon-shoots or other forms of competition in addition to internal inter-platoon shoots and their annual prize meeting. The Rifle Volunteers were encouraged to place equal emphasis on the social side as on military matters. Where a corps was able to provide its own Drill Hall, there might be mess facilities and in many cases the Drill Hall would also provide a social centre. Amongst other things the London Scottish provided a shooting club, a school of arms, a swimming club, a golf club, a revolver club and a football club. The 1st Surrey Rifles boasted a lawn tennis club. Corps would play each other at cricket, football and rugby and athletics was a popular Volunteer pastime. The 19th Surrey Rifles entered a very favourable transaction in 1875 by leasing their drill shed as a roller skating rink. Many corps maintained a band or contracted the services of a civilian band. This would be useful for fund raising. Dances, bazaars, fetes, theatrical performances and smokers' concerts were all commonly taken to this end.

Volunteer emphasis upon the use of the rifle and the contemporary founding of the National Rifle Association was no coincidence. Earl Spencer had set up a committee including volunteer representation for such a purpose in October 1859. Simultaneously a committee was raised by various Rifle Volunteer officers headed by Lord Elcho of the London Scottish and Earl Grosvenor (The Duke of Westminster) of the Queen's Westminsters. After the combination of the two groups, firstly at Earl Spencer's London home and subsequently at the Thatched House tavern in St James, the NRA. came into being. Lord Elcho, the first chairman, in a letter to *The Times* explained that the purpose of the association was to give permanence to the volunteer force by promoting its focus on musketry by the institution of a competition comparable to those central or other national sports, an annual 'Rifle Derby', in fact.

The first annual prize meeting of the NRA was held at Wimbledon on 2 July 1860 in the presence of a large crowd. The Queen and Prince Albert were both in attendance, together with the Prince of Wales and other members of the Royal Family. They were met by the Prime Minister, Lord Palmerston, Lord Elcho and Mr Sidney Herbert, Secretary of State for War, who gave the welcoming address. The Queen and Prince Albert both responded. Such royal approbation in the presence of leading members of the government represented a significant official endorsement of the volunteer movement. After acknowledging the expression of loyalty to the Queen, she proceeded:

> ...and I assure you that I, together with my Royal Consort, have gladly given encouragement to a body whose object is to render permanent an armed force, limited exclusively to defensive purposes and founded upon voluntary exertions.

The inaugural first shot was then fired by the Queen with a Whitworth rifle carefully laid in rest. After a brief explanation of the mechanism by its inventor, Mr Whitworth, the Queen pulled the scarlet silk cord and a bull was scored amid loud cheers from the crowd.

The tangible evidence of the Royal encouragement was to be 'The Queen's Prize', a sum of £250 per year, and the 'Prince Consort's Prize' of £100 per year, known after his death in 1862 as 'The Albert'. These were magnificent sums in Victorian times, 'The Queen's Prize' being sufficient to provide the winner with a small home or to set him up in business, as indeed occurred in the case of George Fulton whose famous family gunsmith's business was founded on his prize money.

Although NRA membership was never exclusive to the volunteers there was a close link between the association and the volunteer movement and the annual prize meeting became a major feature of the volunteer calendar. The Chairman's Reception at which Royalty was frequently present made the meeting an important social event. In 1861 nearly 22,000 people were admitted to the meeting. By 1864 the camp at Wimbledon Common became known as 'tent town' or 'canvas town' covering an area one mile in circumference. There were traders selling all manner of wares. There were caterers, entertainments formal and informal, gymnastic displays, fireworks, concerts and there were volunteer reviews and sham fights sometimes involving as many as 15,000 men. There was no doubt that the NRA made a major contribution to the permanence of the volunteer movement by establishing a principal volunteer activity as a popular sport.

After describing an outline history of the militia and volunteers from early times and that Victorian phenomenon the Volunteer Rifle Corps which dates from 1859, it is time to turn to the subject of this book, *A History of the Artists Rifles, 1859-1947*, a unit that carved its unique niche in the story of our Territorials, and who remain in the service of their country to the present time.

Barry Gregory
Salisbury, 2002

Chapter 1

Cum Marte Minerva

The Grey, Black and Silver
1859-1882

There must be a beginning to any great matter, but the continuing unto it is finished yields the true glory.

Sir Francis Drake

Among the young men in London who were seized with patriotic emotion by the scare of invasion by France was one Edward Coningsby Sterling, a student at Cary's School of Art in Bloomsbury. (Cary's School of Art specialized in preparing students for the examinations for admittance to the Royal Academy Schools.) Edward Sterling's father John, a co-proprietor of *The Times*, had in 1838 founded the Sterling Club in London, which counted among its members such eminent men of letters as Carlyle, Tennyson and Palgrave. Edward was thirteen years of age when his father died in 1844 and he was made a ward of Thomas Carlyle, the Scottish essayist, historian and moralist; F. W. Newman, Professor of Latin at University College, London, and brother of the famous cardinal, was appointed as his guardian.

In 1859 Edward called a meeting of fellow members of the life class with a view to forming a volunteer group to join one of the new volunteer companies which had been created in that year. The result of that first meeting was disappointing; only two decided to join him, but word got round the arts community in London about Edward Sterling's idea, and in the early days of 1860 a meeting took place at the studio of a well-known portrait painter, Henry Wyndham Phillips, which was to recruit 119 members to form a Volunteer Corps of Artists as an entity in its own right. The actual enlistments were made on 10 May 1860 at

Wyndham Phillips' residence and studio which were located at 8 George Street,[1] a red-bricked building situated off Hanover Square. At the meeting it was decided to form a corps of painters, sculptors, engravers, musicians, architects and actors, although at first the artists predominated. Thus was born the Artists Rifles.

The new unit which amounted to one company in strength was named the 38th Middlesex (Artists) Rifle Volunteers, otherwise known as the Artists Volunteer Corps, or Artists Rifle Volunteers (RV). In spite of the Duke of Cambridge's foreboding, the new volunteer corps took its place in the Order of Battle of the British Army in 1863. At first the Artists used a temporary headquarters at the Argyll Rooms, but towards the end of 1860 an official headquarters was established at Burlington House, the new home of the Royal Academy. (Drill was performed in the gardens at the rear of Burlington House which, in 1869, were built on to accommodate more galleries and the Academy Schools.) In 1868 another move was made to the Arts Club, then in Hanover Square; in 1880 the Regiment moved yet again to the West London School of Art in Great Titchfield Street; two years later it found a home at 36 Fitzroy Square; and finally, in 1889, the Artists built their own permanent headquarters and Drill Hall at 17 Duke's Road, St. Pancras.

The first enrolment register shows under 5 October 1860 the following names, *inter alios*:

No. 1 Lord Bury (elected Captain)
No. 2 Arthur James Lewis, tradesman, (elected Lieutenant)
No. 3 Alfred Nicholson, musician, (elected Ensign)
No. 4 Charles Thomas Lane, musician
No. 5 Val C. Prinsep, painter
No. 6 Henry Wyndham Phillips, painter
No. 7 Alfred Wigan, writer
No. 8 Robert William Edis, architect
No. 9 Frederick Leighton, painter, (elected Ensign)
No. 10 Henry Perkes, painter
No. 11 George Frederick Watts, painter, hon. Member
No. 12 Charles Edward Perugini, painter
No. 13 Edward C. Sterling, painter, (elected Ensign)
No. 14 John Everett Millais, painter, (elected Lieutenant)
No. 16 Frederick William Wyon, writer
No. 19 Field Talfourd, painter, hon. member
No. 37 Carl Haag, artist
No. 40 John B. Turner, Professor of Music
No. 46 Frederick P. Cockerell, architect
No. 50 Charles Earles, artist

No. 54   A. Charles White, Professor of Music
No. 63   Arthur Gilbert, artist
No. 69   John G. Waetzig, musician
No. 72   Robert L.L. Underdown, painter
No. 77   William W. Fenn, painter
No. 99   J. Henry Christian, architect
No. 101 Lewis H. Shepherd, architect

The average age of the above recruits was 32.5 years, which suggest that they were of mature stature and already successful in their various professions.

Other early enrolments in the ranks of the Artists were Holman Hunt, John Hullah, William Morris, Dante Gabriel Rossetti, Algernon Swinburne, Edward Burne-Jones, Spencer Stanhope, John Ruskin, honorary member, and William Blake Richmond as honorary secretary.

Presumably Lord Bury (the future Duke of Albemarle) was a friend of the arts community and was elected captain because of his social status but he only remained at the post for one month before resigning after accepting the command of the Civil Service Rifle Volunteer Corps. Edward Sterling, who was to exhibit at the Royal Academy on three occasions, did not play a significant ongoing role with the Artists, dying in middle life. John Everett Millais, Dante Gabriel Rossetti and William Holman Hunt were founding members of the Pre-Raphaelite Brotherhood formed in 1848 by a group of young English artists who shared a dismay at what they considered the moribund state of British painting and hoped to recapture the sincerity and simplicity of early Italian art (i.e. before the time of Raphael, whom they considered the fountainhead of academism).

Millais, who was born in 1829 in Jersey was a child prodigy, at eleven the youngest ever student to be admitted to the Royal Academy Schools. His career as an artist can be divided into two parts: 1) The Pre-Raphaelite period, which by 1853 had been virtually dissolved, and 2) moving away in the 1850s from the brilliantly coloured, minutely detailed Pre-Raphaelite manner, he adopted a more fluent way of painting in a popular style which met the public demand for sentiment and a good story, an example of which was his *Boyhood of Raleigh* (1870). In great demand for his portraits, book illustrations and illustrative material for advertising, of which his best known example was *Bubbles* for Pears' soap, his income is said to have reached a staggering £30,000 a year. Away from work he delighted in country walks, fishing and playing cricket. An easy-going much-liked man, in 1885 he became the first artist to be awarded a baronetcy and in 1896, the year of his death, he was elected president of the Royal Academy in succession to

Lord Leighton, who died in the same year.

William Holman Hunt, who was born in 1827, was the only member of the Pre-Raphaelite circle who throughout his career remained faithful to its aims, which he summarized as finding serious and genuine ideas to express; direct study from nature in disregard of all arbitrary rules; and envisaging events as they must have happened rather than in accordance with the rules of design. From 1854 he made several journeys to Egypt and Palestine, for which he armed himself with a pistol to use in the event of his encountering brigands of both the Moslem or Jewish faith, to paint biblical scenes with accurate local detail. It was as a result of painting works such as *The Light of the World*, which depicts Christ carrying a lantern, that he became immensely popular with the Victorian public and he made a fortune from the sale of engravings of his paintings. In old age he became a patriarchal figure in the art world and he was awarded the Order of Merit in 1905. He died in 1910.

Dante Gabriel Rossetti, born in 1828, was the son of an Italian political refugee who settled with his family in London. Both painter and poet, his sister was the poet Christina Rossetti. It has been argued that the idea to form the Pre-Raphaelite Movement came originally from Rossetti. His *Girlhood of Mary Virgin* (1849) was the first picture to be exhibited bearing the Brotherhood's (PRB) initials and was warmly praised, but the subsequent abuse (the Brotherhood's reputation later being salvaged by the art critic, John Ruskin) that the Pre-Raphaelites received, hurt him so much that he rarely again exhibited, relying on private sales often with the help of John Ruskin, who provided the contacts. In the 1850s he virtually gave up oils and concentrated on water colours. By the 1860s he was earning the very substantial sum of £3,000 a year. However, he returned to oils for the last two decades of his life, specializing in turning models into femmes fatales. Rossetti had joined William Morris and Edward Burne-Jones in 1861, in the decorative arts firm later known as Morris & Co., but business and personal relationships became strained. In his later years Rossetti became an eccentric recluse (he had a menagerie, attached to his home in Chelsea, of unusual animals including a wombat, the death of which occasioned a poem), he fought a losing battle against drugs and alcohol and died in 1882 paralysed and prematurely aged.

George Frederick Watts, who was born in 1817, was a painter and sculptor, who received part of his training at the Royal Academy Schools. In 1843 he won a prize in the competition for the decoration of the Houses of Parliament and used the money to live and study in Italy where the great Renaissance masters helped shape his high-minded attitudes towards art. After returning to England in 1847 he established a solid reputation in intellectual circles, but popular fame did not come until about 1880. Thereafter he was the most revered figure in British art, in 1902 to be appointed to the Order of Merit. His style was early influenced by William Etty, one of the few British artists to specialize almost exclusively in the nude; but the Elgin Marbles and the great Venetian painters (notably Titian) and Michelangelo were his avowed exemplars in his desire to affect the mind seriously by nobility of line and colour. He tried to invest his work with moral purpose and his most characteristic paintings are abstruse allegories that were once enormously popular, but now seem vague and ponderous. His portraits of the great contemporaries, Gladstone, Tennyson, J. S. Mill, etc., to be seen at the National Portrait Gallery have generally worn much better. As a sculptor he is remembered chiefly for his equestrian piece *Physical Energy* (1904). A cast of it forms the central feature of the Cecil Rhodes Memorial in Cape Town, and another is in Kensington Gardens in London. Watts was twice married, his first wife being the celebrated actress Ellen Terry. She was thirty years his junior and the marriage ended in divorce. He died in 1904.

Born in 1833, Sir Edward Coley Burne-Jones was a painter, illustrator and designer; his interest in art was stimulated by William Morris, his fellow divinity student at Oxford, and then by Rossetti, to whom Burne-Jones apprenticed himself in 1856, and who remained the decisive influence on him. Like Rossetti, Burne-Jones painted in a consciously aesthetic style, but his taste was more classical and his elongated forms owed much to Botticelli. He favoured medieval and mythical subjects and hated modernists such as the Impressionists, describing their subjects as 'landscape and whores'. Burne-Jones led the second phase of Pre-Raphaelite(ism). His own ideas on painting are summed up as follows:

> I mean by a picture a beautiful romantic dream, of something that never was, never will be – in a light better than any shone – in a land no-one can define or remember, only desire – and the forms divinely beautiful.

Burne-Jones exhibited little before 1877, but then became quickly famous. His work had considerable influence on the French Symbolists and the ethereally beautiful women who people his paintings, like the more sensuous types of Rossetti, had considerable progeny at the end of the century. Some of Burne-Jones's finest work was in association with William Morris (he was a founder member of Morris & Co. in 1861) notably as a designer of stained glass and tapestries, and as an illustrator of the Kelmscott Press books, which were printed at the private printing press founded in 1890 by William Morris in Hammersmith. Sir

Edward Burne-Jones died in 1898.

Born in 1834, the multi-talented William Morris was a writer, poet, painter, designer, printer, craftsman and a social reformer. As a student at Oxford University he formed a long-standing friendship with Burne-Jones and began to write poetry and study medieval architecture, reading John Ruskin and Augustus Pugin, an English architect, designer, writer and medievalist; one of the key figures of the 'Gothic Revival' and of Victorian design as a whole. In 1856 William Morris was apprenticed to the architect G. E. Street but soon left to paint under Rossetti's guidance – his only completed oil painting being *Queen Guenevere*, which was strongly Pre-Raphaelite in conception. In 1859 Morris married Jane Burden, who appears in numerous paintings by Rossetti as the archetypal femme fatale. Morris's architect friend Philip Webb built the famous Red House, Bexley Heath, for the couple.

With Webb, Rossetti, Burne-Jones, Ford Madox Brown (a painter friend of the Pre-Raphaelites), P.P. Marshall (a surveyor) and Charles Faulkner (an accountant), Morris founded the manufacturing and decorating firm originally called Morris, Marshall, Faulkner & Co. in 1861. After a shaky start, the firm prospered, producing furniture, tapestry, stained glass, furnishing fabrics, carpets and much more. Morris's wallpaper designs are particularly well-known (they are still produced commercially today) and Burne-Jones did some superb work for the firm, particularly in stained glass and tapestry design. Morris repudiated the concept of fine art and his company was based on the ideal of a medieval guild, in which the craftsman both designed and executed the work. He defined art as 'man's expression of joy in labour' and saw it as an essential part of human well-being. As a socialist he wished to produce art for the masses, but there was an inherent flaw in his ambition, for only the rich could afford his expensive hand-made products. His ideal of universal craftsmanship and his glorification of manual skill thus proved unrealistic in so far as it ran counter to or failed to come to terms with modern machine production.

But his work bore fruit in England and abroad, in the emphasis it laid upon the social importance of good design and fine workmanship in every walk of life. He also had an important part to play in the development of the private printing press, through the founding of the Kelmscott Press, which between 1891 and 1898, two years after Morris's death, issued more than fifty titles, including editions of Morris's own works. Deeply influenced by his study of early printing, Morris himself designed most of the type, borders, ornaments and title pages, taking as his basic unit the double page when the book lies open. The press's greatest book, and by common consent one of the world's masterpieces of book production, is the 1896 edition of Geoffrey

Chaucer's works, with illustrations by Burne-Jones. Although short-lived, the Kelmscott Press had an enormous influence on the private presses that followed in its wake. Morris's home at Walthamstow in London and Kelmscott Manor in Oxfordshire contain good examples of work designed by William Morris and his associates.

Apart from Lord Bury, Henry Wyndham Phillips, Frederick Leighton[2] and Edward C. Sterling, the following signatories of that first enlistment are worthy of further note. Arthur Lewis (No.2), who became a captain in the Artists Volunteer Rifle Corps, was a successful tradesman, who lived in a suite of rooms over his own fruiterer's shop in Jermyn Street, W.1. A member of the Arts Club, from which many of those early members were recruited, Arthur Lewis was a great lover of music, an admirable amateur painter, a good whip and a brilliant huntsman, whose weekly hospitality was proverbial. Part-singing was the great entertainment; those who took their share in it were called the Moray Minstrels. On the occasions when they met, celebrities jostled one another in friendly proximity. The group included Frederick Leighton, Holman Hunt, Millais, the novelist Anthony Trollope, Poole, the fashionable tailor, together with a sprinkling of lords proud of being admitted to such an intellectual society.

Valentine Cameron Prinsep (invariably known as Val Prinsep), who was twenty-two when he joined the Artists, was an honorary member of a group of painters called the St John's Wood Clique not associated with the Pre-Raphaelite Brethren, who enlisted in the Artists Corps in 1860. He was in time promoted to senior major. An unsuccessful candidate for the Presidency of the Royal Academy in 1896, he served the Academy as Professor of Painting from 1900 to 1903.

John Ruskin, born in 1819, was the most influential art critic of his time, also a talented water-colourist. His output of writing was enormous and he had a remarkable hold over public opinion, as he showed when he successfully defended the Pre-Raphaelites against the savage attacks to which they were being subjected by Charles Dickens and others. Although Ruskin's worship of beauty for its own sake brought him into affinity with the advocates of 'art for art's sake', his strong interest in social reform and ever-increasing concern with economic and political questions during the second half of his life (he used much of his large inheritance for philanthropic work) kept him from accepting a doctrine of the autonomy of the arts in divorce from questions of social morality. His eloquence in linking art with the daily life of the workman had affinities with the view of William Morris. Ruskin's personal life was deeply unhappy. His marriage to Effie Gray was annulled in 1854 on the grounds of non-consummation. Effie, after the divorce, married Millais who had long admired her. In middle and old age he made young girls the objects of his unhealthy affection. In 1878 he lost a famous libel case against James Whistler, the American painter, whom he had accused, in the case of one of his works, of 'flinging a pot of paint in the public face', and soon after he first showed signs of the mental illness that made his final years wretched. Ruskin's complete works were edited in thirty-nine volumes (1903-12). His most important work of art criticism is *Modern Painters* (five volumes, 1843-60). John Ruskin died in 1900.

Algernon Charles Swinburne, the poet, was born in 1837, the year of Victoria's accession to the throne. Educated at Eton he might justifiably have claimed to be the complete Victorian, delighting as he did in flouting Victorian respectabilities with his poetry. When Swinburne's *Poems and Ballads* was first published in 1866, he was castigated as the 'libidinous laureate of a pack of satyrs'. The themes of moral, spiritual and political rebellion, and sometimes sadistic, pornographic and blasphemous subject matter goaded the Victorian reading public to fury. With his imaginative experiments in both the classical and romantic traditions, his luxurious imagery and metrical pyrotechnics, Swinburne found admirers in an age in which his outrageous virtuosity spoke to those sickened by the conventions of the late nineteenth century. More admired after his death than during his life Algernon Swinburne died in 1909.

John Hullah was a musician, who entertained Mendelssohn on his visit to England in the spring of 1846 and Spencer Stanhope was an orchestral conductor of front rank. William Blake Richmond was the son of George Richmond RA, who specialized in portraiture, those sitting for him including Charlotte Brontë, Edward VII (when Prince of Wales), Cardinal Manning, Sir Robert Peel, Lord Salisbury and William Makepeace Thackeray. His son William Blake Richmond, who was also to become an RA and was knighted, was born in Marylebone in 1842. As, in the case of his father, he specialized in portraits but did paint in other genre and was also a sculptor. As a lad of eleven in 1853 William had raced to Great Portland Street to watch the Guards leave their barracks for the wooden ships which were to take them to the Crimea. A crowd composed of women had assembled at the gate. As William Richmond was later to record in his papers:[3]

> The crowd seemed scarcely to breathe, so intently was each member of it listening. At last through the closed gates and over the band of drums and fifes, rang out military orders in stern, sharp terms. Next the gates were flung open, and the soldiers led by the commanding officers [sic] of the battalion and a full band playing *The Girl I Left Behind Me*, filed out in columns of four.

Then, in an instant, the orderly columns were broken by women, who rushed into the ranks to embrace – in all probability for the last time – brother, lover, or husband. But the long line of men never moved. They stared rigidly in front of them, striving to ignore the unnerving clasp of those agonized arms ... For one moment the women clung to their loved ones; then they staggered back again, weeping, into the crowd which engulfed them.

Three years later William Richmond once again turned out to watch the Guards, this time returning from the Crimea to their Portland Street Barracks. He wrote:

I saw the troops return, corpse-like men with great unkempt beards, far other than I saw go out clean-shaven lads, alert, quick-stepping, and full of promise. There did not seem to be a young man among the returning army. Two years of service had put twenty years on all of them. Those who were not crippled were fagged out, weak and weary – it was a tragic sight.

William Richmond's interest in the military led him, at seventeen years of age, to join the Artists Volunteer Corps, an excellent environment for a budding young artist of talent to mix in, especially as the older artists were bent on taking in hand and evaluating the work of their younger brethren. He was quickly made a drill corporal and later became the Artists' secretary. In his position as corporal, Richmond found that some recruits took to drill with avidity and intelligence, others seemed unable to grasp even the rudiments of collective movement! As he recorded in his papers:

To some the words 'right and left' seemed synonymous! William Morris, for example, invariably turned to the 'right' when the order was 'left'; then, surprised at his mistake, he invariably begged pardon of the comrade to whom he found himself facing and whom he should have followed – it was supremely comical. Rossetti, on the other hand, was apt to argue. He wished to know the exact reason for every movement which he and his comrades were told to execute; but there was no time for elaborate explanations, and he had to fall out or go on with the interminably monotonous regime necessary to effect even the smallest detail of military service.

It was my duty as Corporal to instruct in lock drill. We used the old-fashioned Brown Bess[4] whose lock one would not have thought was conspicuously complicated, but often men having taken the lock to pieces could by no manner of means put it together again. Screws fell on the floor and disappeared under hiding places, or an absent-minded recruit would pocket one or two, and thus lose all sequence of detail in the instructions.

The cleverest recruit in the game of losing and finding was dear Holman Hunt, who, with his accustomed exercise of will and thoroughness, would constantly pocket a screw and spend incalculable time in looking for it exactly where it was not, and could not have been mislaid. Being reminded of the possibility of his having pocketed it, he good-naturedly made a search, and to the amusement of us all invariably brought out the lost article from his trouser pocket, and again, with dogged perseverance, proceeded to readjust the scattered members of the lock, succeeding only after a great deal of talk, reasoning, and argument, together with some practical assistance from me.

Of course, we used ramrods with the Brown Bess, which at times became a source of danger to the skins of onlookers as well as comrades, for it has happened that a ramrod left in the muzzle of a gun after ramming was expelled with unexpected velocity in the rear of the charge that, in one instance, a dog was killed thereby.

The incident, in which the Artists were not involved, took place on Blackheath Common, gave rise to the topical chaff of the London street gamin who enquired of every Volunteer they met, 'Hi, Guv'nor, hev' you killed the dawg?' Another current jest was that of the Volunteer who, informing an enquirer about the avocations of his martial profession, explained 'You see, we never leave England except in the case of invasion.'

It was at the first meeting of the embryo Corps at 8 George Street that young Richmond came into personal contact with both Leighton and Millais, and he at once felt the fascination of the former, just as the latter had appealed to his imagination as a boy. More from the pen of William Richmond:

Leighton was attractive as a young man, though much more interesting as an old one. German education for a time gave a little rigidity to a nature which did not receive it kindly, for Fred Leighton was by disposition spontaneous, intensely emotional, impulsive, and highly artistic. He would be a little inclined to reason in Teutonic fashion why a thing was beautiful – to analyse and pick to pieces a flower – his mission was to accept it, love it, and absorb its beauty.

Drilling on Wimbledon Common in 1859 I first encountered G. F. Watts, England's great epic poet-painter. He was on horseback having ridden from Little Holland House to be present at our skirmishing, then taking place on the high level of the Common near the windmill. Watts had liked some early work of mine, and spoke kindly to me. He looked very splendid; his beard was worn long, was very silky, and was blown about in a fascinating fashion, first over one shoulder and then over the other.

At that date Watts was not much before the public; he had exhibited little; when he did, the R.A.'s of that day treated him badly, hung his pictures ill, and some of them were venomous. But Watts had his public, a select one, and certainly did not find any place amongst the commercial set; he was an artist for artists, a poet for poets, and so distinguished and great a man that he would have been out of place in the halls of Stock Exchange patrons.

Watts became a much-valued mentor as an artist for the young corporal as did Holman Hunt. It would appear from the foregoing that, celebrated as some of these artists were, they were of no great military value to the Artists Corps but they acted as a magnet to more recruits from the Arts' community who, although they enlisted in the Corps for sound patriotic reasons, were much attracted by the possibility of showing to and discussing their work with their seniors.

The rules and bye-laws laid down for governing the Artists Volunteer Corps savoured more of the formation of a private club than of a military body, for they contained provisions for 'General Meetings', 'Election of Officers', 'Election of Treasurer', 'Accounts', 'Audit', etc. Members of the Corps were to be of two kinds, those enrolled for service in Great Britain (who had to provide their own uniform and equipment, pay an entrance fee of 10s. 6d. and an annual subscription of £1.1s. on each 1 January, with the risk of being reported a defaulter if not paid by 1 February), and honorary members, who were under no obligation for military service, but had to pay in addition to the entrance fee of 10s. 6d, a subscription of £2.2s. yearly or £10.10s. in one downpayment.

The names of officers elected by a 'General Meeting' were to be submitted to the Lord Lieutenant, who had power to grant commissions subject to the Queen's approval (later directly by the Queen). The CO had the power to appoint NCOs. The CO was entirely responsible for discipline but under the rules he had the power to convene a court of enquiry (of from three to five members of the Corps, one of whom was to be an officer) to assist him in the investigation of any irregularities, but if any enquiry was to be made concerning the irregularity of any officer, the court of enquiry was to be convened by the Lord Lieutenant. Trigger-happy riflemen would have been out of pocket. On the spot fines by the officer or NCO in charge of a parade: e.g., for 'pointing a rifle, loaded or unloaded, at any person without orders', £1; for 'loading without order' or for 'discharging a rifle accidentally' or 'without permission', or for 'shooting out of turn without leave when engaged in ball practice,' 2s. 6d. on each occasion. For 'hitting the dummy target on the range', 6d. each time, and for 'firing when the danger flag is shown', 10s.

The badge chosen by the Artists consisted of two heads, of Mars (the Roman God of War) and Minerva (the Goddess of Wisdom), to represent the combination of war and the fine arts. It was worn by the Artists as a cap badge throughout their existence as an active unit. The uniform agreed upon was of a light grey colour which was to be worn by the Grey Brigade, the group of London Rifle Volunteers which included the Artists RV. Originally without facing, the uniform consisted of tunic, knickerbockers (afterwards altered to trousers) and black gaiters with a shako hat (having a grey and black ball in front), white haversack, water-bottle, white gloves, and a cape (or sometimes a great cloak) rolled and worn horse-collar fashion across the left shoulder. Reference to the Capitation Grant referred to in the introduction, volunteers failing to complete the required number of drills and time firing on the range had to pay for these uniform components out of their own pocket. The Capitation Grant did not cover the great coat, the wearing of which was optional but all the members of the Corps acquired and paid for the overcoat. The Corps colours were grey, black and silver. The Mars and Minerva cap badge was designed by Artist J. W. Wyon, the brother of F. W. Wyon also an Artist. J. W. Wyon was engraver to the Signet, the Wyon family having provided the Sovereign's Medallist since the days of William IV and before him George IV.

The first marching song, *Cum Marte Minerva* (the Corps' motto) was the inspiration of Artist George Caley, who wrote the words coining the title. It was set to the music of Salvator Rosa (not an Artist) by the musician Artist Alfred Nicholson. Later in the 1880s, this rather highbrow anthem was dropped and *They All Love Jack*, sung to a tune by Captain Michael Maybrick of 'B' Company, better-known under his professional name as Stephen Adams, was substituted. (The words of *Cum Marte Minerva* are to be found in Appendix IV.) In 1860, the Artists were duly represented at the Queen's Levee for Volunteer officers at St James's Palace, where Her Majesty was greeted by a colourful array of uniforms, and also at the opening of the National Rifle Association at Wimbledon. The Corps also attended the great Volunteer Review in Hyde Park in June of that year, marching to their rendezvous by way of Piccadilly, led by their two tallest sergeants, R. W. Edis and Val Prinsep, both being considerably over six feet in height. At the review the Corps seemed to have won high opinion for their good turn-out and appearance. As reported by the journal, *Once a Week*:

Not less admired was the little company of 'Artists'. Such splendid beards; worthy of Titian and such fine faces! Imagine some dirty little scrub of a foreigner picking off his Stanfield,[5] or potting a Millais before breakfast. But there would be plenty of Englishmen left to avenge them and to paint good pictures afterwards.

Just before the end of 1860 the Corps became so strong in numbers that a second company was formed, and Captain Wyndham Phillips was promoted to captain commandant. Frederick Leighton and Arthur Lewis were promoted respectively to command 'A' and 'B' Companies. The consolidating Rifle Volunteer Act of 1863 provided inter alia for the attachment to each Volunteer Corps of a small staff of Regular soldiers; one officer as adjutant and three NCOs to act as sergeant instructors. The act also provided that the Volunteers could, from time to time, be placed under Regular officers of senior rank, for instruction and training; it also provided for an annual 'Inspection' and report for each corps by a Regular officer.

About 1864 'C' Company was raised and subsequently commanded by Captain R. W. Edis. Edis, who was twenty-one years of age when he joined the Artists in 1860, already owned his own architectural practice and in 1864 was President of the Architectural Association, and already embarking on a brilliant career as an architect – the new company being largely composed of architectural students. Soon afterwards in 1865 'D' Company was formed. It originally consisted of members of the arts side of London University. Captain King Harman was its first captain. He was a Regular of the 60th Rifles, and according to tradition was the Artists' first adjutant. He may well have held that post, but the first official record of the appointment of an adjutant for the Artists in the old Army Lists is that of Captain J. A. Ramsay, of the Bombay Army, who was appointed in the same year, 1865.

In 1868, the CO Captain Commandant Wyndham Phillips died and he was succeeded in the command by Captain Frederick Leighton on 6 January 1869, and in the same year (the Corps then consisting of four companies), he was promoted to major. In 1869 also the headquarters was transferred from Burlington House to The Arts Club, then in Hanover Square, and in 1871 the Enfield rifles, with which the Corps was armed, were converted into Sniders. In 1875 black facings and black-edged shoulder straps (with 38th Middlesex worked thereon) were added to the grey uniform. 'C' Company having become over strength, a new 'Architectural' company ('E' Company) was formed with Captain Lacey Ridge in command. This was followed in 1877 by the formation of a new 'Painters' company ('F' Company), largely recruited from 'A' Company, with Captain Val Prinsep in command; and with the strength of the Corps being by this time six companies, the CO, Major Leighton, was promoted to lieutenant colonel and Captain Edis became the major.

In 1877 the Artists' 'School of Arms' was founded. Among the founders were Colour Sergeant Hamilton, a future Olympic fencer, and Transport Sergeant A.G. 'Sammy' Cowell. The School of Arms was lucky enough to secure the services of Corporal of the Horse Macpherson (a fencing instructor of the Royal Horse Guards) as their first instructor, and in a few years' time became one of the most flourishing institutions of the Artists Corps. Instruction in single combat was originally given in bayonet, sword, lance, sabre, foil and quarterstaff, the School of Arms only being dropped in the late 1930s when the bayonet was no longer considered the infantry soldier's necessary weapon. Accommodation during the winter months was, in former days, obtained at the Queen's Road Baths at Bayswater.

The founders of the School of Arms also furnished enthusiasts to initiate the Military Tournament (later the Royal Tournament), which was originally established by Volunteers and run by them annually at the Old Agricultural Hall at Islington, prizes being offered for competition with Regulars as well as Volunteers. The success of the Artists' Corps, particularly with bayonet and foil, at the tournament was nothing short of astonishing right up until the school ceased to exist. 'Sammy' Cowell, who joined the Artists in 1876, was one of the first four privates to be detailed as drivers of the first transport acquired by them, being a beer cart and an ambulance, which accompanied them on their marches. An expert horseman, a printer by trade, 'Sammy' was the star turn at smokers' concerts and children's parties, which he organized for many years.

In 1879 the shako was abandoned, and the helmet introduced as the headgear. The helmet was modelled on the German Pickelhaube with a strictly non-functional spike on the top and which became all the rage in British Police and County military circles. The round forage cap – worn on the right side of the head, tilted just above the right eye – was retained for undress. In 1880 the designation of the Corps was changed to the 20th Middlesex (Artists) Rifle Volunteers. In the same year Captain Ramsay, the adjutant, was replaced by Captain E. Pennell Elmhirst, of the Royal West Kent Regiment. In 1880 two more companies ('G' and 'H') were added to the Corps – 'G' was chiefly an off-shoot of 'D', the London University company, and was recruited largely from the students of the various London hospitals, Captain F. A. Lucas being in command. 'H' Company was a branch of 'A' and 'F' (the two Painters' companies), and was commanded by Captain D. W. Wynfield, the leader of the St John's Wood clique of painters, who were amongst the early recruits of the Corps. Shortly afterwards (the Corps being then eight companies strong) Captain E. H. Busk was appointed as a second (i.e., junior) major.

Around 1880 there was established a very efficient Drum and Fife Band, which was recruited from the late Baroness Burdett Coutts' School at Westminster, commanded by W. H. Baker. Baker, who was then the headmaster of the school and was also a sergeant in 'B' Company, thus became the first drum major. Recruits continued to be drawn from past scholars of the school for some time to come. W. H. Baker was succeeded as drum major in 1887 by G. J. Enguell, at which time the latter was a youth of about twenty years of age and he looked much younger. Enguell, who came from the Royal Marines, was instructed by the Guards and he took the drummers of the Brigade of Guards as his pattern. The drums became renowned for their music, drill and smartness on parade. In 1881, being the twenty-first year of the Volunteer Corps' existence, the Royal Review of Volunteers was held by Queen Victoria at Windsor. The Artists (eight companies plus drums) was among the best of the corps represented on that occasion, and won high praise for their smartness and appearance during a long and very trying day.

Ever since the formation of the Artists' Corps, all recruits had to be introduced by a past or present member (who was responsible to the Corps for his introduction). The minimum age (except for buglers) was seventeen years; the minimum height 5 feet 6½ inches; minimum chest measurement, 34 inches. Officers were always commissioned from the ranks. The Artists' Corps took part in every important Volunteer camp and review that was held in this period. The chief military work done in those early days was undoubtedly drill, followed at a distance by shooting on the range. Bayonet fighting was only taught in the School of Arms. With regard to manoeuvre and field work, towards the end of this period, the Volunteer Corps was granted permission to attend (in provisional companies) a week's camp at Aldershot each summer made up into provisional battalions composed of a mixture of different corps, but these summer camps were by no means popular or largely attended.

The best 'outings' of the Volunteer Corps were undoubtedly at Easter-time when practically all attended, assembling in their thousands at Eastbourne, Folkestone, Brighton, or some other seaside town, which was near suitable ground for manoeuvres and which provided good accommodation with seaside attractions, and the four days of training from Good Friday to Easter Monday inclusive, always culminated in a big field day on Easter Monday under the direction of a senior Regular officer, and resulted in a great amount of marching and firing of blank ammunition. Most of the Volunteer Corps spent Good Friday and

Saturday in marching to their rendezvous, and huge marching columns were the result. The Artists started a detachment known originally as 'The Baggage Guard' and later on as 'the Marching Detachment', which set out on foot from headquarters in London on the Tuesday for their destination at the seaside. The marching on these occasions, all in marching order, was of a strenuous character, and this and also the billeting in a barn or church hall en route was useful training from a military point of view.

Notes
1. Now St. George St., W.I.
2. An account of Leighton's life is given in Chapter 3.
3. A.M.W. Stirling, *The Richmond Papers from the correspondence and manuscripts of George Richmond RA., and his son Sir William Richmond, RA, RCB*, William Heinemann Ltd., London 1926.
4. The Brown Bess was in service in the British Army from about 1700.
5. An RA. but not an Artist

Chapter 2

The Royal Academy and the Artists Rifles

1768-1947

I should desire that the last words which I should pronounce in this Academy, and from this place, might be the name of – Michael Angelo
Sir Joshua Reynolds, the first President of the Royal Academy,
Discourses on Art, 10 December 1790

On 28 November 1768 a memorial, signed by twenty-two of England's most prominent artists, was presented to the monarch namely George III. These are the opening two paragraphs of the memorial:

To the King's most Excellent Majesty

May it please your Majesty, We, your Majesty's most faithful subjects, Painters, Sculptors and Architects of this metropolis, being desirous of establishing a Society for promoting the Arts of Design, and sensible how ineffectual every establishment of that nature must be without the Royal Influence, must humbly beg leave to solicit your Majesty's gracious assistance, patronage, and protection, in carrying this useful plan into execution.

It would be intruding too much on your Majesty's time to offer a minute detail of our plan. We only beg leave to inform your Majesty, that the two principal objects we have in view are, the establishing of a well-regulated School or Academy of Design, for the use of students in the Arts, and an Annual Exhibition, open to all artists of distinguished merit, where they may offer their performances to public inspection, and acquire that degree of reputation and encouragement which they shall be deemed to deserve.

George III received the memorial graciously, said he considered the Arts to be a national concern and promised his patronage and assistance in bringing the plan to fruition. He furthermore desired that the artists' intentions might be more fully explained to him in writing as soon as was convenient. No time was lost over this. William Chambers, one of the signatories of the memorial, consulted as many of his confederates as was possible in under ten days and drew up a sketch plan which was submitted to the king on 7 December. This was approved, written in proper form and signed by His Majesty on Saturday, 10 December 1768. It is known as the Instrument of Foundation of the Royal Academy.

It was deemed to be his Majesty's pleasure that the following persons be the original members of the said Society:

Joshua Reynolds	G. Michael Moser
Benjamin West	Samuel Wale
Thomas Sandby	Peter Toms
Francis Cotes	Angelica Kauffman
John Baker	Richard Yeo
Mason Chamberlain	Mary Moser
John Gwynn	William Chambers
Thomas Gainsborough	Joseph Wilton
J. Baptist Cipriani	George Barrett
Jeremiah Meyer	Edward Penny
Francis Milner	Newton Augustino Carlini
Paul Sandby	Francis Hayman
Francesco	Bartolozzi Dominic Serres
William Hunter	

The above mentioned persons were to be made academicians, which entitled them to the suffix 'RA' after their names. Joshua Reynolds, painter and writer on art, was appointed the first President of the Royal Academy, Chambers as Treasurer, Penny as Professor of Painting, Samuel Wale as Professor of Perspective and Dr William Hunter as Professor of Anatomy. Reynolds at first declined the presidency but he was advised to reconsider by his eminent friends Dr Johnson and Edmund Burke. Joshua Reynolds was knighted on 22 April 1769.

The Academy's meetings, the schools and exhibitions for the first eleven years were held in London in premises on the south side of Pall Mall. They were opposite Market Lane (now Royal Opera Arcade) and on the site of part of the present United Services Club which stretches eastwards along the street from the corner of Waterloo Place. Previously Aaron Lambe, an auctioneer, had his business there and later Richard

Dalton his print warehouse. The accommodation was modest in size and character and had to be used for all the Academy's activities. Reynolds first discourse was delivered there.

The original members were probably a little conscience-stricken at not having admitted engravers at the foundation and as early as 19 January 1769, the council proposed the election of not more than six Associate Engravers. After further thought it was decided to enlarge this idea and include them in a new class of Associates of the Royal Academy, to be chosen from the participants in the annual exhibition, not to exceed twenty in number, not to be apprentices or less than twenty years of age and to comprise painters, sculptors, architects and engravers. These persons were to be Associates of the Royal Academy and bear the suffix 'ARA' after their names.

On 7 January 1771, it was announced as follows:

> Notice is hereby given to the Members and Students, that the Academy is removed to Somerset House, and will open on Monday next 14th Inst., at 5 o'Clo: in the afternoon.

This referred to the old Somerset House in the Strand in connection with the removal from Pall Mall of the schools, library and administration into some apartments there which were put at the disposal of the Academy by George III. Certain royal retainers were made to vacate these rooms and this provided much needed breathing space for the increasing number of students. The exhibitions, however, continued at the premises in Pall Mall up to and including 1779. Meanwhile plans had been underway for several years for rebuilding the old Somerset House and providing the room for specially built accommodation for the Royal Academy in all its activities.

The exhibition was held on comparable dates from year to year and indeed, in 1771, it was laid down that the annual dinner should thenceforward take place on St George's Day (23 April) and that the exhibition should be open to the public on the following day. The company had in fact adjourned to dine after the opening meeting on 2 January 1769, but the first dinner to coincide with the launching of the annual exhibition, and held at the Academy's own rooms, took place in 1770. In the following year, twenty-five gentlemen were invited to sit at table with the academicians. The custom of the Royal Academy dinner arranged for the eve of the opening of the exhibition has taken place every year since with the exception of the years of the two World Wars and the year of the death of a sovereign.

Sir William Chambers, who had now been knighted, was the architect commissioned to rebuild Somerset House for the use of the Royal

Academy, the Royal Society, the Society of Antiquaries and a number of government departments including the Navy Offices. He thus undertook what was to become one of the greatest examples of English civil architecture, though this involved the destruction of some good work by Inigo Jones which had been created just over 100 years earlier. The conception as a whole is grand and the terrace front, which looks southwards over the River Thames, is one of London's finest façades, even though the water can no longer lap against its massive stonework. There is no doubt, however, that the architect lavished extra attention on the Strand block. The Strand block decoration, mostly designed by Cipriani and carved by Wilton, Carlini, Bacon, Nollekens and Cerachi, is beautifully balanced, remaining subordinate to the main lines of the design and yet quietly asserting itself as a foil in the lower storeys and developing into a flourish in the surmounting ornamentation.

With the anticipated growth of the Royal Academy exhibits annually, Somerset House was still not big enough for its needs. These were, for instance, 547 pictures hung in 1781 and 672 in 1791, so that the exhibits still had to be hung from floor to ceiling and the frames touching one another. It must have been an immense jigsaw puzzle for the hanging committee to fit together. The exhibition receipts in 1780 amounted to £3,069. 1s. 0d. and thereafter they grew from year to year so that subsequently the Royal Academy (under the protection of Royal patronage) has always been able to pay its way. Tuition at the schools was free; membership was limited to six years, although students in receipt of gold medals for the outstanding merit of their work were granted free access for life.

Sir Joshua Reynolds reached the age of sixty-six in 1789 and his eyesight began to fail. Although he gave notice that he did not wish to seek re-election as president in December 1791 he was persuaded to carry on, but died two months later. The funeral and burial at St Paul's Cathedral were conducted with great pomp, the body lying the previous night in the Academy's rooms at Somerset House, and so there passed the figurehead of the Academy's first era. Reynolds was succeeded as President of the Royal Academy by the American-born Benjamin West who had settled in London in 1763 and was one of the Academy's foundation members.

In 1793 there were celebrations to commemorate the Academy's twenty-fifth anniversary. A medal by T. Pingo was struck, examples in gold being given to the Royal Family and in silver to the academicians and associates. A loyal address was presented to the King and the President spoke at a special dinner held at Somerset House. The library continued to grow and, in 1810, inspectors were appointed to make biennial surveys of the Academy's books and casts. In 1815 studentship was extended to ten years and the winners of gold medals were continued to free access to the schools for life.

George IV, who as Prince Regent had had close connections with the Royal Academy, came to the throne in 1820. His accession involved a change in the preamble to the diplomas and the substitution of his portrait for that of his father on the obverse of the schools' medals. The reverse of the gold medal was replaced by a design by Thomas Stothard and is signed 'W.WYON MINT'. It shows three figures representing Painting, Sculpture and Architecture with their appropriate emblems and the words 'AEMULA QUAQUE SORORIS'. The reverse of the silver medal was a new version of the Belvedere torso, in lower relief than that of the former example, and signed 'W. WYON'. The word 'STUDY' appears beneath it. Both medals bore the institution's name and date of foundation.

On 30 March 1820, Sir Thomas Lawrence succeeded West as president and was re-elected unanimously each year until his death in 1830. He had been admitted as a student in the Royal Academy Schools in 1787 and was only twenty-two when elected an associate in 1791. He was not quite twenty-five when he was made a Royal Academician in 1794. John Constable was elected a RA during Lawrence's presidency in 1829, after ten years as an associate. On the death in 1830 of Sir Thomas Lawrence he was succeeded as President of the Royal Academy by Martin Archer Shee, who was knighted, as was the custom for the newly-appointed president. Also in 1830 George IV died and he was succeeded by his brother, William IV. His head by William Wyon, then appeared on the medals but the reverses remained the same. William IV died in June 1837 and was succeeded by the young Queen Victoria. Her head, by William Wyon, then adorned the Academy medals but the reverses once again remained unchanged. Sir Martin Archer Shee was granted permission to paint her portrait, full length, as he had done for William IV, and these two pictures were duly added to the Academy's collection.

As early as 1825, a committee had been appointed to take into consideration what may be the wants of the Royal Academy in the event of the erection of a new building and, as the newly-formed National Gallery desperately needed a proper home, thoughts turned to housing the two institutions under the same roof. In 1832 the government commissioned William Wilkins to design a new building for this dual purpose on the site of the Royal stables, or King's Mews, on the north side of Trafalgar Square. Work commenced in 1833 and was completed five years later. The Academy was very much concerned that, in giving up its independence in Somerset House, its rights should not be placed in jeopardy. Shee was a tower of strength in this matter and an agreement was reached under which the National Gallery was to have the western half of the new building and the Royal Academy the eastern half, the latter to be divided into two parts. The Academy moved into the eastern half of the Trafalgar Square building early in 1837. William IV officially opened the new premises on 28 April 1837 but this was to be his last public appearance; he died two months later.

J. M. W. Turner, who had been Professor of Perspective since 1808 but who had delivered no lectures for a number of years resigned from the post in 1837. Turner's neglect of his duties had been an embarrassment to the Academy for some time but his reputation was such that no one dared complain to him. The new students in the 1840s included John Phillip, James Sant, J. E. Millais, W. Holman Hunt, D. G. Rossetti, Arthur Hughes (a Pre-Raphaelite sympathizer), Edward Lear, H.H. Armstead, Thomas Woolner (one of the original Pre-Raphaelites), and Richard Norman Shaw.[1]

Most of them were in their late teens or early twenties but Lear was thirty-seven and Millais only eleven when admitted. Dressed in a long coat, gathered at the waist by a belt, and with a long falling collar on it some four inches in length with goffered edging, he apparently looked even younger. He was nicknamed 'The Child' and was frequently sent on errands to fetch pies and stout for his older colleagues. He tells us:

> I was told off by other students to obtain their lunch for them. I had to collect forty or fifty pence from my companions, and go with that hoard to a neighbouring baker's and purchase the same number of buns. It generally happened that I got a bun myself by way of commission.

Millais worked unceasingly and was acknowledged as a youthful genius. He won the Academy silver medal for a drawing from the antique when he was fourteen, the gold medal four years later for his historical painting *The Young Men of the Tribe of Benjamin Seizing their Brides*.

Millais was still only eighteen years of age when, in 1848, after long discussions with his fellow students Holman Hunt and Rossetti, the Pre-Raphaelite Brotherhood was formed. Born of the enthusiasm of youth, it was in being for only four years or so but its influence has continued into the twenty-first century when millions of pounds change hands in return for the sale of Pre-Raphaelite paintings.

What was the Pre-Raphaelite Brotherhood and what did it stand for? The other four initial brethren were James Collinson, the sculptor Thomas Woolner, and the art critics W. M. Rossetti and F. G. Stevens. Ford Madox Brown was closely allied with them though not at any time a member of the Brotherhood. The movement had a strong literary flavour from the start: the members were aroused to lyrical excitement by the poets John Keats and Alfred Lord Tennyson and published a journal called *The Germ* (financed by Martin Tupper). Rossetti was distinguished as a poet as well as a painter.

Rossetti's brother, William, who edited *The Germ* defined the aims of the Brotherhood as follows: 1) To have genuine ideas to express; 2) to study Nature attentively, so as to know how to express them [sic]; 3) to sympathize with what is direct and serious and heartfelt in previous art, to the exclusion of what is conventional and self-parading and learned by rote; and 4) and most indispensable of all, to produce thoroughly good pictures and statues.

Their desire for fidelity to nature was expressed through detailed observation of flora, etc., and the use of clear, bright, sharp-focus technique and their moral seriousness is seen in their choice of religious or other uplifting themes. The kind of pictures they hated were academic 'machines' and trivial 'genre scenes'. In summary the Pre-Raphaelites revelled in the study of early, primitive Italian art, i.e. before Raphael, whom they considered the turning point in what later were acclaimed to be great works of art in the neo-classical style. Raphael, along with Leonardo da Vinci and Michaelangelo, was one of the trinity of the High Renaissance. His death in 1520 is a mystery, but an artist-chronicler of the time, Giorgio Vasari, believes it was the result of exhausting sexual debauchery.

By 1853, however, the Pre-Raphaelites had virtually dissolved. Apart from their youthful revolutionary spirit and their romantic, if ill-informed, medievalism, the prime movers had little in common and they went their separate ways. Of the original members only Hunt remained true to the PRB doctrines. Millais with his much looser style with his magazine, book illustrations and advertising work became the most popular and richest painter of the day. The Pre-Raphaelite Brotherhood had its followers and critics. Amongst the supporters were Walter Deverell, Arthur Hughes, William Morris, Edward Burne-Jones and John Ruskin.[2] Amongst their critics was Charles Dickens, who called Millais' *Christ in the House of his Parents* 'mean, odious, revolting and repulsive'. John Ruskin led the defence of the Brotherhood against their abusers.

It had been learned from the Prime Minister, Lord John Russell, in March 1850, that 'the Apartments now occupied by the Royal Academy in Trafalgar Square would be required by the National Gallery'. A notice to quit was received a month later but it was announced that it was the intention of the Government to 'vote the sum of Twenty Thousand pounds in the present year, and a similar vote in the next year, to enable the Royal Academy to provide themselves with a Building suited for the purposes of Instruction for Students, and for Exhibition of the works of artists.'

Following the death of Sir Martin Archer Shee, Charles Lock Eastlake was elected president on 4 November 1850 by an overwhelming majority. His first year in office coincided with the Great Exhibition and Albert, the Prince Consort, made a point of attending the Academy Dinner, 'in order to assist what may be considered the inaugural festival of your newly elected President, at whose elections I have heartily rejoiced, not only on my high estimate of his qualities, but also on account of my feelings of regard for him personally'.

Joseph Turner who, as a student, member and professor, had been a staunch supporter of the exhibitions for over sixty years and was, with little doubt, in his day its most brilliant star, died in 1851. Edwin Landseer was probably the best known artist of the time to the ordinary public and was very much in the favour of Queen Victoria. He was given a knighthood in 1850 and this was the year he showed his painting *A Dialogue at Waterloo*. One of his most famous pictures of a stag, now called *The Monarch of the Glen*, was shown the following year.

Edward Poynter, W. B. Richmond, Thomas Brock, Albert Moore, W. L. Wyllie and Ernest George were among the students[3] admitted into the Academy schools during the period 1850-68 and some consternation during this time was caused when it was discovered that 'one of the probationers recently admitted to the Antique School is a woman'. She was Laura Anne Herford, aged twenty-nine, and apparently, as she had put her initials only on her drawings which she submitted, it was not suspected that she was a female. There had in fact never been any resolution prohibiting the entry of women into the schools but it seemed that, until then, none had ever applied!

In 1855 the Prime Minister (Lord Derby) agreed that the Royal Academy had 'a moral claim, should the Public Service require their removal from the present locality to have provided for them equally convenient accommodation elsewhere' and in 1859, the Chancellor of the Exchequer (Benjamin Disraeli), made an offer for the Academy to choose a freehold site at Burlington House in Piccadilly and for the government to erect extra premises there for its use. As this would be at the public cost, he could not promise, however, that the Academy would be free from the interference of Parliament, or future governments, but the government was ready to offer the same site for the Academy to build on out of its own funds and, in these circumstances 'the independence of the Institution could be guaranteed'.

Eastlake, the president, died at the end of 1865 and Sir Edwin Landseer was elected in his place but declined the post due to ill health. The second choice was Francis Grant, well-known in Victorian society, the owner of a hunting establishment in Melton Mowbray, who specialized in painting portraits and sporting pictures. The new president was knighted before the end of 1866. He used all his endeavours to get accepted a new architectural plan devised by Sydney Smirke. This was for the existing Burlington House to be made available for the Academy's administrative purposes and for its exhibition galleries and schools to be built immediately adjacent to it in the northern gardens. In August 1866 the government agreed to grant a 999-year lease at a nominal rent of £1 per annum on the understanding that the Academy would, at its own expense, build galleries and schools as suggested, make any necessary alterations to the house without spoiling the main southern façade (facing Piccadilly), and add a third storey.

Work commenced in April 1867 and, by May 1868, the new building on the gardens was said to be nearly completed. It comprised the present galleries I to XI (though then numbered differently), together with the lecture room, a domed central hall of octagonal plan and a vestibule, all very lofty with glass roofs, and set at first-floor level with storage accommodation below. The schools were built alongside the northern face of the galleries. They consisted basically of two ranges of studios stretching the whole length of the building plus a large room on the east for the School of Architecture, which was concealed from the courtyard by an annexe. This was added later to the old house as living quarters for the keeper. A meeting was convened in the new building on 24 November 1868 and it was available for occupation immediately afterwards, 100 years from the Academy's foundation.

Mention will be made here of the previous history of Burlington House. It was built between the years 1664 and 1668 by Sir John Denham, who was Surveyor-General to Charles II, but it was sold before completion to Richard Boyle, the first Earl of Burlington and second Earl of Cork. The mansion was of two main storeys, together with a basement and an attic, and two rooms in depth from front to back. It was built of plain brickwork and stone quoins, with walls of over four feet in thickness and a hipped roof. There were wings at both ends, projecting some ten feet to the south, and the centre of this main façade, comprising the doorway with two windows on each side was slightly recessed. The whole treatment was very simple, the only structural features being a balcony over the door and a small triangular pediment in the centre of the cornice about it. The house itself stood well back from Piccadilly (then called Portugal Street), with single-storey buildings on the east and west sides of the intervening courtyard and screens linking them to the main gate in a very high street wall.

The 3rd Earl of Burlington, later to become a celebrated dilettante and patron of the arts, came into possession of Burlington House in 1704, when he was only ten years old. Alterations seem to have started in 1712 and, as a result of the young earl's visit to Italy in 1714-15 and subsequent visits, what was a rather uninspiring house was transformed into a palatial, Italianate mansion, which was a marked success, although Denham's north front remained for another 100 years. When the architect, Colin Campbell, had completed the work, Burlington House was a fitting meeting place for soirées for the leading artists, musicians and men of letters of the day.

The 3rd Earl of Burlington died in 1753, and on the death of his widow the property passed to their grandson William Cavendish, Marquis of Huntington and subsequently 5th Duke of Devonshire. It was then tenanted in turn by two of his brothers-in-law, the 3rd Duke of Portland and Lord George Cavendish, and the latter bought it from his nephew, the 6th Duke of Devonshire, in 1815. The new owner (afterwards Earl of Burlington in a re-creation of the title) employed Samuel Ware, an architect, to make further alterations, between 1815 and 1818, which included constructing a great central staircase. The government purchased the house from the Earl of Burlington's descendants, in 1854 for £140,000. The subsequent major alterations were not begun until after the Royal Academy had built its new galleries and premises erected in 1869 for the University of London on the northern boundary of the gardens.

The first exhibition at Burlington House was held in 1869 from 3 May to 31 July. It was preceded by the annual dinner on Saturday, 1 May, but the soirée, instead of taking place at the end of the season, was brought forward to 24 June. The pattern has, generally speaking, been followed ever since but the soirée on occasions has been dropped for reasons of economy. The exhibition was a great success. There were 315,000 visitors and a profit of £15,000. In addition, a total of £14,905 7s. 6d. was reached for the sale of 189 works and thus more artists than usual who were unable 'to make ends meet', as was the custom since the foundation of the Academy reaped direct financial benefit. Over 4,500 works were submitted out of which 1,320 forming the exhibition were hung.

The annual 'Exhibition of the Works of Living Artists' began to be known in the 1870s as the Summer Exhibition. A special day for the press view was instituted in 1871 and, following the Act of Parliament that year making the first Monday in August a Bank Holiday, it was decided that from 1872 the exhibition should be extended to include this as the last day. Opening on the first Monday in May and continuing till the first Monday in August became the standard practice till 1912. The Summer Exhibition during the period 1869-78 had average attendances of around 300,000 visitors. One need only remember such paintings as *The Boyhood of Raleigh* by Millais in 1870, which was the epitome of the Victorian dream – 'Go West, young man' – of adventure and romance on the world stage, or *When did you last see your father?* by W. F. Eames in 1878 depicting an incident in the English Civil War as pictures which attracted the public; but the exhibits of G. F. Watts, John Pettie, Lawrence Alma-Tadema and Briton Riviere, to name but a few, were equally popular.[4] William Blake Richmond frequently protested that exhibitors should be allowed to have glass on their oil paintings but the proposal was always defeated. In 1876, an attempt was made to share more equitably the best hanging places and it was resolved that no artist should have more than four pictures hung 'on the line'.

The growth of the Academy inevitably involved more work for all concerned. Committees were enlarged and it was decided to elect more associate members and the system for voting for associates and full academicians was revised. In 1866 W. E. Gladstone became Professor of Ancient History. The increased accommodation for the schools at Burlington House, together with the fact that their work could now be continuously conducted without interruption on account of the exhibitions, brought about a number of reforms. Probationship was limited to a term of three months. A preliminary class was established to study the practice of oil painting and another to encourage mural painting. Teachers of sculpture and architecture were appointed in addition to the professors and a Schools' Committee (disbanded in 1874) was given the task of supervising the many changes. A Professorship of Chemistry was instituted in 1871, to which F. S. Barff was duly elected and, besides the regular courses of lecturers, single talks were given on such subjects as 'Beauty' and 'Light'. Frank Dicksee, J. Seymour Lucas, Stanhope Forbes, Hamo Thornycroft and Alfred Gilbert were amongst those admitted during the first decade of the new buildings.[5]

The health of the president, Sir Francis Grant, had been declining for some time when, in 1878, he found himself unable for the fourth year in succession, to wait upon the Queen with the annual record of the Institution's business and he died in October. The election of the new president took place on 13 November and it is noteworthy that all forty-two Royal Academicians were present. Frederick Leighton received thirty-one votes, against five for J.C. Horsley, two for Sir John Gilbert, and one each for W. P. Frith and J. E. Millais. Leighton was received by Her Majesty twelve days later and knighted.

Leighton had taken his turn more than once as a visitor in the Academy Schools and Hamo Thornycroft, for one, spoke of him as 'an inspiring master'. He was a sculptor as well as painter and, according to his contemporaries, he was a commanding presence, an eloquent speaker, punctual to a degree in his appointments, absolutely fair in all his dealings, vital in thought and action, catholic in his tastes and masterly in his judgements. It is therefore not surprising that he should have been chosen as president and that he was annually re-elected unanimously until his death in 1896. His period of office marked a peak in the Royal Academy's relationship with the general public and, largely due to him, its standing was impregnable.

Edward Burne-Jones was elected an associate in 1885 and, in a letter to him, the President wrote:

> I am not aware that any other case exists of an Artist being elected, who has never exhibited, nay has pointedly abstained from exhibiting on our walls. It is a pure tribute to your genius and therefore a true rejoicing to your affectionate old friend Fred Leighton.

The event came as a great surprise to Burne-Jones and he accepted only after considerable heart-searching. He replied:

> For many reasons, I cannot forsake the Grosvenor Gallery, they gave me an assured place of distinction from the first ... much that I do would look strange and without reason on the Academy walls ... I do want to make this clear, that there may be no after-difficulties.

Burne-Jones thereafter continued to exhibit at the Grosvenor Gallery, and sent only one painting in to the Academy in 1886. He resigned his membership in February 1893.

A fuller account of the life of Lord Leighton of Stretton is given in Chapter 3.

Lord Leighton died on 25 January 1896 and on 20 February Sir John Everett Millais was elected President of the Royal Academy by thirty-three votes to one for P. H. Calderon and, on hearing the news, Edward Lear is said to have remarked, 'Ah! Now the Millais-nium has come.' As a child prodigy, a founder-member of the Pre-Raphaelites and later the painter of many pictures which had immense popular appeal, Millais had been under consideration for the post for many years and, indeed, had acted as Leighton's deputy in the chair at the annual dinner of the previous year. Unfortunately his period in office was all too brief. Trouble with his throat proved to be a malignant cancer and his last appearance at the Academy was on the next private view day, 1 May. His devotion to the institution was heart-warming. As he said:

> I love everything belonging to it – the casts I have drawn from as a boy, the books I have consulted in the Library, the very benches I have sat on – I love them all.

He died on 13 August and was, like Leighton, buried in St Paul's Cathedral. Thus the Academy lost in a little over six months its two most distinguished members. No dinner was held, the attendance at the Summer Exhibition fell to under 300,000 for the first time in years and the whole atmosphere was one of deep mourning.

Having been deprived of two presidents in so short a time, the members appeared to be greatly divided in their views on the most suitable successor. The election took place on 4 November 1896 and, at the first marking, Briton Riviere received twelve votes, E. J. Poynter eleven, Frank Dicksee five, P. H. Calderon two and there were one each for Luke Fildes, J. C. Horsley, W. Q. Orchardson, Valentine Prinsep, W. B. Richmond and Marcus Stone.[6] Those who had obtained four votes or more were then considered a second time when Frank Dicksee's support remained as before. Riviere and Poynter increased theirs to sixteen and fifteen respectively but, at the final ballot between them, E. J. Poynter emerged as victor with nineteen votes while Riviere stayed on his previous figure. Poynter was the third member of the Artists Rifles in a row to be appointed President of the Royal Academy.

The new president, born in 1836, had at one time been a student in the Academy Schools and had spent a good deal of his younger life in Paris. He had exhibited at the Academy since 1861, been elected an associate in 1869 and an academician in 1877. He became the first Slade Professor of Fine Art at University College, London, in 1871 and, later, Principal of the National Art Training School (now the Royal College of Art) and Director for Art of the South Kensington Museum (now the Victoria and Albert and the Science Museums). In 1894, he was appointed Director of the National Gallery and thus, on his election as president in 1896, he held at one and the same time two of the most important positions in the field of art in this country. He was received by the Queen on 25 November and knighted. His wide culture, with a distinctly French bias, and his considerable experience of art teaching made him a suitable choice and he soon commanded the respect of his colleagues and the outside world – so much so that he was re-elected each year, with no votes ever recorded against him, until his resignation in December 1918, a few months before his death.

The Winter Exhibition of 1897 comprised 293 oil paintings, 107 drawings and 13 sculptures, all by Lord Leighton. It attracted over 50,000 visitors and was followed, in 1898, by one devoted to the works of Millais. This proved even more popular and drew over 80,000 people. G. F. Watts was commemorated in 1905 (over 60,000 visitors). There were only 200,000 people at the Summer Exhibition in 1897 but this seems to have been entirely due to the gloom which had descended on the institution following the deaths of Leighton and Millais. The

Queen's Diamond Jubilee was celebrated on 22 June by hoisting the Royal Standard over Burlington House and illuminating the front, but the whole of the Academy's activities were closed for the day. The attendances were reduced to about 200,000 in the period between the death of Edward VII in 1910 and the outbreak of the Great War in 1914, but, even so, the average over the whole period exceeded 280,000. There was no great change in the style of popular pictures of this period compared with those of the previous twenty years or so. W. P. Frith, G. F. Watts and James Sant, all very elderly, were still at work at the turn of the century. Lawrence Alma-Tadema, Luke Fildes and Hubert von Herkomer[7] were names to conjure with and there were attractive painters among the slightly younger men, such as John Singer Sargent with his brilliant portraits.

Queen Victoria died in January 1901 and was succeeded by her son, Edward VII. No annual dinner was held that year. The schools medals were redesigned by Thomas Brock with the head of the king on the obverse and Poynter painted a full length portrait of him for the Academy's collection. The reverse of the gold medal was to comprise three figures representing Painting, Sculpture and Architecture. It eventually materialized but not until 1910, by which time Edward VII had just died and George V had come to the throne. His head, also by Brock, then adorned the medals until his death in 1936. The reverse of the silver and bronze medals during both these reigns was a new version of the Belvedere torso with the word '*STUDY*' on the left and the inscription '*THE ROYAL ACADEMY OF ARTS INSTITUTED MDCCLXVIII*' on the right.

In 1905 moves were made by the Art Union of London drawing attention 'to the decay of the art of Engraving in England' and urging establishment of a school of instruction in the subject at the Royal Academy and another at South Kensington. The Academy replied sympathetically though no immediate action was taken on these particular lines but in 1906 two engravers, Frank Short and William Strang, were made members and these were the first such elections since 1883. At the same time, it was resolved that 'in order to be eligible for election as an Associate, a Painter must obtain five signatures to his nomination, a Sculptor three, an Architect three, and an Engraver three, all of course from existing members'. In 1907 it was decided to hold an annual conference 'for the purpose of making suggestions with regard to the Schools and the Summer Exhibition' and in 1914 it was agreed that 'all Elections of Associates be held on one of the Members' Varnishing days in the month of April'.

There was talk in 1913 of the formation of a Ministry of Fine Arts but it came to nothing. It was also the period of trouble with suffragettes.

An abortive attempt was made to start a fire in the ladies' lavatory and to hold a public meeting in the galleries while, in 1914, a woman made three slashes with a chopper through the glass and canvas of the portrait of *Henry James*. Another female slightly damaged Sir Hubert von Herkomer's portrait of *The Duke of Wellington* and a third caused serious injury to the painting *Primavera* by George Clausen. The iron railings around the galleries were then set further back from the walls and additional detectives were employed but the Academy did not in fact close its doors as did certain important permanent collections at the time.

Such troubles quickly ceased, however, at the outbreak of the Great War in August 1914 when the use of the galleries was immediately offered for any military purpose and, from October, the eastern half was occupied for a few months by the United Arts Force;[8] their rifles were stored in the refreshment room and drills were carried out vigorously in the courtyard. The building was insured against damage by hostile aircraft for £120,000 and the Academy's possessions for £80,000. The highest individual valuation (£3,500) was placed on each of the following items – the Michaelangelo tondo, the Leonardo da Vinci cartoon, the painting *Temperance* (then considered to be by Giorgione), *Theory* by Reynolds, his *Self-portrait* and his full-length paintings of *George III* and *Queen Charlotte*. Forty of the Academy's chief treasures were stored in a specially adapted 'safe chamber' in the basement together with sixteen pictures from Sir John Soane's Museum.

As the war got into its stride, the majority of the male students enlisted in the armed forces. The Architecture School and the Day Modelling School had to be closed in 1915 followed by all the Evening Schools in 1916. There were no male classes for the duration and all prizes were suspended. The Diploma and Gibson Galleries were closed and no annual dinners or soirées were held. The Winter Exhibition of 1915, called the War Relief Exhibition, took the form of a collection of works by living artists contributed by invitation. The exhibitors received one-third only of the proceeds of sales and the remaining two-thirds together with the profits on running the exhibition, were divided between the Artists' General Benevolent Institution, the British Red Cross and St John Ambulance Association and a fund for the relief of Belgian Artists. Towards the end of the year the galleries in the eastern half of the building were used as ladies' work-rooms for 'sewing shirts for soldiers' and similar purposes.

The number of submissions declined to about 8,000 from 1916 to 1919 but increased again to 10,000 or so in the early 1920s and the total of works exhibited varied from 1,250 and 1,950. Many of the pictures depicted the grimness of war, such as, *Youth Mourning* by George

Clausen, *Defeat of the Prussian Guard* by W. B. Wollen and *A Fight to the Last* by W. L. Wyllie, while others in the same year, such as *Sunny Morning* by Alfred Parsons and *A Spring Revel* by R. Anning Bell, seemed to be specially designed to keep at bay the horrors of the time. William Orpen and R. G. Eves were busy painting portraits of serving officers while heroes and heroines, such as Nurse Cavell, were popular subjects. Incidents in the great battles of Ypres, Verdun, the Dardanelles, Jutland and many others were seized upon, followed by scenes of the Armistice and the signing of treaties. Eventually there was a spate of war memorials and the Academy set up a special committee in 1918 to advise on them. A memorial tablet, to commemorate those students who had lost their lives in the war, was placed under the portico at the western end of the building, and to match this a similar memorial for the Artists Rifles was later placed at the eastern end.

Sir Edward Poynter was over eighty and in poor health when he resigned the presidency in December 1918. A special toast was drunk to him at the next annual dinner (the first after the war and resplendent with admirals and generals) and he died in July 1919. The election of Sir Aston Webb had taken place on 21 January and he received twenty-four votes against two for Sir George Frampton and one each for Reginald Blomfield, Sir Arthur Cope, Frank Dicksee, Sir Frank Short and Henry Woods.[9] Thus for the fourth time in a row the president had been a member of the Artists Rifles. Except for the makeshift appointment of James Wyatt when Benjamin West had been temporarily out of favour, Webb was the first architect to be made president. He was already in his seventieth year and the election was the culminating point of his busy and rewarding career.

Sir Aston Webb had been President of the Architectural Association as early as 1884 and of the Royal Institute of British Architects in 1902. In 1905 he received the latter's royal gold medal and, in the following year, was the first recipient of one awarded by the American Institute of Architects. Webb designed the Imperial College and the Victoria and Albert Museum at South Kensington in 1891 and, in 1913, was responsible for Admiralty Arch, the Mall and the existing front of Buckingham Palace, giving the layout a simple dignity which forms a suitable setting for the pomp and glitter of processions on ceremonial occasions. Sir Aston Webb's former Academy post as treasurer was filled by the appointment of Sir Frank Short. Unfortunately Webb was seriously injured in a motor accident in 1924 when returning home from the annual dinner with Melton Fisher, Sir Luke Fildes and Sir William Llewellyn. He was out of action for nearly a year, by which time he had to resign the Presidency on becoming a Senior Academician. Sir Frank Dicksee was elected in his place and was knighted in the New Year.

Hitherto unaccustomed to cope with the difficulties of business or diplomacy, Dicksee soon had a very ticklish problem on his hands. Charles Sims had been granted sittings in 1922 for a portrait of George V. It was shown in the Academy Exhibition of 1924 and a reproduction of it forms the front page of *The Royal Academy Illustrated* of that year. The king, however, informed Dicksee of his dissatisfaction with the finished picture which, though a splendidly flamboyant composition, was somewhat whimsical. The legs might have belonged to a ballet dancer. Sims duly received his fee (250 guineas) and it was agreed that the picture should be destroyed but he subsequently exhibited it in New York in the autumn of 1925 and had arrangements in hand to show it in Canada. This put the President of the Academy in a very embarrassing position and, on payment of a further 750 guineas, they took possession of it 'unreservedly'. The official records are silent as to its ultimate fate but rumour has it that the head was cut from the rest of the canvas and retained for a short while though both pieces were eventually burned to ashes in the boiler house at the Academy under supervision of the treasurer and the secretary. Meanwhile the Council arranged for a new portrait by Sir Arthur Cope. This was duly approved and Queen Mary always considered it to be the best likeness of George V.

Sir Frank Dicksee died in October 1928 and in December Sir William Llewellyn was elected president in his place. Llewellyn, a good-looking Welshman who always retained the upright bearings of a distinguished courtier, had at one time been a student under Sir Edward Poynter at the National Art Training School and also studied in Paris. He began exhibiting regularly at the Royal Academy in 1884 and soon turned to portrait painting as a profession, one of his most successful works being the State portrait of *Queen Mary* in 1910. He seldom expressed personal opinions but was skilful in summing up at meetings and, when he did speak, it was with an autocratic finality. His manner was pleasant but full of the dignity of his office. His soft, rather twisted smile was inscrutable and his demeanour imperturbable.

The most important feature of Llewellyn's presidency was the series of international loan exhibitions. That of Dutch Art, 1450-1900, from January to March 1929, was followed the following year by that of Italian Art 1200-1900. The loans from Italy were brought about by the personal intervention of Mussolini and they were transported to and from this country in the Italian vessel *Leonardo da Vinci*. The attendances at the exhibition were enormous. Nearly 540,000 persons paid for single admissions and, with the sale of almost 10,000 season tickets, this brought the total number of visits to about 600,000, more than had been recorded for an exhibition at the Academy before. The Italian exhibition was followed by one of Persian Art in 1931, the magnificent array of carpets, jewellery, miniatures and various objets d'art capturing people's imagination. A platform was built in Gallery VIII for the display of a fine collection of the Shah's jewels. On the walls were silk, gold and silver carpets and the whole effect was reminiscent of the Arabian Nights. The exhibition of French Art, 1200-1900, was more usual and palatable to European taste, including an important representation of the Impressionists and Post-Impressionists.

The Commemorative Exhibition of Works by Late Members (Dicksee, Orpen and twelve others) in 1933 was modest by comparison but over 40,000 people attended. This was followed in 1934 by a gigantic Exhibition of British Art, c.1000-1860. There were over 1,600 exhibits and special exhibitions in connection with it were held concurrently at the National Gallery, the British Museum and the Victoria and Albert Museum. Besides about 600 oil paintings and over 200 watercolours, there were large and choice displays of miniatures, drawings, manuscripts, alabasters, ivories, silver, porcelain and sculpture, as well as tapestries, armour and furniture. A conference had been held in 1929 to discuss 'the training of British artists in Design for Manufacturers' and, in his speech at the Royal Academy Dinner in 1932, Prince George (afterwards Duke of Kent) spoke at some length on the possibilities of improving the attractiveness of British manufactured goods. The president took up the same theme and the outcome was the Exhibition of British Art in Industry held at the Royal Academy three years later in collaboration with the Royal Society of Arts.

The next great exhibition was that of Chinese Art in the winter of 1935-6. It comprised over 3,000 exhibits from the earliest times to about AD 1800. The Chinese Government contributed more than 800 items and other examples were procured from almost every major country in the world. A colossal marble statue of Buddha, over 20 feet high and weighing 14 tons, dominated the Central Hall. The exhibition contained paintings, calligraphy, sculpture, porcelain, pottery, lacquer, glass, embroidery, fans and carpets. The bronzes and jades were of superlative quality and the Architectural Room, fitted out as a Chinese interior, was delightful. Well over 400,000 people came to the show and, on the last Thursday, there were almost 20,000 visitors in the one day. The cult of chinoiserie took London by storm and some aspects of it were reflected in the fashions and furnishings for some time to come.

George V died in January 1936 and no dinner or soirée was held that year. His successor, Edward VIII, did not wish his head to appear on any medals except 'King's Medals' and the Academy thereupon commissioned E.G. Gillick to produce a design with the head of its founder sovereign, George III. He did so, showing the king in a tricorne hat surrounded by the inscription *'KING GEORGE III – PATRON PROTECTOR SUPPORTER'*. The reverse had the words *'BENE MERENTI'* separated horizontally by a spray of laurel and surrounded by the inscription *'ROYAL ACADEMY OF ARTS – FOUNDED MDCCLXVIII'*. This design has been used for all Academy schools' medals since that date, in gold, silver and bronze, and whether or not paid for through any trust fund. The abdication of Edward VIII took place in December 1936 and his brother, George VI, then came to the throne. To mark the coronation in the following year, the Academy's royal portraits hung together in the Central Hall as a feature of the Summer Exhibition.

The exhibition of Seventeenth Century Art in Europe held in 1938, was both scholarly and attractive but had no wide appeal, while the exhibition of British Architecture in 1937 drew less than 9,000 visitors in a period of eight weeks. The last loan exhibition before the Second World War, in 1939, was that of Scottish Art. Schemes for exhibitions of American, Japanese, German and Indian Art were under way but all had to be abandoned as Adolf Hitler destroyed the peace of Europe and eventually the world. An era was at an end and once again the Academy had to restrict its activities. Meanwhile the Summer Exhibitions continued steadily in the 1930s. As far back as 1914, the question of a statue of Sir Joshua Reynolds had been discussed and a commission for it was given to Alfred Drury in 1917 through the Leighton Fund. The final model was approved in 1929 and the finished figure, in bronze, was erected in the courtyard in 1931. Two years later, a pair of wrought iron lamp standards, designed by Sir Edwin Lutyens and Sir William Reid Dick, were paid for through this same fund to stand in front of the west entrance of St Paul's Cathedral and, in 1937 and 1939, bronze statues of J.M.W. Turner by William McMillan and Thomas Gainsborough by Sir Thomas Brock were placed in niches at the top of the main staircase in Burlington House. Sir David Murray made a present in 1930 of a stained glass window, which was designed by C. Kruger Gray, for the Diploma Gallery staircase and, after Murray's death in 1933, it was learned that he had left the Academy a large sum of money (about £38,000) to be used for encouraging the study of landscape painting.[10]

Sir William Llewellyn's last year as president was in 1938 and Sir Edwin Lutyens was elected in his place. Lutyens, born in London in 1869, was best known to the public as the designer of the Cenotaph in Whitehall and the most prolific architect of his time, but, to the initiated his name meant much more. It stood for fertility of invention and elegance of style in his work at New Delhi, his civic buildings in this country and his variety of country houses. His wit was crisp and unbounding. He was forever drawing on whatever paper came to hand, on menu cards particularly and even on the tablecloth but, behind the boyish spirits, there was a brilliant brain and a great kindness of heart. He had been knighted in 1918, made a KCIE in 1930 and, in 1942 was awarded the Order of Merit. His presidency came to an end with his death on New Year's Day in 1944 and, unfortunately, his period of office was hampered by the exigencies of the Second World War.

The war had begun in 1939 and the arrangements for an art exhibition that winter of the Art of Greater India, which was well advanced, had to be abandoned. A conference of representatives of seventeen art societies was held at the Academy on 5 October when it was agreed to promote instead a United Artists' Exhibition on similar lines to the War Relief Exhibition of 1915. Eight other art societies subsequently joined in and, in fact, no serious artist in the country, whether a member of any society or not, was debarred from participating. Almost 1,200 artists were represented in the exhibition and there were 2,219 exhibits; 201 items were sold for over £4,000. The artists retained half the selling price while the other half was divided between the Lord Mayor's Red Cross and St John Fund and the Artists' General Benevolent Institution. Plans were put in hand for a similar exhibition in the following year but they had to be set aside when the Academy's glass roofs suffered severe damage from nearby bomb explosions in September and November 1940.

Perhaps the greatest triumph of the war years was to have continued the series of summer exhibitions, dating from 1769, without a break. With so many artists on war service, it is understandable that the number of submissions fell, but most surprising that the total in any one year was never less than 5,500. The attendances slumped to below 50,000 in 1940 and 1941, but reached almost 150,000 again from 1943 and over 200,000 in 1945. With all the permanent collections closed the public was starved of art and, after an initial period of hibernation, was willing to face flying bombs to visit the Academy's exhibitions. Union Jacks were raised along the Piccadilly frontage of Burlington House during the exhibition in 1944 (and indeed for each major exhibition subsequently) and this reflected the determination of all concerned to keep spirits high. Neither the dinner nor the soirée was held through the war. *The Royal Academy Illustrated* could not be published after 1940 owing chiefly to the scarcity of suitable paper. The Academy schools had to close down at the end of the summer term in 1940. No lectures and none of the prize competitions were held until after the cessation of hostilities.

Unfortunately Lutyens, who had been ill for a long period in 1943, died the following New Year's Day. The election for a new president took place on 14 March. After the second ballot A. J. Munnings beat Augustus John by twenty-four votes to seventeen and Munnings was knighted in June that year.

Sir Alfred James Munnings had been born in 1878 in East Anglia and, from 1920, lived at Dedham in the heart of Constable country. From his early youth he had painted landscapes with gypsies, cattle and ponies and, from the days of the Great War, he had more and more chosen horses and their surroundings as his favourite subjects. He scarcely ever missed an important race meeting, though he never placed bets, and eventually he had a studio provided for him at Newmarket. Despite the loss of sight of his right eye by an unfortunate accident at the age of twenty-one, he was the keenest observer of the effects of light. He was a born countryman, bluff and honest, often to the extent of causing embarrassment. He saw no place in art for abstractions and 'isms' and had a very low opinion of their adherents.

Munnings became president at a time when the financial side was beginning to turn temporarily in the Academy's favour. Germany surrendered in May 1945 and that year brought over 200,000 people to the Summer Exhibition. Arrangements were made for the Painting and Sculpture Schools to reopen in 1946, and there was talk of resuming the large loan exhibitions. The first post-war loan exhibition took place in the winter of 1946-7 and was entitled *The King's Pictures*. Over 500 paintings were assembled from the various Royal Palaces and they included masterpieces from the collection of Charles I, Dutch and Venetian pictures acquired by George III and George IV, early Italian works collected by the Prince Consort in the nineteenth century and an unrivalled series of portraits by Holbein, Van Dyck, Reynolds, Gainsborough, Lawrence and others. Such an exhibition would have been bound to attract a large public at any time but, coming as it did immediately after the deprivations of war, people flocked to it and the total number of admissions exceeded 366,000.

Sir Alfred Munnings did not stand for re-election as president at the end of 1947. The voting took place on 8 December and at the second ballot Sir Gerald Kelly defeated Charles Wheeler to become the new president. Kelly, one of the best-known portrait painters of his day, was then seventy but still full of drive. In temperament and methods he was not unlike the famous actor-managers of his youth. He had many friends and acquaintances in high places and, through a number of successful broadcasts on television, he became very popular with a large public. His conversation and speeches were always entertaining and his personal style in letter writing most persuasive. He gathered around him, from outside the Academy, important groups of advisers on finance and the assembling of loan exhibitions but, in judgements on art he would accept no interference with his own intuition and experience. The Royal Academy had survived the war and flourished once again, now well on the road to celebrating its bicentenary on 10 December 1968.

Notes
1. Of these, Millais, Hunt, Rossetti and Hughes were enrolled in the Artists Rifles in 1860
2. Of these, Hughes, Morris, Burne-Jones and Ruskin were founder members of the Artists Rifles (Ruskin was an honorary member).
3. Sir Edward Poynter, a future president of the Royal Academy, Sir William Blake Richmond and Sir Thomas Brock (a sculptor) were all early members of the Artists Rifles.
4. W.F. Eames and G.F.Watts were members of the Artists Rifles.
5. Frank Dicksee and Hamo Thornycroft were members of the Artists Rifles.
6. Val Prinsep and Luke Fildes were members of the Artists Rifles.
7. Sir Hubert von Herkomer was a member of the Artists Rifles.
8. The United Arts Force was an unofficial off-shoot of the Artists Rifles.
9. Sir Aston Webb and Sir Arthur Cope were members of the Artists Rifles.
10. Like Sir Thomas Brock, William McMillan and C. Kruger Gray were members of the Artists Rifles.

Chapter 3

Frederick Leighton, The Royal Academy and the Artists Rifles

1830-1896

He is Colonel of the Royal Academy and President of the Artists Rifles – Aye, and he paints a little!

James Whistler

Frederick Leighton, whose Christian name seems to have been spelt without the final 'k' from about 1891 onwards, was born in 1830 in Scarborough on the Yorkshire coast, the son and grandson of eminent physicians. His grandfather, Sir James Leighton, had been court physician to the Tsar of Russia. His father, Frederic Septimus Leighton, foreshadowed his son's ability. He had, for instance, the gift of languages, learnt Russian in six months, and astonished everyone by passing his medical examinations in Russian at St Petersburg with the highest credit. His flow of conversation was copious and there seemed to be no end to his reading. Part of each day was set aside for the study of Greek and Latin classics. His mother had the gentler virtues. She loved music, had some talent for drawing and was devoted to her family.

There were three children: two girls, the elder, Alexandra, godchild of the Empress Alexandra of Russia; the younger, Augusta (affectionately known as 'Gussie') and Frederick, the only surviving son (the younger son James dying in infancy). By the time the painter was born, his father returning to England, no longer had the economic need nor the inclination to practise as a doctor. (The family fortune had grown in Russia on account of service to the Tsar.) Frederick's father, who was thoroughly intellectual, agnostic and cosmopolitan, began to oversee his son's education with diligence.

From Scarborough the family moved to Bath, but Dr. Leighton was not long in practice there. He grew deaf and the disability that cut him off from his patients turned him increasingly to the world of books and ideas and gave him ample time to train his children and in particular his only son. At ten the boy was well grounded in Greek and Latin and knew more of the legends, the poems and history of the ancient world than he would have been likely to gain at school. An untoward event now became the means of making his education still more exemplary and apprising him of the wonders of Europe.

In 1840 Mrs. Leighton had an attack of rheumatic fever and as a result the family began to travel abroad for the sake of her health. They had never really settled down, and had moved from Bath to London in 1832, living first in Argyll Street and then Upper Gower Street. They now went to Germany and Switzerland and away from the winter to Italy. They visited Berlin, Frankfurt, Dresden and Munich. They wandered, in affluent nomadism, from one Italian city to another – Milan, Florence, Bologna, Venice, Rome, Naples – and Dr. Leighton did not overlook, as well as the beneficial effects on his wife's constitution, those on his son's mind.

At the age of twelve Frederick was fluent in French and Italian, in a year or two more in German too. Meanwhile he began to show a strong bent for drawing and painting, and this Dr Leighton encouraged, without being aware of it. He wanted the boy to be a doctor, for this was the family calling. Therefore he gave him careful instruction in anatomy. He taught him the names of the bones and muscles, described them in action and repose, and insisted that they should be drawn from memory and without mistake. Anatomy was as useful to the student of art as of medicine, and at fourteen Frederick Leighton knew more about the structure of the body than an academy would have taught him. His father was disappointed when he learned that his son wished to be an artist. There was so much that was inexact and uncertain about the career, so much that was alien to his exact mind; yet, if this was to be his son's choice, then, obviously, the best masters must be employed, and the most eminent practitioners had to be consulted.

The expanding scheme of Frederick's education had already called for special tutors, among them a Roman drawing master, Signor Francesco Meli; but before Dr Leighton sanctioned art as a main study for his son, he took the advice of the then noted sculptor, an American living in Florence, Hiram Powers, to whom he showed examples of Frederick's drawings.

'Shall I make him a painter?'

'Sir,' said Powers, 'you cannot help yourself, nature has made him so already!'

'What can he hope for?'

'Let him aim at the highest. He will be certain to get there.'

In the winter of 1842-43, young Frederick Leighton was at the Berlin Academy, and during 1845-6 at the Accademia delle Belle Arti, in Florence. In the summer of 1846 the family settled in Frankfurt, which at this time enjoyed the reputation of one of Europe's most highly cultured cities. It was here that Frederick followed his serious artistic education at the Städelsches Kunstinstitut although the family left the city during the disturbed years of the Frankfurt Parliament (1848-49), when the Leightons spent time with Frederick pursuing his art studies in Brussels, Paris and London.

Frederick was not entirely satisfied with his progress. He needed a master who could develop and control his talents. Returning to Germany a master was found in the Nazarene painter, Jacob Eduard von Steinle. The Germans were thorough – and Frederick had been trained to appreciate thoroughness. They were in earnest, which he was, precise in all that they did, and punctual – qualities which many journeys had already taught him to value. Thorough, earnest, precise was von Steinle, in addition an idealist and a leading member of a school of painters, which in the course of forty years or more, since about 1800, had grown famous.

These painters were called the 'Nazarenes', or one might say the German Pre-Raphaelites, the nucleus of the group being established in 1809 when six students of the Vienna Academy, including Friedrich Overbeck and Franz Pforr, formed an association called the Brotherhood of St Luke (*Lukasbrüder*), named after the patron saint of painting. They believed that art should serve a religious or moral purpose and that since about the middle of the sixteenth century this ideal had been betrayed for the sake of artistic virtuosity. In their desire to return to the spirit of the Middle Ages, the *Lukasbrüder* not only looked to late medieval and early Renaissance art, but also wished to return to a learning and teaching programme based on the workshop rather than the academy. To this end they lived and worked together in a quasi-monastic fashion. In 1810 Overbeck, Pforr and two other members of the Brotherhood moved to Rome, where they occupied the disused monastery of St Isidoro.

Frederick Leighton found Steinle a congenial master and he admired much of the work of the Nazarenes, but he began to have his doubts about the Brotherhood. Von Steinle, like his fellow Nazarenes, was engulfed in a deep-seated and pathological disquiet, which the young Englishman and Olympian in the making could not be expected to understand. The Nazarenes were full of yearning, doubt and complexity. They were, one might say, men fighting desperately for their souls, engaged in an intense spiritual struggle on which even national existence may depend.

It was natural that having imbibed the Nazarene dream in Germany Frederick should take to the revivalists' spiritual home, Rome. He left Frankfurt in August 1852 for Rome where he initially followed the Nazarene form, holding himself apart from the large international colony of artists, regretting the Reformation and hanging works by the Nazarene painters Peter van Cornelius and Jacob von Steinle in his studio. His instinctive independence had perhaps already begun to harden into isolation; for while he had scant respect for the current generations of students in Rome, Leighton also found the veteran Nazarene Overbeck decrepit and religiose and his younger imitators trivial. Rome indeed was the grave of art, with all sense of community lost.

In social terms Leighton did not have to remain entirely lonely, however, for in 1853 he formed a very strong friendship with Adelaide Sartoris, the sister of Fanny Kemble who had herself been a renowned singer until her marriage a decade earlier. She became Frederick's best friend in Rome, and they were soon seeing each other every day. To his mother Leighton made the revealing comment that he feared he would never find a wife to measure up to her. But too much should not be made of his dependence upon Mrs Adelaide Sartoris, as Frederick was still able to enjoy a flirtation with Isabel Laing, the daughter of some family friends, whose portrait he painted in 1853. He mixed happily enough both in Roman high society and with an ever growing circle of English visitors and expatriates.

Among his visitors were William Makepiece Thackeray and Robert Browning and Elizabeth Barrett Browning. When Thackeray, who was in Rome to do the drawings for *The Rose and the Ring* returned to London, he chuckled to his friend, John Everett Millais, 'Johnny, my boy, we always settled that you should have the Presidentship of the Royal Academy, but I have met in Rome a versatile young dog called Leighton, who will one of these days run you hard for it'.

Frederick Leighton was radiant in personality and high-spirited. He was a model of courtesy and irresistible in charm. He talked so well, and so well in many languages, and everyone averred that he was marked out for a splendid career as a painter. No sooner than one superlative quality was noted than another of a counter and complementary kind appeared to balance it. With so many mental gifts was he not studious, stooping, averse from physical exercise? Not so. As he was to prove as an officer and gentleman of the Artists Rifle Volunteers, which he was later to command, he was splendidly active, fond of exercise and an accomplished dancer. 'I don't know what he is like as a painter,' said a girl with whom he had danced, 'but I know he is the best waltzer in Rome.'

Leighton worked in Rome from 1852 and in 1855 he had his first exhibit hung in the Royal Academy. The painting, an oil on canvas, 87½ x 205 inches, entitled *Cimabue's celebrated Madonna is carried in procession on the streets of Florence*, was bought by Queen Victoria for 600 guineas and his reputation was made. He did not, however, settle in London until 1860 and this is the probable explanation of his not being elected an associate of the Royal Academy until 1864, by which time Millais, the Academy's most eminent exhibitor, was already an academician. Leighton himself was elected an RA in 1868.

He built himself a magnificent house designed by George Aitchison in London in Holland Park Road in 1865-6[1] but still continued to travel, particularly in Spain, Algiers and Egypt with frequent visits elsewhere over the years, never neglecting his beloved Italy. No doubt his wide knowledge of foreign works of art led him to be a firm supporter of the Academy's promotion of loan exhibits from 1870, he himself serving on the organizing committees. He was also devoted to the Artists Volunteer Corps, which he had joined when it was formed in 1860.

As we have learned in Chapter 1, when Frederick Leighton joined the Artists Volunteer Corps he was numbered nine in the muster roll. Although he was an established painter and exhibitor at the Royal Academy, he was not the most eminent of the bevy of artists, who had joined together in founding the Corps, an honour attributed at the time, although by 1860 the Pre-Raphaelites had broken up, to Millais, Holman Hunt, Dante Gabriel Rosetti and their ally William Morris. After the departure of Lord Bury (No. 1 in the muster roll) after an abortive spell as captain and the appointment of H. Wyndham Phillips, a distinguished portrait painter but not an academician as captain, Arthur Lewis, a painter, and Millais were elected lieutenants. Frederick Leighton and Alfred Nicholson, a musician, were made ensigns. Just before the end of 1860, what was now known as The 38th Middlesex (Artists) Rifle Volunteers, was granted a new establishment of two rather than one company. Phillips became captain commandant and Lewis and Leighton were appointed respectively as captains of the two companies. As William Blake Richmond, who had joined the Artists Volunteers in 1860 at seventeen years of age, recorded in his papers:[2]

> It was hard work and by no means child's play. Field days were most enjoyable, by these I mean sham fights which were played in pleasant places in Kent or Surrey; when either we marched to the scene of operations or were taken like cattle in trucks, and returned in like manner often very late at night. To do your duty as an Artist Volunteer, there were the daily hours 7 to 9 a.m. and company and Lock Drill from 4 to 7 p.m. in Burlington House Gardens [the open

piece of land on which the extension of Burlington House now stands] or in the earlier days in the old Argyll rooms, where two Companies could be drilled. On Saturdays the whole afternoon, sometimes the whole day, [The Volunteers were often called 'The Saturday afternoon soldiers'] was taken up in drill, route marches and skirmishing upon some open space in London. This, in itself, was exacting, but men really in earnest managed to get in their seven or eight hours' work of painting besides their patriotic duty, and the latter told wonderfully upon the health of us all – never was I so well and full of energy. Leighton was a marvel, so thoroughly did he become a soldier-painter that he learned his job *au fond* and was hard at the study of battalion and company drill at Wellington Barracks with the Guards at 5 o'clock on summer mornings. No wonder he rose to such distinction as a Commander and could hold his own with the best leaders of troops. But then, Leighton had a genius for success in whatever he put his hand to.

Leighton, who certainly did all things well, excelled at these war games. 'I make as bad a soldier as anybody else,' he wrote lightly to Robert Browning, the poet. The German habit of punctuality and thoroughness, acquired in the early days of his art studies, stood him in good stead. But although the founding of the Corps seemed to be progressing satisfactorily there were two opposing cultural camps within its ranks. In the one camp was the former Pre-Raphaelite Brotherhood: their art had been popularly acclaimed by the public that cared for art.

The Pre-Raphaelites were in love with the Middle Ages. They, too, loved less the beauty of the figure than the mystic melancholy of legend. Frederick Leighton represented the opposing camp, his work inspired by the neo-classical tradition upon which the Royal Academy was founded. He, after all, had freed himself from the German 'Pre-Raphaelites' – the pietistic Nazarene Brotherhood. There was not a very close similarity between the German and English artists, but enough to arouse Leighton's critical suspicion. If it came to a preference between Athens and Camelot, Leighton preferred Athens. Millais and Leighton, although brothers in arms and the best of friends, were in a sense artistic rivals but less so through the 1860s when Millais turned to commercial art, including book illustrations, which deservedly made him into an immensely rich man. Leighton and Millais did, however, combine their talents to design the jaunty grey cap worn in the Artists Corps in those early days.

In a way Leighton was feeling his way as an artist and sculptor – sculpture playing a secondary role to his work as a painter – in the 1860s although as we have learned he was a full academician in 1868.

In spite of the demands of his 'military hobby' he made a prolonged grand tour in the late 1860s in the course of which he acquired many of those objects of art which were to delight and astonish visitors in his mansion in Holland Park. He visited Greece and the Grecian islands where he learnt much about the bodily perfection sought by the Greek artists. He went on to Rhodes and Lindos, where he bought much pottery.

He came back to London in 1868, and announcing his arrival, expressed himself 'right glad to be home again'. Yet in the same year he was off again, this time to Egypt where the circumstances of his expedition were of a splendour that was unusual but befitting. He had an audience at once with the Khedive, not as a painter (even an illustrious one) but as a friend of the Prince of Wales. The Khedive was at his palace in Abassia, and if the military review which was then taking place was not for Leighton's benefit, it happily coincided with his arrival and he was much impressed by it. The purpose of Leighton's visit to the Khedive was to seek his help and advice in touring all the sites of interest in Egypt which were worthy of a visit. The Khedive cordially obliged by putting his steam yacht at Leighton's disposal, which would get him down the Nile in considerable comfort.

In 1868 Captain Wyndham Phillips died. He was succeeded in command of the Artists by Captain Frederick Leighton who was elected at a general meeting of the Corps held at the Middlesex Artillery Drill Hall in Leicester Square, on 6 January 1869. In the same year (the Corps then consisting of four companies), he was promoted to major.

In 1875 the strength of the Corps was increased to six companies and the CO, Major Leighton, was promoted to lieutenant colonel, Captain Robert Edis, the architect, being promoted to senior major, or in modern parlance second in command. Three years later the commanding officer having been appointed to be president of the Royal Academy, he was knighted and became Sir Frederick Leighton. He was, as the American painter James Whistler put it when commenting with ironic wit on Sir Frederick Leighton's achievements, 'Colonel of the Royal Academy and President of the Artists Rifles – Aye and he paints a little.'

In his dual management role Sir Frederick Leighton no doubt granted himself permission to hold a battalion parade in the courtyard of the Royal Academy. Mounted on his horse he faced the parade and delivered his order in part before being bucked by the horse and thrown on to the cobbled stones of the courtyard. Scrambling to his feet he completed the order in the standing position. Meanwhile the horse went galloping out through the archway racing down Piccadilly until it was gallantly apprehended by a policeman at Hyde Park Corner. The policeman led the horse back to Burlington House where the commanding officer re-mounted the horse, re-assuming his dignity at the head of his troops. Leighton was unhurt by the mishap but his soldiers could barely conceal their mirth.

Extant regimental records of this period are rather sparse and hence not very informative but it was Leighton as the newly elected president of the Royal Academy who instituted the Academy Guard, which was mounted by the Artists Volunteers in the courtyard at the Royal Academy on the eve of the Summer Exhibition to honour the principal guest, usually but not always of the Royal Family. The guard preceded by the drums consisted of three officers and up to 100 men formed up in four files. At Leighton's first dinner, the Duke of Cambridge, who was still commander-in-chief of the British Army, complimented Leighton on the 'fine body of men' who had stood before the Academy steps to greet the guests on their arrival. It was a welcome change of heart on the part of the Duke, who had so vehemently criticized the formation of the Volunteers. It was the custom that the Guard Commander, a major, would take his place at the dinner, the guard marching back to their headquarters where they were refreshed with beer and sandwiches. The guard was subsequently mounted each year with the exception of those of the two World Wars and the death of the sovereign until 1939 when the Artists Rifles ceased to exist as an active unit.

The first Summer Exhibition under Leighton's presidency (1879) was a huge success. It attracted the greatest number of paying visitors (391,197) ever recorded in the long series of these shows and 2,878 season tickets (first introduced in 1876) were issued. The holders of these tickets would have had to use them at least five times to make their purchase worthwhile, so that with free admissions for exhibitors, press and others, the total attendance must have reached well over 400,000. More than 115,000 catalogues were sold and the excess of receipts over expenditure on the exhibition amounted to £20,814. The largest number of visitors on a single day was 7,643 and the smallest 2,589. This was an exceptional season but the average total attendance yearly over the next twenty years was about 355,000. Sir Frederick Leighton as president was in an impregnable position and he remained President of the Royal Academy until his death in 1896.

The 1880s and 1890s were golden years for Leighton and the Academy. As a painter he was prolific. His varied output included portraits and book illustrations, but he is best known for his paintings of classical Greek subjects, the finest of which were distinguished by magnificently opulent colouring as well as splendid draughtsmanship, as, for example, demonstrated by *The Garden of the Hesperides*. As a sculptor he is best known for the bronze *Athlete Struggling with a Python*.

In 1881 the title 38th Middlesex was changed to 20th Middlesex (Artists) Rifle Volunteers and in 1883 Lieutenant Colonel Leighton resigned as its commanding officer. His work at the Royal Academy had become too much for him to handle both appointments. He did however as honorary colonel attend the regimental dinners and smokers' concerts right up until his death thirteen years later. In 1886 he was made a baronet and, in the New Year's Honours List of 1896, he was awarded a barony. He thus became the first British professional artist to be raised to the peerage and, on 24 January, the day before his death, he assumed the title of Lord Leighton of Stretton, a village in Shropshire where his ancestors had lived. Leighton contracted a slight bronchial cold in the week before his death but he gave strict instructions that no news of his illness should be made public. It is often said that he died of exhaustion and his last words were 'Give my love to the Royal Academy'. To carry out the wishes of their brother, Lord Leighton's two sisters subsequently gave £10,000 to the Royal Academy. His coffin rested at Burlington House from the Thursday before the funeral. The coffin lay in state in the Central Hall; it was covered in rich embroidery and raised on a bier, surrounded by innumerable wreaths and palms, on a dark-coloured floor covering. A bronze bust of the artist, decorated with the president's gold medal and chain, was set at the head on a white marble pedestal draped in black crepe. His palette and brushes were placed on the pall-cloth at the foot of the coffin and his many orders and medals were displayed on crimson velvet cushions. In the centre of this profuse array, the plain laurel wreath from his colleagues stood in simple dignity.

Lord Leighton was buried at St Paul's Cathedral on Monday 3 February 1896. He was buried in the crypt alongside Sir Joshua Reynolds, the first president of the Royal Academy. His coffin was escorted by a detachment of the grey-clad Artists Volunteers. The coffin was smothered in wreaths from the highest in the land to the merest private in the ranks, the Queen Empress Victoria sending a wreath from Buckingham Palace. The obituaries were extensive both nationally and internationally, confirming Leighton's position in the art world and in society, his death marking the end of the glorious 'Golden Age of the Living Painter'. Tributes came no less from the military world led by General Sir Garnet Wolseley, the former 'very model of a modern Major General'.

Notes
1. Now the Leighton House Museum.
2. From A.M.W. Stirling, *The Richmond Papers, from the correspondence and manuscripts of George Richmond RA, and his son Sir William Richmond RA, KCB*, William Heinemann Ltd., London, 1926.

Chapter 4

Sir Robert W. Edis, KBE, CB, VD, JP, FSA

1839-1927

He who has an art, everywhere has a part.

Old English proverb

Sir Frederick Leighton PRA was succeeded in command of the 20th Middlesex (Artists) Rifle Volunteers by his senior major, Robert W. Edis FSA, who shortly after his appointment as lieutenant colonel was promoted to full colonel. Number 8 in the original nominal roll of Volunteers in 1860, he was made a sergeant in the same year. He reigned as commanding officer from 1883 to 1902, thereafter holding the rank of honorary colonel until 1921. Knighted in 1920 at the age of eighty-two for services in the Great War, he thus served the Regiment making a prodigious contribution to its development for over sixty years.

Unlike his predecessors as CO Edis did not sport the long flowing beard which had become fashionable in the Army after the Crimean War but what he may have lacked in moral fibre as a result, in the view of many Victorian military men, he made up for with his exceptional height (6 feet 2 inches). His handsome appearance – he curled his hair, which partly hung in ringlets over the top of his forehead – was also of advantage to him in professional and social circles in London and elsewhere.

His early days are obscure. Born in Huntingdon in 1839, the eldest son of bookseller parents, he went to the Brewers' Company School at Aldenham in Hertfordshire, then trained for five years as an architect, before setting himself up in practice in London. Sergeant Edis was quickly awarded a commission in the Corps and in 1864 (in which year he became President of the Architectural Association), he largely helped to form the new Architectural Company ('C' Company), recruited chiefly from architectural students, which he was to command. In 1877 (six companies having been formed) the Regiment was permitted to have a senior major as second in command and Captain Edis was promoted major accordingly.

The ongoing biographical material on Sir Robert Edis will be divided into two parts. 1) His role and achievements as commanding officer in the organization and development of the Artists RV (1882-1902) and 2) his career as an architect. He was to combine both career aspects of his life, which were inevitably intertwined with complete devotion and outstanding merit.

Colonel Edis' military career.

On assuming the appointment as commanding officer, Robert William Edis formed a strong 'General Committee' to oversee the running of the Regiment, which otherwise might have been described as an 'assembly of senators' drawn from eminent members of society. The committee included among its soldiers General Viscount Wolseley (then Adjutant General), Lieutenant General Higginson, Major General Gipps (then commanding the Home District), Colonel Moncrieff and Colonel Stacey (then commanding the Scots Guards). Among the painters, many of whom were ARAs and RAs and former serving members of the Regiment, were such distinguished artists as Sir Frederick Leighton PRA (then honorary colonel of the Artists), Millais, Alma-Tadema, Armitage, Armistead, Calderon, Vicat Cole, Frith, Hodgson, Hull, Horsley, Long, Stacey Marks, Ouless, Pearson, Pettie, Saint, Stocks, Marcus Stone, Yeames, Birch, Boughton, Brett, Burgess, Luke Fildes and the multitalented William Morris. The sculptors were represented by Boehm and Hamo Thornycroft.

The committee also included the Regiment's first captain commandant, Lord Bury, Sir Thomas Gore-Browne, the serving director of the National Gallery, the president of the Royal Institute of British Architecture, the president of the Architectural Association; also the great physician, Sir William Jenner (physician to the Queen), and the distinguished war correspondent, Archibald Forbes; among the musicians were Sir Arthur Sullivan and Michael Maybrick (better known in the Regiment and to the public as Stephen Adams); and representing the theatre, the greatest actor of the day Henry Irving, also J. L. Toole, Arthur Cecil, George Grossmith, Rupert D'Oyly Carte and Pellegrini; a many and varied task force of expertise brought together by the energy and persuasion of Colonel Edis.

When Colonel Edis took command, the 20th Middlesex (Artists) RV was quartered at No. 36 Fitzroy Square. The accommodation included the dining room on the ground floor converted as the officers' mess; two small rooms at the back as the CO's office and orderly room; the double drawing room on the first floor as a canteen (also for drilling, lectures, smoking concerts and many other purposes); the rooms above being the sergeants' mess, committee room and changing room respectively, leaving room for quarters for one of the members of the permanent staff, who acted as caretaker, in the attic above; accommodation was also provided in the basement for an armoury and stores. Although Fitzroy Square was an improvement on previous headquarter premises, now with eight companies the space available had become inadequate. In 1887 Colonel Edis resolved to obtain a building site in London for a purpose-built Drill Hall, to be funded by past and present members and friends of the Regiment.

Colonel Edis established a headquarters' fund to which some money held in the regimental funds was diverted but the main source of income was to be the Art Union, under the auspices of which a wonderful collection of pictures, gratuitously contributed by leading artists of the day (not by any means all members of the Regiment) were raffled. The contributing artists included Leader, MacWhirter, the Hon. John Collier, Du Maurier, Carruthers Gould, Harry Furness, Seymour Hayden, Charles Keane, Blair Leighton, Laslett Poll, Frank Dicksee, Linley Sambourne, S. J. Solomon, Dendy Sadler, Chevallier Taylor, Tenniel, Waller and Whistler. Smoking concerts to augment the fund were arranged at the house in Fitzroy Square, at which some of the best talent in London freely gave their services, including Lionel Brough, Charles Bertram, C.A. Capper, Charles Colette, Charles Coborn, John Le Hay, Eugene Stratton, Michael Maybrick and Brandon Thomas (then a private in the Corps).

The result was that a large sum of money was raised and in 1888 a suitable plot of land was secured (just behind St Pancras Church in the Euston area), and was taken for ninety-nine years on a building lease at a reasonable ground rent. The new headquarters, the official address of which was 17 Duke's Road, St Pancras, was built under the supervision of Colonel Edis and in accordance with his plans. The façade of the new building was designed in the Renaissance style, with red terracotta dressings. The large medallion over the entrance was executed by Thomas Brock ARA (the future Sir Thomas Brock RA), then serving as a lieutenant in the Corps. On the ground floor was a large entrance, 10 feet wide, with orderly, committee, officers, the commanding officer and adjutant rooms, which led up steps to a spacious Drill Hall, 100 feet long x 52 feet wide, top-lighted with a gallery at the south end, 52 feet x 15 feet. In the basement were the armoury, rooms for quartermaster stores, lavatories and dressing rooms for the men. On the first floor was found a large general room for the men with canteen facilities, 52 feet x 20 feet wide, with a lift to the kitchen on the top floor, and sergeants' room. The top floor also contained dressing and bathrooms for officers and sergeants and living quarters for headquarters' staff. The total cost of the new building was £6,500. The work was carried out under the honorary architect, Colonel Edis, by Messrs Kynoch & Co., building contractors of Clapham.

The new headquarters was formally opened by the Prince and Princess of Wales (the future King Edward VII and Queen Alexandra) on 25 March 1889, at a special matinée concert given by the Regiment, aided by the following first-rate talent, namely: Edward Lloyd, Trebelli, Antoinette Stirling, A.D. Commager (with his banjo), Edward Terry, John Le Hay, Lionel Brough, George Grossmith, Herbert Standing and Charles Collette, along with Michael Maybrick, Brandon Thomas and many other members of the Corps. The Prince, smoking his customary cigar, was said to have greatly enjoyed himself, laughing and applauding the various turns heartily. Ten years later an opportunity arose to purchase the freehold ground of the headquarters, which was taken advantage of, the money required (a good round sum) being borrowed on easy terms from a sympathetic insurance company on security of the land and building, coupled with the guarantee of Colonel Edis and three of his senior officers. Every penny of the loan, however, was gradually and eventually paid off out of funds subscribed by members of the Corps, and the freehold of the headquarters was freed of all debt, incurred either before or after the purchase.

The massive response in Victorian Britain to the Rifle Volunteer Act of 1863 had been essentially a middle-class phenomenon. The Industrial Revolution in the latter part of the eighteenth century had given birth to a new rank of society comprising the factory owners and their executives, and the merchants and businessmen at various levels who traded in the raw materials, largely imported, to feed the factories and in marketing the finished product at home and to the four corners of the earth. The prosperity of the middle class steadily increased in the nineteenth century and it was natural that such a crisis as was incurred in the late 1850s by the threatened invasion by France should provoke the apprehension of the bourgeois, who were anxious to take up arms to defend the homeland, which lay at the hub of an ever-widening and prosperous empire.

By the 1880s, the Artists Corps had broadened its original scope for recruitment to include members of the legal profession, civil engineers and numerous other trades and professions. In a battalion census taken in 1893 the breakdown of numbers included in each membership category was as follows:

Artists (painters and sculptors),	4.54 per cent
Architects (and students),	11.79 per cent
Legal Profession (and students),	12.39 per cent
Medical Profession (and students),	10.33 per cent
Civil Engineers (and students),	5.99 per cent
Civil Service, Banking, Insurance, Stock Exchange, Accountants and miscellaneous occupations,	54.96 per cent.
Total	100.00 per cent

Although the Corps was no longer primarily an Artists' regiment, the past and serving painters and sculptors still wielded an enormous influence in the body of the ranks, who freely acknowledged their contribution to the formation of the Regiment and were proud to be known as 'The Artists'. Although the only actual qualifications to join the Corps were to be between the ages of seventeen and forty-nine and a minimum height of 5 feet 6½ inches with a chest measurement of 34 inches, it went without saying that relying largely but not exclusively as the Regiment did on the public schools and universities for recruits, that the unwritten rule was that each candidate should be of 'good social background and education', or a 'gentleman' in the broadly accepted sense of the term.

Every recruit had first to be nominated to a company by a past or serving member of the Regiment. On being sworn in he was required to sign an agreement to make himself efficient for a term of three years. In return during his second year of recruit training he would be provided with items of uniform, free of charge, including cape, water bottle, haversack and kit bag, but he would be expected to provide at his own expense a great coat (price 23s), a canvas fatigue jacket (5s 9d. and a red (brewer's) cap (1s 6d.), obtainable from Messrs. Hobson & Co., Golden Square, W. In addition, recruits were recommended (especially when attending camp) to provide themselves with a serge tunic (price 10s, also obtainable at Hobson's) for the dirty work. Any member who failed to make himself efficient during the three-year period, thus failing to earn the capitation grant for each year would be liable for the proportionate cost of his uniform, which he would have to pay over to the colonel commanding.

All the new Volunteer regiments were governed by the Rifle Volunteer Act of 1863, with subsequent amendments and additional clauses, but the instructors and not least the volunteers themselves were often confused and frustrated by the plethora of booklets, pamphlets and Army orders that were obtainable to enforce the provisions of the Act and ensure the efficient organization and training of the Volunteer units. A major contribution to the successful administration and training programmes of the 20th Middlesex (Artists) RV was made with the publication in 1889 of its *Standing Orders and Instructions*, a pocket-sized book (price 1s) which was to become known as *The Grey Book*. Sponsored by Colonel Edis, the compilation of the book was the work of Captain H.A.R. May, a rising star amongst the commissioned officers of the Regiment, who was inspired by Lord Wolseley's *Soldier's Pocket Book*, the first book of its kind to give tips for the welfare of the common soldier both in barracks and in the field. May's proposal to the commanding officer was that the existing *Field Exercises* and *Musketry Instruction*, which all volunteers were required to possess, should be supplemented with a third book, which contained all the 'Standing Orders and Instructions' that it was necessary for each volunteer to know by heart if they were to be proficient in performing their duties as part of the squad, company and battalion. Reading *The Grey Book* today, which runs to over 200 pages, it has to be said that all ranks were presented with a bewildering array of facts and procedures to comprehend and master in performance. A second edition of *The Grey Book* was published in 1893.

The Grey Book contained information on the volunteer's obligation to his country; the names and addresses of all officers, NCOs and men holding definite appointments in the Corps and the full regimental standing orders on every subject. Full instructions were given to recruits joining the Regiment as to his obligations, uniform, equipment and many other personal matters; junior NCOs and sergeants were given full instructions as to their duties and, in the case of the sergeants, as to the sergeants' mess. Officers were fully briefed as to their duties, and as to the officers' mess; full information, instructions and regulations being given with regard to such branches of the Corps as signalling, ambulance, transport and cycling; and as to squad, company and battalion drill and musketry, including prize shooting. Full information was given about duties on guard, entraining, marches, camp, barracks, bivouacs, tent-pitching, cooking, bugle calls (with easily remembered words to assist recognition) both in barracks and in the field.

Full information and rules were given also about the NCO's school for junior NCOs and sergeant and officer training, both sergeants and officers being required to do courses of instruction with the Regular Army, the various regimental courses, the Regimental Club, School of Arms and regimental institutions. Also chapters were provided in considerable detail on elementary tactics, dealing with simple principles, rules and duties in advance and rear guards, outposts, reconnoitring, attack and defence, woods, defiles, villages, hedges, walls, houses, trenches, convoys, obstacles and other matters – written especially with the intelligent private in mind. *The Grey Book* became the bible of the Corps and was studied, carried about, referred to and produced as an authority on all occasions by all ranks, and helped to settle many disputed points, discrepancies and lack of uniformity in numerous regimental customs and habits. It is not possible within the scope of these pages to replicate all the contents of *The Grey Book*, although some of its more interesting features will be reviewed in this chapter. Fuller accounts of the procedures for company and battalion drill, camp, and elementary tactics involved in a battalion attack will be found in the book itself.

At the initial interview with their company commander, recruits were told they would be required to 1) attend at least sixty drills during the first two years and nine drills in the year afterwards; 2) fire at least sixty rounds on the range passing a certain standard of shooting and 3) attend the annual inspection in Hyde Park, which was convened so that the Corps could earn its capitation grant if the volunteers were considered by a high-ranking officer to be efficient in every aspect of their training.

Recruits

The recruits were divided into thirty-man sections or squads as follows:

1st Squad. Squad Drill with intervals and in single rank. This involved drill in standing at ease, dressing, turnings, saluting and 'balance step'. i.e, standing on one leg and slowly swinging the other to and fro from front and rear, all by numbers, and all as an introduction to the 'slow march', which was given in much detail. After twelve drills the volunteers were passed on to the 2nd Squad, at the discretion of the instructor and approval by the adjutant.

2nd Squad. The manual and firing exercises, which consisted of twelve drills, the volunteers moving on to the 3rd Squad if passed out by the instructor and adjutant.

3rd Squad, which also consisted of twelve drills, was performed in two ranks, including instruction on skirmishing, attack and defence, and piling arms. The same inspection was conditional on passing on to the 4th Squad.

4th Squad. This covered sentry duties, tent-pitching, elementary tactics and the musketry course, the drills numbering sixteen. On completion of the final leg of the recruit course, the Adjutant authorized the successful volunteers to join their companies. Those who failed to pass out from any of the squads were required to do that part of the overall course again.

Musketry

The simulated musketry course consisted of:
1) aiming drills
2) a lecture on theoretical principles
3) clearing arms drill and position drill; half-an-hour being devoted to each drill. After completing this instruction the drilled volunteers, as they were now called, proceeded to the rifle range, the facilities for which were to be found at Runnymede, Harrow, Staines and Wormwood Scrubs.

Third-Class range firing consisted of:
Ten rounds at 100 yards, five kneeling and five standing.
Five rounds at 200 yards, five kneeling and five standing.
Five rounds at 300 yards, lying down.

All men making forty-five points and upwards in this class were passed into the second class and became second-class shots.

Second Class range firing consisted of firing:
Five rounds at 400 yards
Five rounds at 500 yards
Ten rounds at 600 yards

All men making forty points and upwards in this class passed into the first class and were regarded as first-class shots, and were allowed to fire in that class on the same day should time permit.

First Class Range Firing consisted of two parts:
1) Five rounds at 700 yards, five rounds at 800 yards, any military position.
2) Ten rounds commencing at 300 yards and ending at a 100 yards, two rounds at every fifty yards, with sight fixed at 200 yards and sword-bayonet fixed at a third-class figure target without bull's eye or centre, first four rounds lying down, second four kneeling, the last two standing. All men making forty points and upwards in this class ranked as marksmen.

A third-class target was six feet high and four feet square, with bull's eye of one foot diameter, and centre three feet. A second-class target was six feet square, with bull's eye of two feet diameter, and centre of four feet. A first-class target was six feet high and eight feet wide, bull's eye three feet in diameter and centre five feet. A bull's eye counted four points, a centre three and an outer two, the outer in each case being the remainder of the target. Hits on the figure target (but not ricochets) counted as three points. The rifle used at this time was the Martini-Henry, which had replaced the Snider as the Regiment's main firearm. With the Martini-Henry the breech was opened by means of a lever through which bullets were fed individually by hand.

Uniform for Other Ranks

The Volunteers were usually measured up for their uniforms in the second year of their recruit training and there was much commotion and consternation in the Drill Hall until the quartermaster adjudged the uniforms to be of a proper fit and the accoutrements worn in the fashion laid down by uniform regulations. Instructions for putting on dress and accoutrements were as follows:

The forage cap was to be worn well down on the right side of the head. The chin strap and also chain of the helmet were worn down (under the lip), except when marching at ease. Trousers had to be tucked into leggings and turned down over them to within twelve inches of the ground. Haversack, water bottle and equipment were to be put on with the accoutrements in the following order:

    1) The haversack slung over the right shoulder and hanging over the left hip. When empty the haversack was to be neatly rolled up.

    2) The water bottle slung over the left shoulder and hanging over the right hip and below the bottom of the tunic.

The equipment fitted as follows:

Waist belt – It was important that this fitted tightly, and that the side buckles were taken in or let out to the same hole on each side. This was important, otherwise the brace Ds in the rear were thrown out of position.

Frog and Pouches - These were slipped on to the belt – the pouch for separate rounds on the right – and the belt fastened.

Braces -These were passed over the shoulders and under the shoulder straps of the tunic, and buckled on to the rear angle Ds. The front supporting straps were passed through the loop on the waist belt, then through the loop on the pouch, through the slide on the strap, hauled tight and buckled to the carrier. When the brace was in position, the Ds for fixing the valise were positioned just above the shoulder blades and to the rear of the shoulder straps. It was important that the braces were buckled up sufficiently to take the weight of the waist belt off the hips.

Great Coat – This was to be rolled as directed and fastened with the coat straps nine inches apart, the tail end of the coat downwards and to the rear, the buckles to the front. The attaching loops of the coat straps were passed through the waist belt inside the brace Ds and downwards, the locking studs being secured. Specific instructions were given on how to roll the great coat when equipment was worn, and how to roll it horse-collar fashion when equipment was not worn.
Mess tin – Placed on the coat, flat side to the back. The strap of the mess tin was passed through the cross of the braces downwards, through the centre loop of the waist belt and buckled tight to the front. The waist belt with bayonet and pouches passed over both straps of the water bottle. The bayonet rested through the straps of and underneath the haversack and under the hooks of the tunic. All straps were to pass under the shoulder straps of the tunic.
Capes (when carried) – Should be rolled, and worn in horse-collar fashion over the left shoulder, the two ends strapped together under the right arm. Specific instructions were given on how to roll the cape.
Review Order for privates and non-commissioned officers was tunic, trousers, helmet, waist belt with side arms, right pouch (at back if no ammunition), leggings and white gloves.
Marching Order – As above, with full equipment, pouches, haversack, water bottle, great coat, mess tin, and capes rolled.
Field Day Order – Same as Review Order, with both pouches.
Drill Order – As Review Order with forage cap in lieu of helmet.
Note – Sergeants, on all occasions (except in Marching Order), were to wear cross-belts in addition to the above-mentioned accoutrements.
Guard Duty - Parade in Marching Order; sentries to wear Review Order. In inclement weather great coats and capes were to be worn.
Church Parade Order – Review Order, without pouches or leggings.
Guard of Honour – Review Order.
On Picket Duty – Drill Order.
Fatigue Dress – White canvas jacket, trousers leggings and red (brewer's) cap. Non-commissioned officers in charge of fatigue parties, going out of camp or quarters were required to appear in Drill Order with side arms, gloves and stick. White duck trousers were sometimes worn in camps of instruction.
Note - Every member was advised to notice in the Drill Calendar, issued monthly, whether 'capes rolled' were ordered for any special parade and to dress accordingly.

Whenever the helmet was worn on duty by either officers or men the chin chains were to be worn down. When the helmet was worn on occasions other than duty, the chin chains were to be fastened to the hook near the top of the helmet – except that at church parade, chin chains were to be hooked up.

Promotion for Other Ranks

No private was recommended to the commanding officer for promotion to lance corporal until he had shown himself efficient and diligent in drill, and anxious to promote the welfare and efficiency of his company. The lance corporal's main job was to drill the recruit squads but before this duty was entrusted to him he had first to pass a preliminary examination under the supervision of the adjutant. The course of instruction for potential lance corporals consisted of three parts – the first a series of classes at which lectures were given on tactics and other military subjects, special attention being given to the actual practical duties of lance corporals in the Drill Hall, on parade and in the field. The second part consisted of squad and company drill, and the third part of battalion drill, in which members of the course were instructed practically in the duties of markers, guides, subalterns and captains.

Standing Orders do not mention special promotion courses for corporals and lance sergeants, although a junior NCO's main step forward to the rank of sergeant is dealt with in some detail. The award of three stripes was also made at the discretion of the commanding officer after junior NCOs had passed an appropriate examination to obtain a Certificate of Proficiency from the adjutant. This certificate was only awarded after:

1) A practical examination in the drill manoeuvre of a company.
2) Practice in the command of a company in battalion.
3) Duties of guard commander, mode of marching reliefs and posting sentries were tested.
4) Practical knowledge of the manual and firing exercises – aiming drill and blank firing – was mandatory.
5) Knowledge of and competency to superintend target practice was also required. After promotion, sergeants were encouraged to go through a special course on sergeant's duties with the Scots Guards, to whom the Artists were attached, at Wellington or Chelsea Barracks. For advanced training in musketry, the sergeant had to find more spare time to attend the School of Musketry at Hythe. For purposes of a course of instruction in machine gunnery at that time a course was available to sergeants with the Royal Marine Artillery. After promotion a sergeant earned the Corps an additional yearly capitation grant of 50s. With a normal progress of events it would take a private on enlistment in the Regiment seven years to reach the rank of sergeant.

Officers' Uniform

As newly commissioned officers tended to buy their uniforms from different outfitters there was often a variation in quality if not in pattern.

The rules for wearing uniform, equipment and accoutrements were as follows:

Review Order – Full dress tunic, trousers, helmet, leggings, cross-belt, sword-belt, white gloves.

Field Day Order – As above, except patrol jacket in lieu of tunic.

Marching Order – As Field Day Order, but with great coat, haversack and water bottle.

Drill Order – As Field Day Order but with forage cap in lieu of helmet.

Regimental Duties – When on these duties officers wore patrol jackets and forage caps, with cross-belts (serges and service caps could also be worn). Whenever the tunic was worn, or when the cross-belt was worn outside, swords should always be hooked up. Laced boots were compulsorily worn with leggings. Without leggings, half-Wellingtons, boots or plain-faced, elastic parade boots were to be worn.

Officer's badges were in gold on the shoulder straps of the tunics and mess jackets, and silver on patrol jacket, serges or great coats. Sword knots were in buff leather, and mounted officers wore steel spurs. Officers could, if desired, on state occasions or at balls, wear silver cross and sword-belts, silver sword-knots and silver stripes on the trousers, but they were not allowed to wear silver belts or silver stripes on the trousers on any parade. At levees and Drawing Rooms silver stripes were not to be worn on the trousers without silver belts; patent leather boots were to be worn. The sword was to be hooked up. Silver sword-belts and cross-belts were not necessary but permitted. Officers were required to carry whistles, pencil and paper on all parades (except church parades), and a compass in addition at manoeuvres.

Mess Dress was to be worn in the mess on all ordinary occasions. When not on duty white collars and black neckties were to be worn. Officers on duty would wear the mess jacket hooked up at mess and wear pouch belts. Mounted officers wore spurs. Patent leather, half-Wellington, or plain-faced parade boots and straps were to be worn with mess dress.

Promotion for Officers

All officers were recruited from the ranks and before appointment they were required to pass an examination in similar subjects to those set for the sergeants. Passing the examination and obtaining his Certificate of

Proficiency conferred the letter P after the officer's name in the Army List, which again earned the Corps an additional yearly capitation grant of 50s. All subalterns and officers newly appointed to field rank (major) were expected, within twelve months, to attend the Scots Guards School of Instruction at Wellington or Chelsea Barracks, and pass higher examinations awarding a Certificate of Proficiency which conferred on the newly-commissioned officers the letters PS after their names in the Army List, in turn again earning the Corps a further yearly capitation grant of 50s.

The courses of instruction were as follows:

For Subalterns
1) Squad Drill
2) Company Drill, which had to be learned by heart before attending the school.
3) Firing Exercises (including firing by numbers), standing and kneeling, to be learned by heart; the rules of aiming drill also to be learned by heart.
4) Battalion Drill; the positions of the Guides, Markers, Subalterns and Captains, and taking command of the Company.
5) Guard Mounting, Sentries' Duties, Duties of Corporals and Commanders of Guards.
6) Battle formation.

For Field Officers
1) Squad Drill
2) Company Drill
3) Battalion Drill
4) Brigade Drill (enabling the officer to command a battalion when in brigade)
5) Route Marching
6) Guard Mounting
7) Battle Formation
8) Must be able to ride

All officers of Volunteers were expected to make themselves available for examination in tactics, military law, field fortifications and military topography as set for officers of the Regular Army in the manner laid down in Queen's Regulations. The subjects would be taken separately. An officer who obtained half marks in any one of these subjects would receive a pass certificate. Captains and field officers were examined on papers set for captains; subalterns on those set for lieutenants. In the case of tactics (only) those who passed had a distinguishing letter (a large or small T) inserted after their names in the Army List, earning the Corps an extra yearly capitation grant this time of 30s. All officers of the Corps were expected to pass the examination in tactics within two years of their appointments.

On passing through the Recruit Squads and being admitted to companies, the Volunteers were given the opportunity to learn Army signalling and the work of the ambulance, transport and cyclist sections (if vacancies existed in the latter two sections).

Signals

Visual signalling was an accurate and rapid method of communication between fixed points and could be used with advantage at various distances depending on the state of the atmosphere. In clear weather, with no intervening obstacles in terrain, flag signals could be read with the help of a service telescope up to twelve miles. There were several methods of visual signalling based on the transmission of the Morse code, each letter of the alphabet comprising a series of dots and dashes translated into short and long intervals of time. The signaller using flags could work from left to right or from right to left, or he may turn his back upon the station to which he was signalling, according to the direction of the wind, so that each flag could be waved from the normal position against the wind. The large flags (representing the dashes) were three feet square, of two colours, namely white with blue horizontal stripes for use with a dark background. The pole to which the large flag was attached was five feet six inches long and held in the right hand; the small flag (representing the dots) held in the left hand being two feet square was white, attached to a pole three feet six inches long. The hands were to be held higher on the smaller than on the large pole, the arms being nearly straight, the left hand being not lower than the chin. A favourite venue for signalling practice was Hampstead Heath, which would be followed by a route march back to Duke's Road.

The heliograph was an instrument for directing the reflected rays of the sun on and off a distant station. A mirror was mounted with trunnions on a U-frame fixed to a plate, which moved horizontally on another plate fixed to a tripod stand. By the action of two screws, one giving the mirror a horizontal motion, the other altering the inclination, the light from the mirror could be kept steadily on any selected point. To make signals the latter screw rod was pressed down against a spring, and after a short or long pause released, thus throwing the light on the distant station for the space of a dot or a dash. The fitful appearance of the sun and the crowded nature of the terrain did not, however, make the heliograph an ideal means of communication in the United Kingdom. It was used to advantage though on the North-West Frontier of India, service on which was of course beyond the remit of the Artists RV!

The hand lamp was an ordinary bull's eye, with a flat double 1½-inch wick fed by colza or other vegetable oil. Between the light and the lens was a metal disc, which was raised and lowered to expose and shut off the light by means of a key on the outside of the lamp, acted on by a spring, which maintained the disc in the obscuring position. The wick had to be placed with its edge turned towards the bull's eye. Practice with the hand lamp usually took place after dark in Regent's Park. In the heliostat the mirror had a slow motion similar to that of the heliograph, in order to follow the sun, but it was not moved for making the signals. This was accomplished by means of a shutter, which intercepted the reflected light. There were various other kinds of apparatus for day signalling such as the shutter apparatus and collapsing drum. Intersection communication in close proximity in the field was made by agreed hand signals and the imitation of bird and animal noises. The complement of signallers for the battalion was two non-commissioned officers and four men, or two complete parties, and a number of trained men as supernumeraries, amounting to one per company. Signalling under the signals sergeant took place through the winter months at Duke's Road. An examination took place annually, when a prize was awarded by the commanding officer to the most efficient signaller. Officers on being commissioned were also required to take a course in signalling.

Ambulance

Two men at least per company were trained as stretcher-bearers of the Corps, according to the instruction in ambulance and stretcher drill, and in rendering first aid to the wounded, as laid down in Army Medical Regulations, Part II. In proceeding on active service field stretchers were drawn up in the proportion of one per company. The stretcher bearers were responsible in training and in the field to the Corps Medical officer, who held the rank of surgeon captain. On commissioning, officers were required to take an ambulance course. Acting as a stretcher bearer was by no means a 'cushy' assignment as humping bodies in difficult country was a strenuous affair. The duties of the bearer were primarily to search for and succour the wounded by administering them water and stimulants, by supplying a temporary dressing such as the nature of the case may require, and by removing them and their arms and accoutrements to a place of safety. The training, as a general rule, comprised twelve lectures and drills, the theoretical and practical portions of the training being carried out at the same time.

As to the theoretical training, instruction was given in the following subjects:
1) The outlines of the anatomy of the human body, including a brief account of the osseous system and the circulation of the blood.
2) Two different appliances used for temporary dressings, namely field splints, tourniquets, lint bandages, the first field dressing, etc.
3) The immediate treatment of gun-shot wounds and other cases of emergency such as bleeding, sunstroke, frostbite, burns and scalds, the apparently drowned, etc.
4) A description of ambulance materials generally and arrangements for the transport of the wounded was given, the instructor being careful to dwell on the importance of the bearer's calling.

Transport

The Transport Section, originating in 1877 grew from an ambulance wagon and beer cart to a fleet of horse-drawn vehicles largely borrowed from the Regulars and hired from civilian firms. This section was led from 1878 to 1907 by Driver-Sergeant 'Sammy' Cowell, who was also a leading light at The School of Arms and as an organizer of, and entertainer at, smoking concerts and children's parties. There was only a limited number of vacancies at any time in the transport section and it was most important that all applicants were prepared to devote the amount of time necessary for the grooming of the horses, and the cleaning and maintenance generally of the vehicles. Height of the drivers was not to exceed 5 feet 8 inches, and weight 11 stones. Cost of a driver's kit for which the member was responsible amounted to about £7.10s. All members were expected to be good riders before joining and have adequate knowledge of the care of horses.

Attendance at the Flying March at Easter was essential, and for the week before the event and the camp at Aldershot or Woking, the drivers were expected to sleep at the Regular Army barracks to which the stables were attached. 'Rouse' was sounded at 5 a.m. when each man had to be up and ready for 'stables'. The drill consisted of grooming, harnessing and wagon drill until 8.30 a.m. when the men were dismissed. Members were instructed in cavalry sword exercise and harness drill at Duke's Road on the days and at the times appointed for that purpose.

The Cyclist Section

The Artists' Cyclist Section, originating early in 1890, was one of the first complete sections of cyclists to be formed in an infantry battalion. The cyclists' role was to replace the cavalry, which traditionally went ahead of the brigade or battalion, also covering their flanks, to spy out the land and dispositions of the enemy. To be a proficient military cyclist, in addition to well-developed leg power, each man had to be a good rifleman, navigator, signaller and skilled in military map sketching. The Artists' Cyclist Section was formed as a result of the initiative of certain members of the Kensington Football Club, who happened also to be Artists. They were keen infantry soldiers, anxious for new worlds to conquer and for them the bicycle – cycling just then coming into fashion with the public – was an ideal means of achieving that goal.

The formation was due to Sergeant S. W. H. Dixon, who commanded the section until 1894, when Lance Sergeant H. C. Yockney took over command. He was succeeded by Lance Sergeant A. E. Dodd in 1897, followed by Lance Sergeant H. C. Travers in 1899, and later in the same year by Lance Sergeant H. Turner. In 1900 a second section was formed and the whole placed under the command of Lieutenant C. J. Blomfield. Together with the signallers, the cyclists made a new company – 'L' – in the battalion organization. Sergeant H. C. Yockney became colour sergeant, the section leaders being Sergeant H. Turner and Corporal A. J. Aspinall. The numbers recruited up to the end of 1901 totalled fifty, two more sections having been added. The Cyclist Section for practically all purposes was treated as a unit, but its members technically belonged to the various companies of the Regiment.

For Drill Order bandoliers and gloves were worn. For Heavy Marching Order bandoliers, haversacks and gloves were worn and when mounted valises, capes rolled and water bottles. The Regimental Regulation bicycle, to which regulation clips and carriers were to be fitted, was purchasable at the members' own expense from Messrs. Hillman, Herbert and Cooper of Holborn Viaduct, or Messrs. Trigwell & Co. of Brixton Rise, S.W. The weight of the bicycle and equipment was heavy and the cost of the machine was expensive, but an allowance was made for 'fair wear and tear' on military duty. A cyclist should invariably carry a watch, compass, and notebook and pencil when scouting or on patrol. An endurance test took place annually, the distance to be covered being 100 miles. The efficiency of the Cyclist Infantry depended in a very great degree on the power of making rapid and long marches in compact order. On the march the maximum distance allowed between each cyclist was two yards. Cyclists should never halt at or near the bottom of a hill. During long halts bicycles had to be stacked and a sentry posted. The bicycles had to be carefully examined at each halt. An advance guard of three men would always precede well forward of a section on the march. Chains were to be thoroughly painted with blacklead and paraffin oil before starting out.

Members of the Cyclist Section competed for various efficiency prizes and other awards, including one for signalling and prizes were awarded at the School of Arms. The Bisley Challenge Cup was open to all members – shot at Staines, the competition called for riding three-quarters-of-a-mile, ten shots to be fired at 200 yards, time allowance eight minutes. With the advent of the Territorials in 1908, cyclist companies were disbanded, but this was not the last the Artists RV was to see of its cyclists.

Prize Shooting

Proficiency in shooting was greatly improved by the numerous company and battalion prizes for competitions that were organized during the training year. There were four series of battalion prize competitions during which different numbers of shots were fired on the range at different ranges under the National Rifle Association's regulations for the current year. The Hartley Challenge Cup and a Champion Jewel of the value of £3.10s. were taken by the man making the highest aggregate score in Series I, II and III, and the two best scores in the monthly cup competitions in May, June, and July. In the company team competitions the Brock Challenge Prize was awarded for skirmishing, the prize for which was a life-size bust by Lieutenant Brock himself of Sir Frederick Leighton, the Honorary Colonel, to which was added a smaller replica, also designed by Brock, for the member making the highest score in the winning team. Further to this was the adjutant, Captain Lamb's prize for the company team making the highest number of points in Field Practice, Section Attack-Infantry, under the rules laid down in *Musketry Instruction (Martini-Henry)*, which involved ten men firing at targets at various distances under their section commander.

The Boutcher Cup was awarded for inter-company competitions by teams of six men from each company. Monthly cup competitions took place at the beginning of each of the eight months of the shooting season. The regulations and ranges were the same as those laid down for the first stages of the Queen's Prize. A battalion team, after qualifying competitions, was annually to shoot against other regiments. The Regiment was entitled to send a team every year to the National Rifle Association meeting which took place at Wimbledon; the team consisted of no more than three men per company, together with two nominees by the colonel, to compete for the Queen's Prize and St George's Challenge Cup. The Artists competed also for various other prizes at the National Rifle Association meeting.

The Regimental Club

The Regimental Club was open to all members and honorary members of the 20th Middlesex (Artists) RV. Honorary members, who had been efficient in the Corps for at least three years but who were no longer serving were admitted on payment of an annual subscription of 12s. 6d., or on making a donation to the headquarter's Building Fund of 10s., and were eligible to join as honorary members, as were members of Her Majesty's Forces on payment of a donation of £5. 5s. Persons who had been of special service to the Corps may also have been admitted to the Regimental Club without contribution on the approval of the commanding officer. All candidates for honorary membership had to be nominated by at least six full members of the Corps. The Regimental Club was administered by Canteen, Entertainment, School of Arms, Tennis and Swimming sub-Committees. The canteen was open every week day from 5 p.m. to 11 p.m. The only games allowed to be played were chess, whist, draughts, cribbage and dominoes. No gambling was allowed; the only liquor to be consumed was to be sold at the canteen bar.

The School of Arms and the Military Tournament

The School of Arms and the Military Tournament, which as we have learned was started in 1877, played an ever-increasing role in the life of the Regiment. All serving members were expected to join, as skill-at-arms helped the participants to keep healthy and develop their physique and combat aggression; the most important reason perhaps being that it was only at the School of Arms where the use of the bayonet was taught and practised. By the 1890s, instruction was also being given in gymnastics, wrestling, fencing, dumb bells, single sticks, rope climbing, Indian clubs, boxing and physical drill (open to members of the Corps only). Persons who were not members of the Regimental Club could join the School of Arms on being introduced by a member and elected by the sub-committee. They had to be re-elected every year. The subscription was 10s. for each season (during the winter months) for members and 15s. for non-members. Five or six instructors were involved, leaders being chosen from the more advanced members. Dressing rooms were provided, with hot and cold showers, and a toilet. A competition was held for School Badges at the end of each season. One entertaining feature of the School's activities was the assault-at-arms, which was staged several times during the year as the second part of a smoking concert, and in which School members were able to display their skills to an always appreciative audience.

The founders of the School of Arms furnished the enthusiasts who helped to initiate the Military Tournament (later called the Royal Naval and Military Tournament, later still the Royal Naval Military and Air

Force Tournament and finally The Royal Tournament), which was originally established by Volunteers and run annually at the Old Agricultural Hall in Islington until it later moved to Olympia. Prizes were offered and fought for by Regulars as well as Volunteers. At the first tournament in 1882, Transport Sergeant A.G. 'Sammy' Cowell won first prize for the Artists in the bayonet v. bayonet and sabre v. sabre competitions, the first of a bountiful harvest of prizes to be reaped at the tournament by the Artists in the years to come.

Entertainment, Tennis and Swimming Clubs

Smoking concerts (music, sketches, recitations, etc.) were held fortnightly at Duke's Road during the winter months. The charge made for a single admission was 1s. Season tickets were available for all concerts. The entertainments were arranged by the entertainment sub-committee, composed of one or more members from each company, appointed by the colonel. The Corps was not short of talented performers but professionals were usually invited to perform as an added attraction, the canteen becoming a thespian club much frequented by the entertainment world. The Drill Hall had been constructed with a view to it being used as a tennis court, the floor being formed from wooden blocks laid on concrete. Members and their guests were allowed to play on the court at the rate of 1s. an hour, with an extra 1s. for the use of gas light. The Swimming Club was introduced for the encouragement of swimming, floating and diving, and life-saving classes were provided. Participation in water polo was encouraged, practice taken and matches arranged. The club met once a week throughout the year at the St Mary-le-bone Baths in Marylebone Road, close to Edgware Road station but simulated classes of instruction in life-saving took place at Duke's Road. According to the battalion census taken in 1893, 75 per cent of the whole battalion, 85.71 per cent of the officers and 82.27 per cent of the NCOs could swim a quarter-of-a-mile in still water.

Of the personalities other than painters, sculptors and architects who served in the Corps in the late nineteenth and early twentieth centuries we will mention here just three who are particularly worthy of note.

Sir Leander Starr Jameson, 1st Bt, as he was to be known in later life, was born in Edinburgh in 1853 and studied medicine at London University, from which he graduated as a doctor in 1878. It was during his time as a medical student that he served with the Artists RV. Shortly after leaving King's College he went to South Africa where he was to form a lifelong association with the empire-builder Cecil Rhodes. Dr Jameson was appointed Administrator of Rhodesia and Director of the British South Africa Company but his name is best remembered for the

Jameson Raid (1895), a fuller account of which is given in Chapter 5, in which he assembled an irregular force of cavalry and artillery in Bechuanaland and led them into the Transvaal against President Kruger's Boer government to support a planned rebellion by the *Uitlanders*, the non-Boer (mainly British) residents, who had flocked to the Transvaal in search of gold and diamonds, and who believed themselves to be badly treated by Kruger as non-citizens who were not entitled to the vote.

The raid, conceived and financed by Cecil Rhodes, who dreamed of the united states of South Africa as part of the British Empire, was a disastrous failure and Dr Jameson and the men who survived were captured by the Boers at Doornkop on 2 January 1896. Jameson was handed over to the British with the demand that he should be punished. He was put on trial in London for his role in the affair and sentenced to ten months' imprisonment, but was released early due to ill-health. He was a survivor. He was elected a member of Cape Town's Legislative Assembly for Kimberley in 1900, and in the same year was appointed Director of the De Beers Consolidated Company. He followed Cecil Rhodes as Premier of the Cape Colony between 1904-08 and he died in London on 26 November 1917.

On a more humorous note, Brandon Thomas, author of the world-renowned farce *Charley's Aunt*, was a member both as other rank and officer of the Regiment from 1883 to 1903, during which time he was acclaimed throughout the Corps as the regimental jester. Born in Liverpool in 1856, Brandon Thomas, actor and playwright, made his mark in his youth in comedy on the stage and as a writer of songs which he sang himself in the music halls. He made his professional debut in the West End of London with the Kendals in 1879, remaining with them until 1885. He wrote about a dozen plays, one of which, *The Colour-Sergeant*, was inspired by his service with the Artists. *Charley's Aunt* was first produced at the Royalty Theatre on 21 December 1897 with W. S. Penley in the title role. On the first night, the Duke of Cambridge is said to have fallen through his seat helpless with laughter but the Prince of Wales was less impressed as the 'aunt' reminded him too much in appearance of his mother, Queen Victoria!

The farce nearly did not reach the stage at all. After a desperate forty-eight hours, Brandon Thomas failed to find the £1,000 necessary to back the play. He offered Penley, for whom the part was created, all the rights for fourteen years if he would manage the play. Penley raised the money in the nick of time from a man who went bankrupt the very next day. *Charley's Aunt*, which initially ran for four years with Brandon Thomas himself later taking over the title role from Penley, has been regularly performed on stages throughout the world ever since in

English and many translations and at one time the play was running simultaneously in forty-eight theatres in twenty-two languages, including Afrikaans, Chinese, Gaelic, Russian and Zulu. The play was made into a musical comedy, *Where's Charley?* and performed in New York in 1948 and London in 1958 and there have been several successful film versions.

Brandon Thomas, who retired from the Regiment with the rank of major in 1903 due to pressure of business, was immensely popular with all ranks, including the commanding officer; Colonel Edis once remarking that 'he would have made an excellent Regular officer if he had not been cashiered in the first fortnight'. He greatly enjoyed organizing regimental entertainment and in particular the smoking concerts. On one occasion a Regular unit with whom the Regiment camped at Easter put on a concert of a very high standard. The Artists were, in turn, invited to stage a return performance. In spite of the great wealth of theatrical talent in the Regiment, a banjo-player was vitally required but non-existent. Brandon Thomas hired an American professional, who was all the rage in London at that time and, dressing him in Artists' uniform, put him in the concert. It was a great success and infinitely superior to that of the Regular unit, although Colonel Edis was puzzled as to the identity of the 'volunteer' he did not recognize!

At his first camp as a recruit, Private Brandon Thomas, who incidentally always wore a monocle, decided that as the cookhouse meals were not entirely to his liking he would dine out one night in style at the Queen's Hotel in Aldershot. On entering the coffee room in uniform and carrying his rifle, he called loudly for a steak and a bottle of Burgundy. The waiter although much impressed by the guest was obliged to inform the new arrival that privates were not allowed to dine at the hotel – only officers, to which Brandon Thomas replied: 'Good heavens, man, I'm not a General, I am, indeed, as you say a private. Give me, therefore, a private room.' The bemused waiter led him to a private room, where he was able to assuage his hunger and thirst in good measure before returning to camp. He lost his way but on approaching the camp was challenged by a sentry with 'Who Goes There?' He replied: 'I am Brandon Thomas of 'B' Company of the Artists. My Regimental number is 3327 and the number of my rifle 6701'. The sentry responded with a touch of irritation 'Who Comes There?' for which the reply was 'I have already told you that I am Private Brandon Thomas of 'B' Company of the Artists. My Regimental number is 3327 – it is written in my great coat – and my rifle number is 6701.' After several more challenges the exasperated sentry – an Irish militia man – finally giving up, retorted, 'Why the divil don't you just say friend?'

In Easter 1892 the Regiment was quartered with the Marines at Walmer and the battalion was due to parade on the square in marching order for some early field work. Newly-commissioned as a subaltern, Brandon Thomas, dressed as for a levee in full tunic, was on his way to the parade ground when he was stopped by a fellow subaltern who informed him that he was wearing the wrong uniform and accoutrements. Panic-stricken, he hailed a passing milk trolley and, climbing aboard, ordered the driver to drive him to his quarters, whereupon he re-emerged dressed and equipped for marching order. Colonel Edis who witnessed the incident angrily demanded to know the name of the officer sabotaging his parade but was graciously forgiving when told 'it was only Brandon Thomas.' When detailed to inspect his first guard, Brandon Thomas spent the previous evening practising the orders that he must give to the guard. His fellow officers were so intrigued that they all turned out the following morning to see him perform his duties. Inevitably he bungled the orders, throwing up his arms whilst shaking with laughter. Only Brandon Thomas could have got away with it.

Amongst his many extra-curricular services to the Regiment, he rewrote the drill manual in rhymed verse, which he claimed would be easier to understand. It was turned into a song with music by J. W. Ivimey, and which became a standard work in the regimental social repertoire. Brandon Thomas died in 1914.

Another interesting recruit to the Regiment from the world of the theatre was Sir Johnston Forbes-Robertson, a leading light on both the classical and popular stage of his day. Sir Johnston was born in 1853 and educated at Charterhouse and Rouen. His father was a distinguished art critic, and he himself trained as a painter, studying at the Royal Academy Schools. Indeed, he always disclaimed acting as his true *métier*; his profession is given in the Regimental Muster Roll, in which his name is entered in May 1876, as 'Artist', though he had then been on the stage for three years. He served in the Corps until the early 1880s during which time he was promoted to drill sergeant, those drilling under him vouching for his flair for delivering his lines with true dramatic skill.

He made his first appearance on the stage in 1874, his first outstanding success being at the Haymarket theatre in *Dan'l Druce, Blacksmith* (1876). Two years later he joined the Bancrofts appearing successfully in Sardou's *Diplomacy* (1878), Albery's *Duty* (1879) and T. W. Robertson's *Ours*, also in 1879. He was then engaged by Wilson Barrett to play opposite Modjeska, and in 1882 went to the Lyceum under Henry Irving, later touring with Mary Anderson with whom he made his first appearance in New York as Orlando to her Rosalind in

1. *(above left)* Edward Sterling.

2. *(above right)* Captain Commandant Henry Wyndham Phillips.

3. Lieutenant Colonel Frederick Leighton.

4. John Everett Millais.
(National Portrait Gallery)

5. Dante Gabriel Rossetti.
(National Portrait Gallery)

6. William Morris.
(National Portrait Gallery)

7. Edward Burne-Jones.

8. One of the original officers.

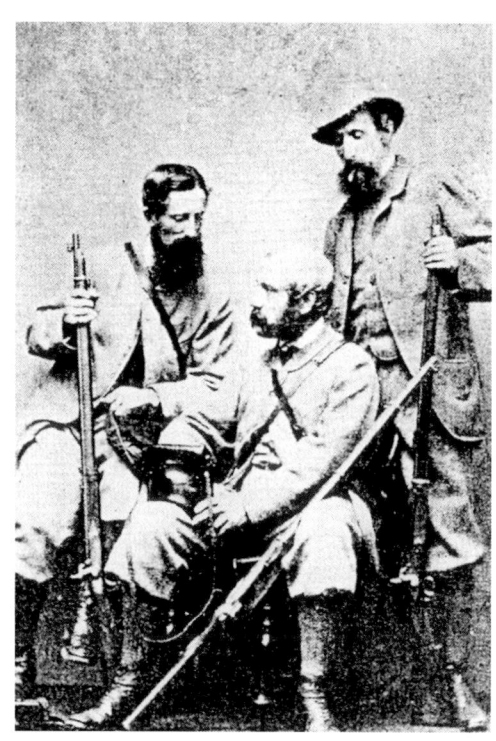

9. Three of the original privates.

10. *Go West Young Man: The Boyhood of Raleigh* by John Everett Millais.

11. Colonel Sir Robert Edis KBE, CB, VD, JP, FSA.

12. *(above)* Artists Rifles Uniforms 1859-1913 by Lieutenant A. Egerton Cooper

13. *(left)* Marching order in the 'Eighties'.

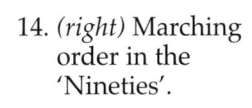

14. *(right)* Marching order in the 'Nineties'.

15. Colour Sergeant Hammond dressed for the Boer War. *(By kind permission of Tony and Joan Poucher)*

16. Bubbles, the famous advertising slogan for Pears Soap by John Everett Millais.

17. *(top left)* Regimental badge of the Artists, designed by Private J.W. Wyon in 1860.

18. *(top right)* The Mars and Minerva insignia.

19. *(above)* The School of Arms. The bayonet team (and reserves) for the Royal Navy and Military Tournament, 1913.

20. *(left)* Three Artists, members of the City Imperial Volunteers, at Johannesburg, 1900.

21. Lieutenant Colonel Walter C. Horsley CB, VD, TD, JP.

As You Like It. Returning to England he went back to the Lyceum to give an outstanding performance as the Duke of Buckingham in Irving's production of *Henry VIII* in 1892. In 1898 he went into management. His first production was *Romeo and Juliet*, in which he played Romeo to Mrs Patrick Campbell's Juliet. He was seen for the first time as *Hamlet* at the Lyceum in 1897, and proved himself to be the finest player of the part of his generation. Outstanding later roles included Mark Embury in *Mice and Men* (1902) by M. L. Ryley, Dick Helder in Kipling's *The Light that Failed* (1903) and, above all, the stranger in *The Passing of the Third Floor Back* by Jerome K. Jerome, with which he managed his last season as actor-manager at the St James Theatre.

Sir Johnston Forbes-Robertson was knighted in 1913, in the same year making his last appearance as Hamlet at Drury Lane. In 1914 he gave a series of farewell performances, including a transatlantic tour, in the course of which he was made an honorary MA at Columbia University. During the Great War he made several silent movies, including a production of *Hamlet*.

Forbes-Robertson was one of four brothers, all of whom served in the Artists RV. His brothers – Ian, Eric and Norman, of whom Ian was the best known – were also in the theatre. Ian first appeared on the stage at the age of twenty-one, later going to America where he acted for ten years with many famous stage personalities. After returning to England he appeared with Irving, and later managed some of Sir Johnston's stage successes, writing plays and acting in them himself. Ian Forbes-Robertson served in the Corps for five years from 1871, thus preceding Sir Johnston in the Regiment. Sir Johnston married in 1900 Gertrude Elliott who acted with him until 1913. One of their three daughters, Jean Forbes-Robertson, was also on the stage and had the distinction of being the actress who created the title role in J.M. Barrie's *Peter Pan*. Sir Johnston Forbes-Robertson died at St Margaret's Bay in 1937 aged eighty-four.

Another long-lasting institution created in the Corps was the Philhurst Club, which was formed about 1890 by Captain (later Major) C. A. Philip, who was a quartermaster of the Regiment. It was established at Gresham Road, Staines, for the recreational benefit of 'D' Company, other companies ('G' and 'H') being admitted later. 'A', 'E' and 'I' Companies had tented camps known as 'Holes' on Datchet Island in the Thames but these compared unfavourably with Philhurst with its house in Gresham Road, its tennis court and its landing stage on the Thames River bank. The idea behind St Philip's Monastery, as it was popularly called, was a club on the river at which members could spend the weekend after musketry practice at the Wraysbury rifle ranges. Some of the club rooms and dormitories were fitted with rifle racks. There were shooting competitions in which every member had to shoot his instructional before 31 May in each year. Boating naturally was the main source of weekend entertainment and an annual regatta was held in June or July. A Goose Supper took place in September at which the captain of the club presided and carved the goose or geese with garden shears!

In 1900 when large numbers of men were joining, the Regiment received a remarkable gift in the form of two Vickers-Maxim machine guns from two former serving members. The donors were the brothers Wagg; Arthur, the late captain quartermaster and Edward, a late private. The machine guns came complete with harnesses and limbers. The two brothers were partners in the well-known stock exchange firm Herbert Wagg & Co.

Sir Robert Edis as an Architect

Robert Edis, well-known in the Regiment for the large cigar he smoked on drill nights – a gift of the Prince of Wales as he invariably put it – was an outsize man in every way. Influenced by the architect Burges, who sponsored his membership of the Regiment in the first place, in the 1850s he made a tour of the early Gothic churches in northern France and in 1862 he visited William Morris's famous Red House in Bexley with Burges. Edis's warehouses in Southwark Street and Paul's Wharf in the 1860s and early 1870s show something of Burges' Gothicism and so do designs of schools for the London School Board and some of his early houses. However, he was soon confident in exercising his own influence. At only twenty-six, he was president of the struggling Architectural Association and, during two years, managed to make it financially stable. In 1867 he was nominated for Associateship and Fellowship of the Royal Institute of British Architects.

By the late 1870s Edis was married with a house in Fitzroy Square and six children, and had widened the scope of his practice. He had even visited the USA (where he shot buffalo) to plan a small town in Kansas, and served as aide-de-camp to Lord Bury, the official British observer at the Franco-Prussian War of 1870-71. He had seen Paris burning in 1871 and written a paper on fire prevention. Now he was in demand for designing shops in Bond Street and the City, insurance offices in Fleet Street, a school of art, minor ecclesiastical works, memorial fountains and especially private houses. Never an innovator in style, the secret of Edis's architectural success was undoubtedly his ability to keep up astutely with fashion, or fashion as his clients saw it.

This now meant leaving Gothic behind for 'Queen Anne Revival' or 'Old English'. 'Picturesque' was the word most used by contemporary architectural journals to describe his work, but in minor ways he toyed with new ideas. His shop at No. 64 New Bond Street (1877) had the upper floor entirely faced with ornamental hanging tiles – a novelty in London street architecture. Tiles were an important topic, too, in his prolific writings on interior decoration and sanitation, which included a handbook, *Healthy Furniture and Decoration*, for the 1884 International Health Exhibition.

In 1880 he delivered the six Cantor Lectures before the Royal Society of Arts, calling them 'plain practical lectures on decoration and furniture'. These became a book, popular with growing suburban middle classes, entitled *Decoration and Furniture of Town Houses*. It advised, with costs, on each room, cleanliness and functionalism. Edis's aims and their implementation did not always coincide. 'Anything that holds dust is essentially out of place on the walls of our rooms' was actually illustrated with a 'double flock paper raised in different thicknesses' and 'a dado of paper stamped in imitation leather'. Nevertheless he did pinpoint the over-ornamented clumsiness of much contemporary furniture, and the rooms he illustrated were space-saving and neat.

By the 1880s and 1890s his style had changed again – and his clients were wealthier. Drawings for the handsome six-storied terracotta Constitutional Club, Northumberland Avenue (1883-5), which were hung at the Royal Academy, were Renaissance, more or less. Two other clubs, the Badminton and the Junior Constitutional, also Renaissance, shared ingeniously a complicated site in Piccadilly. The former (1885) edged behind the latter (1890), with a comparatively narrow frontage to the road. Both used marble freely and luxuriously, and had lavish public rooms and staircases. The Junior Constitutional had a ground-floor smoking room, then rare, and the Badminton three hand-powered service lifts. Edis was himself a member of all three clubs and of the Arts Club in Hanover Square, where he designed the interior. As demonstrated as colonel of the Artists RV, Edis was sociable and gregarious, sponsoring the smoking concerts at the Drill Hall in Duke's Road and giving 'At Homes' at Fitzroy Square, which were attended by leading members of the arts community, politicians, lawyers and senior Army officers.

He built several huge country houses too. For the brewery family, Bass, he designed houses in the Midlands. In Staffordshire, in the 1880s, came the red brick Smallwood Manor for G. A. Hodgson, a member of the Inner Temple where Edis had already made highly praised sympathetic additions to the medieval library. Smallwood Manor used electricity from the start, Edis designing all the fittings. In 1883 the Prince of Wales employed him to design a new ballroom at Sandringham. It was in flamboyant 'Jacobean' style and large enough for the Royal Family to cycle around on wet afternoons. Edis was honorary architect to the Royal Commission for the 1893 World Fair in Chicago and designed Victoria House, the British office there: 'a red brick, half-timbered cottage (with twenty rooms) in the style of Henry VIII'.

Frederick Hotels commissioned him for the Great Central Hotel at Marylebone in 1899. His yellow and red Jacobean terracotta overshadowed the station, and apparently provided another unusual cycle track, this time on the roof. Inside, plain Burmantorfts tiles were praised for their unusual constraint at a time when patterns rioted everywhere. In 1903 came the Abercorn rooms. These were a vast extension of red brick and terracotta built on to the Great Eastern Hotel at Liverpool Street Station. These later buildings may now seem ostentatious and pompous. At the time they pleased the clients, and certainly fulfilled Edis's own aims to 'avoid monotonous walls and street fronts' and 'the dismal commonplaces of grey and stone colour'. And they illustrate his professional competence: the Abercorn Rooms did not overwhelm Charles Barry's hotel, while at Sandringham his additions after a fire matched elegantly with the earlier 'Jacobean' lower floors of the 1860s. In 1894 Edis brought a surprisingly plain Georgian house in Ormesby, Norfolk, and, though his wife lived only three years to enjoy it, he soon gave up his house in Fitzroy Square and spent a long retirement in the country, well known in local affairs and looked after by his one unmarried daughter.

By the end of Colonel Edis's term as commanding officer, the Corps had risen to twelve companies. Early in 1900 he supervised the organization of the Artists' contingent which was hurriedly enlisted, equipped and despatched as part of the City Imperial Volunteers (CIVs) to South Africa, (see the next chapter). He also set up, under the chairmanship of Major H. A. R. May, a Clothing Committee to overhaul the Corps uniform – slouch hats and field service caps replaced the helmets and forage-caps for all ranks: a new grey serge, a 'Sam Browne' belt and a new (roll collar) mess dress were introduced for officers; also brown boots and leggings in place of the long black boots for mounted officers, besides other changes. A detachment of the Artists RV helped line the route through London at the funeral of Queen Victoria on 2 February 1901. Colonel Edis's last camp was at Yarmouth in 1902, from which he was recalled as the longest-serving senior Volunteer officer to command, with the temporary rank of brigadier, a large parade of London Volunteers to mark the coronation of Edward VII. He died on 23 June 1927 at the age of eighty-eight; his reign as commanding officer marking an especially formative era in the early history of the Corps to which he was devoted for so many years.

Chapter 5

The Boer War and the Artists Rifles

1899-1902

The next best thing?

Alas I am too old. My son commands your company. God be with you – I cannot!

>The parting message of Colonel Robert Edis, commanding officer of the 20th Middlesex (Artists) Rifle Volunteers, on the occasion of the Artists contingent to the City Imperial Volunteers (CIVs) departure by train from Nine Elms Station in London to Southampton for embarkation for South Africa, 20 January 1900.

Our attention now turns from sham fights and parades in London parks, on common land and camps in southern England, to war in a hotter clime in far distant southern Africa. The Boer War (1899-1902) was the culmination of over a century of antagonism between the Boers, the descendants of the Dutch colonists who had made the first white settlement in southern Africa during the seventeenth century, and the British, who had seized control of the Cape of Good Hope from the Dutch in 1806. In 1820 many Boers started the 'Great Trek' north from the Cape, across the Orange River. These transplanted Boers, the *Voortrekkers*, eventually founded the independent states of the Transvaal (1852) and the Orange Free State (1854).

Conflict between the Boers and the African tribes they dominated, which threatened all of South Africa, led to the British annexation of the Transvaal in 1877 which, though peaceful, was opposed by Paul Kruger, the protagonist of supreme Afrikaner domination of the indigenous tribes. In 1881 armed hostilities called the Boer Insurrection, or First Boer War, culminated in a British defeat at Majuba Hill, whereupon the

British Prime Minister, William Gladstone, ordered the restoration of Transvaal independence, excepting for matters concerning foreign relations.

Until the fabulous gold strike of 1886, the watershed (*Witwatersrand* or *Rand*- Afrikaner for 'ridge' – the land south of Pretoria) was empty veld. The rapid influx of prospectors, miners and traders – mainly British but they came from many other countries – created the city of Johannesburg almost overnight. Though rescued from bankruptcy, the Boers regarded the horde of fortune-seekers (*Uitlanders* or foreigners) as a threat to their customs and independence. The *Uitlanders* had other grievances against President Kruger's government which they, in company with the British Cape Colony administration, generally regarded as corrupt.

Joseph Chamberlain, the British Colonial Secretary in the new Conservative-Unionist government of 1895, was a staunch imperialist and had a champion in Cecil Rhodes, who was premier of the Cape Colony, head of the huge De Beers diamond monopoly and mine owner on the *Rand* and who dreamed of a single British African nation, stretching from the Cape to the Sudan, a country fit for Englishmen, more populous than the United States of America. Rhodes's own personal prosperity was enhanced by the granting of a Royal Charter to his British South Africa Company, or Chartered Company, which entitled him to exclusive mineral rights in the British territories, which made them to all intents and purposes under his control.

Continued provocation of the *Uitlanders* in the Transvaal led to the formation in Johannesburg of 'The Reformers' who plotted rebellion, although it has to be said the 'foreigners' were very divided in their attitude to the Boers. There were those who unreservedly preferred the status quo, others who were willing to serve Kruger under a more liberal Boer government, and others who wanted to see an end to Kruger and his regime. Dr Leander Starr Jameson, the former member of the Artists Corps of Volunteers whom we met in the last chapter, a close friend of Rhodes and fellow African pioneer, conceived of a plan backed (but later repudiated) by Rhodes to lead a raid into the Transvaal to support the *Uitlanders'* uprising, and who would be assisted by arms and ammunition smuggled into Johannesburg by Rhodes in oil barrels.

As the Jameson Raid may be said to have triggered off the Second Boer War, it is appropriate to look into its conduct and outcome in more detail. (Jameson's early years and subsequent career after the raid are mentioned in Chapter 4.)

A plan began to take shape. The *Uitlanders* would rise up against Kruger and Jameson, the conqueror of Matabeleland and administrator for Rhodesia, would ride to their rescue at the head of Rhodes's private army – Kruger would be overthrown and Rhodes would have the Transvaal. Jameson had done it before in Matabeleland and could do it again! He was gung-ho. 'Anyone,' he told Rhodes 'could take the Transvaal with a dozen revolvers.' His force was recruited from Rhodesian policemen, many of them in their teens, and he chose as his base Pitsani in Bechuanaland, close to Mafeking, on the Transvaal border. A string of supply depots was to be set up between Pitsani and Johannesburg.

On Sunday, 29 December 1895, Jameson's raiding force of 510 Rhodesian policemen, reinforced by a few policemen from Mafeking with seventy-five African drivers rode into the Transvaal, armed in addition to their personal weapons with eight Maxim machine guns and three field guns. The Boers, surprisingly unaware of Jameson's raiders at Pitsani and consequently of their intentions, soon learned however that something was afoot. It was too early for the Boers to strike. They had no machine guns and their artillery had been tied up in a distant punitive action against African insurgents. For the moment, Boer horsemen were content to trail and circle the column at a safe distance, leaving Jameson in no doubt that his every movement was being watched.

At heart Rhodes willed the mission to succeed although he and some British officials wanted it to stop. Jameson ignored their pleas and reached Krugersdorp, twenty miles from Johannesburg. There had been a few light skirmishes with the Boers but they had not so far made a stand. Now the Boer tactics suddenly changed. Here at the approaches to Krugersdorp the terrain was broken up by gullies and boulders that afforded protection against bombardment and the indiscriminate sweep of machine-gun fire. The Boer riflemen now had a chance against Jameson's field artillery and Maxims. Willoughby, Jameson's senior officer, brought up his big guns and bombarded the Boer positions. Not one Boer was hit. Deceived by their silence, Willoughby ordered his men to charge. The Boer marksmen were waiting for them. Crossfire rained down on the raiders from the front and flanks. Thirty men were killed or wounded. Willoughby ordered a retreat.

Dusk was gathering and Jameson agreed to abandon the attack on Krugersdorp and attempted an all-night march to Johannesburg instead, but hardly had the force started when they heard heavy firing from the direction of Krugersdorp. The fracas was a Boer celebration of the arrival of their long-delayed artillery. Jameson and Willoughby made the fatal assumption that the rebels had arrived from Johannesburg (they had not started out) and were engaging the Boers. Leaving their carts and pack animals on the road, the raiders advanced to Krugersdorp to assist their imaginary allies. They had not gone far when the distant firing stopped and instead of friends they found a large Boer force facing them, and others closing in from the flanks. Ordering his men back to the road, Jameson knew that a night march to Johannesburg was no longer possible.

It was now almost dark and it was decided that the only sensible course was to bivouac for the night. Intermittent rifle fire made sleep virtually impossible and at first light Jameson ordered his men to move out. They had been on the march for eighty-six hours and had eaten nothing since the morning of the previous day. A running fight continued for about ten miles until Jameson's men discovered that they had been driven into a cul-de-sac. Ahead of them was a large Boer force on top of a low cliff. It was impossible to skirt the cliff and impossible also to retreat, as the Boers in the rear were closing in.

Jameson's men were exhausted, surrounded and heavily outnumbered, but they put up a brief fight. Men and horses were shot down, and when the Boers brought up their artillery there was no hope left for the raiders. Jameson raised the white flag: the Jameson Raid had ended in failure. Seventeen of the raiders had been killed and fifty-five wounded. The Boers lost four men. The actual surrender took place at Doornkop on 2 January 1896. Jameson and his officers were taken to Pretoria in carts, his men on horseback. After being paraded around the market square for the benefit of the jeering crowds, they were marched off to Pretoria gaol and forbidden to communicate with anybody. President Kruger and his Executive Council decided to hand over the raiders to the British Government. They knew this would be unpopular with the Boer subjects, who demanded blood, but wisely calculated that it would not benefit the Boer cause in the Transvaal to make martyrs of the Jameson Raiders. Let Britain be placed in the difficult position of punishing them. Jameson and his officers faced trial in London and received prison sentences but after a short spell behind bars Dr Leander Starr Jameson returned to South Africa where he became a leading figure in Cape politics after the Boer War was over.

The Jameson Raid resulted in the hardening of the Boer attitude toward the British Colonies and the *Uitlanders*. A strong defensive relationship was formed by the Transvaal and the Orange Free State and a hastily begun arms build-up was intensified, the Boers' principal supplier being Germany. President Kruger's intransigence over the granting of full citizenship to the *Uitlanders* led to the rebels sending a petition to Queen Victoria demanding British protection, which won the widespread sympathy of the British public. For the British High Commissioner in South Africa, Sir Arthur Milner, the issue was no longer the franchise for the *Uitlanders* and Transvaal independence, but a Boer threat to the paramountcy of Britain in South Africa. He saw war as the only solution.

Britain had only 12,000 soldiers spread around South Africa and an additional force of 10,000 men, mainly from India, was embarked under Sir George White. Orders were immediately given in Britain for the mobilization of an army corps (50,000 men) under the command of Sir Redvers Buller, VC. Military thinking in Britain still centred around the tactics of the Crimean War and, although there had been widespread reforms in the Army, the military had no experience of fighting an enemy in the vast open spaces of South Africa. The Boers could muster some 35,000 men (their army eventually rose to about 60,000), but they were expert horsemen who were to fight from shelter, usually a hill. They were able to manoeuvre quickly, their handling of supply wagons making them independent of the railways. Forming 'Commandos', the Boers were to strike swiftly causing havoc in British strongpoints and defensive positions before vanishing from the scene of battle as quickly as they had entered upon the fray. The Boers were armed with modern artillery supplied by Germany, along with the crews to man the guns.

Initially the main British force was concentrated in Natal, which prompted President Kruger to send an ultimatum to the British Government demanding their withdrawal. When Joseph Chamberlain, the Colonial Secretary, rejected the ultimatum, the Boers launched an attack westwards which led to the sieges of Mafeking and Kimberley. The invasion south-eastwards into Natal did not lead initially to the same success for the Boers. Sir Redvers Buller arrived in Cape Town on 31 October and immediately planned a counter-offensive. He split his army corps into four forces, one under John French and another under Sir William Gatacre, which he sent to fight holding actions in the western Cape, while a column of 13,000 men under Lord Methuen marched from the Orange River Station for the relief of Mafeking and Kimberley. At the same time a column of 18,000 men under Buller's own command headed for Ladysmith, which was now also besieged by the Boers.

'Black Week' for the British, which started at dawn on 10 December 1899, saw Gatacre disastrously defeated by the Boers on a hill side near Stromberg, leaving behind him in retreat 600 of his men who fell prisoners to the Boers. On 11 December Methuen was checked on the Modder River where, spearheaded by the crack Highland Brigade, his force was confronted by 4,000 Boers under Piet Cronje. Methuen was forced to retreat after suffering nearly 1,000 casualties. On 15 December Buller launched a three-pronged attack against Botha's 8,000 Boers at Colenso, the battle ending in another alarming defeat for the British Army, Buller's force taking 1,180 casualties.

The three battles of 'Black Week' caused a convulsive reaction in

Britain. Lord Roberts ('Bobs'), with Lord Kitchener as his chief-of-staff, was sent out to take charge in South Africa. Britain was gripped by almost hysterical patriotism as men rallied to the Empire for service in South Africa, or for home defence in the face of marked hostility from Germany, France and Russia. Smaller nations, however, recalling British liberalism, remained friendly, while the United States maintained an officially neutral but sympathetic position. The Boers themselves did not share the rest of the world's surprise at their defeat of the British, who they considered were being destroyed by the judgement of God. On the other hand, Queen Victoria was confident that God was on the side of the Imperial cause. When A. J. Balfour, the First Lord of the Treasury, went to Windsor with the gloomy news of the reverses of 'Black Week', she cut him short with the sharp retort: 'Please understand that there is no depression in *this* house; we are not interested in the possibilities of defeat; they do not exist.'

The depressing news of the Boers' early successes in battle and the sieges of Mafeking, Kimberley and Ladysmith was nowhere more keenly felt than at the hub of the Empire in the city of London. After 'Black Week', the Lord Mayor of London, Sir Alfred Newton, approached the War Office and offered to raise a regiment of infantry with mounted infantry attached, and to clothe, equip and transport them to South Africa. The offer was accepted by the War Office and thus was formed the City Imperial Volunteers (CIVs for short). The Corps was placed under a colonel commandant, Colonel W. H. Mackinnon, Grenadier Guards; Lieutenant Colonel Cholmondeley, London Rifle Brigade, was appointed Commander of the Mounted Infantry and the Earl of Albemarle was to command the Infantry Battalion. The CIVs also included a field battery of the Honourable Artillery Company (HAC). A quota of one officer and forty men to serve in the Corps was granted to all London Volunteer units and by 4 January 1900, 1,365 officers and men had been sworn in at the Guildhall and all made Freemen of the City of London.

The first contingent of Volunteers marched to the Guildhall on 2 January, as reported in the *Standard*:

> The detachments of the various Metropolitan Volunteer Battalions who have volunteered to serve in South Africa in the newly-raised City of London Volunteer Regiment assembled at their various headquarters early this morning preparatory to marching to the Guildhall to be enrolled. The authorized strength of each contingent is 40 rank and file and one officer, but at present some of the drafts are incomplete, owing, it must be stated, to the policy adopted in raising the Regiment. Each of the Volunteer Corps furnishing men

was required to send in 40 names without delay. The result of this is that the moment a sufficient number had volunteered their names had to be forwarded without regard to the fact that they had not passed the medical inspection, and that there was no time to examine their complete fitness for service. In several cases the men offering themselves were not 21 years of age, and their parents objected to them going out. The parade of the volunteers attracted large crowds to the various headquarters, who waited patiently in the fog and damp in order to give the men a cordial send-off. As each detachment represented the flower of the battalion between 21 and 30 years old, marksmen, and unmarried – all the men being physically sound – it can be taken for granted that the City of London Imperial Volunteers will prove a regiment of high efficiency and capacity.

The contingents marched to the Guildhall headed by their bands playing patriotic airs. Large crowds assembled in Cheapside and King Street, and loudly cheered the men as they marched up.

The first to arrive was a fine detachment of the Artists, 50 strong, with Colonel Edis and Lieutenant Croft. The band played the regimental quick-step 'They All Love Jack,' composed by Mr Maybrick, who was at the time an officer in the Corps. The men, in grey were quickly followed by the 3rd London, under Captain and Adjutant Jenner. This scarlet-coated contingent marching to the 'Soldiers of the Queen', was enthusiastically cheered by the spectators. Colonel Mortimer Hancock, accompanied by two officers attended in mufti...

In his address the Lord Mayor stated *inter alia* that:

> We have been forced to the arbitrament of war, and we shall not sheath the sword until our supremacy in South Africa is established [cheers] – a supremacy which will be universally welcomed as securing in that country equality before the law to all nationalities, and, in consequence, real freedom in its best and only true sense. Gentlemen, your splendid patriotism is deeply appreciated. To you signally belongs the honour of leading a movement, which stirs every city, town and hamlet throughout the Kingdom.

The Lord Mayor informed the Volunteers that all arrangements were being made for their clothing and equipment, the first batch of 500 men and their officers being scheduled to embark for South Africa on 13 January. Each Volunteer was presented with a newly-minted Queen's shilling bearing the date of the year, 1900.

On leaving the Guildhall the newly-established soldiers passed through the streets lined with dense crowds, who suddenly ceased singing verses of patriotic and national songs, in which they indulged from the very commencement of the proceedings until the end, to welcome them with stanzas of 'Soldiers of the Queen', followed by hearty cheering. In fact the passage of the Corps through that portion of the City was marked by an outbreak of patriotism of a most unusually fervid and moving description.

By 12 January special khaki uniforms and equipment had been drawn (the infantry rifle was the Long-Lee-Enfield) and the following day about 500 CIVs embarked at Southampton and sailed to Cape Town. About 800 of the Infantry Battalion also sailed from Southampton on 20 January, which embraced the Artists contingent, whose quota had been increased to three officers and sixty-eight men. This was the largest single element of the London Volunteer units from which the Infantry Battalion was drawn. The Artists had already been posted to 'F' Company, which included Volunteers from the London Scottish, Queen's Westminster, Civil Service, Bloomsbury Rifles and the Inns of Court. 'F' Company was commanded by Captain Wilkie Edis of the Artists Rifles (son of the commanding officer).

Before entraining at Nine Elms Station in London, the CIV attended a service conducted by the Bishop of London at St Paul's Cathedral and that evening were entertained to dinner with 'real good English food and flagons of ale' by the Benchers at Lincoln's Inn and Gray's Inn. In addition to the founding of the City Imperial Volunteers, the Imperial Yeomanry had been rapidly expanded, countrywide, and many Artists enlisted in the Yeomanry unit of their choice. The part-time soldiers contributed a 'newfangled accent to the British Army, the Gentleman trooper' – Rudyard Kipling was right: 'Never had war looked so democratic.' Over half of the rank and file of the Imperial Yeomanry and City Imperial Volunteers, raised in the whirlwind of patriotism that followed 'Black Week', were from the middle class.

The vessel in which 'F' Company embarked was ordinarily used for ferry trips to the Baltic and the troops were in for a rough passage until the warmer weather approached. A brief stay for coaling at St Vincent, Cape Verde Islands, proved a welcome respite but misgivings about inoculation, which was still in its infancy, while in the tropics, proved itself to be a blessing in disguise in view of the number of deaths that occurred in South Africa from enteric (typhoid) amongst soldiers who had not been inoculated. The CIV contingent was landed in Cape Town after twenty-six days at sea. After camping on the coast at Green Point, on the outskirts of Cape Town, the Volunteers entrained for the interior.

While at Green Point 'F' Company was visited by the unofficial Poet Laureate, Rudyard Kipling, who was serving in South Africa as a war correspondent, and a number of Artists who remembered his visits to Duke's Road on social occasions had an interesting 'pow-wow' with him in his tent at Green Point.

The Commander-in-Chief, Lord Roberts, secretly prepared a new army of 13,000 men behind Methuen's camp on the Modder, mounting as many as he could. To forestall a Cape rising by the Boers, to relieve the besieged towns, where starvation was fast feeding disease, and to restore Britain's international security, he struck on 11 February, before he was quite ready. Relying on wagon transport, he boldly left the railway line. His cavalry under French right-hooked around Cronje at Magersfontein to relieve Kimberley on 15 February. Cronje's escape bid was cut off at Paardeberg; after a dramatic ten-day siege he was compelled to surrender with 4,000 men, on 27 February. On the same day Buller at last asserted his strength properly and forced the Tugela to relieve Ladysmith. The Boers were wildly on the run everywhere, quitting the Cape and offering only token resistance at Poplar Grove and Abraham's Kraal. On 13 March Roberts entered Bloemfontein unopposed.

Delayed at Bloemfontein by problems of reorganization, epidemics and brilliant Boer raids east of the town (led by the new Orange Free State Commander Christian de Wet), on 3 May Roberts commenced his long march north to Pretoria with 38,000 men. Other columns, including Methuen's from Kimberley and Buller's from Ladysmith, also converged on the Transvaal. Hopelessly outnumbered, the Boers fought holding actions at Karee Siding, Brandfort, Vet River and Sand River but continually fell back or dispersed before the three columns. To Britain's delirious delight, Mafeking was relieved on 16 May. The most solid Boer resistance was outside Johannesburg (28-29 May), but Roberts captured the city and after another action, entered Pretoria. His advance from Bloemfontein to Pretoria, 300 miles in thirty-four days ranks as one of history's great marches but was inconclusive in effect.

Returning to the CIVs arrival in South Africa: after the long climb from Cape Town, the Volunteers were detrained at the Orange River Station where they were assigned to guard duties. The Volunteers were bucked to hear that Lord Roberts had accepted the colonelcy of the Corps and that they were to be shortly brigaded for the push north to Pretoria. Next the Volunteers entrained for Naaupoort where they made camp near a large hospital. They were not pleased to find that there were 'funeral parties going on all day. We got sick of hearing the "last post" and were only too glad when we left the place.' Thus spoke an unnamed diarist from the ranks of the Artists, whose diary entries were to be published in the early issues of the *Artists Rifles Journal*, first appearing in 1916. 'F' Company practised a lot of field firing in the area, our diarist commenting:

> In a wide range of kopjes we fixed up head-and-shoulders targets, attacked them across country starting from about a thousand yards and opening fire at unknown ranges. We finished up with a match against the Hampshire Yeomanry; a team of twenty from 'F' Company was chosen as we had done best in the practice, and we succeeded in getting nearly double the numbers of hits of the Yeomanry. We were lucky in having quite a number of men who, at home, had shot in the *Daily Telegraph* Competition at Pirbright.
>
> After about ten days we journeyed on to Springfontein where we camped alongside the 2nd Battalion, Scots Guards, and then trekked for seven days to Bloemfontein. There was a lot of rain on this trek, thereby greatly hampering our transport.

The CIVs were shortly embodied in the 21st Brigade, with the Royal Sussex, the Sherwood Foresters and the Cameron Highlanders, and commanded by Bruce Hamilton. The Brigade formed part of Ian Hamilton's division in which was also included the 19th Brigade, commanded by Horace Smith-Dorrien. They pushed on in the general advance on Pretoria and the CIVs were now definitely in the battle area. As our diarist put it:

> We first came under fire at Zand River, and between there and the Vaal River we contacted the Boers several times, but they never stood their ground and soon faded away when we got our guns on them. It was all very exasperating, foot-slogging after them, and they with two horses a-piece. Crossing the Vaal on 26th May, then about eighteen inches deep, we bared our feet and slung our boots, but regretted the rocky bottom.
>
> Our first real action was at Doorn Kop where, following an eighteen mile march, and after four hours fighting, we drove the enemy out of his position, and this cleared the way for the advance on Johannesburg, which place we sighted the next day. By passing the town, as it was dealt with by the division on our right to whom it surrendered, we pushed on to Pretoria, where we arrived on 5th June, bivouacking a mile or so outside. With other troops we marched through the city in the afternoon. Lord Roberts took the salute.

Horace Smith-Dorrien, who was in command at Doorn Kop, gave Colonel Mackinnon an extract from his after-battle despatch:

The features of the day were the attacks by the Gordon Highlanders and the CIV. That of the CIV convinced me that this Corps at any rate of our Volunteers is as skilled as the most skilful of our Regulars at skirmishing. The skill and dash of movement and taking advantage of every fold of ground in spite of terrific fire from several directions, enabled them to drive the enemy from every position with comparatively little loss.

After the fall of Pretoria Lord Roberts waited confidently for the surrender of the Boer forces. It was not until 10 June that he decided he was waiting in vain and sent his army back into battle. By this time his own fighting force at the front had been reduced to 16,000. The Boers, on the other hand, had succeeded in scraping together 5,000 Transvaal burghers. The battle that followed (called 'Diamond Hill' by the British, 'Donkerhoek' by the Boers) was another resounding anti-climax (12-13 June). From Pretoria the Volunteers trekked south-east and were engaged in small actions before going into action with the Guards Division at Diamond Hill. The Boers held a very strong and commanding position on a high range of kopjes running for about three miles in a crescent formation. This was attacked across ground with very little cover and under heavy rifle and machine-gun fire, and it was not until late afternoon that further artillery support on the left caused the Boers to abandon Diamond Hill.

The Transvaal Boers, now commanded by Louis Botha, drew off along the Delagoa railway line with President Kruger, who soon went into exile in Europe. After Diamond Hill, Roberts continued his pursuit of the Boers, linking up with Buller, who had driven north from the Natal-Pretoria railway. The last pitched battle of the war was fought at Bergendal on 27 August, where Buller led the British breakthrough, but although the Orange Free State and the Transvaal were annexed to the British crown, the war was far from over. The conflict now entered into a second phase in which the Boer rebels engaged in guerrilla warfare against the Imperial forces who were hell bent on rounding them up. Lord Roberts returned to Britain in December 1900, leaving Chief-of-Staff Kitchener in charge.

In this new phase of the war, the CIV now found themselves involved in the thankless task of preventing the Boer Commandos from harassing and destroying convoys, railway lines, blowing up trains carrying reinforcements and essential supplies. The Volunteers now left 21st Brigade and with various other units formed Mackinnon's Force. Towards the end of August the CIV arrived back in Pretoria for the third time. At the end of September Lord Roberts spoke to Colonel Mackinnon about sending the Corps home, declaring that, though he could ill afford it, the

Volunteers had done so well that he was determined to let them go, as he knew how important to them were their jobs at home. On 2 October, Colonel Mackinnon wrote in his diary:

> Lord Roberts inspected the whole Regiment and our camp and made us a splendid speech in which he dilated on the work we have done, told us how proud he was to be our Colonel and ended by saying, 'one word more men. When you arrive at home give a thought to me who, although absent from you in body, will be present with you in spirit, and whose ambition it was, as your Colonel, to ride into London at your head.'

The Second Boer War did not end until 31 May 1902 when with the Treaty of Vereeniging the Boers finally accepted British Sovereignty. The City Imperial Volunteers had spent nine months in a sun-drenched far off land where, as Kipling put it:

> Then scorn not the African kopje
> The kopje that smiles in the heat,
> The wholly unoccupied kopje
> The home of Cornelius and Piet,
> You can never be sure of your kopje
> But of this be you blooming well sure
> A kopje is always a kopje,
> And a Boojer is always a Boer!

Our anonymous diarist of the Artists CV concludes the story of the City Imperial Volunteers in South Africa and their return to London:

> On 7th October we arrived in Cape Town and all embarked on board the *Aurania*. It was a good voyage home, but saddened by the death of five men from enteric. Many messages of welcome, including one from Queen Victoria, were received when we arrived at Southampton on 28th October: we disembarked the following day.
> Coming to London in four trains, arriving at Paddington about 1.30 p.m., we marched to St Paul's Cathedral for a Thanksgiving Service, then to Guildhall where we were formally welcomed by the Corporation, and finally to Finsbury Barracks where we handed in our rifles and side arms. Then we went to a banquet in the HAC headquarters: several Artists friends turned up there and helped to see us home.
> Naturally we were all glad enough to be home again, but I feel sure that one and all, in spite of hardships and discomforts, would

not have missed the venture for anything in the world. Friendship and adventure made in war stand out in the lives of all who have shared it, and will always be treasured in our memories.

Apart from the wonderful reception we received in the streets of London, the one at the Artists headquarters on 1st November was something never to be forgotten. There was a reception, a dinner and then a smoking concert with Col. Edis presiding. All the Artists members of the CIV were present, and the guests included the Commandant, Col. Mackinnon, Col. Lord Albemarle and Capt. The Hon. J.H. Bailey (Adjutant) of the CIV, also Gen. Turner and the Earl of Denbigh.

The Smoking Concert was outstanding: many famous on stage and music hall came and gave of their best, and these included H. B. Irving, Dorothea Baird, Rutland Barrington, Florence Collingbourne, Edmund Payne, Katie Seymour, Ada Reeve, Brandon Thomas, Bertha Moore, Dan Leno, Beerbohm Tree and Mrs Tree, and others, many of whose names are not unknown. I must not omit mention of Capt. Bailey, who sang some of the songs he made up in South Africa, delightfully topical, and which he used to sing out on the march. He was a grand fellow and one of the finest Guards officers.

After being feted every night for a week, I was glad to get down to Cornwall for awhile and enjoy the peaceful calm of the countryside, and then refreshed I returned to my job in the City.

On 25 April 1903 now Major General W. H. Mackinnon CVO CB unveiled a war memorial tablet at Duke's Road in memory of the three Artists who had fallen in the South African War. This was unveiled in the presence of a large number of members of the Corps and their friends, including relatives of the men who had died.

The memorial tablet reads:

ON ACTIVE SERVICE
SOUTH AFRICA
1900

TO THE MEMORY OF

PRIVATE ALEXANDER CARDEN
PRIVATE W. FRASER COOMBS
PRIVATE CLIFFORD W. HAWKES

BY THOSE WHO CAME BACK

Chapter 6

Walter C. Horsley, CB, VD, TD, JP

1855-1934
The Haldane Army Reforms,
The Territorial Force and
The Mobilization Plan

If you can talk with crowds, and keep your virtue
  Or walk with Kings – nor lose the common touch ...
Rudyard Kipling

Walter Charles Horsley succeeded Robert Edis as colonel of the 20th Middlesex (Artists) Rifle Volunteers on 25 April 1903. 'Walter', as he was irreverently but affectionately known throughout the battalion, was born of Kentish stock in Cranbrook in 1855, the son of John Callcott Horsley RA, a distinguished painter and eminent figure in Victorian society, and his second wife Rosamund Haden. Walter Horsley bore the distinction of being a godson of Queen Victoria. Brought up in the Cranbrook Colony of Painters formed by his father, Walter was himself a talented landscape painter, but as he did not paint for a living he was the first commanding officer of the Regiment not to have made a profession of one of the arts.

He had two younger brothers, one Sir Victor Horsley who, as a medical student, was a member of 'D' Company for a short while and who became a famous brain surgeon, and the other, Gerald Horsley, who was a one-time president of the Architectural Association. Sir Victor had three sons – Oswald, Siward and Vivian – all three being enrolled in the Artists before being posted as officers to other units in the Great War. Oswald was killed in action while serving with the Royal Flying Corps and Siward died as a result of the influenza epidemic that broke out at the end of the war; Sir Victor himself died on active service in the war in Mesopotamia.

It was in 1873, at the age of seventeen, that the young Horsley, No. 1040 in the muster roll, joined up, on the introduction of Major Frederick Leighton, the other sponsor being Major Val Prinsep. As a painter he joined the old 'F' Company, in which he served in every rank from private upwards, eventually becoming its captain and later a major and second in command to Colonel Robert Edis. On gaining the rank of sergeant, Walter Horsley's name became indelibly associated with 'The Baggage Guard' later to be called 'The Marching Detachment', an explanation of which event in the Artists' calendar is contained in the following paragraphs.

In this early period of the Regiment it was the custom for practically all Volunteers to join, in their thousands, in a big field day when a 'sham fight' took place on the Easter Monday Bank Holiday. This field day was held in various parts of the country, where ground was available and accessible, mostly near a big seaside town. It became the custom for large numbers of Volunteers to be quartered in the town from the Good Friday or Saturday evening, until they returned to town on the Monday, or very early on the Tuesday, each Volunteer taking part contributing a sufficient sum to cover the expenses involved. In the early 1880s this custom developed a little further and big marching columns were frequently arranged starting very early on the Friday morning, entraining at a convenient railway station as a starting point, billeting on the way on the Friday evening, resuming the march early on the Saturday night, in time for a clean up, a big Church parade on the Sunday morning, the remainder of the day being spent resting at the seaside.

The Artists, however, always had to go 'one better' than the rest of the Volunteers, and from the very early days it had been their custom to send their ambulance wagon and beer cart (the only two vehicles the Regiment possessed of its own) with sometimes two or more military or civilian wagons, borrowed or hired to carry the officers' and men's kits. This little horse-drawn transport party, commanded by Transport Sergeant 'Sammy' Cowell, started on its journey from London on the Tuesday or Wednesday, a few days before the departure of the main body of men. It was Sergeant Horsley who first conceived of the necessity of having a 'baggage guard' to escort the little convoy on its journey until it met up with the battalion.

The original guard was only a sergeant's command (i.e. was commanded by Walter Horsley himself), but it grew in size as its founder and natural commander progressed in rank over the years. The 'baggage guard', or 'marching detachment' as it was later termed, was eventually enlarged to a party of two or more companies, commanded by a captain, or even a major, i.e. generally by Captain Walter Horsley or Major Walter Horsley. It became one of the most instructive and important events of the year, to which Artists, who were looking for promotion, clamoured to belong. The 'baggage guard' grew from a small escort party consisting of its commander, a corporal and less than a dozen men to a half company, then a full company and finally to several companies with fife and drums, complete with officer commanding, who specially selected his adjutant, quartermaster and sergeant major each year.

In 1893 there was a vacancy in the Regiment for a junior major and Captain Horsley (the painter), who commanded 'F' Company was appointed to the post. When in 1903, Colonel Horsley took command of the Regiment it consisted of eight companies. A man of independent characteristics, he was an outstanding commanding officer in every way. His looks, the way he wore his uniform and character made him unique amongst the commanding officers of the Regiment. He was so modest that few realized his extraordinary ability and immense physical strength. As no profession appears to have been recorded against his name, it is to be assumed that he was a 'gentleman of means' but there were few professions and callings that he would not have really excelled in, few subjects in which he was not keenly interested. He knew the countryside and his strategic and tactical skills, if seemingly casual, were sound. A typical sample of his orders on an exercise would be 'Scatter them along – well beyond those woods – but keep a good lump in reserve, somewhere about here' (indicating the position on the map). The actual position of each company and other details would have to be left to others!

The colonel earned the reputation of being over-enthusiastic on the subject of battalion drill, his favourite movement of the men at his disposal on the parade ground being a 'battalion wheel in quarter column', which he considered the best exercise of every kind of drill to practise. This led to the composition of a well-remembered song, in which all would join lustily in chorus at smoking concerts, which went something like this: 'Wheel us round once again, Walter, around, around, around', which usually elicited the response from the Colonel: 'Oh, all right I will.' And the next time on parade, he *did*!

Under Horsley the Regiment prospered with the introduction of new ideas for training and novel prize-winning competitions. He was eager to learn all he could from foreign armies attending annual manoeuvres on the Continent, the countries visited being France, Holland and Switzerland. But his greatest test was to come in April 1908 with the advent of the new Territorial Force, which signalled a new role for the Artists CV in the lead-up to the Great War.

The Haldane Army Reforms and the Territorial Force

By far the most important series of events in Britain affecting the military in the first decade of the twentieth century were the Haldane Army Reforms. Although Volunteers had responded grandly to the Imperial cause in South Africa, with victory their patriotic fever had subsided and in the happy-go-lucky Edwardian era the public in Britain sat back and let the world roll by. But there were some keener observers of international affairs in the country who still feared invasion from the long-standing enemy, France, and were apprehensive to say the least by the threat posed by the Imperial Russian Army, seemingly poised on the North West Frontier of India for an incursion into the sub-continent. As the Edwardian years progressed, a very real menace emerged, however, in the person of the King's nephew and grandson of Queen Victoria, Kaiser Wilhelm II, and German imperialism, who and which threatened the security of Europe. The Kaiser's intention of starting a war was implicit in the German High Command's Schlieffen Plan of 1906, which envisaged a two-front war against France and Russia.

Pleas for conscription in Britain by the National Service League led by Lords Roberts and Kitchener were rejected by successive governments, but steps were taken by Sir Henry Campbell-Bannerman's Liberal government, which took office in January 1906, to modernize the Army. The job of introducing these reforms fell to Richard Burdon Haldane (1856-1928), Secretary of State for War in the new government. Haldane, a Scot, was educated at the universities of Edinburgh and Göttingen, where he read the German philosophers and absorbed a good deal of German culture. He admired the German determination born of the Bismarck era to establish the Reich as a national identity, although he roundly opposed its imperialistic aims. Perhaps the most useful thing Haldane learned from the Germans was their thoroughness which he practised to good effect in creating a two-line national army, capable of despatching an efficient fighting force overseas in the event of war. It was rumoured that, among Campbell-Bannerman's potential cabinet ministers, Haldane was the only one who would accept the post of Secretary of State for War. It was perhaps because of Haldane's Scottish background and grounding in German culture that Campbell-Bannerman is said to have remarked: 'Let's see how Schopenhauer gets on in the kailyard.'[1] Haldane (he was elevated to the peerage in 1911) faced a formidable task. He himself was not well versed in military systems, so he was wise enough to employ as his military secretary Colonel Gerald Ellison from the War Office, who proved to be an invaluable assistant. Although in the trauma in military circles that followed the South African war, Arthur Balfour's Conservative

Government (1902-5) had made some progress with Army reform, the Tories now in opposition would inevitably criticize much of the detail of Haldane's proposals, and to add to his worries the Liberals were divided between Imperialists and Radicals, who opposed the expansion of empire and any expenditure aimed at enlarging and improving the efficiency of the fighting services.

Haldane in 1906 quickly specified the principles which would underpin the reform of the Regular Army. He contended it would have to differ from that of any other nation in order to meet its unique, long-distance, overseas commitments. He affirmed that the country needed a highly-organized and well-equipped striking force (in the event it was called the Expeditionary Force), which 'can be transported, with the least possible delay, to any part of the world where it is required'. To sustain such a force in numbers and efficiency for the duration of hostilities a sufficiently large reserve was necessary. Only the Militia, argued Haldane, could provide adequate numbers, but he refrained at first from suggesting that the Militia should be liable for service abroad but rather that it should relieve the Regulars of the responsibility for home defence.

After a month's deliberation he expanded upon these views, claiming that the Militia (and Yeomanry) would have to furnish not only drafts in the early stages of war, but also a whole range of ancillary services for the striking force. By tapping skilled labour resources in the civilian community, Haldane contended that a striking force of three Army Corps could be mobilized without breaching a financial ceiling of £28 million. Further expansion could be met by the third constituent of the triad of auxiliary forces – the Volunteers – by the creation of a Territorial Army from the Volunteers en bloc and those portions of the Militia and Yeomanry not required for the striking force. Haldane, in short, proposed a rationalization of the existing Regular and Auxiliary Forces into two lines able to undertake and sustain an overseas campaign while maintaining the security of the homeland.

As Haldane wrote in a memorandum in 1907:

The National Army will, in future, consist of a Field Force and a Territorial or Home Force. The Field Force is to be so completely organized as to be ready in all respects for mobilization immediately on the outbreak of a great war. In that event the Territorial or Home Force would be mobilized also, but mobilized with a view to its undertaking in the first instance systematic training for War. The effect of such training given a period of at least six months would be, in the opinion of all military experts, to add very materially to the efficiency of the force. The Territorial Force will, therefore, be one of support and expansion, to be at once embodied when danger threatens, but not likely to be called for till the expiring period of six months.

The proposals for the Regular Army differed little actually from the Field Force which had been in existence since 1895. The professionals consisted of seventy-four paired infantry battalions (the 1st and 2nd Battalions) alternating between home and overseas service and six Battalions of Guards, four Brigades of Cavalry with supporting units, mainly artillery and engineers. (Over 50,000 officers and men were stationed in India and the minor colonies.) With the contribution of the Special Reserve of a further seventy-four battalions, Haldane earmarked six large divisions and supporting units numbering approximately 150,000 officers and men. This constituted the striking force, or British Expeditionary Force (BEF), which went to France at the outbreak of war in 1914. There was little need, in fact, to reorganize the Regular Army as such but there was an acute shortage of Regular officers and artillery and urgent steps were taken to remedy these deficiencies. Haldane made changes at the highest level, pumping new blood into the General Staff and eliminating some of the bureaucracy for which it was noted. The General Staff was shortly to become the Imperial General Staff to coordinate but not oversee the interests and requirements of the Dominion Armies for their own benefit and that of the mother country. Exchanges of officers were made, the Dominion officers attending Staff College to facilitate their promotion to field rank.

Haldane never doubted that the Auxiliary Forces required reform. They cost about £4 million per annum and, unless reorganized, were of questionable military value. The semi-professional Militia, the 'old Constitutional Force', had the distinction of being the oldest military force in the kingdom, yet its contemporary weaknesses were all too evident. It boasted an establishment of 131,000 men, but the Militia was short of officers and its actual strength was only 85,000 officers and men. Of its 124 battalions, forty-six were under 500 strong. Officered by country gentlemen, the Militia's ranks were filled by casually employed or unemployed labourers, many of them too young for overseas service. Some 10 per cent deserted annually and 25 per cent left through premature discharge.

The condition of the Yeomanry, on the other hand, was more satisfactory. Reorganized in 1901, the fifty-six Corps of mounted landowners and farmers numbered 25,585 of all ranks. Prepared to train annually over a period of from fourteen to eighteen days, in addition to the preliminary instruction, the Yeomanry was potentially a useful force. Yet it lacked a wartime role. Indeed it had mushroomed since its origins in the French Revolutionary Wars without regard to strategic requirements and without concern for efficiency or economy. The Yeomanry, however, remained a nucleus from which the second line of Cavalry might be formed.

The Volunteers, as we have learned, were formed by the Rifle Volunteer Act of 1863 to repeal a threatened invasion by France. Mustered in exclusive military clubs, the Volunteer Corps were originally self-sufficient units, only dependent on the State for 25 per cent of their rifles. By 1906 these social conditions and financial circumstances had radically changed. The Volunteers by then were recruiting the vast majority of their rank-and-file from 'artisans', that is from the more respectable sections of the urban working class. The force had become progressively less and less middle class. Indeed by the end of the Edwardian years about one quarter of the recruits came from the ranks of unskilled workers.

This social change necessitated an increasing dependence by the Volunteers on the government for financial support, amounting to £1,750,000 per annum when Haldane entered office. Still this sum, disbursed through the capitation grant for each efficient soldier with allowances for uniform, equipment and attending camp, was not sufficient. Haldane replaced the capitation grant with a block grant designed to put each Volunteer unit's finances in order so that they could function efficiently as part of the new Territorial Force. Undoubtedly the worst hit individual financially had been the commanding officer, who bore the main financial responsibility for his Volunteer unit, and who was often forced to raise additional funds by public subscription. As Haldane observed: 'the unfortunate commanding officer of a Volunteer battalion is an even greater patriot than is popularly supposed; he risks not only his life but his fortune.' Indeed some Volunteer COs had oversubscribed recruits to increase the capitation grant, which was not generally speaking conducive to military efficiency. Another factor which militated against efficiency was the right of any individual Volunteer to leave his unit on giving three months' notice. In summary, the Volunteers were badly in need of reorganization. One consideration was that the Volunteers were bereft of transport and supplies so necessary for mobilization.

Haldane formally moved the Territorial and Reserve Forces Bill before a thinly attended House on 4 March 1907. He stated that the Bill, if passed, would empower the Army Council to create County Associations headed by the Lords Lieutenant to administer (but not command) the Territorial Force and the Special Reserve. The Bill would also enable the Army Council to expand the category A Reserve. The second reading of the Bill was taken on 9, 10 and 23 April, whereupon the government, aided by some Labour members, steamrollered the Bill through by 388 to 109 votes. On 6 May, at the opening of the committee stage, the Prime Minister announced that a guillotine procedure would operate throughout the discussion. The House debated the Bill on eight different days, before taking the third reading on 19 June. The Liberal majority dominated throughout, securing the final passage of the Bill by 286 to 63 votes. (It was said that the Labour and Liberal radical members who supported the government did so in the hope that, having passed their first act of parliament dealing with the means of defence of the realm, that the government would now devote its energies to alleviating the plight of the working class by improving the social conditions which prevailed at the time in an otherwise prosperous nation!)

Haldane did not make his changes in the Auxiliary Forces without bitter opposition from the Militia colonels, who were anxious to preserve their traditional privileges and who resented the interference of the government and the County Associations in what they regarded as their private army. Although it was stipulated in the Bill that the Territorial Force would not be liable for service overseas, it was understood that the TF could be mobilized in the event of war on government advice by Royal Warrant. The Territorials [2] were to be organized into field divisions and equipped with ancillary services such as transport and artillery. Political and public opinion, however, caused the government to reduce Haldane's target of twenty-eight divisions to fourteen with fourteen cavalry brigades and Corps troops. Many Volunteer units were embodied as a whole in the Territorial Force, while seventy Militia battalions were allocated to Regular Regimental Depots to form the new Special Reserve. The Territorial Force (TF) actually came into being on 1 April 1908 and in that year the first annual fortnight's training camp took place. By the beginning of 1910, as a result of energetic recruiting, the Territorials numbered 276,618 officers and men, 88.5 per cent. of the proposed establishment. The TF was (almost) a complete vindication of Haldane's hopes.

Another of Haldane's creations was the 'Officer Training Corps' (OTCs), which were and still are special Corps formed at universities and at public schools for the express purpose of manufacturing and providing trained material for future officers in the Regular Army, or more especially the Territorial Force. The OTCs were of two kinds, the senior OTCs, which were designed for the universities and composed of students while in residence there. They went to camp in their summer vacation and were instructed by Regular officers and NCOs; and the junior OTCs, designed for the public schools, i.e. manned by the boys while actually at school with some of their masters as officers and

Regular NCOs attached to the school for drill, musketry and tactical instruction. Haldane travelled far and wide throughout the country visiting the universities and public and grammar schools to explain his scheme, and he was greatly disappointed when the grammar schools rejected the idea of being included in his proposals. Haldane, however, was responsible, in addition to his many other achievements, for the Army Cadets, which State-educated boys could join in their own locality at fifteen.

When the Artists under Colonel Walter Horsley in 1908 were embodied into the Territorial Force, the 20th Middlesex (Artists) Rifle Volunteers were re-titled the 28th Battalion County of London Regiment (Artists Rifles). This was the third unit designation that the Regiment had borne since it had been raised, although it was more familiarly referred to in the military world and in London life in particular just simply as the Artists. The Artists were now part of the 2nd London Division (TF). The new role was not entirely to the liking of the stauncher traditionalists in the Regiment. Some thought the Artists had lost their upper crust appeal. The differences in service were not great but were significant. The former undertaking of three years' service now became a legal liability for four years and discharge was made more difficult.

Each member could re-engage for a further definite period, not exceeding four years at one time, as may be fixed by the County Association, instead of merely staying on from year to year until they sent in their resignations as they did in the old Volunteer Force. In the Territorial Force also, as in the old Volunteers, men were able to resign before the expiration of their definite period of service (except when the force had been embodied for active service), provided they gave three months' notice, gave up all their arms and equipment in good condition, and paid a fine, not exceeding £5 as may be laid down; the amount of which fine, generally speaking, varied with the term of service unperformed. In the old Volunteers, it will be remembered, the amount that a man had to pay the CO on resignation before the expiry of his first three years of service (when not embodied for active service) was, in accordance with his agreement on joining, such a sum, if any, as might be necessary to make up the total amount earned by him in capitation grants, since his enrolment, to the sum of £4 10s, the actual cost to the Corps.

By 1907-8 the new Volunteer could get his military training practically free of cost, except for his annual Corps subscription (of £1 5s in the case of the Artists), and his personal expenses of Regimental dinners, and of meals taken in the canteen. The Territorial Act of 1907 provided not only money to recoup the expense of journeys to and from his headquarters, his drill ground and the range but also certain personal bounties, pay and other allowances as pecuniary remuneration to the man himself for military services. The annual bounty was £1 10s (being £1 for drills and camp and 10s for musketry). A bonus of £5 (besides the usual Army pay and allowances) would be made as a one-time payment on mobilization. In future khaki uniforms and equipment would be freely provided, the rifle adopted at the time being the Long-Lee-Enfield. Payment for service at camp and on courses was made at Regular rates for the rank held.

Officers on first appointment received an 'outfit' allowance of £40, out of which they had to provide, besides their service uniform, a mess dress, a patrol jacket, their sword, revolver, Sam Browne belt and compass, but full dress was not required. The officers, like the men, also received routine allowances and payments at Regular rates at camp and while attending courses. Horses were also supplied by the authorities for use in camp or when required for other training sessions for such officers who were entitled to them, instead of officers having to provide their own horses, as had been the case in the old Volunteer days. Officers would nevertheless still have to dig into their own pockets if they could not make the £40 allowance cover the Regimental requirements for dress, etc., which in many cases was very likely.

Both Colonel Horsley and his second in command, Major May, who were responsible in the Artists' case for implementing the requirements of the Territorial Act, were agreed that the Territorial Force held out better prospects than the old Volunteer Force ever did. The TF was now made up of complete divisions, containing a proper proportion of all arms, and was administered (under the War Office) by the County Associations, which relieved the Regiment of a good deal of paperwork in running the Drill Hall, etc. The commanding officer had been relieved of practically all his financial responsibilities, which in the old days was a very real one, largely restricting the command of Volunteer Regiments to gentlemen of private means.

The opponents of the scheme from within the ranks of the Artists were convinced that service with the TF was rather like paying the 'Gentlemen' to play cricket. 'Gad sir, it is like being tipped by the Army for military service, which had in the past been freely given without resentment.' So what with hurt feelings and increased responsibilities, and loss of freedom of the freelance, there was a fall in strength of the Artists when the time came for attestation in the Territorial Force. This, however, was only a temporary lapse for within a couple of months the Artists were one of the strongest TF battalions in the country and in 1908 turned out for the first fortnight's camp with the 2nd London Division (TF). The camp was in north Kent. The Artists, who were assigned as Corps troops and not brigaded, were called in at the last moment to act as the third battalion of a Regular brigade, which contained only one battalion each of the South Wales Borderers and the Duke of Cornwall's Light Infantry, and who were to act as 'the enemy'. It was generally agreed at the end of the exercise that the Artists were a credit to their training and discipline.

Following the introduction of the Territorial Force, the War Office gave some consideration to the old Grey Brigade in the order of battle of the key London Volunteer units. The Grey Brigade consisted of the Kensington Rifles; the London Scottish Rifles; the Civil Service Rifles; the Queen's Westminster Rifles; the Inns of Court Rifles; and the Artists Rifles. It was decided that the first four regiments should be retained as infantry of the line but that the Inns of Court and Artists should be turned into senior OTCs. The Inns of Court accepted the War Office's proposal but it was rejected out of hand by Colonel Horsley. He argued that the Artists were trained to fight as an infantry battalion: all officers were promoted from the ranks; it took on average ten years for a man to be selected for commissioned rank and the CO considered that ten years was about the right amount of time needed to turn out a good officer. No OTC could offer cadets that scale of thoroughness in training as potential officers. The War Office, who might well have thought Colonel Horsley's views over zealous, if not a trifle ponderous, nevertheless accepted his argument and the 28th Battalion County of London Regiment (Artists Rifles) remained in the Grey Brigade (now khaki-clad) as its fifth member. The War Office did not, however, give up the idea of turning the Artists into an OCTU, as we shall see later in this book.

Colonel Walter Horsley resigned his command in 1912 and was succeeded by Lieutenant Colonel H. A. R. May. (Colonel Robert W. Edis remained honorary colonel, Horsley being appointed to the post in 1921.) Towards the end of his period of command Horsley saw the death of Edward VII in 1910 and the succession of George V, the Artists contributing to the contingents of troops lining the way on the occasions of the funeral and coronation. (Edward VII had always been a keen supporter of the Volunteers.) Colonel Horsley's final act as CO, assisted by Major May – as the storm clouds gathered in Europe – was to put into effect the Mobilization Plan, which would put the Artists on a war footing.

The Mobilization Plan

The Regimental plan based on the War Office's Mobilization Instructions for the Territorial Force dated April 1910 and signed by E.

H.H. Lees, Captain and Adjutant, was posted from headquarters at Duke's Road during that month to every serving member of the Regiment. Set double-column in small type on one side of a quarto sheet of paper, it was a remarkably comprehensive document, which covered all possible contingencies in preparing all ranks for war. As a preliminary, advice was given on the proper care and maintenance of uniform, other clothing and all items of kit. Boots were to be well-oiled and kit regularly cleaned. Hair was to be kept short and toenails cut.

The document stressed that every man should at all times keep himself in readiness for immediate mobilization. A maximum of twelve hours were allowed to elapse between the receipt of the mobilization telegram and the arrival of the soldier at headquarters ready to proceed to the war station. Before leaving home all items carried on the body, in the haversack and in the kitbag, as listed, were to be thoroughly checked. These items included field glasses on a sling (if available), a clasp knife and water bottle filled with drinking water.

The contents of the haversack (and pockets of the tunic) for the men were to include the following – a notebook, notepaper, two pencils, a whistle and materials for cleaning kit and rifle, a toothbrush, soap in case, razor in case, shaving soap and brush, a small tin for salt, small (1d.) tin of Vaseline (for feet or boots), a small book of plasters, matches, tobacco and pipes (if desired), fork and spoon, a small tin of cocoa and meat lozenges or soup tablets, a small towel and one (possibly two) big silk or cotton handkerchiefs (useful for carrying food), spare bootlaces and cash. Space remaining was to be filled with food (such as hard-boiled eggs, sugar, cheese, ham, bread rolls), to be replenished on every available occasion. Moist food was to be carried in the mess tin.

The kitbag with blanket strapped to the outside (not obscuring the name) was to be packed as follows – spare pair of marching boots and laces, two spare flannel shirts and vest, drawers and three pairs of socks, spare khaki tunic, trousers, puttees (if available), spare handkerchiefs, enamelled plate and mug, small towel, housewife with sewing items, tin of dubbin for boots, small clothes brush and small hairbrush. In addition, such articles mentioned above which could not be carried on the man or in the haversack should be put into the kitbag. Civilian dress and medals were to be left at home.

Before setting out for headquarters each man was advised to inform his employer (if any) of mobilization and to fill in a simple will and form provided by the Regiment assigning 'power of attorney' in his absence at war to his wife, or if single to his next of kin. On arrival at headquarters each man must:

1) Report himself to an officer of his company
2) Be medically examined

3) Draw his identity disc
4) Draw his field dressing
5) Draw his paybook (and give any special instructions as to allotment of pay)
6) Get his bayonet sharpened
7) Draw his emergency ration
8) His rifle and service ammunition to be drawn from the armoury.

Having fulfilled all these commitments, the man was ready to march. In addition to the above requirements for the men, officers and NCOs must carry (on the man):
1) Field glasses
2) a whistle on the lanyard on left arm
3) a magnetic compass and
4) the 'Field Report Book (Army Book 153)'.

Further, in the case of officers they were required to carry (on the man):
1) revolver, government ammunition to be drawn from the armoury
2) Pouch (with ammunition on belt)
3) Wire cutters
4) 'The *Field Service Pocket Book*' and
5) Officer's mess tin. In place of kitbags, officers should bring,
6) a 'Wolseley Valise', the contents as above specified for the men,
7) a portable portfolio with writing materials
8) a canvas bucket and
9) a collapsible lantern. Every three officers (e.g. from each company) should also bring
10) a sealed pattern of officers camp kettle.

Mounted officers[3] must bring (on the horse):
1) Nosebag with feed of corn
2) Head and picketing ropes
3) Picketing pegs
4) Shoe case containing fore shoe and hind shoe (made to fit) and nails
5) Horse blanket
6) a Dandy brush
7) Horse rubber, and
8) Pad for surcingle.

The aim of all ranks had to be that the battalion (as a unit) was ready to march within twenty-four hours of the receipt of the Mobilization Orders. Men who had placed their names on the list as willing to take a commission in the event of mobilization should be prepared to obtain an officer's equipment at a few hours' notice. As advised by the adjutant, these orders were to be hung up, for instant reference, in the bedroom of every member of the Corps, over a box containing the various items specified for inclusion in these instructions. Needless to say all articles, wherever possible, should be marked with name, rank and company.

Notes
1. Kailyard, or Kaleyard school: a group of nineteenth century fiction writers, including J.M. Barrie, who described local town life in Scotland in a romantic vein with much use of the vernacular.
2. The Territorials were generally referred to as the Territorial Army, although their official title was the Territorial Force. They were not officially called the Territorial Army until 1921.
3. These were the commanding officer, second in command and field officers.

Chapter 7

H. A. R. May CB, VD

1863-1930

Glory to man in the highest
For Man is the master of things
Algernon Swinburne

Henry Allan Roughton May (more commonly referred to throughout his long service with the Artists CV as H. A. R. May) was born and brought up in London in the Bloomsbury district in 1863. Public school educated, he started work at eighteen as an articled clerk in a firm of London solicitors in Fetter Lane. A fellow clerk with whom the young May had struck up a firm friendship enlisted in the Regiment and after a glowing account of his time spent at camp in Aldershot in the summer of 1882, May was persuaded to join also, which being of tidy mind he did on 1 November, the beginning of the next Volunteer year. He was sworn in and after kissing the New Testament was assigned to 'H' Company, commanded by Captain D. W. Wynfield, the leader of the St John's Wood clique of painters who had joined up in 1860. The new recruit was at first ill of ease since he had no connection with the arts, but Captain Wynfield, every inch an artist in appearance and manner, wished him well, expressing the opinion that he would do well in the Corps.

Right from the start May deduced that success in the Artists required constant attendance, infinite patience and a passion even for the most minor of details. There were two drill nights – Tuesdays from 5.30 p.m. to 7.30 p.m. and Fridays from 6.00 p.m. to 8.00 p.m. – when the battalion met at Westminster Hall or at headquarters at 36 Fitzroy Square, and there was also a training session on Saturday afternoons, which was usually held in the University College grounds in Gower Street. In his spare time when not applying his attention to his law books, he devoured all the instruction manuals that he could lay his hands on, particularly admiring Garnet Wolseley's *Soldier's Pocket Book*, which was to be his mentor and guide throughout his military career. Wolseley's remarks that all military reforms since 1860 in the British Army had first been introduced by the Volunteers made May conscious that he had a part to play in upholding a proud tradition.

After completing his first year recruit and musketry courses, in 1883 he volunteered to take part in an Ambulance and Hygiene course, which was conducted by Surgeon Captain Jackson. In the same year he took part as a stretcher bearer in the Easter Monday sham fight on the Downs in the Brighton area. After passing out as an ambulance man, May turned his attention to musketry and after shooting his way through the various courses under the tutelage of Sergeant Instructor of Musketry John Hampton, a permanent staff Rifle Brigade reservist, he qualified as a marksman. In 1883 May attended the Annual Inspection in Hyde Park and also took part in the eight-day summer camp at Cove Common, Aldershot, where in addition to performing all the required duties, he acted as an assistant to the Regular Rifle Brigade cookhouse sergeant, who taught him all he needed to know about the culinary art. His progress thus far earned May a commendation for 'General Excellence' from his company Commander, Captain Wynfield.

Soon after 1 November 1883, when signalling was first introduced into the Regiment, May was one of twenty-seven volunteers for the course which was to last one year. He did so well on the course that at the end of the period of training he was promoted to lance sergeant and made Regimental Signalling Sergeant, an unparalleled achievement for such a young recruit, it on average taking seven years for a man to attain the rank of sergeant. May's appointment was greeted with considerable resentment by senior members of the sergeants' mess and May considered handing back his stripes. However, the adjutant, Captain Charles Haggard, Royal Irish Rifles, would have none of it and the sergeants received a further rebuff from Colonel Edis, who informed them that not one of them was qualified to make Signalling Sergeant as not one had been keen enough to volunteer for the course! Lance Sergeant May did his first stint as Signalling Sergeant on the Easter Field Day 1884, which was based on the Royal Marine Artillery Eastney Barracks near Portsmouth. On this occasion May, to his delight, managed to get a place in Lieutenant Horsley's 'baggage guard'.

Captain Haggard got on to a friend, a Captain Ricardo, who was adjutant of the Grenadier Guards Battalion stationed at the time at Wellington Barracks, and asked him if he would take on May for a month's training in the all round duties of a Regimental Sergeant. Ricardo responded by saying that it would take at least two months to train a Volunteer however good he was. May intended to give up his summer vacation for the course, but his employer would not allow him to take eight weeks off. A compromise was made and his employer gave him seven weeks of absence from the office, which Lance Sergeant May looked forward to with relish. He would receive no pay or ration allowance from the Guards and would not be quartered in barracks.

May reported to Wellington Barracks in May 1884 and was at once involved in long hours of drill instruction on the parade square, after which he was expected to give the orders himself, during which he eventually achieved the adequate and articulate voice projection necessary to activate the guardsmen temporarily under his command. About halfway through the course at Wellington Barracks the Grenadier Battalion was posted to Egypt and May was sent on to another battalion of Grenadiers at Chelsea Barracks, where a friendly Sergeant Brisbane, a very smart and efficient Guards NCO, was assigned to him as instructor. The Regular Army had recently adopted the Martini-Henry rifle but May questioned the necessity of learning how to use it, as the Volunteers were still armed with the Snider. He was told, however, in no uncertain terms, that he would have to learn how to drill and shoot with it, an asset as it happened, as he was the only man in the Artists capable of giving instruction on the Martini-Henry when it eventually replaced the Snider in the Volunteer Force. Sergeant Brisbane got May enrolled in the sergeants' mess, the members of which rose to toast the 'Volunteer Sergeant' with glasses of beer on his last day at Chelsea Barracks.

In 1884 May attended 245 drills, a record never surpassed in Artists' history. In the same year he formed a class for lance corporals and corporals and in 1885 was promoted to full sergeant in 'H' Company. In that year Captain H. Gore-Brown, 60th Rifles, who had succeeded Captain Haggard as Regimental Adjutant, established the NCOs school and Sergeant May was appointed the senior NCO instructor. In May's own words:

> In our course of instruction and with the help of the permanent staff we first put our pupils through a really sharp 'refresher' course of squad and company drill and musketry. We then instructed them in the art of drill and instructing others, including the giving of clear and correct instructions and cautions and words of command, in discipline, duties on guard, dress and equipment, tent pitching, duties in camp, cooking, fatigues, outposts, advance and rear guards, marching, care of men, care of feet and boots, bugle calls (with the help of a piano and a bugle), topography and scouting (the Adjutant's two favourite subjects) and also such domestic things as singing on the march, organizing impromptu smoking concerts and

miscellaneous matters in connection with the Regiment.[1]

In 1887 May was promoted to be colour sergeant in 'H' Company and was thereupon allowed to instruct and drill all the NCOs (including the sergeants) in one class, and he organized special classes for all the NCOs of 'H' Company. In 1888 he was awarded a commission and the adjutant thereupon gave up his work in the NCO school (except as an occasional helper) and May was given complete charge of it, also of recruit instruction, and was permitted to suggest the NCOs who were to be assistant instructors, all of which he undertook. In 1886 Lord Wolseley brought out a new edition of his *Soldier's Pocket Book*, which May read and studied avidly. He was greatly struck by Wolseley's invaluable suggestions as to the care of men which, with associated subjects such as sanitation, billeting, justice, etc., he incorporated into his 1886-7 training programme syllabus. He found in his dictionary that the word sergeant was derived from the Latin *Servio* ('I Serve') adding 'Serving' to the title officer and the men they commanded in the battalion. In 1889 he published his *Grey Book*, the contents of which have been described in some detail in Chapter 4. It was to be the bible of the Corps for many years to come.

By 1893 May had progressed from being junior subaltern to senior subaltern in 'H' Company and one of the senior subalterns in the Corps and he began to wonder if he would make captain. In the early 1890s the Corps still had a strong connection with the Arts, more especially as regards its officers. Of its eight companies six were what was then known as 'Professional Companies', i.e. 'A', 'F' and 'H' Companies were Painters' companies, 'C' and 'E' were Architects' companies and 'B' was a Musician's company. Two companies were 'Non-Professional' ones, 'D' and 'G', both of which were founded in connection with London University. The 'Professional Companies' were all originally and afterwards commanded by a captain of the profession to which his company belonged and it was the wish of the CO (Colonel Edis) that in the 'Professional Companies' two of the officers (out of three) should also be of the company's profession and that in the 'Non-Professional Companies' at least one of the officers (out of three) should be from the Arts community, so as to keep up the artistic character of the Corps. This rule had been broken on occasions before 1893 but by the middle of the decade the Corps was beginning to lose touch with the Arts. However, the impression was still given that being a full-time practitioner of the Arts carried weight in the election of NCOs for promotion to commissioned rank, and also in the promotion and selection to be captain in command of a 'Professional Company'.

In 1893 there was a vacancy for a junior major and as was expected,

Captain Horsley of 'F' Company was appointed to the post and, as neither of his former subalterns (Lieutenants F. S. Howarth and S.S. Higham) were painters, it was expected that another painter would be brought in to command 'F' Company. Contrary to tradition, May, now a qualified solicitor, was given the command. Topped only by 'D' Company, 'F' was next in line in the Regimental company order of merit, and Captain May set his heart on making 'F' the best company in the battalion. Lieutenant Howarth, a stockbroker who was good with figures worked out the average score of performances in every discipline throughout the Regiment and May gave notice to his men that their scores should never fall below that average figure. In addition 'Volunteer Godfathers' were appointed from within the company to help underperforming individuals with their work, particularly shooting. Improvements immediately took place in every direction. By the end of the first year the company, which had been considerably below strength, rose to full strength, which at that time was 100 men. By the end of the second year it produced a record number of marksmen, although they were still below 'D' in numbers. The average number of drills per man improved as also the number of 'efficients before inspection'. In addition, 'F' Company introduced many new innovations, such as the Weldon range finder, map reading classes and some novel shooting competitions. Also at the end of the second year, 'F' Company was furnishing all the instructors (with the exception of the permanent staff) for the battalion NCOs School of Instruction.

In 1897 the figures of merit of 'D' Company and 'F' Company were the highest of all companies of London Volunteers ('D' being slightly ahead). In 1897 every man in 'F' Company was 'efficient before inspection', and in the same year 'F' obtained a record attendance at the Easter manoeuvres. The company's strength increased well beyond establishment, so much so that in 1900, when Colonel Edis decided to increase the strength of the battalion from eight to twelve companies, 'F' Company provided the nucleus of some seventy men to form 'I' Company, which was placed under the command of Captain Brandon Thomas with Lieutenant L. H. M. Dick (late of 'D' Company) as his senior subaltern and C. E. W. (Pane-eye) Austin (supplied by 'F' Company) as his junior subaltern. During Captain May's period of command the company's marksmen were increased fourfold, the second-class shots were reduced from forty-two to six and there were no third-class shots at all.

Captain May continued in command of 'F' Company until 1900 when he was promoted junior major. In his new post Major May greatly missed his duties as a company commander but his time was taken up as President of the Band committee, which gave him supervision of the band and drums and Chairman of the Clothing committee, in which capacity he was responsible for the new dress regulations described in Chapter 4. He attended the Field Officers' Course at Wellington Barracks and afterwards devoted more time to the NCOs School, which he had always regarded as his special child. He was allowed to start a new class for junior officers, i.e. for all under the rank of captain, and in this class he endeavoured to carry on with, among other subjects, the instruction in map reading, topography and military sketching introduced by Captain Horsley a few years earlier. He was also given leave to run a special course of instruction for the previous year's recruits, i.e. for men during their second year of service, on all kinds of military subjects, including mobilizing, sanitation, bugle calls, billeting and care of men.

Major May realized the truth of Lord Wolseley's broad and frequently quoted dictum that all military training should have 'preparation for active service' for its ultimate object and he was very conscious that no amount of drill in the Drill Hall and tactical exercises in parks could be realistically practised even in ingeniously conceived simulated war conditions. In order to improve the battalion's performances the men were drilled in rapid reaction to orders given in the attack and in defence, as well as the reorganization by officers and NCOs of a retreating column. He also had ideas on speeding up the battalion on the move, which he modelled on the retreat to Corunna in the Peninsular War, in which the fastest pace that could be kept up along a road by a large body of men was first to make six paces of quick marching and then six paces doubling, then six paces of quick marching, then six paces doubling – and so on. This march in quick time – christened 'the lope' by the younger rankers – was tried out on Hampstead Heath and after a half pint at the Spaniard's Inn on the road back to Duke's Road, when the 'lopers' caused much amusement to the onlookers. The 'lope' was not adjudged to be a success and was never used by the Artists in the Great War. Major May also tried out an unusual type of shooting competition after buying up the bankrupt stock of a crockery store in Woking. The cups, saucers, plates and jugs, etc. were to be used as targets on a field firing range. It was May's belief that marksmen would get more satisfaction from destroying objects rather than merely hitting conventional targets. Be that as it may, the edge was taken off the afternoon's shooting by the bill rendered by the range authorities for clearing up the litter. It was perhaps fortunate that there were no other shops in the Regiment's orbit with a supply of crockery ready for disposal for 'any reasonable offer'.

Early in the year 1903, in which Colonel Horsley was appointed commanding officer, May was promoted as second in command with the rank of lieutenant colonel. At the same time he received the Volunteer Long Service Medal, having completed twenty years of service in the Regiment. He was appointed chairman of the Finance Committee, which was responsible for administering both the Public Funds of the Regiment, which consisted of the capitation and other official grants to the CO by the War Office to enable him to carry on the Regimental work and the Private Funds, being the private subscriptions of £1 5s each, and any other sums contributed by members of the Regiment individually, and which were spent by the CO, more or less as he thought fit, for the benefit of the Regiment and its members. Meetings of the Finance Committee were held almost every week to sign cheques and otherwise carry on the financial work. Strict accounts were of course kept and a detailed report (as to the financial position of the Corps) was made each year by the Finance Committee to the CO, and a printed copy of the report was, by the direction of the CO, sent each year to every member of the Regiment, as would be the case with any good club.

In 1906 Colonel May was given a chance to demonstrate his talents as a showman when the Artists were invited by the Royal Military Tournament authorities to give a torchlight display at the annual May meeting at Olympia. May, who considered that a brilliant display would not only be good for the Artists but for the Volunteer Force as a whole, evolved a long series of complicated manoeuvres to be performed by about 200 Artists formed up in four files and carrying lighted torches. The display, which was of course to be performed in a darkened arena, was aided by both the battalion's brass band and drum and fife band. May's problem was for his performers to find the time to attend the number of rehearsals he considered necessary to ensure success. With the assistance of twelve enthusiastic NCOs, instruction was reduced to three hard drills of two hours each. At the first drill correct marching in file was practised; at the second correct dressing and carrying torches; and at the third the NCOs and bands were introduced with the contingent of 200 men divided into four lines of fifty each, marching in single file, with torches, through the evolutions, without words of command with one of the twelve NCOs at the end of each file, so all the leader of the next file in line had to do was to follow him. (This left four NCOs to act as understudies.) On the night of the display, which was to be repeated the following night, the continuous moving maze of lights in the darkness, to the music of the bands, going through ever more complicated evolutions without words of command proved very popular and was greeted by the audience with a prolonged round of applause. It was to the credit of the Artists that not one of the NCOs or men lost their heads, carrying out the evolutions with a speed and precision which was much to be admired.

In the years 1907-08 both Horsley and May were actively engaged in the integration of the Artists Corps as part of the new Territorial Force but the Mobilization Plan, which was in place by 1910, was May's work in its entirety – accepted and approved of, of course, by the commanding officer. The Mobilization Instructions as issued to each member in April 1910 have been covered in the last chapter, but a considerable amount of administrative work was necessary for the arrival of some 800 men of the Regiment at headquarters when the time came.

Regulations required that all 800 officers and men should be medically examined before being passed as 'fit for service'. This was too much work for the two Regimental medical officers, so a team of ten civilian medical practitioners was recruited to assist in the 'medical'. Arrangements were made for a firm of West End hairdressers to send a gang of haircutters, and three chiropodists, to overhaul the hair and feet of those members who had not already complied with the relevant clause of the Moblization Instructions. Mobilization telegrams, in addition to those to be despatched to the men, were written out and ready for despatch at a moment's notice to all such doctors, haircutters and chiropodists and also to all officers and to certain selected NCOs whose services would be required at headquarters before the arrival of the main body of men.

As to accommodation for the officers, May entered into an agreement with a small hotel in Bloomsbury possessing rooms for thirty-seven guests, by which in the event of mobilization, the rooms would be vacated and placed at the disposal of the officers and certain senior NCOs, at agreed rates. As to accommodation for the men, May obtained through the proper authorities written permission so that when the balloon went up, the Regiment might, at once, have the exclusive use of two London County Council schools close at hand – one in Lancing Street, WC and the other in Manchester Street, WC – which would be immediately vacated by the children and teachers. Both schools were surveyed by an officer of the battalion (a well-known architect) and rooms allotted for each company for dormitories, medical examination, hair cutting and chiropody, and recreation to meet requirements.

It was recognized that when war was declared many former members of the Regiment would apply to re-join and they and new recruits anxious to enrol in the Artists would descend on headquarters once mobilization had been announced. So a fair-sized flat adjacent to HQ was earmarked to assemble the recruits, interview them and enrol them. The recruits were to be drilled by specially selected NCOs on the big squares in the neighbourhood and on the recreation ground at University College in Gower Street. As to horses each officer entitled to a charger was made responsible for bringing his own on mobilization, and the military authorities concerned undertook to indent to military contractors and civilian firms for transport horses. Arrangements were made with the Midland Railway Company to allow the Regiment to stable sixty horses in the arches at St Pancras station, the company further providing a team of their horse keepers to assist in the grooming and care of the horses in general.

As regards the stores, May prepared complete lists of everything that would be required on mobilization and ascertained from the secretary of the TF Association (himself an old Artist) from whom each type of store would have to be obtained. Some would come from the Tower of London, some from contractors and tradesmen, but some the Regiment would have to buy in for themselves. May also satisfied himself as to what transport would be necessary to call for all these stores, as well as the size of the party, in each case, to be told to collect them. He also prepared lists specifying how the stores were to be allocated to companies, to wagon loads and to individuals. The spaces to be allocated to each company's stores as listed were to be marked with chalk lines in the Drill Hall. The quartermaster was made responsible for the provision and collection of stores and the distribution to the companies, wagon loads and men, the transport officer being responsible for the packing of stores and their safety in transit.

Besides the above, careful lists of special duties were prepared for many of the officers and NCOs, each as to his practical work in the general scheme. May himself was responsible for the mobilization of the officers as a class. The junior major had the job of selecting, enrolling and training the recruits. He kept a mobilization box up to date, containing the scheme of training, list of qualified instructors, note of training grounds, and all forms and documents necessary for him to perform his duties. Every officer had his understudy. Carefully thought out instructions were prepared for the systematic training of the battalion, if opportunity permitted, at Regent's Park or on Hampstead Heath. Special instructions were issued to the adjutant, each of the medical officers, the quartermaster, the transport officer, the signalling officer, the officer i/c depot, and each company officer – every one of whom had his own mobilization box, the contents of which were to be up-to-date and ready to act upon. Similar instructions were also given to various of the NCOs, such as recruit instructors, and those in charge of cooks, the newly re-formed cyclist section, pioneers, and the parties detailed to draw stores.

At the end of 1912 Colonel Horsley resigned his command and was succeeded by Lieutenant Colonel H. A. R. May as commanding officer of the 28th Battalion London Regiment (Artists Rifles). The objectives of the new CO were to maintain the battalion in a state of readiness for war. He carefully overhauled and endeavoured to improve upon the instruction of recruits, particularly the second year men, of officers and of NCOs. He kept all existing classes of instruction and in addition instituted a series of weekend 'Rapid Solution Courses' for officers and NCOs to solve tactical problems on the ground. He also practised whenever possible all his 'stunts', such as practical team shooting etc.

In the summer of 1913 King George V held a special review of London Volunteers in Hyde Park, when a large number of Volunteers marched past His Majesty at the saluting base. Lieutenant Colonel May headed the Artists contingent, who were attired in their Grey No. 1 Dress. Practice mobilizations were in part carried out in the springs of 1913 and 1914.

On Sunday, 2 August 1914, the battalion attended annual camp at Perham Down, arriving at 1.30 p.m. on that day, but the same night, soon after 10 p.m., it was ordered at once to return to London. The battalion accordingly left camp at 7 a.m. the following morning, Monday 3 August, and arrived back at Duke's Road at 10 a.m. The men were dismissed and allowed to go home until, at 6.30 p.m. the same day, they were ordered to attend again at headquarters. On arrival (no orders having been received by the Regiment in the meantime) the men were again allowed to proceed home but warned to keep themselves in readiness for further orders. The next day, Tuesday 4 August, at 8.45 p.m., definite orders TO MOBILIZE were received at Duke's Road. The mobilization telegrams were at once despatched, and all other orders were posted by 10 p.m. Britain was at war and the long-prepared Mobilization Plan had at last been put into operation.

Note
1. From Colonel H.A.R. May CB,VD, *Memories of the Artists Rifles*, Howlett & Son, London 1929.

Chapter 8

The Artists at War

1914

We came to Sarajevo, Herr Burgomeister, *and have a bomb thrown at us.*
The last public utterance of Archduke Franz Ferdinand of Austria-Hungary before he died in company with his wife at the hand of a Serb nationalist assassin, an act that was to provoke World War, 28 June 1914.

When on 28 June 1914 Gavrilo Princip, a nineteen year old Serb nationalist killed Archduke Franz Ferdinand, the heir to the throne of Austria-Hungary, in Sarajevo, capital of the Austro-Hungarian province of Bosnia-Herzegovina, he triggered a war which the aggressive foreign policies of Russia, Austria-Hungary and, most of all Germany, had been pursuing during the preceding decade. Austria-Hungary gave Serbia, an independent state, forty-eight hours to reply to an ultimatum demanding that their officials be allowed to investigate Serbian complicity in the assassination and to enforce the suppression of subversive movements in Serbia itself; to no one's surprise Serbia rejected these demands.

An offer from the British government to mediate was curtly rejected by Germany as 'insolence' and Austria-Hungary, at Germany's prompting, declared war on Serbia on 28 July. Russia immediately mobilized in support of fellow Slavs in Serbia, Germany in support of Austria-Hungary and France, which together with Britain was a member of the 'Triple Alliance', in support of Russia. After a last effort to salvage an agreement had failed, Britain joined the hostilities alongside France and Russia on 4 August after the German invasion of Belgium: 80,000 members of the British Expeditionary Force (BEF) were sent across the Channel to France within a few days. After a month 16 million men had taken up arms across Europe. France recruited from its colonies in Africa and Indo-China; Britain from Australia, Canada, India and New Zealand.

Immediately war was declared by Britain, a mass of work became urgently necessary in London: certain localities had to be protected; known enemy aliens living and working in London had to be arrested, imprisoned and guarded; arms and other military equipment had to be collected and distributed, etc. Major General Sir Francis Lloyd, KCB, CVO, DSO, who then commanded London District, at once detailed two battalions for this kind of work, namely a battalion from the Scots Guards, and the other a Territorial battalion – the 28th London Regiment (Artists Rifles). The Artists were required to find numerous parties and to carry out various duties in different parts of London during the evening and night of 5 August, the first day of mobilization, by which time headquarters at Duke's Road was flooded with men in response to the Mobilization Instructions and by applicants wanting to join or re-join the Regiment. In the days and nights that followed the Artists had much work to do in small parties all over London.

Colonel May, who had now been a practising solicitor for thirty years, found acting as full-time commanding officer a very real challenge. He applied his usual meticulous planning skills to the choice of the NCOs in charge of these 'fatigue parties', a task he was assisted in by Staff-Sergeant Peter Emslie, a former Scots Guards Regular. Perhaps the most onerous job assigned to the Artists in those early days of the war was the guarding of German and Austro-Hungarian prisoners at Olympia, a task they took over from the Scots Guards. At Olympia the prisoners lived and slept in the arena, which was surrounded by barbed wire. In the arena were three sub-enclosures, one named by the rank and file of the battalion the 'knut' and another the 'House of Lords', which was reserved for alien enemy of high rank. Each of the latter category was allowed as a privilege to have a batman, being one of the prisoners from the general enclosure, and also a small bed to sleep on (instead of a straw mattress on the tan for the ordinary prisoners), along with a portmanteau in which to keep his belongings. The third sub-enclosure was known as the 'dangerous enclosure', which was used for prisoners who displayed a tendency for violent behaviour, and who were watched day and night by an armed guard. Each prisoner was issued with lists of his 'Prisoners' Obligations and Prisoners' Rights', which were chivalrous but to the point. Colonel May, who inspected the arena twice daily, suffered the indignity on one occasion of being spat upon by two Prussian officers.

All men who were not assigned to the fatigue parties were assembled daily at their temporary barracks, the two requisitioned LCC schools near Duke's Road, at ten o'clock in the morning for a route march to Hampstead Heath, led by one of the majors. The route taken was through St John's Wood via Fitzjohn's Avenue, and this being a broad, spacious thoroughfare, the marchers made a habit of having their first halt there. The residents in the area of Fitzjohn's Avenue came to expect the daily arrival of the Artists and supplied them with refreshments. The young ladies and a few of the older ones got to know the names of many of the Hampstead contingent forming temporary friendships, which raised the morale of the soldiers in no small measure. The Artists' quarters at the schools in Lancing Street (by day) and Manchester Street (by night) were not well suited as accommodation and, moreover, a hindrance to the pupils' education, so after three weeks the battalion was moved to Lord's Cricket Ground, where the Artists' headquarters or officers' billets were located in a hotel, leaving the rank-and-file to live in tents in the grounds, messing facilities being provided in the luncheon arbours. After remaining at Lord's for another three weeks, during which time the Artists assumed most of the 'London Duties', the battalion was suddenly transferred to the Tower of London to replace a resident Guards battalion which had been sent to France.

The Artists were the first Volunteers to be stationed at the historic Tower and take over guard duties there. Colonel May, riding on his charger behind the Regimental Drums, led the battalion through the City to the Tower where the Artists received a warm welcome from the governor, Major General H. Pipon, CB, and the permanent staff of Yeoman Warders quartered at the Tower. The Artists did their best to learn and carry out all the traditions and customs of the establishment. Colonel May put up only one black. Exercising grounds for the horses were hard to find in the City so the CO set up and conducted a riding school for the officers and transport men to exercise their horses in the Tower ditch. Using the ditch for this purpose May discovered too late it was unheard of and had not been used for riding practice for upwards of 200 years. The Colonel received a pardon for his blunder but the Regimental Surgeon (Dr C.S. Segundo), ignorant of the proceedings of the previous day received a stern rebuke for riding round and round the ditch the following morning.

The Artists had only been at the Tower for a few weeks when Colonel May heard that a feud existed between the general commanding London District and the general commanding the 47th (2nd TF) Division, which was exercising near Watford, Hertfordshire, prior to embarkation on active service. At the heart of the matter was the fact that London District wanted to retain the 28th London Regiment (Artists Rifles) for 'London duties' but the 47th Division to which the Artists belonged wanted them under their active command. The 47th Division won the day and on 17 October the battalion was posted to Brickett Wood, then a wasteland sparsely wooded with trees and bushes and thick undergrowth some three miles from Watford. The Artists had only been stationed at Brickett Wood training with the 47th Division for a week when on Saturday 24 October, Colonel May, who was seated with his officers at lunch, was called to the telephone. He was informed that written orders were on the way to embark at Southampton for France on Monday 26 October. May was surprised to learn that it was only the Artists who were committed to France; the remainder of the 47th Division were to stay at Brickett Wood pending further orders.[1]

The battalion had two days in which to prepare for embarkation. Men who had been sent on weekend leave were hastily recalled and it was with heavily laden packs that the Artists' contingent arrived at Watford railway station at midday on the Monday. A crowd of well-wishers, including wives and families, girlfriends and members of other regiments of the Grey Brigade with its brigadier had assembled on the station platform. It was with pride and feelings of apprehension as to what the future held in store for them that the Artists entrained for Southampton. It had been a ruling at the War Office that as a condition of being allowed to go abroad, a second training battalion of Artists should be formed based at its depot at Duke's Road. The 2nd Battalion (2/28th) was already in existence therefore when what would henceforth be called the 1st Battalion (1/28th) joined their ship at Southampton. After marching to the docks at Southampton, the Artists went aboard the SS *Australind* at 7.15 p.m., which was to sail at midnight for Boulogne.

The transport ship was soon crammed with men, horses and stores, not only from the Artists but from detachments of other regiments as well. The horses were packed in between decks with little more than standing room for the men and their equipment on the main deck. The *Australind* was one of many troopships in harbour awaiting the Royal Navy to escort them across the Channel. At midnight, Captain S. Angel, the skipper of the *Australind*, informed Colonel May that their departure would be delayed as one of the transports en route for France had hit a mine. On the following day the *Australind* anchored opposite Netley Hospital, departing at 6 p.m. and arriving after an uneventful voyage at Boulogne at 8.30 p.m. Disembarking the following morning, the battalion replenished its rations and marched to the railway station heartily singing the *Marseillaise* before entraining (with their horses) for a long and tiring journey to St Omer, where they moved into a French infantry barracks in the town.

The 1st Battalion had not been at St Omer for more than a few hours when a staff officer of very high rank arrived to inform Colonel May that the Commander-in-Chief of the BEF, Field Marshal Sir John French, was about to pay the Regiment a visit but that no special parade was to be arranged for his arrival at the barracks. Colonel May believed that Sir John French intended his visit as a welcoming gesture on the arrival of a Territorial battalion in France, so the CO was surprised to find that the C.-in-C. subjected him to a cordial interrogation as to how well the Regiment had performed its 'London duties' and to give him some idea of the Artists' pre-war training and the state of their preparedness for war. Sir John French was particularly impressed by the fact that all members of the Regiment had joined as privates and that promotion to NCO and commissioned rank had been entirely on merit. Colonel May emphasized that the Artists were all drawn from the same social class and were to be rated as above average as Territorial soldiers. The C.-in-C. then toured the ranks, asking each individual soldier about his personal background, and when he arrived at the cookhouse he expressed surprise at meeting the 'gentleman cooks' who had taken to the culinary art to be of real service to the Regiment rather than shirking action in the frontline. The significance of Sir John French's visit to the 1st Battalion at St Omer will unfold later in this chapter.

In the early afternoon of 29 October, the battalion assembled their packs and equipment and marched to Helfaut, a village in the neighbourhood. At Helfaut the men were provided with billets in the village, Colonel May being privileged to be quartered at the official residence of the *Maire* (Mayor). After a discussion with the *Maire*, the Colonel arranged for a small sum to be paid to 180 villagers providing accommodation for his men, the service to include supplying coffee at 8 a.m. and soup at 8 p.m.; one middle-aged lady, who had a husband and son serving in the French Army, adding a drop of cognac to the morning coffee of the eighty men billeted in her barn. At Helfaut the Artists enjoyed their first real rest since leaving England. Soon after their arrival in the village, Colonel May was approached by an Army chaplain, the Revd. John Gibb, on horseback, who enquired if he could be of service to the Artists. The CO was not sure with so many men of different religious denominations in the ranks as to of how much practical use an official Church of England chaplain would be to him. May, however, delighted Gibb (a Cavalry officer before being ordained a priest) by accepting his offer; the CO suggesting that a Holy Communion service should be held the following day, a Sunday, and as it happened All Saints Day. It was decided to hold the service in the local school but on the day so many men assembled at the entrance that it was impossible to accommodate them all in one sitting. The service was transferred to the common where there was plenty of room for all of them, a memorable service being held, administered by six padres, five of whom were serving as privates in the Regiment.

It was during the service that orders were received for the Artists to take their place as part of the 7th Division in the Ypres Salient. After the retreat from Mons and the Miracle of the Marne when the Germans were turned back in sight of Paris, the Allies advanced to the River Aisne, where the opposing armies dug the first series of trenches of the war. The final actions of the 'Race to the Sea' by the Germans were fought in Flanders at the Battle of the Yser (18 October – 30 November) and in the bloody first Battle of Ypres (30 October – 24 November). The 1st Battalion immediately departed Helfaut for Bailleul in a fleet of omnibuses, the CO, adjutant and quartermaster travelling in a motor car. The column was halted in a secluded part of the countryside on a muddy road on the approach to Bailleul. There the Artists found a senior officer of the HQ staff, who turned out to be Colonel C. F. Romer, Royal Dublin Fusiliers, as it happened an Artists adjutant in 1902. Colonel Romer informed Colonel May that he had been charged with conveying the order from Sir John French at his headquarters at St Omer that the Regiment was not to proceed beyond Bailleul where they were to await further orders.

Although the CO was not surprisingly anxious to know what the Field Marshal had in mind, he was urgently beset with the problem of finding accommodation for the Regiment in Bailleul, but the challenge was not as difficult to solve as he had at first thought. With the help of an officer on the staff of the Town Commandment, May allocated his transport section and specialists to a brewery, where there was plenty of available room; two companies were billeted, one each in the two grape-houses which were empty but for a mass of grapes; headquarters was set up in a central house in the Rue de la Gare; his other six companies were divided up, three being placed in facing houses, on either side of the headquarters house. About a week afterwards, early on Thursday 12 November, Field Marshal Sir John French himself arrived at Bailleul. The C.-in-C. was very distressed informing Colonel May that losses in the Battle of Ypres had been colossal, especially among the officers of the 7th Division, and there were simply not enough of them left to lead the division, which was due back in the trenches the following Sunday.

Sir John French went straight to the point. He was satisfied that the Artists as a Regiment were of the 'officer class'. Would the Regiment immediately supply *that day* fifty junior officers for the 7th Division? Colonel May questioned the C.-in-C. as to whether he would be allowed to present the one-star badge of rank as a second lieutenant on completion of his course of instruction, so that although they would be wearing their Other Ranks' uniforms, they would be accepted by the 7th Division as officers. French concurred with this suggestion and May immediately contacted his company captains requesting them to hand lists of suitable officer candidates to RSM Peter Emslie as soon as possible after lunch. On seeking the advice of two of Sir John French's senior staff officers on how to conduct the afternoon training session, one of them told Colonel May that all potential officers should be given three months of hard drill, and the other that it took two years of training to merit commissioned rank.

It was hardly an encouraging start for the CO, but on being handed fifty-two names he resolved in the few hours at his disposal to concentrate all he had learned as an instructor since he had given his first course as a lance sergeant in 1884. His discourse was based on four essential points:
1) 'leading'
2) 'serving'
3) to stress the privilege as a Territorial of being allowed to take the place of and complete the task of a Regular officer killed in the service of his country
4) underlying the preceding three points, to uphold at all times the honour and reputation of the Artists Rifles.

To elaborate on this theme, May insisted that each of the fifty-two men should note down and memorize the essential points that their men were entitled to: food, pay, leave, comfort, justice and recreation, etc., all in due season, urging especially that as officers they should combine the love of their men with emphasizing the need for discipline and obedience. He gave them all such tips as he could hastily gather from Lord Wolseley's *Soldier's Pocket Book*, and since there was no time to go into tactics in the field, each man was presented with a copy of *The Field Service Pocket Book*. Towards the end of the afternoon Colonel May affixed a star to the shoulder straps of each man, shook him by the hand and wished him good fortune as an officer in the British Army. All the above took place on Thursday 12 November. On Sunday 15 November when the 7th Division went back into the line there was at least one Artist in each of its companies. In some companies the Artist was the only officer and thus the company commander. The next Colonel May heard of his young men was from a letter received from the commander of the 7th Division, Sir Thomas Kapper KGB. 'The young men you have sent have done splendidly ... . They are keen fighters and their men almost worship them ... . I am telling the Commander-in-Chief what I think of them.' It was not surprising therefore that Sir John French asked Colonel May if he could supply any more officers for the BEF and after five days of training sixty-two more Artists were commissioned as second lieutenants, and many more followed as required. The officer training was carried out for the time being at Bailleul.

The reputation of the Artists' officers was soon established. General officers along the front line were soon clamouring for them, and during the Great War with the help of the 2nd Battalion at home over 10,000 young officers were produced from within the ranks of the Artists Rifles and sent to practically every Regiment of the British Army, including the Royal Flying Corps and later the Royal Air Force. This chapter is concluded with the words of the now Lord French[2] expressed at a gathering of the Artists Corps after the war:

> I shall never, never forget the first visit I paid to the Artists after they landed in France, or the wonderful impression they left on my mind of the possibilities which were in that Corps of furnishing a want which was so terrible to all of us at that time – the supply of officers. What really influenced me in trying the experiment I had to try was the appreciation I had of the splendid material of which I saw you were composed, and of the marked aptitude of Colonel May and those who helped him for organizing and commanding such a Corps. Just at the period I am speaking of we had suffered fearful casualties, and the proportion of losses in officers was higher than in any other rank, and it was going on every day. I was really positively at my wits' end, suffering almost agony, to know where I could get officer reinforcements. You all know how any fighting force must deteriorate, and deteriorate badly, unless this supply of officers is kept up properly and regularly.
>
> Well in this trouble and difficulty the Artists came to my help, and I shall never forget, as long as I live, the courage, the determination, the skill and the organizing power which they displayed in trying to meet my wishes. By day and by night, almost under the enemy's guns and very often under close rifle-fire in the trenches, they commenced, they carried on, and they developed this work to the very highest standard of efficiency, and they showed clearly what men of energy and skill could do in this direction when they knew how. They taught us, indeed, a very great lesson, among the many lessons which all we Regular soldiers had to learn in the war. We never knew what the possibilities were before. We used to talk about it taking two years to train an artillery driver, and, above all things, we said we could not turn out officers under a certain considerable length of time. Well, the Artists showed us we made a mistake there, because they turned out a most efficient body of officers, and kept up everything they said they would. From that moment they became the model for and example to that large number of training establishments all over France, which to the end

of the war turned out officers with the utmost speed and the utmost efficiency. What they suffered in doing it is recorded in this book which I now hold in my hand. [*The Artists Rifles Regimental Roll of Honour, 1914-1919*], and I may recall at this moment, without frivolity, the fact these boys, all of them, looked death straight in the face, laughing and smiling, and that the Artists earned at that time the sobriquet of 'The Suicide Club'. That perhaps is the highest honour that could be paid to them.

Of Colonel May's 'First Fifty', twenty-four were subsequently killed in action or died of wounds, another met his death as a result of an accident and another died of influenza. Of the survivors 1030 Private Harry Willans was a future commanding officer of the Artists Rifles (1933-38). He won both the DSO and MC during the war

The First Fifty[3]

Roll of NCOs and men of the Overseas Battalion who went into action in November 1914, as probationary second lieutenants in the 7th Division.

20th Infantry Brigade
1st Grenadier Guards
1076 Cpl Crisp, F.E.F.
1634 Pte Edlmann, F.J
1464 Pte Hillas-Drake, R.F.
1186 Pte Moller, A.A.

2nd Border
392 Cpl Close, M.A.
1614 Pte Cuthbertson, F.T.
1551 Pte Sampson, H.F.
1613 Pte Wornum, T.H.

2nd Gordon Highlanders
691 Cpl Chater, A.D.
1437 Pte Horsley, O.
1436 Pte Horsley, S.M.
997 L/Cpl Mulock, E.R.

21st INFANTRY BRIGADE
2nd Yorkshire
2220 Pte Crosse, M.E.B.

2nd Wiltshire
1823 Pte Carden, R.H.
1138 Pte Kitcat, A.J.
1536 Pte Shepherd, W.S
1725 Pte Strawson, F.M

22nd INFANTRY BRIGADE
2nd Royal Warwickshire
1101 Pte Herbage, P.F.W.
1285 Pte Monk, G.B.
539 Pte Pearce, G.V.
787 Sgt Standring, B.A.

2nd Royal West Surrey
693 Sgt Austin, C.F.
1372 Pte Humphreys, D.F.
1390 Cpl Messom, H.
1371 Pte Rought, C.G.

1st Royal Welsh Fusiliers
954 Cpl Jones, L.
608 L/Cpl Parkes, H.F.

1167 Pte Cuttle, G.
2255 Pte Hollis, H.L.
1794 Pte Pickup, A.J.

1429 Pte Rees, J.T.
1934 Pte Winters, J.W.
NOTHING

2nd Bedfordshire
1260 Pte Brewer, C.H.
1929 Pte Dabell, N.V.
1033 L/Cpl De Buriatte, H.
1030 Pte Willans, H.

1st South Staffordshire
706 Cpl Frost, K.
1744 Cpl Mackintosh, H.L.
1087 L/Cpl Silcock, A.
1399 Pte West, F.

2nd Royal Scots Fusiliers
1760 Pte Raymond-Barker, C.L.
1755 Pte Stewart, J.R.
1578 Pte Wallace, J.R.
1573 Pte White, L.S

ROYAL ENGINEERS
1150 Hunter, J.W.
1491 Hutt, H.V.
NOTHING
NOTHING

Notes
1. The London Scottish, which was also a part of the 47th Division, being the first Territorial unit to cross the Channel, was already in France at this time.
2. Sir John French was raised to the peerage in January 1916 as Viscount French of Ypres and of High Lake, County Roscommon.
3. There are forty-six names in this list as published in the Regimental Roll of Honour.

Chapter 9

The Artists at War

The Duke's Road Depot, The Regiment Expands and Gidea Park 1914-15

Plus ça change?

A soldier should be a young man, sound of all his limbs, of good resolution and quick of apprehension, rather pleasant than sullen and a hater of idleness, let him company with better than himself, and if he means to rise by the warres, let him make a pleasure of the greatest toile. He must keep a good clothes to his back as he can get, and his Armes bright and handsome and a good sword by his side when he walketh abroad, with a good tongue in his head, and be obedient to his officer, and above all to serve God, whom I pray to protect him.

Joseph Ward, 'Military Discipline', 1636

The Artists in August 1914 were not in any doubt that their well-established reputation would attract an inundation of new recruits to their ranks. Mobilization recruiting posters were placed in the foyers of London hotels advertising the attractions of joining the Regiment and the London telephone book was searched for the names of 'gentlemen with good addresses', the chosen subscribers receiving hand-delivered invitations to join the Regiment through their letter-boxes. Recruiting for the 2nd Battalion commenced on 31 August and by the end of the first week in September 5,000 recruits had applied for admission. During that week there was such a crowd assembled outside the front door in Duke's Road that several NCOs changed into civilian clothes and mingled with the crowd. Those men they liked the look of were presented with a card requesting their presence at an interview the following day, the remainder being ignored and left to draw their own conclusions. Four thousand of them had perforce to be refused and, if unsuccessful in joining the H.A.C., London Scottish or other leading London Territorial units, formed the nucleus of the Royal Fusilier and other Public School battalions established in 1914-15.

The War Office had wanted to appoint a non-Artist to command the new battalion but Colonel May saw to it that Colonel Walter Horsley was recalled from retirement to do the job. Colonel Horsley's adjutant was Captain A. J. Neame, TD, and his second in command Major W. Shirley, CMG, later succeeded by Major Passmore Edwardes, TD. Captains Keene, Foster and Thompson were among the company commanders, and Captain F. R. Light, the quartermaster. Designated the 2/28th London the 2nd Battalion for a time had no uniforms or arms, but the whole battalion somehow or other, from Jermyn Street to Petticoat Lane, succeeded at their own expense in clothing themselves in khaki and eventually some old Martini-Henry carbines were dug out to arm them by 'Q' Branch of London District. The only other item of equipment provided was a regulation water bottle for each man but with no means of attaching the same to the soldier. Mufti overcoats were worn *en banderole* and rations were carried in neat brown paper packets tied on to the waist-belts.

Drills and other training, interspersed with much strenuous route-marching, were carried out in Russell, Gordon, Tavistock and Euston Squares, and in Regent's Park and on Hampstead Heath. Journeys were made into Kent by strong working parties to assist in the construction of 'the last ditch' to defend the land against invasion. At the end of 1914, the 2/28th now properly equipped with Long-Lee-Enfields moved into new quarters at Dover House and Roehampton House (later the War Hospital), and after that to a big tented camp in Richmond Park, where the Artists also initiated a Machine-Gun School. Like many similar units the Reserve Battalion was soon drained dry after supplying drafts to the 1st Battalion in France. It also furnished officers for Kitchener's New Army[1] and some other Territorial units. Colonel Horsley, fast running out of men to command, was appointed to the command of the 104th Provisional Battalion for Home Defence, stationed at the Tower of London, and eventually ended up his forty-two years' service in the Artists by going overseas to a staff appointment as an Area Commandant at Englebelmer in France. (It was during this posting that Colonel Horsley produced a remarkable series of water-colour paintings depicting scenes on the Western Front, which were much admired when later exhibited in London.)

On 1 January 1915, by which date old Artists and others were beginning to arrive from Imperial parts,[2] a third battalion (3/28th London) was launched (at first severely restricted to two companies under a major) in which all subsequent recruits had to be enrolled. The new battalion, which was enlarged was placed under the command of Lieutenant Colonel William Shirley, an old friend of the Corps who had been acting as second in command of the 2/28th, and who was the brother of a long-standing serving Artists officer, Dr H.J. Shirley. Although not an Artist by training, William Shirley brought special qualifications to the post. Originally gazetted in 1887 to the King's Dragoon Guards, he transferred to the Bengal Cavalry two years later. Appointed Assistant Commandant Burma Military Police in 1893, he rose to Commandant in 1898. Shirley commanded the Escort Burma-Yunnan Boundary Delimitation Commission, 1897-8. He became instructor Rhaniket, India, in 1902, and an instructor at the Royal Military College, Sandhurst, for which post he was recommended by the Viceroy and Commander-in-Chief, India, in 1907. He retired from the Indian Army in 1913 as lieutenant colonel in order to take up the appointment of Director of Military Studies at the University of Cambridge, an appointment he was to hold until 1922.

On occasions the 3rd Battalion, which was principally officered in the first instance by senior NCOs sent home for the purpose from 1/28th in France, was over 3,000 strong and in three-and-a-half years 9,352 recruits had passed through its ranks. After a period of recruit training at Duke's Road, which included the construction at Kenwood (Hampstead Heath) of a series of entrenchments and dugouts on the most up-to-date Continental models, the 3rd Battalion went into camp with the 2nd at Richmond Park, the latter absorbing the former, the new entity being titled the 2nd (Reserve Battalion) Artists Rifles, or 2/28th London Regiment. In May 1915 an Officers' School of Instruction was formed within the 2nd Battalion, very much on the lines of the Officers' School in France. (See next chapter.) To this were attached for training, newly-gazetted officers of the Territorial Force in England and, by March 1916, upwards of 1,500 officers had passed through the school courses and examinations. In July 1915 the revamped 2nd Battalion moved from Richmond Park to High Beech in Epping Forest, thence to Hare Hall Camp, Gidea Park, near Romford, Essex, where it remained until 1918, finally ending up in Berkhampstead in Hertfordshire. In November 1915, the Regiment was officially recognized by Army Order 429a as an Officers Training Corps and the Home Battalion became the 2nd Artists Rifles OTC.

Gidea Park, which formed the Hare Hall Estate, was owned jointly by two brothers, Majors C. E. and V. E. Castellan. It was a hutted camp, although tents were often used to accommodate an overspill of recruits with modern camp facilities but when the Regiment moved in, the camp was painfully lacking in a toilet system. This deficiency was hastily rectified by Corporal Barnes Wallis, a trained marine engineer with Vickers Ltd., who joined the Artists in early 1915 and was at Richmond Park. He was later commissioned in the Royal Naval Air Service. This was the same Barnes Wallis who after the war designed the R-100 airship and went on to produce the Wellesley and Wellington bombers. During the Second World War he designed the famous 8,000 lb 'Bouncing Bomb' with which Wing Commander Guy Gibson, VC, and his 617 Dambuster Squadron so effectively breached the huge Möhne and Eder dams, all important to Germany's munitions supplies. This was the precursor of the 12,000 lb 'Tallboy' and 22,000 lb 'Grand Slam' bombs. Other of Barnes Wallis's inventions were responsible for sinking the German warship *Tirpitz* and the destruction of V Rocket sites. He was made CBE in 1943. Chief of Aeronautical Research and Development, British Aircraft Corporation, Weybridge, 1945-71, he was made a fellow of the Royal Aeronautical Society in 1967 and knighted a year later. Sir Barnes Wallis, CBE, FAS died in October 1979 at ninety-two years of age.

Barnes Wallis incidentally was a close, life-long friend of A. Egerton Cooper, a fellow Artist, each having served as best man at the other's wedding. Cooper also joined the Regiment in 1915 and was later commissioned in a staff appointment as official Artist to the Royal Air Force. At the time of his death in May 1973 at the age of ninety he was one of the oldest and best known of Chelsea artists. A member of the Chelsea Arts Club he had many pictures hung at the Royal Academy and Paris Salon exhibitions. His most famous picture was of Sir Winston Churchill, copies of which went all over the world during the Second World War. Other portraits were that of King George VI and of his old friend, Sir Barnes Wallis.

A. Egerton Cooper's work made an important contribution to Regimental history, an outstanding example of which, the remarkable series of paintings of uniforms worn to date by the Artists Corps since 1859, is reproduced in this book.

The Home Battalion, whose functions were almost entirely those of training rightly developed the sporting side very strongly. Sport was considered essential to develop physical fitness, the team spirit and leadership qualities. The Regiment and individual companies formed rugby, soccer, hockey, cricket and tennis teams, participating in athletics and shooting competitions which were conducted on a Regimental and inter-Company basis. Among the many sportsmen who joined the Regiment in 1914 was J. G. Greenwood, who was promoted colour sergeant before he was commissioned in the East Surrey Regiment, subsequently transferring to the Grenadier Guards. Greenwood played rugby for Cambridge in the University Match five times, being captain of the side in 1912 and 1919. He played for England thirteen times, captaining the team in all the international matches in 1920. He was president of the Rugby Union 1935-39 and a senior trustee of the RFU.

The most outstanding cricketer to join the Artists was D. J. Knight, or 'Dolly' as he was popularly known, who served as drill sergeant. Born in 1895, in five seasons, two of them as captain, in the Malvern School XI from 1909 to 1913 he displayed such ability that he hit 2,860 runs at an average of nearly 47, and during his schooldays he appeared for Surrey. At Oxford he gained his Blue as a freshman in 1914 and played again in the University Match in 1919. In the latter season he enjoyed special success, sharing in a number of splendid opening stands for Surrey with Jack Hobbs and scoring altogether 1,588 runs, average 45.37. His nine centuries included 114 and 101 in the match with Yorkshire at the Oval and he scored 71 and 124 for the Gentlemen against Players at Lord's. Knight became a master at Westminster School in 1920, in which season he received a heavy blow on the head when fielding at short-leg and never again recovered his old form. All the same he played but without success in two Test matches at Trent Bridge and at Lord's for England against Warwick Armstrong's Australians in 1921. Thenceforward he played little cricket, but in 1937, at the age of forty-two, he was persuaded to take part in twelve matches for Surrey, scoring 584 runs, including 105 against Hampshire at the Oval, average 24.33.

Important sporting fixtures at Gidea Park were invariably followed in the evening by smoking concerts and there was no shortage of actors, musicians and singers, including well-known professionals, to provide the entertainment. The battalion formed a first-class Concert and Entertainment Party, which did continuously excellent work at the many hospitals in and around London. The Companies boasting names like 'The Star Shells' and 'The Artistics' competed with each other in their efforts to put on a first-rate show, favourite sketches, songs and monologues being frequently repeated by popular acclaim.

The headquarters at Duke's Road remained open for recruits throughout the War. At first called The Depôt, it was commanded from November 1914 until 1919 by Captain C. J. Blomfield, TD, FRIBA. A genial character, Charles Blomfield had enlisted in the Artists CV in 1882 and was soon commissioned. When the Cyclist Section was formed he was the first officer to command it. He resigned twice from the Regiment, re-appearing as an officer for the third time in August 1914. An architect by profession, 'Blommy', to give him his nickname, was the son of the painter Sir Arthur Blomfield ARA and himself no mean artist. As an architect, Charles Blomfield carried out some important works, especially at Wellington College and Southwark

Cathedral. He was a keen yachtsman having designed and sailed a 10-ton yawl for many years. Considered too old for active duty, command of the depot was nevertheless no sinecure, Captain Blomfield interviewing over 47,000 applicants to join the Regiment during the War and in so doing exercising extraordinary patience, coupled with a lively sense of humour, at all times steadfastly upholding the Artists' strong sense of tradition and efficiency.

In his book *Once an Artist Always an Artist*, published after the War, Blomfield – himself a Charterhouse man – had this to say about the Artists' preoccupation with recruiting public schoolboys:

> In the earlier days of the war we were rather prone to look askance at any applicant who was unable to show that he had been at Public School, but later we took a wider and more liberal view of this, as also of other points. If we had not done so we should not only have missed many a good man who subsequently did extremely well, but, at one time, if we had tried to stick closely to the qualifications obtaining in pre-war days and in the earlier part of the war, we should have been hard put to it to find enough recruits to maintain our strength.

Blommy and his staff of one sergeant, Smith by name, and four corporals were constantly on the alert to receive inspections by generals and other senior Regular officers, who for the most part were sceptical about the true value of the Territorial soldier. In the case of one inspection, as quoted in his book:

> The General arrived; and as soon as he got into the building began finding fault with everything.
> 'Each platoon when I have inspected it will stand at ease and stand easy. Now then, what did I say? – that leading platoon is not standing easy, the men are standing badly at ease – don't you know the difference between standing at ease and standing easy?'
> I thought that this all foreshadowed a bad report on the Depôt, but as I walked up the hall with the General, he said,
> 'Well I don't know what sort of officers they will make, but as private soldiers they will be magnificent, and the turn out is excellent.'
> This cheered me up a lot.
> 'Now I should like to see the men separately.'
> Whereupon, having conducted him to my room, we had a number of men brought in, in succession.
> 'Let them take off their caps when they come in, so that I can see what they are like.'

'What are you?'
'Chartered accountant, sir.'
The first six men were all of that calling.
'Are they *all* chartered accountants?' said the General; and then to the next man -
'Are you a chartered accountant, too?'
'No, sir, a planter.'
'Oh, what do you plant?'
'Bananas, Sir.'
'"Good God, what, in Hyde Park?"
'No, Sir, in Jamaica.'
We all laughed tentatively and judiciously at this, and the General then became quite genial.
'Well, now that I have had the opportunity of inspecting the men quietly and having a word with them, which I could not do in camp, I must say that I am entirely satisfied with the type of man you are taking and I am very pleased.'
After the trouble Camp got into, this was very gratifying, and I thought, 'Here is a chance for Charles,' so I said,
'Very pleased you think so, sir, as I selected all the men you have seen.'
'Ah, indeed, very good, I congratulate you.'
Exeunt General and ADC.
This General is a celebrated 'nut', or, as we should have said years ago, a 'masher', and at a big concert which the Corps gave at the London Opera House in 1915, he appeared on the stage as an 'extra turn' to deliver an address. A certain well-known cricketer (who was also an officer in the Army) was with my party, and when the General came on he yelled out,
'Hullo, Harry Tate,[3] by gad, splendid!' and proceeded to applaud vociferously.
'Shut up, you ass' I said. 'It's the General!'
'General be blowed, it's Harry Tate, I tell you. Ha! Ha! Splendid! Good old Harry Tate, Haw! Haw! Haw!'
But it *was* the General and the celebrated cricketer's applause gradually petered out.
'My *aunt*, do you think he heard?' he said.

One of Captain Blomfield's greatest problems was the number of would-be volunteers applying to join up who were under age. Again as recorded in his book.

One youngster gave his age as seventeen years six months and was duly enlisted. Two days later a choleric father was shown in.

'I understand, Sir, that you have enlisted my young son without my permission or authority.'

Having looked up the roll of men recently taken, I informed the father that as the son had given his age as seventeen years six months, and appeared to be otherwise eligible, he had, of course been taken.

'Seventeen-six! And do you know his real age, Captain Blomfield?'

I explained that I concluded the age he had given was correct.

'I see, but his real age is fifteen – nine and *I've paid his fees for next term at school.*'

'Ah,' I said, 'that's bad.'

'Yes, damn it, very bad,' replied the father.

'Well, Sir, I am afraid this is a very serious business; your son is liable for prosecution for fraudulent enlistment.'

'Dear me, dear me, is that so? Look here, Captain Blomfield, will you take an ashplant and give him a damned good hiding? If you will, I shall be much obliged to you.'

I explained that I couldn't very well do that.

'Well, look here, Captain Blomfield, he smokes. He oughtn't to smoke, ought he?'

Having smoked with determination at the same age myself, I of course, heartily agreed that it must not be allowed.

'Ah, I am glad you agree, and do you think you could manage somehow to stop his smoking?'

'You leave that to me,' I replied, confidently.

After that the choleric father cooled down a lot. As a matter of fact, he was really immensely pleased and proud of his boy, but the paying of fees for the following term had been a nasty facer. Other fathers will appreciate this point.

After the father had blown away I sent for Private, No. – , and he reported, looking smart as paint, and a credit to any corps (he had been a corporal in his school O.T.C.).

'Now then...what age did you give when you joined?'

'Seventeen years six months, Sir.'

'Quite so; and what is your real age?'

'Fifteen years nine months, Sir.'

'I see. Now look here young man, there's going to be big trouble over this, but I'll give you a chance. You smoke, don't you?'

'Oh yes, Sir.'

'Oh, it's "Oh yes," is it? Now listen to me – if you will undertake not to smoke until you go overseas, your punishment washes out, but if *not* you are in for a very bad time. Now, which is it to be?'

'Oh, I don't think I could give up smoking, Sir!'

'What!' I said. 'A boy like you unable to give up smoking! Don't talk rot. Now, make up your mind, which is it to be?'

He then got very red and shuffled about on his feet, but suddenly drew himself up – he was a smart lad.

'All right, Sir, I'll promise.'

He kept his promise, at any rate for a considerable time, and did well in camp, eventually wangling his way out to the 1st Battalion, his real age only being discovered after he had been in the trenches for some weeks, when he was promptly sent home again.

What was it like to enlist in the Artists Rifles in the Great War? We are firstly indebted to H. Rowland Bate for the following extract from an article he wrote for *Blackwood's Magazine*, which was published in November 1975, sixty years after enlisting in the Regiment. At the outbreak of war young Bate was studying for the priesthood at the College of the Resurrection at Mirfield in Yorkshire. The present author had the privilege of spending the afternoon with the Revd. Canon Bate, MC, aged ninety-seven, at his retirement home near Bath in the summer of 1993. He died in 1994. His memories of Duke's Road and Gidea Park were fading but the name of one of the instructors stood out above all the others, Sergeant Freddie Beausire, a long-serving Artist, who was later commissioned.

> Unlike Germany and France, we British were unused to conscription and compulsory military service. The Army was looked upon as a fit and proper profession for officers who were gentlemen of private means; its soldiers were recruited largely from the ranks of the under-privileged and the unemployed. It needed the Retreat from Mons to open the country's eyes to the immense challenge which lay ahead, and to face it. Then the recruiting offices became crammed with eager volunteers. The Army Ordnance Department could not compete with the demand for khaki uniforms, so that some recruits had to wear the blue-grey jackets and forage caps of the Old Volunteers and others began their drills in plain clothes. Everyone was filled with patriotic fervour and idealism, joining in a war to end war.
>
> I had just reached the age of eighteen. The head at Mirfield told me that I must complete the year of academic training due to finish in September 1915. I stayed on to take the intermediate BA examinations at Leeds University. Then laying down my pen after finishing the last paper on 3rd June, neither knowing nor caring what the

results would be, I caught an early morning train to London. Inspired by a senior college friend who had joined the Artists Rifles in August 1914, I went to their headquarters near St. Pancras Station. After being medically examined, I swore loyalty to the King and was inoculated, kitted in khaki, and given the King's shilling. Those of us without London homes were issued with three blankets, but no mattresses or bed boards and were allowed to sleep on the floor of the Drill Hall.[4]

The Artists Rifles had gone to France in 1914 as a fighting unit. The many casualties in the Battle of Neuve-Chappelle caused authority to decide that such practice was a wasteful use of officer material so the Regiment was withdrawn to take over guard duty at Haig's GHQ at St Omer and it was decreed that in future its private soldiers were to be commissioned into regiments in the field and posted to battalions as required.[5] By the time I joined, it had been decided that we would be posted to a battalion in training at home.

We did our drills in Tavistock and Gordon and Russell Squares. On Fridays came the weekly route-march. Led by the regimental band we went past Lord's Cricket Ground, along Finchley Road to Hampstead Heath.[6] On the Heath we did field-exercises and afterwards we were dismissed so we could refresh ourselves at Jack Straw's Castle before we returned to our billets in our own time. Later we went into camp at Epping Forest for more advanced field-exercises and route marches to such villages as Ongar, Nazeng and Theydon Bois. In the autumn we were moved into newly-built huts, thirty men to each at Hare Hall Camp at Gidea Park. One of the men in my hut was Wilfred Owen. At that time he had written little and published nothing and I did not know he was a poet.

In December our training finished and we returned to London. After commissioning I was posted to the 2/6th Battalion of the Manchester Regiment at that time based at Crowborough in Sussex.

Wilfred Owen (1893-1918) from whose pen we record the second set of impressions as to what it was like to enlist in the Artists Rifles in the Great War, had indeed resolved to be a poet before he was ten years of age but when he joined the Regiment in late 1915 he had yet to catch the eyes of the literary editors. Born in Oswestry and educated at state schools in Liverpool and Shrewsbury, he was the son of a railway clerk who rose to be a station superintendent. Wilfred failed to gain sufficient marks in his London Matriculation Examination to win a university place. After a brief spell as a lay assistant to a vicar in Dunsden, near Reading, which he hated, Wilfred was fortunate to obtain a post as an English teacher at the Berlitz Language School in Bordeaux. When war broke out he was bound by contract until the summer of 1915, but he was intrigued when on vacation in London he saw a poster displayed by the Artists Rifles in the Regent Palace Hotel. He determined to write, on his return to France, to his mother to ask her to find out more details about this Regiment that offered young, French-speaking English gentlemen 'home from abroad' commissions in the Army after four months training by the Artists. Wilfred had considered joining the French Cavalry and Italian Cavalry, displaying a romantic but war-like streak, but as a well-read young man, he knew something of the history of the Regiment for as he put it in a PS to his letter to his mother: 'Lord Leighton, Millais, and Forbes Robertson were in the Artists Rifles.'

When this author had the opportunity to discuss Wilfred Owen as a fellow occupant of Hut 6A at Gidea Park with the Revd. Canon Bate in 1993, he said that Wilfred seldom if ever had a smile on his face and did not mix well with his comrades. Perhaps the poet best expressed himself on paper for *Wilfred Owen Collected Letters* edited by his brother Harold Owen, Oxford University Press, London, 1967, reveals that he had a sense of humour, was determined to be a good officer and was steadfastly loyal to the men under his command. Interest in Wilfred Owen's short life and poetry reached a peak in 1993, the 100th anniversary of his birth, when the literary public was deluged by new editions of his poetry and new biographical studies. His reputation as the greatest poet of the Great War was given birth paradoxically by the surge of the anti-war movement of the 1960s.

On 21 October 1915 Wilfred wrote the following letter to his mother, Susan Owen, from Les Lilas, a small hotel at 54 Tavistock Square, WC, two minutes walk from Duke's Road. This and other letters written at the time not only make an important contribution to the military and social history of the Artists Rifles, but are examples of his fastidious nature, his sense of fun, and his instinctive confidence that as a young man of literary talent with no privileged wand to guide him on the path to success, he was taking a step in the right direction by joining the Artists Rifles.

Dearest of Mothers,

I [several words illegible] attacked the day by going straight to headquarters. It was found that the Doctor had not given his signature to my papers so I was examined again – and passed. Three others at the same time were refused. One was mad about it and insisted on knowing why. 'I don't think you *look* a strong man' was the first reply. (But he *did!*) More expostulation.

Dr. 'I shouldn't like to risk you – with those teeth in your head.'

Recruit. 'They can come out.'

Dr. 'Well, if you must know, your heart murmurs sometimes.'

And so on with apparently robust fellows!

I still did not 'swear in' but spent the afternoon hunting for rooms.

Four hours I passed on this job, and finally chose a French Boarding House, where Guests, Conversation, Cooking and everything else is French.

This should be quite valuable to me; but I don't know if the price is too high – 35s. a week. Bed and Breakfast at other places is 17/6 a week. I scarcely think it could come much cheaper, if I took proper meals at A.B.C.[7] Moreover there are no A.B.C.'s near at hand. I am two minutes from headquarters. Only 3 minutes from Imperial Hotel, and 5 from Waverley,[8] so I am at home in the region. Tavistock Square is a replica of every other Bloomsbury Square; wadded with fog; skeletons of dismal trees behind palings, and the usual pervasion of ghostly aristocracy. In London I cannot be unhappy in my surroundings for what in Manchester would be dismally forlorn is here mysterious. What in Liverpool would be detestably sordid, is here romantically free and easy; what elsewhere seems old dinginess is here suggestive of Antiquity. (I have a notion that Dickens lived in Tavistock Square.)[9]

In the middle of this letter I was called to lunch; and then went to swear in. This time it is done. I am in the British Army! Three of us had to read the oath together, the others were horribly nervous! and read the wrong Paragraph until the Captain stopped them! 'Kiss the Book' says the Captain. One gives it a tender little kiss; the other a loud smacking one!!

After that we had to be inoculated for Typhoid. And that is why I am in bed since four 'o'clock! The delightfully kind, confidence-inspiring doctor gave us full instructions. There were scores of Tommies taking the ordeal before me, and believe me some were as nervous as only fine, healthy animals can be before doctors. One fainted before his turn came, merely as a result of the Doctor's description of the possible symptoms!

You will be glad to hear that though it is three hours ago, I have no constitutional symptoms whatever! Merely a local soreness! Some will have fever and 'influenza pains' all night! (My ink is running out.) I quite expected such myself but I feel so physically happy that it might have been Morphine injected! We have sick leave until Monday morning. The hours are 9.30 to 5! Jolly reasonable.

The Poetry Bookshop is about 7 minutes walk![10]

A crowd of Belgian ladies fleeing from Brussels through Holland are staying here today on their way to Paris.

There are just one or two hitches in this pleasant time in bed. First, I have broken the bridge of my specs, and can't read without risk of headache; second, I daren't smoke (Doctor's orders); Third – empty pockets!

You will like me to write again tomorrow. This I promise, if only you lived near London.

Fondest love to Father, Mary and the Dearest of boys[11]

From your lovingest of boys, Wilfred.

After a month or so at Duke's Road, Wilfred Owen in late November 1915 reported to Hare Hall Camp, Gidea Park, for training as an officer cadet. Cadet W. E. S. Owen, 4786, was posted to 'C' Company and billeted in Hut 6A. On 28 November he wrote a postcard to his mother which read:

I was put on Guard Duty from 9 a.m. yesterday to 9 a.m. today. Miserable time; not allowed to take off packs or boots during 24 hours. I was Sentry from 11 to 1 and 5 to 7, etc. a. and p.m. I was with fellows that I don't like – chumps all of them. We got enough to eat; and I made toast with my Bayonet. There was not much Challenging to do. I am one of the orderlies again tomorrow, this Camping is beginning to get troublesome...

Your W.E.O.

Wilfred spent Christmas in camp and after long hours of drilling and spit and polish, in February 1916 he was ordered to attend a ten-day course in London where he was left to find his own lodging. He made a bee-line for Devonshire Street where he found an attic room in a house near Harold Monro's Poetry Bookshop, his spare time being devoted to writing poetry for Monro to circulate to his poetry circle. When Wilfred returned to Gidea Park, it was not to Hut 6A but to the Officers' School at Balgores House, which was located to the south of the park on the corner of Squirrel's Heath Avenue. The work was hard, the day beginning with drill or a lecture at 6.30 a.m. and ending with a period of cleaning, polishing and preparations for the next day, 7.30 to 9 p.m.

The results of his first exam as an officer cadet were satisfactory. He did well in musketry, reconnaissance and drill for which he received full marks, and only in military law did he do really badly. Noting his results in a letter home he mentioned that he was present at a performance of the Artists Drum and Fife Band, which he found 'thrilling' and was further excited later that night when he saw an enemy Zeppelin airship make good its escape from searchlights and shellfire. Early in May 1916 Wilfred sat his final exam as a cadet, and on the 19th left

22. *A Wild Dream of the Future* by Captain C.L. Potts.

23. *Hesdin.* Sketch by Lieutenant Alner W. Hall.

24. *Our Billet at Bailleul* by Private Ernest Kennedy Smith.

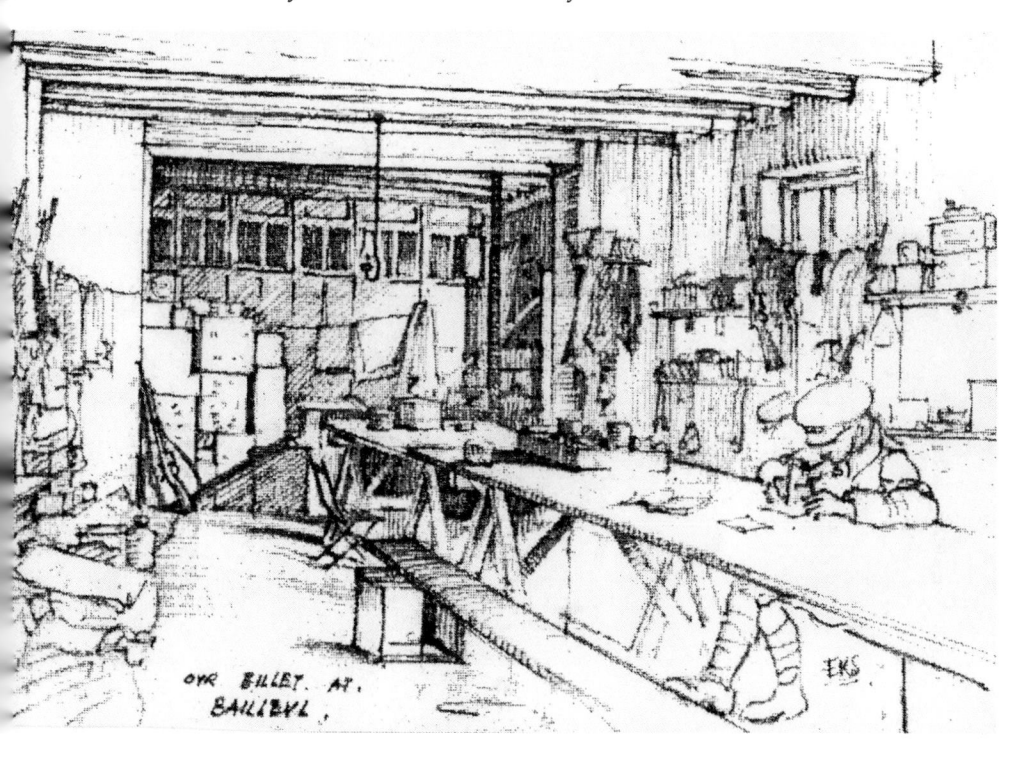

25. Colonel H.A.R. May CB, VD.

26. *St Omer, Tower St Martin* by CQMS H.J. Chetwood.

27. *St Omer, Caserne de Bueil* by CQMS H.J. Chetwood.

28. *Over the Top.* The 1st Artists Rifles at Marcoing, 30 December 1917 by John Nash.
(Imperial War Museum)

29. Four painters, 1916. *Left to Right:* Gerald Ackerman, James Thorpe, Adrian Stokes RA and Edward Handley-Read MBE.

30. Lieutenant Colonel William Shirley CMG.

31. RSM Peter Emslie.

32. Lieutenant Colonel S. J. Chatfeild-Clarke.

33. Wilfred Owen.

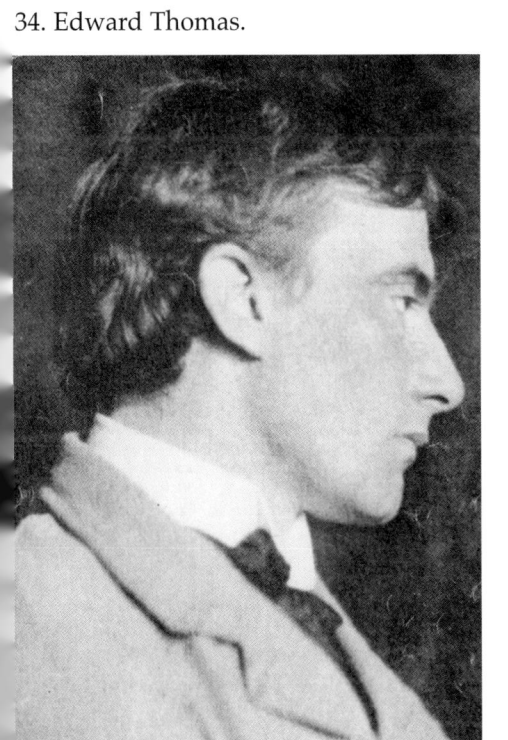

34. Edward Thomas.

35. Lieutenant D.J. Dean VC.

36. Embryo officers at St Omer, 1915.

37. Embryo officers at Gidea Park.

38. Second Lieutenant G.E. Cates VC.

39. Captain, the Revd. E.N. Mellish VC.

40. Second Lieutenant A.J.T. Fleming-Sandes VC.

41. Lieutenant E.P. Bennett, VC, MC.

42. Lieutenant G. St G.S. Cather VC.

43. Second Lieutenant R.P. Hallowes VC, MC.

44. Lieutenant Colonel B.W. Vann VC, MC and Bar, Croix de Guerre.

45. Lieutenant Colonel H. K. Eaton Ostle MC, TD..

Gidea Park on 'Leave Pending Gazette', which he spent first in London and then with his family in Shrewsbury. On 4 June 1916 he was gazetted as second lieutenant in the 5th Battalion of the Manchester Regiment.

The period between Wilfred Owen's commissioning and his death in action on the night of 3-4 November 1918 is not strictly speaking part of the Artists's story, but although it goes beyond its allotted time scale this chapter will conclude with a brief outline, as it was during these remaining months of his life that his reputation as one of the outstanding poets of the twentieth century was forged, as well as his conduct as a gallant officer.

On 6 January 1917 he was posted to France where he was attached to the 2nd Manchesters, a Regular battalion, which had recently suffered heavy losses in the Beaumont Hamel area during the Battle of the Ancre. Wilfred's early letters home contained vivid accounts of the living conditions, the difficulty of movement, the discomforts of mud everywhere and the fierce cold, in which men could and did freeze to death. But in one letter to his mother he assured her, 'I cannot do a better thing or be in a righter place.'

Early in February Wilfred was sent on a Transport officers' course at Amiens where he remained for a month before returning to the line where he re-joined the 2nd Manchesters as they moved forward as part of an offensive to pierce the Hindenburg Line, which ran close to St Quentin some miles to the east of the Somme. During the fighting on 11 March Wilfred fell into a cellar, which had been blasted into a deep hole, in pitch darkness, where he lay badly concussed for twenty-four hours before evacuation to a Casualty Clearing Station at Gailly on the River Somme. Wilfred rejoined his men on 2 April: it was whilst his battalion was engaged in constructing a main line trench in Savy Wood in the Beaumont Hamel area that a German shell blew him half asleep into the air as he lay against the side of a railway embankment. The battalion Medical officer found Wilfred 'shaky, tremulous and confused in memory' and sent him back to Gailly. Diagnosed as suffering from neurasthenia, or severe shell-shock, he was evacuated to Netley Hospital in Hampshire, from which he was transferred for specialist treatment at the Craiglockhart War Hospital, near Edinburgh, where he arrived on 26 June 1917.

At Craiglockhart Wilfred was assigned to the care of Captain Arthur Brock of the Royal Army Medical Corps and his colleague Captain W. H. R. Rivers. His doctors' philosophy was to bring disturbed patients back to a civilized and natural relationship with the everyday world. Wilfred responded well to the treatment, making many friends in Edinburgh and going for long walks in the Pentland Hills. He was able to use his literary talents as the editor of *The Hydra*, the hospital journal. In mid-August the course of Wilfred's life as a poet changed with the arrival at Craiglockhart of a patient, Siegfried Sassoon, already a published poet, who had chosen the savagery of war as his theme. Wilfred became devoted to Sassoon, an older man of a different social background – he was educated at Marlborough and Clare College, Cambridge – who encouraged him to write poems about his own experience of war and Wilfred's confidence was greatly enhanced when Sassoon acknowledged that as a poet the younger man was his peer.

In October 1917 Wilfred was passed fit to leave Craiglockhart but not yet ready for active service. He was posted back to the 5th (Reserve) Battalion of the Manchester Regiment who were then stationed at Burniston Barracks in Scarborough on the Yorkshire coast, and later when medically upgraded to the Northern Command depot at Ripon. It was during the ten months following his discharge from Craiglockhart that Wilfred wrote the bulk of the poetry by which he is remembered today. As a result of introductions by Siegfried Sassoon and the poet Robert Graves, fellow officers of the Royal Welch Fusiliers, that Wilfred made more acquaintances in the literary world meeting Arnold Bennett, H. G. Wells, Osbert Sitwell, Charles Scott Moncrieff and Robert Ross, the literary agent and friend of Oscar Wilde. As a guest at Robert Graves's wedding, Wilfred was introduced to the other guests as 'the poet Owen', which must have greatly boosted his morale as yet as an unpublished poet.

On 10 August 1918 Wilfred had another medical inspection and was passed fit for draft. He was offered a job in the War Office and as an instructor at the Artists OCTU in Berkhampstead but he turned down both options in favour of returning to the front line. On receiving the medical board's report Wilfred said, 'I am glad. That is I am much gladder to be going out again than afraid. I shall be better able to cry my outcry playing my part.' On the last day of August Wilfred landed in France once again, over a year since he returned to England in 1917. On 13 September he re-joined the 2nd Manchesters at Corbie, a few miles from Amiens.

The summer of 1918 had been one of movement and alarm for the Allies as the pattern of static trench warfare had broken up with the onslaught of the great German spring offensive, which had once again placed Paris under threat. The Allies were on the attack now, as the Germans exhausted by the ferocity and initial success of their strategy, were pushed back to their own frontiers, and the war moved into what was to become known as 'the last hundred days'. In late September, when the 2nd Manchesters re-joined the British Fourth Army at Vendelles, the line had been driven back eastwards once more nearer to

St Quentin.

Wilfred was posted to 'D' Company, officially assigned as Bombing officer. From Vandelles, the battalion moved forward through Verguier to the next German line of defence where the St Quentin Canal formed part of the Hindenburg Line. As they approached the front line there were casualties close to Magny-la-Fosse, a village tucked almost invisibly into the folds of a hill. The Manchesters and the units with them prepared to attack the strongly-held Beaurevoir-Fonsomme Section of the Hindenburg Reserve Line. It was during the action that followed that Wilfred Owen was awarded the Military Cross. The citation reads as follows:

> OWEN, 2/Lt, Wilfred Edwards Salter 5/Manchester
> FONSOMME LINE, 1/2 October, 1918. For conspicuous gallantry and devotion to duty in the attack. On the company commander becoming a casualty he assumed command and showed fine leadership, and resisted a heavy counter-attack. He personally manipulated a captured enemy machine gun from an isolated position and inflicted considerable losses on the enemy. Throughout he behaved most gallantly.

The battalion was relieved on 3 October but was back in action a fortnight later. The line between the advancing British and the retreating Germans continued to shift north and east; by the end of October the battalion was close to the Sambre-Oise Canal east of Le Cateau and preparing to cross the canal itself. The 96th Infantry Brigade, which included the 2nd Manchesters, took over the line west of the canal during the night of 30-31 October. The attack on the Sambre Canal took place on the night of 3-4 November. Rain had fallen and a thick mist had settled in the valley. All along the line the offensive was greeted with a hurricane of fire from the far bank. The canal bank had been inundated with water and thus the crossing on rafts made difficult in the extreme. Throughout the deluge of artillery, mortar and machine-gun fire, the small figure of acting Captain Wilfred Owen was seen walking backwards and forwards encouraging his men. He was last seen at the water's edge, a lone figure humping duckboards when he was hit and killed.

The *Poems of Wilfred Owen*, edited and introduced by Siegfried Sassoon, the first complete work of his poems to appear in book form, was published by Chatto and Windus in London in 1920.

Notes
1. Lord Kitchener was said to have an abhorrence of Territorials.
2. As most of the Artists who went to the Dominions would have joined their own

national armies, the largest contingent of arrivals at Duke's Road from overseas came from the Argentine and other South American countries. The OC Depot, Captain Charles Blomfield, a noted humorist, posted orders in both English and Spanish!

3. Harry Tate, the popular comedian of the heyday of the music hall.

4. Some took rooms at their own expense at the many small hotels that abounded in the Bloomsbury district.

5. This is not strictly accurate. The Artists did not take part in the Battle of Neuve-Chapelle (March 1915). At the time referred to, Sir John French was still C.-in-C., and it was his decision to commission the 'First Fifty' rankers on the Artists' arrival in France in late 1914. On 17 December 1915, Field Marshal Sir John French – blamed for the failure at Loos – was relieved of the command of the BEF by General Douglas Haig at the GHQ at St Omer. It is not true that all other ranks of the Artists Rifles received commissions.

6. There was an alternative route via Kentish Town and Highgate. The marchers were allowed to walk back in twos or threes, or take a tram if they could afford it.

7. ABCs were a popular chain of inexpensive cafés. Duke's Road did not have sufficient cooking facilities for providing meals for the recruits.

8. Wilfred had stayed at the Imperial and Waverley hotels in Holborn on pre-war visits to London.

9. He did, at Tavistock House from 1850-56 where he wrote *Bleak House* and *Hard Times*.

10. The Poetry Bookshop was located at 33 Devonshire Street (now Buswell Street), off Theobald's Road, WC. It had been opened by the poet Harold Monro in January 1913.

11. Wilfred Owen had one sister, Mary, and two brothers, Harold and Colin. Harold was in the Navy and Colin later joined the Royal Flying Corps.

Chapter 10

The Artists at War

With the 1st Battalion in France
1915

This is described as the finest club in Northern France, founded in November 1914 and situated on thick clay soil, 30 metres above sea level and within five minutes of the station, also within range of the enemy's artillery, etc. Sub, 2 francs per week. Proposers and Seconders required.

Extract from the brochure of The Artists Rifles, Cooks Club, Bailleul.

The work of the 1st Battalion at Bailleul was varied, interesting, strenuous and continuous – by day and night. Bailleul was the nearest point to the fighting line at which troops could detrain or from which they could entrain. Fresh battalions, both British and French, were arriving almost hourly at the railway station, which was situated opposite the Artists' headquarters in the Rue de la Gare. The British Army headquarters' staff, including the C.-in-C., Sir John French, were frequent visitors. Battalions just back from the trenches for a short rest spell were often quartered at Bailleul, or in the neighbourhood, and from these locations the badly wounded were despatched back to England, as well as the men due for leave. At these locations also the battalions received their new drafts and new equipment, and it was here they reorganized, refitted and prepared often in great haste to take their places once more in the line. The trenches could be observed from high ground to the north of Bailleul, and the town itself was within range of the German heavy artillery and even at times machine-gun and sniper fire, the railway station being a favourite target for enemy aircraft dropping their albeit tiny bombs.

The experiment of attaching Artists to the Old Contemptibles as probationary officers having proved successful, further batches were called for and early in 1915 the C.-in-C. directed that selected Artists officers and NCOs were to be transferred to run a separate Officers Training Corps, the remainder being retained as a fighting unit to be used as occasion demanded. Sir John French referred to the matter in this despatch.

> I established the battalion as a Training Corps for officers in the field. The cadets pass through a course, which included some thoroughly practical training as all cadets do a tour of 48 hours in the trenches, and afterwards write a report on what they see and notice. They also visit an observation post of a battery or group of batteries, and spend some hours there. A Commandant has been appointed, and he arranges and supervises the work, sets schemes for practice, administers the school, delivers lectures, and reports on the candidates. The cadets are instructed in all branches of military training suitable for platoon commanders. Machine-gun tactics, a knowledge of which is so necessary for all junior officers, is a special feature of the course of instruction. When first started the school was able to turn out officers at the rate of 75 a month. This has since been increased to a 100. Reports received from Divisional and Army Corps Commanders on officers who have been trained at the school are most satisfactory.
>
> [The length of the course varied but it was usual to turn out an officer in about three months.]

The School in France was originally run by Colonel May (his substantive rank was actually lieutenant colonel), his officers, the RSM and other senior NCOs, but presently, as the enemy pressure relaxed, he had the advantage of the assistance of Regular officers, one of whom (a major) being appointed 'Commandant of School', and gradually, as additional candidates began to arrive from other regiments, the original 1st Battalion and the OTC were worked as separate units.

The Artists' normal method of officer training was for all drafts when they first came out to France to undergo a hard tour of service in the ranks. The selection of the men to be trained as cadets was in the hands of the company officers, aided by their NCOs, Colonel May placing great store on the advice of his RSM, Peter Emslie. (Early in 1915 the number of companies in the battalion was reduced to four to conform with Regular Army practice.) The men selected, nicknamed the 'Embryos', were then put into the 'Colonel's Class', taken off all other duties, and were kept hard at their special training. As Colonel May recorded in his book, *Memories of the Artists Rifles*, Howlett & Son,

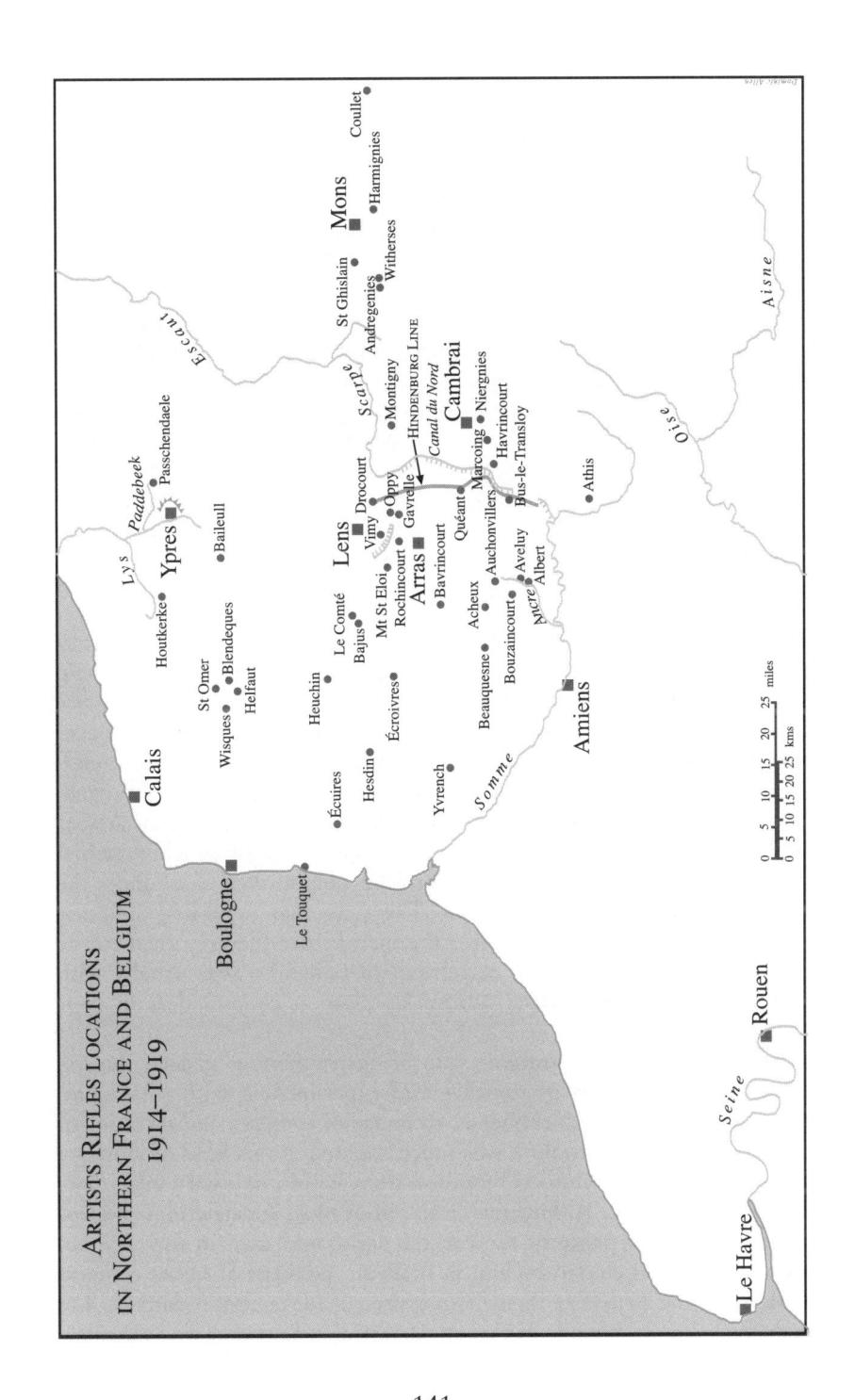

ARTISTS RIFLES LOCATIONS IN NORTHERN FRANCE AND BELGIUM 1914–1919

London, 1929:

> I was always most anxious to superintend myself their *first* special training as young officers, so as to impress upon them, at the very commencement of their new career, good sound principles with regard to the actual leading of men to fight, the care of their men under them in all circumstances, and the maintaining of the traditions and reputation of the Artists Rifles in everything they did. I had, perhaps, the most wonderful opportunity that had ever existed of giving men not only theoretical instruction, but actual illustrations from the events taking place all round, of the many kinds of military problems that were then being enacted. For instance, they could be shown actual examples of troops worn out by strenuous hard work, and of others, newly arrived from England, bursting with enthusiasm, and could be shown the best ways of helping each, and, indeed, of the best ways of dealing with the manifold military problems they were sure to have to encounter when they become officers.

With regard to 'care of men', the Colonel delegated the captain quartermaster, J. A. Smith ('Jacko'), to form squads of Volunteer Embryos who would contact the CO of a battalion returning from the line to enquire if any assistance in billeting was required, an offer that was never rejected. The Embryos would then see to it that billets were found, cleaned out, straw laid down and baths and cooked meals arranged. Due to the generosity of their relatives and friends in Britain, the Artists had a surplus of cigarettes and chocolate, quantities of which were distributed voluntarily by the Embryos to the 'men in their care' under the supervision of the quartermaster. The QM also organized smoking concerts and football matches for the men before they returned to the trenches and when they did march out of Bailleul it was usually with newly commissioned Artists officers as platoon commanders in their ranks.

As part of their programme for the instruction of cadets, the 1st Battalion dug sections of trenches and experimented with periscopes, super posts, dugouts, duckboards, drainage of trenches and methods of revetting, etc. The battalion was much assisted in this kind of work by the engineers and architects recruited from within its own ranks. The Pioneer sergeant, L. R. Huggins, was full of ideas for new innovations. He manufactured some of the earliest periscopes used in the trenches using mirrors purchased by him in Bailleul. GHQ at St Omer came to look upon the Artists as their main source of ideas and initiatives. On one occasion a squad of seven electrical engineers was urgently despatched from Bailleul to sort out a problem at St Omer followed later on by a team of twenty chartered accountants (one of whom was Colonel May's batman), presumably to lend professional assistance to GHQ in rendering accounts on the cost of the BEF to the Treasury. On another occasion there was a requirement for interpreters in connection with the imported Chinese labour employed on the Western Front and three qualified men from the Artists were immediately produced for the purpose. Landscape sketching (originally introduced to the Regiment by Colonel Horsley) was a means used at observation posts to indicate gun positions, sniper posts, sentry posts and other targets in the opposing trenches. The cadets were taught a carefully thought out system by Lieutenant W. E. Newton, an architect and Artists officer. The idea was to pass on the sketch to the relieving officer at the observation post, which usually took place at night-time, so that targets could be instantly recognized if the morning light permitted. Well defined landmarks were indicated on the sketch along with compass bearings from the OP to assist in the location of the actual targets.

In April 1915 by order of the C.-in-C., the 1st Battalion and the OCTU were transferred from Bailleul to St Omer, a further thirty miles back from the trenches. It was thought that Sir John French's main motive in moving the Artists to St Omer was to spare them the risk of casualties which were being caused by the German shelling on Bailleul. The 1st Battalion, which was quartered at the French Infantry Barracks where they had been temporarily billeted shortly after their arrival in France in 1914, was named the GHQ (or headquarters) Battalion responsible for town security. The Cadet School was established at Blendecques, a large country house (some called it a château) located in spacious grounds about two miles from St Omer. At Blendecques the Cadet School was divided in the school tradition into Houses, of which there were three, each with seven divisions or classes. The Artists, who came out in drafts together with NCOs from Cavalry, Artillery, Canadian and other units sent up for instruction in Infantry work, were then put in the 'Colonel's Class' and on passing out went to this school until July 1916, when the battalion was specially authorized by General Haig, the new C.-in-C., to send candidates approved by their CO direct to commissions. The bulk of the original NCOs and men soon obtained commissions in their various regiments, while senior captains had been promoted to command battalions in the field.

In June Colonel May was invested with the CB (Military Division) by King George V while on leave in England. The ceremony took place at Windsor Castle and after the investiture, during the luncheon that followed, the King reminded the Colonel of the sham fights that had taken place at Hatfield House (Lord Salisbury's seat) between the Eton

College OTC and the Artists Rifles, which the King had witnessed and greatly enjoyed. In October the King visited St Omer, the Artists being entrusted with the task of providing the guard of honour, his personal bodyguard and the protection of his private quarters. Both the King and Sir John French expressed complete satisfaction with the performance of their duties.

Among their duties at 'G.H.Q. Troops', besides having to post sentries and guards over certain buildings in St Omer, the Artists were responsible for the picqueting of the town and for ensuring that no one obtained access to it or left it unless authorized by an official pass to do so. Colonel May could see that the task of excluding unauthorized persons, without giving occasional unintentional offence to some of the authorized ones might be difficult. He discussed the matter with his adjutant and RSM Emslie (whose business it was to instruct the guards and sentries) and they were determined to make a 'bull's-eye' of this job. The Artists proceeded on the following lines. After a careful survey of the ground around the town, it was discovered that it was along sixteen roads only and past sixteen points only that access could be gained. Each of these points was placed in the middle of a straight piece of each of the roads, with wire-netting on each side of the road for 100 yards before arriving at a control point to 100 yards after passing it. Each control post was joined up by barbed-wire entanglements to the next control post on each side, so that anyone seeking entrance to the town had, of necessity, to come along one of the roads and past one of these control posts, at each of which a sentry was placed. At these control posts escape was impossible except directly up or down the road, which was controlled by the sentry, and the sentry was, in almost every case, himself under systematic and constant observation from some house or building (well on the town side of the control post), from which an armed guard or other assistance could be instantly furnished to the road.

Every guard had direct access by telephone to all the others and to a place where a reserve of men was waiting, and would be sent for if required. All this prevented any possibility of a control post being 'rushed'. The Artists also arranged with the French authorities that a French sentry (as well as the British) should be placed at all of these control posts to deal with French inhabitants and persons with French passes. A new form of British pass was issued and circulated, all the old ones being called in and cancelled. Each of the Artists, before being allowed to act as a sentry, had an intensive course of training which enabled him to instantly recognize all 'good' passes and also instantly to spot a forged or cancelled one, and each had to pass severe tests before being certified as 'fit for control post duty'.

The Artists had to learn their way to all parts of the town, and also exactly where each branch of the HQ and any special officers and regiments quartered in the town could be found for the information of persons, often very distinguished ones, who were entitled to it. They were also instructed always to be courteous, willing and helpful to all persons producing passes, but adamant to all who could not do so, and never to be irritated by anybody under any circumstances whatsoever. The effect of these instructions at first was amazing. Round each control post groups of noisy persons, all talking at once would collect. Persons who wanted to pass in and out of the town, but who had forgotten their passes, including sometimes high-ranking persons who considered their face a sufficient passport, or who sometimes were testing the sentry out in his work, were closely investigated. The Artists' security system, exercised with a great deal of patience, was a distinct success and no German spies infiltrated into the headquarters of the BEF at St Omer.

Although the Artists Rifles in France were mainly known for their proficiency as an OCTU they provided another service which was greatly to benefit the British Expeditionary Force. In the late autumn of 1914 a Major (later brigadier) C. D'A. B. S. Baker-Carr of the Rifle Brigade, a senior instructor at the Hythe School of Musketry, called to see Colonel May in his office in Bailleul. Baker-Carr informed the Colonel 'in confidence' that machine guns were considered by high military authority to have become of overwhelming importance for infantry regiments, which were to be increased in strength. The visitor had been appointed to take charge of a Machine Gun School attached to GHQ at St Omer. Baker-Carr confessed that he had only two staff sergeant instructors and he urgently needed 100 to train 1,500 to 2,000 NCOs a month in machine gunnery. Colonel May said he would have no difficulty in finding suitable material amongst the Artists but the men would have to be trained as instructors from scratch. This the Major undertook to do in a fortnight and two lance corporals and fourteen privates were accordingly posted to the school, which was accommodated in the Cavalry Barracks at St Omer. The lance corporals were J. Lee and F. G. E. Sheehan and the privates were F. N. Bath, E. G. G. Bax, D. F. Belchamber, R. B. Clark, H. J. H. Dicksee, A. H. Douglas, A. S. Foskett, F. S. Griffiths, F. G. Judd, N. Leighton, O. P. B. Marshall, H.J. Mills, E. H. Orton and H. H. Young. More Artists followed and by the end of December Major Baker-Carr, with assistance also from other units, had his 100 instructors.

At the Machine Gun School GHQ, trainees were introduced to the Maxim and Vickers but early in 1915 the Lewis, which was to be the primary weapon of its kind used by the British Army in the Great War, came into use for the first time. Each of the new instructors was promoted to sergeant but the Artists amongst them retained their Mars and Minerva cap badges, adding to their repertoire by running smoking concerts at the end of the fortnightly courses. At one of these concerts (shortly before the Battle of Loos) the Guards Division supplied the talent, which included the Welsh Guards choir and pipers of the Scots Guards, the Prince of Wales being present as a guest. The School shortly moved to more rural surroundings at Wisques only a few miles from St Omer, and a few months later a second Machine Gun School was set up at Grantham in England. Approximately 800 machine gunners were trained every fortnight. In July of 1916, about forty Artists' instructors started a Lewis Gun School at Le Touquet where they trained over 200 new instructors to cope with an intake of 2,000 pupils a week.

Towards the end of 1915, the strain of command both before and after the outbreak of war had made its mark on the Colonel, now aged fifty-three. He was suffering from insomnia and the deprivation of sleep was seriously affecting his performance as commanding officer of the Artists Rifles in France. The senior Regimental Doctor, Surgeon Major C. S. de Segundo, was so concerned that he asked a specialist to come out from England to examine the Colonel, who was advised to take three months' complete rest. Admitted to the Military Officers Hospital at Wimereux, after a short stay he found himself on a hospital ship bound for home where he was committed to the care of his wife. He was succeeded in his command by Lieutenant Colonel S.J. Chatfeild-Clarke VD, a veteran Artists officer, who had been acting as Colonel May's second in command. Once at home, the Colonel found it difficult to keep away from Duke's Road where his services were used to lecture on the Artists' experience in France to drafts from the 2nd Battalion hung up in London pending embarkation for St Omer. Passed fit for home duties, Colonel May wrote to Lord French now commanding Home Forces, on Horse Guards, in September 1916 and appealed to him to find him a job. Lord French reacted swiftly and the Colonel was appointed to the important post, which he held to the end of the war, of Commandant at Tidworth of the Southern Command School of Instruction for Infantry officers, where over 14,000 officers (including 5,000 Australians) passed through his curriculum. At Tidworth Colonel May also organized a 'Chaplain's Course' (1917-18).

In concluding this chapter on the Artists Rifles in France in 1915, our attention now turns to the fortunes of one individual Artist, namely 1990 Private Ernest Kennedy Smith, an architect and talented artist, who joined the Artists at Duke's Road, along with six colleagues, all members of the Architectural Association, shortly after the outbreak of war. Ernest Smith was included in a draft from the 2nd Battalion to the 1st Battalion in France and arrived at Le Havre on 31 December 1914.

During 1915 Ernest wrote many letters to his family living in Muswell Hill, in north London, mainly addressed to his mother, but also to his father, three sisters and two brothers, and also to other relations and friends living, for the most part, in the London area. The following are extracts taken at random from his letters,[1] which reveal that although life with the 1st Battalion could at times be monotonous and discomforting, he and his comrades recognized the justness of the cause for which they were fighting. They will also remind the reader the Army was not paid very much in those days.

After landing at Le Havre the Artists contingent moved to Rouen and later to Bailleul, which Smith was not allowed to give as his location in his letters.

Jan 20th 1915

My Darling Mother,
...Nothing very particular has happened, we have now adopted the 4 Company organisation used throughout the Regular Army. I am now in 'C' company and No. 11 'Platoon' ...

On Sunday we went to Service in the morning in some kind of hall, and in full marching order.

It seemed a very new sensation standing up armed to the teeth, covered with ammunition and singing 'The King of Love my Shepherd is'! One could not help feeling it incongruous though I hope it was not a contradiction, the whole effect was impressive anyhow...

Today we did a practice attack over wet and heavy ground, principally for the benefit of those of us who have applied for a commission.

Jan, 22nd

It is good news about the cakes and tobacco, please thank Amanda very much from me.

A little Players Navy Cut occasionally would be welcome, but tobacco is served out fairly regularly and I had an anonymous present of some from the weekly Dispatch. Now for the list [of his requirements]:

Cake of soap (carbolic or something powerful)
Small towel
Matches
Handkfs
Shirt
Envelopes ...

Jan, 31st 1915

My Darling Mother,
...A day or two ago we had a little excitement in the shape of 4 bombs dropped on the town by a German Aeroplane, only one child was killed, 2 or 3 being wounded.

One of them fell on some open ground about 100 yards from our billet, so did no damage – we were out drilling at the time and itching for the order to be given to fire on the thing, which much to our disappointment never came ...

4th February 1915

My Darling Mother,
...It is very satisfying to know what you feel about the commission; as a matter of fact the money would not go quite as far as you think, but there are other considerations which make me feel that I ought not to go out of my way for a commission, as I said to my company commander, that is to say that I can imagine circumstances when it might be my duty to take one, but not as things are at present..

Today we went on a route march and got a good view of the battle from a hill, the aeroplanes too have been very active, the weather being fine and there has been a lot of firing on German craft, we had another over the town the other day. (I should like to know, by the way, if anything I have written has been censored.)

22nd February 1915

My Darling Mother
...Tell Maurice I have been playing Rugger a bit, we had a game last Monday which I enjoyed immensely, in spite of the fact that we had a sort of water jump in the middle of the field. We have several quite 'star' men in our company and some of the officers play too.

Thurs 25th
...I had another scratch game of rugger yesterday in the snow, which, by the way, is quite thick on the ground today.

March 12th 1915

My Dearest Mother,
...By the way there is a possibility of some of us (privates) having

a go in the trenches, but as we are now admittedly on O.T.C. this will probably be more a sort of 'Cook's Tour' business than anything else, I should think, i.e. for the sake of experience...

March 16th
...Ford and I spoke to Capt... tonight and asked if we could be taken into the officers' class together. He said that I (being the right age) would probably have been taken next anyway (having said I was willing if necessary) and that he would push Ford forward too (as he is rather older than they really want)...

P.S. Oh yes! Would you please enclose 'Infantry Training 1914' (a little red book which Father gave me) next time you send.

It will probably be in my room somewhere

April 3rd 1915

My Dearest Mother,
...We have left our comfortable billet at Bailleul and bidden pathetic farewells to our sundry friends and acquaintances, some of them in tears!...

We are now at General headquarters of the British Expeditionary Force (I expect you know the name of the place) having travelled on motor lorries, which was considerably better than marching, as we had a colossal amount to carry as you may imagine. I managed to bring away a certain number of useful things, which I had accumulated as our transport took a limited amount of stuff for each man.

Our quarters here are in a large French barracks which is a great come-down from our last billet which had acquired a certain amount of human atmosphere of which this place seems totally devoid at first. On arrival we were promptly told off for various duties – guards innumerable and endless 'fatigues' and all sorts of funny jobs which have necessitated putting off the new officers' class for a bit owing to the number of men required for the said duties.

Easter Day 6th
A gloriously fine day as seems appropriate to the day...

Last Wed'y we had a special address from the Bishop of London. I thought it rather disappointing. I hear too that he is here today...

April 9th 1915

My Darling Mother
...I have several bits of news to tell you this time. First of all, I have left the 'Police Force' having been put into the officers' Class,

and with Ford and several other men whom I know and like especially...

The next bit of news is that I am now a Lance-Corporal! Why they made me one I don't know, but there it is...

They have started a drill at 7.0 a.m. for N.C.O.'s and subalterns which is rather amusing ...

Now as to the new daily programme – Reveille at 6.30. The aforementioned drill at 7. Breakfast – 7.45. Parade at 9.25 for drill – at intervals we each get a turn as company commander, platoon commander, platoon sergeant, section commander etc. so as to be familiar with the part each man has to play. Normally, a 2nd Lieutenant is a platoon commander, I may say. After this there are two more hours during the day for the same thing. Then a lecture from the Colonel at 3.45...

Cadet School

June 15th 1915

My Dearest Mother,
We are in what has been at any rate a most lovely house, almost a chateau! About 2 miles from where the battalion is.

Of course everything is absolutely bare and everything in sight has been whitewashed, but it is most beautifully clean and has to be kept so.

There is a most extraordinary variety of regiments here besides ourselves. Highlanders, Canadians, Cavalrymen, guardsmen, dragoons, etc., etc., over 100 in this house, which is one of 3. The aforementioned men of course were exceptional men in their regts, from an educational point of view, who applied for commissions and have been sent here to be trained, so you see the Artists do not by any means monopolise the place.

In 'Marlborough House' (ours) there are 7 'Divisions', similar to forms in a school, except that all seven go through the same course simultaneously.

Each division is instructed separately by a regular officer (usually a captain) and all of them straight from the front, and conspicuously full of practical tips, wise saws and modern instances!

June 16th
I and another Artist were lucky enough to get a tiny room to ourselves, so I really have more privacy now than ever before.

The country round is quite beautiful and lectures under the trees are delightful in this weather...

Cadet School

June 22nd 1915

My Dearest Father,
Thank you very much for your card of a few days ago.

Already I am able to say how long our course here will last, the date of completion being officially announced as July 24th! This comes on a Saturday but according to what has happened on previous occasions, I think it very likely that we may leave here on the previous night (Friday) and arrive at Victoria about 2.0 p.m., the following day.

This, of course, is a long way ahead yet but I thought you would all like to know.

Cadet School

July 4th 1915

My dear Father,
My division – with three others, went up for a spell in the trenches on Thursday and on Friday last, which I know you would like to hear details about – or as much as I can tell you.

We left here at midday on Thursday on motor-buses and reported towards the evening at the Head Quarters of the Brigade we were to be with, in a town just behind the line.

We then marched some way by road till we arrived at the rear end of the communication trench.

This was very wet and muddy after the heavy rain, and being only just wide enough to get along, one found it difficult to go at any decent pace with one's equipment. The idea is to have the trench as 'curly' as possible, so the impression one gets is rather of the Hampton Court maze with shells buzzing overhead at intervals.

After about a mile of this sort of travelling, we arrived at the battalion headquarters, which sounds rather more 'magnifique' than it really is, being a sort of collection of smugglers' caves with labels outside.

There we were told off by the adjutant in batches of about 4 or 5 to each company, so we toddled off again and reported to the company Commander in the front line trenches, which as trenches go, I should say were quite palatial!

Well, the captain and all the company officers were absolutely as nice as they could be to us, insisted on our messing with them (not that it required much insistence on their part), offered us pretty well everything they had got in the way of drinks and things and helped us with the reports we each had to write.

I was rather afraid we were crowding them out rather too much, but the O.C. Company always sent a servant round when meals were ready, so I don't think they minded at all.

Naturally I cannot give you very much detail in a letter, but I think we learnt all there was to learn in the time – we stayed up with the officer who was on watch about half the night, went with him on his rounds, and crawled out in front of the barbed wire entanglements to listening posts and all sorts of things.

As far as the 'Boches' were concerned things were comparatively quiet, a slow fire was going on all the time, and a few light shells came over which really did no damage.

As a matter of fact we were so close to the enemy that I suppose the heavy artillery could not do much if they wanted to in case they should hit their own men.

The firing bucked up a little at night – as it always does and the machine guns started a little. We got back here about 10 o'clock on Friday night.

On completion of the course at the Cadet School at Blendecques on 24 July Ernest Smith was awarded his commission. He then embarked for five days' home leave with his family spending some of the time shopping for officers' kit in London. On his return to France he was posted as a second lieutenant to the 1st Battalion, the Buffs.

In the first half of 1915 the BEF was engaged in many bloody battles, including the Second Battle of Ypres, during which heavy losses were sustained, the fighting continuing into the autumn and winter, the BEF again suffering heavy casualties at the Battle of Loos (25 September – 8 October).

During the period August-December Second Lieutenant Ernest Smith, a somewhat diffident private in the Artists Rifles, turned out to be a born leader and very popular with his men. On 21 December 1915 the 1st Buffs went into the trenches on the Second Army front. Leading his men 'over the top', a German shell burst in front of him, one fragment hitting him in the head and a second piercing his thigh. He was not thought at first to be seriously wounded but he was transferred from the casualty clearing station and conveyed to the field hospital where he died on the operating table whilst the surgeon attempted to extract the shell fragment from his head. Second Lieutenant Ernest Kennedy Smith, who was in his early twenties, is buried in the Lijssenhock Military

Cemetery at Abeele – A, plot 2. He had been looking forward to spending New Year's Eve on leave in London.

Note
1. Extracts are taken from *Letters from France – Service with the Artists' Rifles and the Baffs, December 1914 to December 1915*, by Second Lieutenant Ernest Kennedy Smith, published by J. Cobb, London, 1994.

Chapter 11

The Artists at War on Two Fronts

The 1st and 2nd Battalions at Work
1916

A Penny Flag Means 14 Fags!
Lady Denham, nicknamed 'Lady Nicotine', launches an appeal for 'Fag Day' on behalf of the Smokes for Wounded Soldiers and Sailors Fund, 7 June 1916.

On 21 February 1916 the German Army began a massive assault on the French stronghold of Verdun, the bastion of the Allied defences on the Western Front. This continued until July when the Allies under General Douglas Haig, the new C.-in-C. of the BEF, launched a 'big push' along a fifteen mile front on the River Somme in Picardy: twenty-six British divisions, all volunteers, took part in the initial assault which followed; the French contingent was reduced to eighteen from the promised forty divisions following the carnage of the five-month Battle of Verdun. Haig's offensive proved disastrous in terms of casualties and the gains were minimal; at the point of deepest penetration a mere five miles of territory was gained and the shattered remnants of many divisions withdrew to their original positions. On 1 July the British infantry, following a rolling artillery barrage, had assaulted the highly organized defensive positions of the German Second Army. By nightfall the British had lost about 60,000 men, 19,000 of them dead – the greatest one-day loss in the history of the British Army. The Battle of the Somme lasted until October when the British casualties totalled 350,000, 40 per cent of the total on both sides. During 1916 248 officers commissioned by the Artists Rifles and serving in other regiments were killed in action or died of other causes, including thirty-nine on the Somme. A further twenty-nine were killed or died as a result of an accident or disease in other theatres.

At St Omer Lieutenant Colonel S. Chatfeild-Clarke continued as commanding officer of the GHQ Battalion and of the OCTU, which met with the approval of the new C.-in-C., General Douglas Haig, who had formerly served as I Corps Commander. Chatfeild-Clarke, a strikingly handsome officer, had enlisted in the Artists CV in 1882 when their headquarters was at No. 36 Fitzroy Square. He was present on the great day in 1889 when the new headquarters was opened by His Royal Highness Prince Albert Edward, Prince of Wales, accompanied by Her Royal Highness Princess Alexandra and suite. In the *Artists Rifles Gazette and Regimental Orders*, No. 65, of April 1939, Colonel Chatfeild-Clarke, VD, DL, recorded his memories of that historic occasion, some of which are reproduced below:

... The time of the opening was fixed for October 3rd. The platform was at the end of the Hall, which was gaily decorated with bunting. A special easy slope was built to lead up to the dais, as owing to a stiff leg the Princess could not mount steps easily. Chairs were arranged in blocks, front blocks 10s. 6d. each, back blocks and gallery 7s. 6d. and 5s. I was a sergeant at that date, and was detailed to show people to their seats in one block. Colour-Sergeant Louis H. M. Dick was in charge of general arrangements in the Hall.

Their Royal Highnesses were received by a Guard of Honour posted outside the Hall, with the brass band which we then possessed. There was red baize everywhere. Escorted by Col. Edis and the Majors, the Royal party processed down the Hall to the dais. Speeches were made, and His Royal Highness declared the headquarters open. What struck me most was the strong guttural accent of H.R.H. – he rolled his r's like a German. During his speech he referred to 'my dear friend Sir Frederick Leighton'. Leighton, our Honorary Colonel, who was sitting in the front row, got up and made a most courtly bow.

There was a short variety programme afterwards, in which Michael Maybrick, Brandon Thomas, Capt. W. H. Thomas and Major White took part. When this was over the Royal party processed back down the Hall to the officers' mess. Much amusement was caused by Colonel Edis hurriedly putting on his helmet with the badge in the rear!

Sergeant Chatfeild-Clarke rose as a captain to command 'C' Company and as a major sailed on the *Australind* for Boulogne in 1914 as Colonel May's second in command.

Early in 1916 the 1st Battalion, being GHQ troops, were transferred from St Omer, one half going to Ecuires (Montreuil) with part of

General Haig's GHQ, and the remainder (including headquarters) to Hesdin, where the training of officers, still the most important activity of the Corps, was carried out (the Officers' School remained at Blendecques). Certain detachments went forward with advanced GHQ under Captain Keene at Beauquesne in 1916 and Captain Miéville at Heuchin and Bavrincourt in 1917.

The GHQ troops on 'special duty' were spread out in detachments somewhere along that indefinable entity the British Front Line, many of them doing very useful work as orderlies in the Casualty Clearing Stations. As one member of the Corps, S. H. Jennings, put it in *The Artists Rifles Journal*, Volume 1, No. 2, September – October 1916:

> I have been dumped down about five miles behind the Line on police duty of a special character. Our work is done at night, and we relieve one another half-way through the night, so we do our patrol in one bite, and are then free to sleep until 11 or to the next morning. Our party was split up into twos and threes and posted all over the place, and I managed to 'work' things so that we got put together. We are miles away from civilization, but being on top of a very high hill we have a magnificent view of some miles of the battlefront. We have seen some pretty hot bombardments, gas attacks, etc., and as we are in the zone of artillery fire have a fairly exciting time. I would not have missed this job for a good deal. When the officer dropped us at our post he said, 'I am sorry there is no accommodation for you, and that I have no blankets to give you. You will have to rig up some sort of bivouac. Pretty choice, eh? After barracks.'
>
> We managed to 'make' a number of empty boxes from the nearest A.S.C. dump, a quantity of sacking, etc., and during the last three or four days have erected quite a respectable dog kennel for ourselves; it measures 9ft. long, 5ft. broad, and 4ft. high, so we can just about make ourselves cosy. We have frequent visitors in the shape of rats, mice, beetles, etc., *but* I manage to live pretty comfortably in spite of them. Of course, we had gas helmets served out to us, and have to carry them wherever we go. I have to do about eight miles every night over rough country roads in any sort of weather. I was appointed 'interpreter' at this post by the officer in charge of our party, as I am the only one who can speak French. I have to do quite a lot of talking to the French Gendarmes, and this is by no means the least interesting part of the work. We are on one of the main roads so we see and hear plenty of what is going on.

On occasions the Colonel, as if to assure his men that there was a war on, would detail a detachment to join a battalion actually serving in the trenches. As another member of the Corps recalled, this time in the *Artists Rifles Journal*, Volume 1, No. 5, November 1916:

> At six o'clock we arrived at battalion headquarters, and were shown our cellar quarters for the night. There we were regaled with tea and any number of bloodthirsty tales.
>
> The battalion was to go into the trenches on the next day. Some expert witness amongst our hosts told us we should get badly 'told off' if we carried anything other than our equipment. We believed him, with the result that when we had got all our necessaries into our haversacks (we were not allowed to carry packs) we had no room for any food. When we moved off I noticed that nearly all the men of the Umpteenth Blanks were carrying sandbags full of all kinds of things. The result was that we lived on charity for the rest of the day, and determined to carry at least two sandbags on our next visit to the trenches.
>
> Half way up we had a halt, during which I heard a sergeant say to a Sub, 'We are very short of men, sir.' 'Yes, I know,' replied the Sub, 'but you can, of course, use these Artists' people.' This made me think we were in for it...
>
> We spent a fairly uneventful eight days [in the trenches]. Every morning and evening Fritz insisted on shelling and trench mortaring (or 'trench motoring' as a Corporal called it) a disused trench. Only one night did he strafe, and that was because he thought we were going to raid. This did not last long, as his iron ration ran out after the fifteenth shell. He must have found another put away somewhere as he sent it over an hour later, but it had been in the damp cupboard too long and failed to explode.
>
> After coming out of the trenches we went into rest billets for eight days. The men are still looking for the humorist who named these billets 'Rest', because we go on a working party either from 8.30 a.m. to 5. 30 p.m., or from 5.30 p.m. till midnight....
>
> The O.C. Company said to me one day: 'I have put you down to go on night patrol with Sergeant .... The object of it will be to see if there are any gaps in the enemy's wire.' Later Sergeant ...... came to my dug-out, and after blowing out his chest saying that he had volunteered to go on night patrol, began a good grouse that the DCMs and MMs were given to men for single deeds, and that people like himself who were always volunteering for dangerous jobs never got anything.
>
> I met him in the front line at 9 p.m. and he looked more like a backwoodsman than a soldier, a cap-comforter on his head, a

revolver in his belt and a pocket full of 'booms' (as he called the bombs). After explaining to me kindly, so that the officer might hear, what I was to do, he led the way over the parapet. I followed very gingerly, and we got through the first part of our wire and lay down for an hour. There he explained carefully how he could see the enemy's wire and freshly-dug chalk on the enemy's parapet. At about 10.5 p.m., he said: 'I think we will retire.' I was too cold to reply, but silently followed him back to the trench, where, with a wealth of detail, he told the officer how he had been over to the enemy's wire and had found no gaps and that the Huns were very busy deepening their trenches.

I afterwards heard that the Sergeant volunteered for night patrols for two very good reasons -
1. Because he got the rest of the night off.
2. Because he got a drop of Scotch after coming in ... .

The time arrived for us to return to our regiment. We left for the ration dump at 7 p.m. At 10 p.m. we got into the limbers and drove to the transport, where we spent the night. Next day we were away in the homeward bound char-à-banc.

There was a notable guard of honour commanded by Captain Bare for HM King George V in August 1916 in the grounds of Château Bryas. The Artists by this time were well used to providing guards of honour for royalty, including foreign kings and generals visiting GHQ, but on this occasion they made a special effort to chiffy up[1] for King George's second visit to the BEF. The King, who had been taken ill on his previous visit, was this time in better health. In the words of Corporal Ernest Blaikley, already a 'name' as an artist, who was a member of the guard, as later reported in the *Artists Rifles Gazette and Regimental Orders*, No. 30, February 1936:

> A group of important officers was standing inside the entrance of the hall [of the château] at the top of the steps. Suddenly a shouting was heard and the young Prince of Wales dashed down the inside staircase, hailing these grave and middle-aged men, who turned about to greet him with solemn bows. He was a cheering and inspiring sight and seemed to be in high spirits. Capt. Bare was then summoned to an inner room and the King decorated him with the Victorian Order. Then we were submitted to several preliminary inspections and it was during the last of these that an unfortunate affair took place. Whilst I was standing stiffly a hungry horse-fly lit upon my left cheek and drove his proboscis into my flesh. By a winking movement I attempted to dislodge him, whilst Lord

Stamfordham was coming down the line on my right. It was very painful. It seemed to me that the sentries opposite gazed at me in astonishment. I winked and winked, felt the brute pull his biting-apparatus out of my cheek, take a stroll around and got down to it again on a spot near my nose. Along came the officers, passed by, fortunately without noticing my predicament. Then out came the King. We gave him the finest Royal Salute that has ever been seen. I heard his one word 'Wonderful!' and we felt sufficiently rewarded. His Majesty then came down the lines, followed by the Prince of Wales. I was told that when he came to Peter Emslie, whose appearance was somewhat distinctive, he stopped and asked him what regiment he belonged to. Peter, that brave and loveable, if terrifying, man, stood rigidly and replied, in his peculiar accent, 'Skuts' Gairds. Your Majesty!' and when the Prince was passing behind me just afterwards, I heard the King ask, '*What* regiment did that extraordinary-looking man say he belonged to?' and the Prince replied with an excellent imitation, 'Skuts' Guards, Your Majesty!'

After that, we placed our caps (or were they tin-hats – I forget) on our bayonets and gave three hearty cheers as His Majesty and the Prince of Wales drove off. And when the tension was relaxed and my neighbour, happy and triumphant, turned to me to exchange views, he exclaimed 'Good Lord! What's all that blood on your cheek?'

During 1915 British engineers experimented with various types of armoured combat vehicle, a notion inspired by Winston Churchill's belief that a land battleship with caterpillar tracks, capable of firepower, was what was needed on the Western Front to break the stalemate by rolling over the enemy's barbed wire and trenches. 'Little Willie' first ran on 3 December 1915, by which time the battle model – at first called 'Centipede', then 'Big Willie' and finally 'Mother' stood almost complete. She ran on 16 January 1916 and showed beyond doubt that the specification had been satisfied and the pioneers' claims as to its combat capability were justified. The mysterious new armoured fighting vehicle was christened the 'tank', as a measure of deception to deflect enemy attention from the machine's real purpose and nature. It was a name which was to lead to many misunderstandings and misrepresentations. The first fighting tanks went into action during the last phase of the Battle of the Somme on 15 September 1916 and were Mark Is, almost identical to Mother. Their dramatic impact on friend and foe won only marginal successes, but their very appearance sufficed to ensure for themselves a second chance in action. It would not be until the Second World War that the tank revolutionized land warfare.

When the huge crates labelled 'tank' were first delivered to France in August 1916 the vehicles' first base and training centre was at Yvrench where the Artists Rifles provided a guard to protect the tanks from unauthorized surveillance. One Artist described Mother as a 'giant slug' and made the observation that this new combat vehicle was 'no health resort'; the Artists nevertheless being completely in awe of the tank's technical construction, its armaments, and the proficiency and courage of the crews that handled the 'monster'. One platoon of the Artists was specially trained in the manipulation of the Inglis portable bridge to surmount river barriers. After the establishment of the GHQ Cadet School at Blendecques large numbers of warrant officers, NCOs and privates from other regiments were attached to the Artists Corps for preliminary training before being admitted to the school. The system by which the regiment completely trained its own members for commissions without any final training elsewhere was put into operation until the 1st Battalion OCTU ceased to function in June 1917 when the Artists went into the line as part of the 190th Brigade of the 63rd (Royal Naval) Division. Early in 1916 some 150 TBs (Temporary Base Details), lads too young for the trenches, who had got to France in error or by guile, were sent to the Artists and trained. The arrival of a large draft from Gidea Park towards the end of 1916 ensured the supply of cadets for the time being but by June 1917 it had begun to dry up and it was then that the decision was taken at GHQ to send the 1st Battalion into action for the first time.

Meanwhile in 1916 Gidea Park was a hive of military and sporting activity. In March 1916 the Director of Staff Duties converted the Officers' School into four companies of cadets for the training of officers of men from the 2nd Artists Rifles OTC, and the battalion from March to August 1916 consisted of four OTC companies and four cadet companies, all under the command of Colonel Shirley. In September 1916 the four cadet companies were transformed into No. 15 (Artists Rifles) Officer Cadet Battalion, which was separated from Shirley's command, its commanding officer being Lieutenant Colonel E. St. L. Shaw, a Regular officer of the East Surreys. No. 15 OCB was nevertheless staffed almost entirely by officers and NCOs from the 2nd Battalion, its adjutants being successively Captains Abbot-Anderson and Willis, both Artists. Numerous other Officer Cadet battalions were at the same time established in various parts of the country, the training, it might be said being based on the same system introduced by Colonel Shirley in 1915. In addition incidentally to commanding the battalion, he was OC troops of the Romford District and President of No. 6 Quartering Committee, which embraced a considerable area of Essex and was responsible for the quartering and billeting of many thousands of troops of all branches in the area.

The Artists Rifles Regimental Association (ARRA) was inaugurated at a mass meeting of all Artists available on 29 June 1916, at the 2nd Battalion's headquarters at Gidea Park. The Honorary Colonel Robert W. Edis presided, supported by Colonel May, representing the 1st Battalion, Captain Horsley representing the (old) 2nd Battalion, and Colonel W. Shirley representing the 2nd (old 3rd) Battalion. The Association was registered as a company not for profit, and limited by guarantee under the Companies Act by Articles of Association giving the objects of the Association which may be summarized as follows:

> To form a centre and rallying point for all 'Artists': to obtain and distribute information with regards to emigration; to act as a patriotic association to further and support British interests throughout the world; to publish a magazine; to act as an employment bureau for 'Artists'; and to establish charitable and benevolent organizations in connection with the Corps.

The Association proved a success from its very inception. The membership was open to all Artists, or ex-Artists, and a few others who had rendered valuable service to the Corps. Those latter required to be specially elected by the council, and amongst them may be noted General Sir Cecil Romer, Colonel Sir Charles Lamb, General R.J. Kentish and Colonel R. Campbell.

The principal work of the Association was connected with the establishment of its headquarters together with the Artists Club at 17-19 Craven Street, Charing Cross. In addition to being the registered offices of the association, these premises were furnished with all the amenities, including providing lunch, tea and dinner for members, but with the exception of sleeping accommodation, of a good club. The Artists Club served as a meeting place for all Artists and ex-Artists who were in London on leave. From this developed the Artists Rifles Regimental Club: the Secretary was Arthur Drewry, late of 'F' Company. Membership of the association was free to all Artists and ex-Artists. The Club subscription was £2 per annum for town members and 10s. for country members, whose home was over thirty miles from London. A house dinner was held on the third Wednesday evening in each month at 7.30 p.m. The Artists Rifles Regimental Association (ARRA), re-titled the Artists Rifles Association (ARA) after the Second World War, is still in existence today.

The Artists Rifles Journal was first published in August 1916, the second number in September/October and the third in December of that year. The *Journal* measured 10½ x 8 ins and each carried a striking cover illustration reproduced from a painting depicting a Mars and Minerva theme by Lieutenant A. Egerton Cooper. It was distributed to all members of the Regiment in France and England, where it was offered for sale on the book stalls. The cover price was 6d. The first editor was Douglas Spencer, who was followed by J. H. Elder Duncan and R. F. W. Rees, all Fleet Street men. There was a wealth of literary and artistic talent available to contribute to the magazine, including Alfred Leete, Fred Buchanan, C. H. Bretherton, Tom Purvis, S.C. Strube, Bert Thomas, R. F. W. Rees, and many others. The first issue was mainly devoted to the formation of the Artists Rifles Regimental Association by Colonel Shirley, reference being made to the ARRA Professional Directory in which members were invited to enrol, stating their work experience and qualifications and requirements for post-war employment. There was also a long article entitled 'The Artists Rifles Since Mobilization' by Colonel H. A. R. May.

A feature of the second edition, which was to be continued until the end of the war, was the Roll of Honour, compiled by Major S.S. Higham and his small staff, which listed those original members killed in action, wounded, taken prisoner or missing, medals and awards, as well as those Artists appointed to commissions and the regiments to which they were transferred. These regular compilations were to form the basis of 'The Regimental Roll of Honour and War Record of the Artists Rifles', which was to be published after the cessation of hostilities. The first issue, in addition to photographs of personalities and scenes in France and England, included paintings (reproduced in black and white) by Colonel Walter Horsley, Sergeant Gerald Ackermann and Sergeant L. Pattison, a dry point by Corporal W. P. Robins; sketches by Second Lieutenant W. Lee Hankey and Corporal Ernest Blaikley and several cartoons by S.E. Strube. Sidney Strube (pronounced Stru-bee) – known universally as 'George' – was, of course, an established Fleet Street cartoonist, who was famous between the wars and after for his 'Little Man' cartoons in the *Daily Express*. A tremendous humorist, he served on the guard room staff and as an enthusiastic bayonet instructor at Gidea Park. He was in the habit of making a portrait of each inmate which he presented to the miscreant after his stay in the cells. As a sergeant, Strube was transferred from the 2nd to the 1st Battalion in 1917 when he took part in the Battle of Passchendaele contracting trench fever and trench feet, which were probably the cause of his death from heart failure at the early age of sixty-four in March 1956. From 1916 right up to the time he died 'George' Strube contributed hundreds of cartoons to the various regimental journals, and for presentations and programmes, etc. to mark regimental events.

In January – February 1916 an 'Exhibition of Paintings and Etchings by Members of the Artists Rifles' was mounted by Ernest Brown & Phillips at the Leicester Galleries, Leicester Square, London. Many of the young men cited in the following list of artists and their exhibits were to become Royal Academicians and Associates of the Royal Academy.

Entrance Gallery
1. Cadet Ernest Cole. *Study for Sculpture.*
2. 2nd Lieut. W. Lee Hankey. *The Knitting Lesson.*
3. Cadet Adrian B. Klein. *St. Omer from the Abbey.*
4. L.-Corp. A.H. Mason. *The Landlord's Daughter.*
5. Capt. Charles J. Blomfield. *Rood Screen at Swaffham Prior Church.*
6. L.-Corp. W.P. Robins. *A Shed by the Stour.*
7. L.-Corp. W.P. Robins. *Interior of a Barn at Datchworth.*
8. Cadet John Wheatley. *Study for a Painting.*
9. 2nd Lieut. W. Lee Hankey. *The Flight from Belgium.*
10. L- Corp. James Thorpe. *The Edge of the Moor.*
11. L.-Corp. E.L. Pattison. *Magdalen, Oxford.*
12. Cadet John Wheatley. *Mother and Child.*
13. L.-Corp. James Thorpe. *High Beach, Sept, 1915.*
14. L.-Corp. W.P. Robins. *Driver's End.*
15. Cadet John Wheatley. *Portrait of a Young Girl.*
16. L.-Corp. James Thorpe. *'Publicity'.*
17. L.-Corp. Malcolm Osborne. *After the Storm, Amberley.*
18. L.-Corp. Malcolm Osborne. *Evening Glory.*
19. L.-Corp. E.L. Pattison. *A Still Day.*
20. L.-Corp. E.L. Pattison. *Evening.*
21. L.-Corp. Malcolm Osborne. *Loches Castle.*
22. L.-Corp. Malcolm Osborne. *Tours Market-place.*
23. L.-Corp. A.H. Mason. *Time Study.*
24. L.-Corp. A.H. Mason. *Study.*
25. L.-Corp. A.H. Mason. *Time Study.*
26. Cadet John Wheatley. *Mother holding her Child.*
27. Cadet Charles F. Wallis. *Sunlight in the Wood.*
28. L.-Corp. A.H. Mason. *Candlelight Study.*
29. L.-Corp. James Thorpe. *Arthur Morrison, Esq.*
30. Sergt. C. Maresco Pearce. *Mentone.*
30A. Sergt. Garrad. *The Pool of London* (Lithograph).
31. L.-Corp. W.P. Robins. *Interior of a Barn.*
32. Pte. Alfred Hayward. *Willows and Poplars.*
33. Pte. E. Findlay Smith. *The Cranes.*
34. Cadet Ernest Cole. *Study for Sculpture.*

163

35.	2nd Lieut. T.H. Hughes.	*Proposed Government Building for Ottawa.*
36.	Cadet Ernest Cole.	*Study for Sculpture.*
37.	Cadet Ernest Cole.	*Study for Sculpture.*
38.	Pte. E. Sharpe.	*Lion.*
39.	Capt. Charles J. Blomfield.	*House at Stansted, Essex.*
40.	Capt. Charles J. Blomfield.	*Wellington College New Dining Hall.*
41.	L.-Corp. James Thorpe.	*Tom Binks.*
42.	L.-Corp. James Thorpe.	*Handley Cross.*
43.	L.-Corp. A.H. Mason.	*A Head Study.*
44.	Capt. A.H. Hall.	*Christchurch, Hampstead.*
45.	Capt. A.H. Hall.	*St. John's Chapel, The Tower.*
46.	Capt. A.H. Hall.	*London Bridge.*
47.	Capt. A.H. Hall.	*Hampstead Heath.*
48.	Cadet John Wheatley.	*Susannah* (Etching).
49.	Pte. Eric Sharpe.	*Ypres, April, 1914.*
50.	2nd Lieut. W. Lee Hankey.	*The Belfry, Bruges.*
51.	L.-Corp. Malcolm Osborne.	*The Heart of Scotland.*
52.	Sergt. C. Maresco Pearce.	*Porta della Carta.*
53.	L.-Corp. James Thorpe.	*Souvenir of Westward-Ho.*
54.	2nd Lieut. W. Lee Hankey.	*The Shepherdess.*
55.	L.-Corp. Malcolm Osborne.	*Chinon Castle.*
56.	Cadet John Wheatley.	*Portrait Study.*
57.	Pte. E. Findlay Smith.	*The Liner.*
58.	Capt. Charles J. Blomfield.	*St. Mary's Church, Welwyn, Herts.*
59.	Pte. Denys G. Wells.	*Mother and Child*

Reynolds Room

60.	Pte. Alfred Hayward.	*A Forest Glade, Radnorshire.*
61.	Corp. Gerald Ackermann.	*Richmond Castle.*
62.	2nd Lieut. W. Lee Hankey.	*The Belfry, Bruges.*
63.	Corp. Gerald Ackermann.	*Across the Common.*
64.	Pte. Alfred Hayward.	*Showery Morning, Wales*
65.	Corp. Gerald Ackermann.	*Corfe Castle.*
66.	Capt. Gerard Chowne.	*The Cliff.*
67.	L.-Corp. James Thorpe.	*Home.*
68.	L.-Corp. Lance Thackeray.	*A Drinking Place, Dierout, Upper Egypt.*
69.	Pte. H.J. Lotz.	*The Thames, from Tower Wharf*
70.	2nd Lieut. Adrian B. Klein.	*Flemish Mill, Ypres.*
71.	Pte. H.J. Lotz.	*The Bridge.*
72.	Sergt. C. Maresco Pearce.	*Mentone.*

73.	L.-Corp. Lance Thackeray.	*The Thames at Moulsford.*
74.	2nd Lieut. W. Lee Hankey.	*France in 1914-1915.*
75.	Pte. H.J. Lotz.	*Brighton Houses.*
76.	Corp. Montague Smith.	*Entrance to a Temple, Yokohama.*
77.	2nd Lieut. W. Lee Hankey.	*Luxembourg.*
78.	2nd Lieut. W. Lee Hankey.	*France in 1914-1915.*
79.	Corp. Gerald Ackermann.	*The Chalk Pit.*
80.	Sergt. C. Maresco Pearce.	*The Well Head.*
81.	L.-Corp. Lance Thackeray.	*On the Thames near Wallingford.*
82.	L.-Corp. Lance Thackeray.	*Villeneuve-les-Avignon.*
83.	Capt. C.W. Pike.	*Sunset on the River Thames.*
84.	Capt. C.W. Pike	*Afterglow, River Thames.*
85.	Pte. Paul Nash.	*Tree tops.*
86.	Capt. C.W. Pike.	*From under Hungerford Bridge*
87.	2nd Lieut. W. Lee Hankey.	*The 'Artists' Billets, Bailleul.*
88.	Pte. Theodore Newman.	*A Landscape.*
89.	Capt. Gerard Chowne.	*Grusse.*
90.	Corp. Gerald Ackermann.	*The End of the Harvest.*
91.	Pte. Paul Nash.	*Summer Garden.*
92.	L.-Corp. W.P. Robins	*Burnham-on-Staithe, Norfolk*
93.	Sergt. E. Handley-Read.	*Somewhere in France.*
94.	Pte. Paul Nash.	*Moonrise over Orchard.*
95.	Pte. Paul Nash.	*Silverdale.*
96.	L. Corp. W.P. Robins.	*Mannacott, N. Devon.*
97.	Sergt. C. Maresco Pearce.	*St. Malo.*
98.	Corp. Gerald Ackermann.	*The Downs, above Steyning.*
99.	L.-Corp. Lance Thackeray.	*Afterglow, Damietta, Egypt.*
100.	L.-Corp. Lance Thackeray.	*Wallingford Bridge.*
101.	2nd Lieut. A. E. Cooper.	*Colonel Shirley, C.O., 2nd Batt., Artists Rifles.*
102.	Corp. Montague Smyth.	*A Castle in Switzerland.*
103.	Corp. Montague Smyth.	*A Norfolk Garden.*
104.	Sergt. Edward Handley-Read.	*Willow Baby.*
105.	Pte. Alfred Hayward.	*La Petite Modiste.*
106.	2nd Lieut. A. E. Cooper.	*The Pardon.*
107.	L.-Corp. E.L. Pattison.	*Le Château*
108.	L.-Corp. F. Dobson.	*The Wooded Byeway.*
109.	Sergt. E. Handley-Reed.	*A Ferry, South Holland.*
110.	Col. Walter C. Horsley.	*The Disciple, Mosque of Almas, Cairo.*
111.	L.-Corp. F. Dobson.	*The Lane, Cornwall.*
112.	2nd Lieut. Adrian B. Klein.	*Rotherhithe.*
113.	2nd Lieut. A. E. Cooper.	*'And He healed them'* (Sketch for

	decoration.)
114. L.-Corp. E.L. Pattison.	*La Fontaine.*
115. Pte. Denys G. Wells.	*The Cornelian Necklace.*
116. Corp. Montague Smyth.	*The Shore, St. Jean-de-Luz.*
117. L.-Corp. A.H. Mason.	*Dinham, Ludlow.*
118. Corp. W. Hounsom Byles.	*The Sheep Wash.*
119. Corp. Montague Smyth.	*A Sandy Coast.*
120. L.-Corp. F. Dobson.	*The Red Dress.*
121. L.-Corp. A.H. Mason.	*In the Net of the Sun.*
122. L.-Corp. E.L. Pattison.	*The Deserted Barn.*
123. Corp. Montague Smyth.	*The Blue Lagoon.*
124. L.-Corp. F. Dobson.	*A Sultry Day.*
125. L.-Corp. A.H. Mason.	*Sunlight and Shadow.*
126. Cadet Ernest Cole.	*Adam and Eve Mourning the Death of Abel, Cain Repentant* (Wax).
127. Cadet Ernest Cole.	*A Woman Created.* (Wax)
128. Pte. W.H. Fisher.	*Cloisonné Enamel Bowl.* (Enamel).
129. Pte. W.H. Fisher.	*Enamel from an Illumination*

The exhibits were for sale incidentally, prices to be negotiated with the artist.

Note
1. 'Chiffy up', in Artists' language, to smarten up. Chiffy = Smart

Chapter 12

The Artists at War

Passchendaele: 'Over the Top' 1917

Though victory is difficult, defeat is impossible.
Prime Minister David Lloyd George launches five shilling War Loan bonds at the Guildhall, 11 January 1917

In spite of Lloyd George's cautious optimism, no one in 1917 really knew who was going to win the Great War. In Britain the year began with a shocked assessment of the financial cost of the war. British costs were running at £5.7 million a day; the government issued War Loan stock and the Prudential Assurance Company invested £20 million at 5 per cent payable in 1947. By the end of the month £1,000 million of War Loan stock had been bought. In July it was announced that Britain's daily war expenditure stood at £7 million.

There was success for British, Canadian and Australian forces on the Hindenburg Line at Arras, but a French assault at Chemin des Dames gained 600 yards at the cost of 120,000 casualties. The Third Battle of Ypres, also known as the Battle of Passchendaele, began on 31 July and ended on 10 November with the capture of the village of Passchendaele itself by Canadian troops. The avowed objective of breaking through to the Belgian ports could not be realized in the appallingly muddy conditions, which accounted for many of the deaths among the 300,000 plus British and Imperial casualties.

Once the winter frost had given way, from February to April 1917, the 1st Battalion, less the cadets retained at Hesdin for officer training, were impressed into navvy work doubling the single railway line from Étaples to St Pol. A new draft from the 2nd Battalion arrived in time to join in the work, its members expressing no little surprise that their first job in France was to be 'navvying' on a railway. On 14 June the warning order was received by the Artists that the battalion was to go into the line as part of the 63rd (Royal Naval) Division, replacing the Honourable Artillery Company (HAC) in the divisional order of battle. On the 19th an officer of the HAC arrived at Hesdin to assimilate the Artists' commissioning system, which the HAC were to take over. The next few days were devoted to overhauling kit and equipment, drawing and fitting gas helmets, disposal of surplus battalion stores and personal kit, etc., etc. The battalion's able and tireless QM, 'Freddy' Light, with CMS Hack ('Quack') and his efficient staff worked long hours to ensure that the battalion had a good send-off in matters of equipment.

Movement orders were received on 24 June and on the following day battalion headquarters, 'A' and 'B' Companies embussed in the barrack square at Hesdin for Bajus, where the Artists were visited by staff officers of the 63rd Division. The 63rd (Royal Naval) Division consisted of three Brigades, each of four battalions as follows:

188th Inf. Bde.	189th Inf. Bde.	190th Inf. Bde.
1/ R.M.L.I.	'Drake' Bn.	1/ Artists.
2/ R.M.L.I.	'Hawke' Bn.	4/ Bedford
'Anson' Bn.	'Hood' Bn.	7/ R. Fusiliers.
'Howe' Bn.	'Nelson' Bn.	4/ Shropshire L.I.

On the 27th the Artists marched to Écoivres, just behind Mont St Eloi, where the 190th Brigade had established its headquarters. On 2 July they moved forward to Aubrey Camp, near Rochincourt, where they were joined by 'C' and 'D' Companies, under Major H. E. Edlemann, TD, and the Revd. Harry Dickinson CF, who had been posted to the battalion as padre. It pleased the Artists that they were referred to as the '1st Artists', wearing the 'Artists' shoulder-title (grey worsted with black lettering), which had been authorized by GHQ, and not as the 'I/28th London' with its unimaginative metal plate shoulder-title bearing the designation 'I 28 County of London Battalion'.

From July to September 1917 the 63rd Division was in the front line ('R3' and 'R4' Sectors, Oppy and Gavrelle) and, with the exception of a few casualties, nothing of special note occurred during this period so far as the Artists were concerned. After a normal tour, the division was relieved by the 47th (formerly 2/London) Division, to which the Artists had originally belonged, the Artists themselves being replaced by the 22/London, commanded by Lieutenant Colonel C. F. H. Greenwood, a former Artists officer, and moved to La Comté. On coming out of the line, the commanding officer Colonel Chatfeild-Clarke, who was over fifty years of age and had reached the age limit for battalion commanders, was obliged to resign his command. Chatfeild-Clarke had been a popular and efficient CO: it had been his idea, approved by the C.-in-C., that cadets on passing out from Hesdin should be commissioned without further training before joining their regiments as officers, and his passing from their ranks was greatly deplored by the 1st Battalion. He was succeeded by Major Edlemann, a veteran Artists officer who, as it happened, was also over fifty, but was allowed to command the battalion during the brief period of interregnum before a new colonel was appointed. It was recognized, however, that pooling, not only of reinforcements but of COs was now inevitable: that as no other battalion overseas was being exclusively fed from its own regiment, the Artists could not expect different treatment. During the ensuing twelve months the Artists in France had six new commanding officers, all drawn from other regiments.

In October the 63rd Division was ordered to the Ypres front; the Artists journeyed to Houtkerque, thence to Reigersburgh and on the 28th left camp for their first big fight. The CO, Major Edlemann, brought the news that, owing to the impossible state of the ground, the divisional front had not been advanced so far as had been expected, so that what was to have been the jumping-off line would now be the objective. During the next thirty hours the Artists suffered casualties from long range artillery fire, 'D' Company losing their CSM C.W.W. King. Minute details of the battle for the Passchendaele Ridge, as far as the Artists were concerned, are not necessary: the story is soon told. Other divisions before the 63rd had been taking their share in the slow process of gaining ground in this water-logged area, at tremendous cost. The 188th Brigade was the first of the RN Brigades to attack, and advancing under a terrific artillery and machine-gun barrage they were able to make some headway, but suffered very heavily.

The 190th Brigade, which included the Artists, attacked on the early morning of the 30th, also under a very heavy barrage: the artillery averaged one gun to every nine yards across the whole divisional front. To reach their objective on the ridge, the Artists had the Paddebeeke to cross, according to the map an almost insignificant streamlet, but in actual fact at this time a wide and almost impenetrable swamp. 'A' Company (Captain W. S. Miéville) and 'B' Company (Captain A. E. Bare, MVO) were in the front line of the attack, 'A' Company being on the right and in touch with the Canadian Corps, and 'B' Company on the left and in touch with the 4th Bedfords: 'C' Company (Lieutenant E. S. Chetwood) was in immediate support and 'D' Company (Captain A. F. Royds) in reserve. Immediately the attack started the forward troops came under intense machine-gun fire from an almost unseen enemy, who were cunningly posted in carefully chosen tactical positions, having taken refuge in pillboxes during the intense bombardment; the supporting troops meanwhile were suffering heavy casualties from enemy artillery. The ground to be traversed was nothing but a deep sea of mud, and many men were drowned in the mud-filled shell holes, particularly those who were already wounded. Further, the mud clogged up rifles and Lewis guns in the first few minutes of the attack and rendered them entirely useless.

Consequently it was not long before the attack was brought to a complete standstill and the very attenuated battalions proceeded to consolidate as best they could on their side of the Paddebeeke. All this time the Canadian Corps was advancing on the right, and being on the higher, and consequently drier ground, they were able to advance further, so that there was eventually a rather dangerous gap between them and the 63rd Division. This necessitated sending up the 4th KSLI, who had been in reserve, to fill the gap. It was interesting to note that the Canadians attacked in extended order, with all the attacking troops keeping as close up under their own artillery barrage as possible; and their casualties were relatively far smaller than in the 63rd Division, who started the attack in artillery formation (section groups). There was considerable discussion at this stage of the war as to the respective merits of the two methods and the Artists' experience of this battle was that the method adopted by the Canadians was actually the more satisfactory of the two.

Some time after the battle it was learned from the Canadians that several Artists had succeeded in crossing the Paddebeeke before being killed, and these same Canadians were loud in their praises of the way in which the Artists had pressed forward in the attack. They went into the battle about 470 strong, and their casualties numbered about 350, of whom about 170 were killed. Among those killed were Captains Bare, Chetwood, and Gordon Williams, Lieutenants Haslam and Howe, and the padre, Captain Harry Dickinson. More of the wounded would have died had it not been for the efforts of the Artists' Medical officer, Captain Dr Mathew, who never rested from the work of collecting and dressing the wounded. With the casualties sustained from the bombardment during the thirty hours before the attack, Dr Mathew was almost continuously at work during the whole of the seventy-two hours that the battalion was in the line and the fact that eight bearers were needed to carry each stretcher down to the Advance Dressing Station will show how heavy this work was rendered by the mud. Once the Artists had started to consolidate after the battle Dr Mathew and his orderlies worked all the time in full view of the enemy under cover of one very small Red Cross flag, and the enemy (with the exception of his artillery) paid scrupulous respect to the flag. Meanwhile a large enemy bearer-party opposite the Artists could quite clearly be seen waving a

Red Cross flag looking more like a good-size tablecloth. Dr Mathew was awarded the Military Cross for his gallantry and devotion to duty in the battle for the Passchendaele Ridge.

After the battle was over the 1st Artists moved out of the line to refit at Eringham, where they received a special message of sympathy in respect of their losses, and congratulations on the part they had played in the battle, brought direct from Field Marshal Haig.[1] The following remarkable description of the final stage of the Third Battle of Ypres is taken from a letter written to his sister on 2 November by a young private in the Artists Rifles, Mark Yewdall, after the attack which gained no advantage at a very high price:

> Thank God I'm alive to write to you... Oh, it was horrible, horrible. And the hopeless folly of it all. The newspaper says today we advanced slightly at heavy cost. My dear, we hardly exist now. Only 156 of us left – all others mown down and blown up before my eyes. Poor Mr. Williams is killed, so is our dear Chaplain and our captain – but I needn't (and can't) go on – only to say that six have come back to my platoon. I being mercifully among them. For miles and miles the enemy shells cover every inch of the ground. You are in a shell hole one minute, the next moment it has gone and another almost in its place. One can only rage at the system that employs infantry in a war of shells. And people that can say that anything is worth it can only be devils. Every step took one over the knees in gripping slime. I saw many sucked down and drowned and I had a near escape myself. A shell blew my section into a shell hole – all wounded but me. For hours we lay there with thousands and thousands of shells falling all over and around us and covering us with debris, but none came right in. Why, I daren't ask. I had a terrible time with the wounded – they kept sinking into the slime and I had to pile rifles and haversacks and equipment – anything – under them to save them. In desperation we struggled out at last and wallowed and struggled in the open to the aid-post and eventually to the dressing station. It was a fearful distance and shells covered it all.
>
> If we have another stunt of this sort, I can't possibly hope to survive again. I do hope we shan't – it is too much to ask of a human being.

After a period of rest and reorganization in December, during which Lieutenant Colonel John Harington, 3/Rifle Brigade, took over command, and substantial reinforcements, including six officers, arrived from Gidea Park, the battalion was on its way back to the Passchendaele sector, when the successful British offensive before Cambrai was checked and the Germans began to press back the wedge that had been driven into their line there. Thereupon the 63rd Division was sent to the Somme district, and at the end of December the Artists moved into the front line in the Marcoing Salient (Couillet Wood sector). On the 30th the enemy launched a terrific attack and succeeded in penetrating the front line to the east of the Welsh Ridge Salient. The Artists, who were in support at this point, were detailed for a counter-attack which had to be made without artillery support. It was pressed for all they were worth but resulted in very heavy casualties without achieving their objective.

Order of Battle
'A' Company (Captain Pike) – 'B' Company (Lieutenant Skinner).
'D' Company (Captain Barnett) Support.
'C' Company (Captain Lepingwell) Reserve.

In spite of their failure, however, the Artists subsequently learned that their efforts were not in vain as the enemy, deceived as to the strength of the opposing available reserves by the promptitude and determination with which the counter-attack was delivered, refrained from exploiting their initial success. Had they done so, it is conceivable that driving the British troops from the Welsh Ridge might have been attained.

A very gruelling night followed, consolidation having to be carried out on ground which had been frozen hard. Sufficient praise cannot be given to the Medical staff under Captain Mathew, MC, who were again working all day at high pressure and all night and who did much to assist in the recovery of the wounded men who were lying out in front of the line. Excellent work was accomplished by 'D' Company, under Captain Barnett in forming a defensive left flank, by Captain Miéville in reconnaissance, and by Lieutenant Holland, these officers being awarded hard-earned Military Crosses. Their citations read as follows:

BARNETT, Lieut. Raimond Austin   1/Artists
   S. of Marcoing, 30th December, 1917. For conspicuous gallantry and devotion to duty. He led a bombing party with great determination and drove back the enemy, who were occupying part of our lines. He inflicted heavy casualties on the enemy and re-established the position.

MIÉVILLE, Capt. Walter Stokes   1/Artists
   S. of Marcoing, 30 December, 1917. For conspicuous gallantry and devotion to duty. When ordered to support a counter-attack he walked forward across the open to one of the advanced companies under machine-gun fire and obtained information of the utmost

value. His coolness and gallantry were a splendid example to all those under him.

HOLLAND, 2/Lt. Arthur Leslie   1/Artists

S. of Marcoing, 30/31 December, 1917. For conspicuous gallantry and devotion to duty. He took command of a company when his company commander became a casualty and successfully led it to a new position which he consolidated. He brought in several wounded men from the front of the lines under heavy fire, and set a splendid example of coolness and courage to his men.

A further Military Cross was awarded to Lieutenant Margetson in recognition of his good work in the maintenance of signal communications. His citation read as follows:

MARGETSON, Lieut. Edward   1/Artists

S. of Marcoing, 30th December, 1917. For conspicuous gallantry and devotion to duty. He kept up communication during an enemy attack under the most difficult conditions, laying telephone lines and personally carrying messages under heavy fire. He showed great initiative and skill.

RSM Emslie did much to keep things going by the organization of carrying parties to get hot food up during the night. One Corporal did yeoman service to his company by going back under heavy fire, crossing a gas-filled valley and bringing up the company water supply which had had to be abandoned in the rush of the morning.

The Artists' casualties were 6 officers and 110 other ranks. Lieutenants Salisbury, English, Skinner and Lightfoot, with the Machine Gun officer (Groom) and the Intelligence officer (Godfrey) were killed, while Pike, Lepingwell and Holland were wounded, and from this date the battalion ceased to be exclusively officered by Artists. But although officers and men came to the Artists from many other regiments the spirit and traditions of the Corps were maintained to the end: one of the most striking features in connection with the arrival of reinforcements from other units was the rapidity with which the new men assimilated Artists' ideas and methods of getting things done.

The first Official Artist, a painter commissioned by the Government to execute pictures destined for the Imperial War Museum, was appointed in 1916, since it was felt that permanent records of typical episodes in the Great War should be preserved for the nation. For the greater part these were young men, perhaps because the then older painters were unable, by their outworn conventions, to convey the clash of modern war in adequate expression. Two brothers, John and Paul Nash, both from the Artists Rifles, were among these Official Artists, and one of the best-known paintings to be hung at the Imperial War Museum then in South Kensington was 'Over the Top – 1st Artists Rifles at Marcoing, 30 December, 1917' by John Nash, then a sergeant in the Regiment. As already recorded in this chapter, casualties were severe and four officers were awarded the Military Cross. A replica of 'Over the Top' was painted by the artist and presented to the Regiment by Colonel H. A. R. May. It hung outside the door of the canteen at headquarters and was later transferred to the small lounge.

John Northcote Nash, who was born in 1893 and educated at Wellington but had no formal art training, joined the Artists in September 1916, going to France in November. In January 1918 he was appointed an Official Artist and gazetted to the New Armies the following May. Another of his large paintings on view at the IWM was 'Oppy Wood, 1917 – Evening', which shows two men of the Artists in a trench observing the British shells bursting over the German trenches; blasted trees, broken wire, corrugated iron are shown in a fine composition with a fiery pattern of sky. Of his other paintings 'The Bridge over the Arras – Lens Railway' shows troops working at fatigues in the railway cutting, a spot well-known to all members of the 1st Battalion in 1917, where they lived for some weeks when it was part of the Reserve Line; 'An Advance Post – Day' depicts men asleep under a shelter. His watercolours consist of 'Near Houdkerk, Belgium' – bean poles in a field near the camp of the 1st Artists Rifles; 'An Advance Post – Night' – sentries listening and watching, a star shell having just burst, sharply defining light and darkness; 'Stand To before Dawn' – a dramatic composition, the figures looking really as cold as this dawn must have been; and 'A Bombing Post in the Snow' – four men in a shell hole amidst the barbed wire, two on watch, and two asleep, snow falling. Yet another interesting watercolour is 'A Lewis Gun – Anti-Aircraft Pit' at Aubrey Camp, Arras; this was just behind the front line at Rochincourt, at the southern end of Vimy Ridge, where there was an enormous area covered with tents and huts; the 1st Battalion was quartered there. Bursts of AA shell in the air, in a pit the Lewis gun mounted on a post, the gunner observing, and the emptiness of the rows of tents, make a striking pattern. In the post-war years John Nash was a painter and illustrator who excelled in meticulous flower drawings for botanical publications. He was elected ARA in 1940, RA in 1951, and in 1967 was given a major retrospective exhibition at the Royal Academy. He died in 1977.

The other brother, Paul Nash, who was the elder and in the long term the more famous of the two, studied at St Paul's and the Slade School, joined the Artists Corps in September 1914 and became an instructor in topography. As a lance corporal he was commissioned into the 15th

Battalion, The Hampshire Regiment, in December 1916. During the next year he was wounded, but returned to France as an Official Artist. Paul Nash enjoyed a distinguished career as a painter, book illustrator, writer, photographer and designer. He was one of the most individual British artists of his period, taking a distinguished place in the English tradition of deep attachment to the countryside, whilst at the same time responding imaginatively to European modernism. He died in 1946.

We are indebted to an 'Old Artist', signing himself R.A.I. for the following account of the action at Marcoing, which appeared in the *Artists Rifles Gazette and Regimental Orders*, February 1935, No. 19.

'OVER THE TOP'

The picture 'Over the Top' has always been of particular interest to me because the first time I saw it, some years after Nash painted it, it immediately recalled in every detail the early morning scene at Welsh Ridge on December 30th, 1917. As I happen to be the only survivor of the particular incident depicted still serving in the Regiment today, your Editor is of the opinion that an eye-witness account of it would be of interest. I will, therefore, attempt to paint a picture in words so that they who are unable to see Nash's picture as I see it, may perhaps appreciate it better.

At Christmas 1917, the 1st Battalion Artists Rifles were holding the salient at Marcoing and at night, on December 29th, were relieved, the battalion front being taken over by another battalion of the Brigade, the Artists Rifles going back into the support line. Owing to the snow and the bitterly cold weather, the Regiment had had a somewhat trying spell in the front line, and the less gruelling conditions 'in support' were anticipated with a certain amount of satisfaction. Unfortunately, however, the Regiment had scarcely taken over the support line, which was actually in the well-known Hindenburg Line, when it was ordered to 'stand to', for just before daybreak on December 30th the Germans – taking advantage of the mist – launched an attack, capturing most of the positions which had been held by the Regiment up till the previous night. As a result of this, the Regiment was called upon to deliver a counter-attack and recapture the lost positions. The attacking companies were 'A' and 'B' with 'D' in support and 'C' in reserve.

Just before daybreak the Regiment moved up to the front line, which may sound quite an easy operation today, but which was actually – owing to the fatigued condition of many of the troops, and the difficulty of making reasonable progress caused by casualties also heavy shelling – a very tedious and trying movement. As a matter of fact the move was so slow that my own company ('B') only arrived in the front line at zero hour and had to jump out 'Over the Top' immediately upon arrival. This is what you can actually see in Nash's picture! The snow and mist; men of 'B' Company characterized by the blue square on the upper arm of their greatcoats; the sergeant with a Lewis Gun, already the sole survivor of his Lewis Gun section, and later a casualty himself.

As for me, there is little to tell.

My platoon consisted of about fifteen men and included a Lewis Gun team. It was on the right flank, and when we jumped out of the trench we moved forward into the mist, judging the direction by the movement of the troops on our left. At about thirty yards distant from the front line, we walked into a Machine-Gun barrage. On my left men were getting hit, and on my right a handful of men were moving forward comparatively untouched, and with them the Nos. 1 and 2 of my Lewis Gun team. I edged away to the right somewhat, and after continuing about fifty yards, came upon the German wire at about twenty-five yards distant, and beyond the wire – somewhat distinctly through the mist – I could see the heads and shoulders of the German troops. They commenced to fire at us with their rifles, and before we could get down they had caused further casualties including my Nos. 1 and 2 Lewis Gunners. The remainder of my platoon, now only four men – two of whom were wounded – and myself, took cover in a shell hole. From this spot we were able to be of some use with our rifles, as we were able to make the Germans keep their heads down. This may possibly have helped 'A' Company, who had got into the German line on our left, and were bombing down the trench.

About midday the German artillery and machine gunners eased up. Taking advantage of this lull in activities, H. E. Frank, who was then company sergeant major of 'B' Company, joined us in our little post. He had a bullet wound in his arm, but was otherwise his usual cheerful self.

As soon as it was dark we got in touch with battalion headquarters, and were withdrawn from our position.

That is all there is to tell, excepting to say that 'B' Company's casualties were very heavy. Out of eighty officers and men who moved up to the attack in the morning, when we called the roll that night there only remained two sergeants and ten other ranks.

Note
1. Haig was promoted field marshal in December 1916: he was not made an earl until 1919.

Chapter 13

The Artists at War

The Year of Victory
1918

Every position must be held to the last man, there must be no retirement. With our backs to the wall and believing in the justice of our cause, each one of us must fight on to the end.

Field Marshal Sir Douglas Haig delivers a personal message to all ranks after a three-week period in which 400,000 Allied troops died.
13 April 1918.

German troops, freed from the Eastern Front following the collapse of the Russian Army and the peace talks between Germany and Russia at Brest Litovsk, were drafted to the Western Front to meet the new challenge of American forces arriving in France in what was to become the decisive phase of the war. Using new tactics – specific assaults by 'shock troops' at weak points following artillery bombardment, instead of a blanket infantry assault – the German General Erich von Ludendorff smashed through the Allied lines in the Arras sector in March and threatened to push British forces back to the Channel in a 40-mile advance. Some 80,000 prisoners were taken in an offensive involving over 3 million men. In April Ludendorff broke through the lines at Ypres: Marshal Foch, Chief of the French General Staff, took over as head of Allied operations. The high point of the German offensive, in which half a million Allied soldiers died, was reached in June as Soissons was taken, Rheims threatened and Amiens destroyed. 'Big Bertha', a 420 mm gun named after the wife of the German arms manufacturer Gustav Krupp, pounded Paris with 1,764-lb shells from a range of sixty-five miles.

The Allied counter-offensive began on 22 June as German troops were halted forty-five miles from Paris and slowly turned back. After a four-week lull caused by the influenza epidemic, a 'Big Push' began at the end of July. In the change of Allied tactics, the Germans had found Allied front lines lightly defended and had pushed on; now with German supply lines fully extended and American troops arriving at the rate of 300,000 a month, the Allies hit back. Twenty divisions, spearheaded by 400 tanks and supported by low-flying aircraft, went into action at Amiens and German forces were pushed back to the Hindenburg Line. By the end of September the German Army was in full retreat across the whole Western Front. With its people in a state of insurrection, Germany surrendered on 11 November, the Armistice being signed at 11 a.m. in a railway carriage in the forest of Compiègne. The total cost of the war was estimated at £120,000,545 for the Central Powers (£37,775,000 for Germany) and £82,25,545 for the Allies (Britain £35,334,012; France £24,265,583; USA £22,625,950). Total Central Powers military casualties were 15,404,477; 3,386,200 died including 1,773,700 Germans and 1,200,000 from Austria Hungary. Total Allied military casualties were 22,064,427 of whom 5,142,633 died; 1,700,000 Russian, 1,357,800 French, 908,371 British and Imperial, 650,000 Italian and 116,516 American. The influenza epidemic that swept the world in 1918-19 claimed 20 million lives, roughly the same as the combined military and civilian toll after four years and three months of war.

During January and February 1918, the Artists put in further tours of duty in the front line, which by this time was liquid mud several feet deep. The CO, Colonel Harington, left the battalion to command 2/Rifle Brigade and was succeeded by Major Lathom of the Royal Fusiliers. After Colonel Harington the Artists had six commanding officers, none of whom were Artists in origin. They were:

> Major Lathom, 7th Royal Fusiliers, wounded in March near Beaulencourt, and replaced by -
> Major F.S.B. Johnson, Royal Lancs, wounded in April, in Aveluy Wood, and replaced by -
> Lieutenant Colonel H.G. Wilkinson, London Rifle Brigade, wounded in August near Amiens, and replaced by-
> Lieutenant Colonel J.F. Legge, Reserve of Officers, replaced by -
> Lieutenant Colonel R.H. Goldthorp, Duke of Wellington's (West Riding), who held the appointment from September 1918 to February 1919.

Meanwhile there had been changes in command at Gidea Park. Colonel Shaw was replaced in command of No. 15 (Artists Rifles) Officer Cadet Battalion by Colonel Gascoigne and in July 1918, Colonel Shirley was compelled by ill-health to resign his command of the 2nd Battalion, his successor being Lieutenant Colonel Ostle, who had gone to France with the 1st Battalion as a Junior Captain.

On 2 January the 190th Brigade, which had suffered far more severely than the other two Brigades of the RN Division and had put up a 'very fine defence', was relieved by the 53rd Brigade of the 19th Division and on 23 January the whole of the RN Division by the 2nd Division. A few days later came the reduction of Brigades to three battalions each, involving the transfer of the KSLI to the 19th Division. The German test barrages and gas attacks preparatory to their March offensive caused many losses before the terrific storm broke on the 21st, the Artists being in reserve at Havrincourt Wood. This was the beginning of the historic retreat of the British Fifth Army. At midnight on the 21st the RN Division withdrew to the intermediate system (the Hindenburg Line), and on the 22nd to the second line (the old British front line), thence to the Metz switch line, and the Green line, further back, on the 23rd.

After dusk touch with the 47th Division was lost and the officers commanding the Artists, Drake and Bedfords decided to withdraw from the Green line and to form a defensive flank in front of the Royal Engineers dump at Ytres-Bus-le-Transloy. At 10 p.m. the ammunition dump, which had been burning, blew up and the Artists had certain casualties. On the 24th there was a further withdrawal, the Artists having to cross open country, a racecourse, north-west of Bus, suffering many losses, and being unable to bring away their wounded. The new line for the division was at High Wood, and then eventually from Martinpuich to Bazentin-le-Petit, the Artists being in Brigade reserve at Courcelette. On the 20th the division was on the Ancre line in front of Hamel, the Artists being in Aveluy Wood, Bouzaincourt, under the command of the 12th Division, on the right of the 17th Division. On the next day, at 7 p.m., they drove back the Germans from the Aveluy-to-Bouzaincourt Road to the very outskirts of Albert. The burden of the attack fell on the Artists and the Bedfords, who lost their VC Colonel. This was the end of the great retreat so far as the Artists were concerned. The Ancre line was saved. On 15 April the Great German Spring Offensive being ended, the RN Division went back for a rest to Puchevillers, the Artists being at Acheux.

On 8 May the RN Division relieved the 17th Division in the Hamel-Aveluy Wood sector, and during the month was subjected to continuous raids by the enemy on the 190th Brigade posts. Counter-raids were made and no ground permanently lost. On 4 June the RN Division was sent back for three weeks' rest in the Toutencourt area. Here the Artists put their SMLE Lee Enfields to good effect, upholding their peacetime tradition by winning the divisional musketry competition. From 23

June to 25 July, a fairly quiet period, they took over the line in front of Auchonvillers, opposite Beaumont-Hamel.

Good news was now coming in. On 20 July Marshal Foch's counter-strokes had thrown the enemy across the Marne and on the 21st Château-Thierry was retaken. The Germans were in retreat. The war of positions had begun. The first rumour of dramatic events reached the RN Division on 8 August in the form of unexpected orders to move to the Montigny area, south of the Albert-Amiens road. Then the RN Division moved north, marching only at night, between 15 and 19 August. Subsequent operations, which most unfortunately included the death in action of RSM Peter Emslie on 23 August (he was succeeded by RSM Fox) found the Artists, in connection with the attack of 25 August, the first troops to enter Le Barque, the first great initial success. By the 31st the RN Division was three miles west of Hindecourt. On 4 September the 190th Brigade relieved the rest of the division. Then came the great Hindenburg line battles. On 27 September, in the successful attack to secure the crossing of the Canal du Nord at Moeuvres, the Artists fought their way south along the Hindenburg line. Yard by yard the Hindenburg system was cleared but the story of 27 September is better told in more detail by Colonel Goldthorp, who had just taken over command of the 1st Artists. (The extract is taken from the Regimental *Roll of Honour*).

>...I took over from Acting-Captain Hermelin, who was then in command; Besch was the Intelligence officer; Morris, Signalling officer; Nelson, the 'Doc'; Hewitt, Acting Adjutant; Light, Quarter-Master; Prentice, Transport officer; Robinson, Padre; and Wyler our Interpreter.
>
>Very early a batch of officer-reinforcements arrived, and it became obvious we were in for a show the nature of which we could only guess, but for my part I should like to say that from the very first I had every help from officers, NCOs and men, and my work was made easy by the spirit they all showed of welcoming me as one of themselves from the start. I shall never forget those first few days and the solid foundation of trust and comradeship they laid for what was before us.
>
>On the 26th September we left our camp for the old trenches just outside Quéant, where we were to assemble prior to a march on to our 'tape' between Moeuvres and Inchy, and we knew when we left (having received all the barrage tables, etc.) that we were in for one of the biggest battles fought by the British Armies during the whole of the War, as the division had to cross the Canal du Nord and take the Hindenburg Line, in conjunction with the Canadians on our left,

and the Guards on our right. This was only to be the first phase, and as far as the Naval Division was concerned, the 190th Brigade was the first to kick off. Afterwards, the other Brigades were to go through us and capture Anneux and get on as far as they could.

I was rather pleased to find that it fell to the Artists to do the lion's share of the work of our Brigade, i.e. we had to capture the Hindenburg Line after the Fusiliers and the Bedfords had crossed the Canal, a very delicate and involved movement which required a great deal of preparation and explanation.

We arrived at our Assembly Point without trouble and at midnight started off – a pitch black night, in a deluge of rain. We made very slow progress; it was a difficult job keeping in touch and following the line, which was marked out by white-washed posts, most of which had either been knocked down by the Artillery or obliterated by the rain. Without Hewitt and Goacher, we should have found it very difficult indeed, and might easily have had the same misfortune as was experienced by another battalion, who missed the track somewhere outside Pronville and got too much to the left. But there these two officers did splendidly, and we eventually arrived at a trench which marked our then front line. I halted the battalion and they laid down and soon went to sleep. We waited about, hoping against hope that the other troops would arrive, but finally gave up all expectation of seeing them and got the battalion out into shell holes slightly in advance of our previous position.

Seeing that the situation was exceedingly vague, I decided to put every available man on the line, and issued orders to the company commanders, telling them that unless the missing battalion turned up, we should have to tackle their job as well as our own on our immediate front, and that in the advance up the Hindenburg Line we should take half their objective, and the Canadians would look after the other half.

About 4.30 a.m. everything was ready as far as we could foresee, and there was nothing further to be done then but wait, and what a long time the last half hour before zero seemed! However the time arrived at last and so did the Boche attempt at retaliation. It seemed to come down on our trench for some reason or other, and soon the doctors were very busy, and after what seemed an age Morris arrived back to say that all was going well, that the battalion was in the Canal taking a lot of prisoners, that our barrage was as near perfection as anything he had ever dreamed of, and that the Boche barrage was falling well behind our men – all of which was good news. With my H.Q. and runners, I started off at once.

What a change from the night before! It was a lovely morning, and once out in the open, going towards the Canal, it was a wonderful sight to see our barrage and the men following it up. I cannot describe the feeling I had watching the Artists in action – to me for the first time. From behind it looked as near drill-perfect as you could wish for. We were not long in getting across the Canal, where we saw one of our tanks stuck, and met many wounded coming back, among them being Fergus Young, who was supported by a Boche prisoner about twice his size. He was very worried about his company, though as it turned out he had no need to be – they were carrying on all right, away on in front. As we got nearer the front line things seemed to get very busy. There were crowds of prisoners coming down – batches of 200 at a time in charge of one or two men – all their officers wanting to go down into dug-outs to collect their belongings, but I do not suppose they found many, because the ground was literally on fire, and after walking a short distance between the Hindenburg Line one's feet were quite hot from the heat of the earth. Soon messages began to come back – that the first objective had been taken – then the barrage moved on again, so did our men, and our messages came fast. 'Cannot get on for machine-gun fire.' 'No sign of the Bedfords on the right flank,' and with like messages from the left.

It then appeared that things were sticking a bit, so we pushed on to see what was really happening, and found things pretty well mixed up – our men short of bombs, having used everything they had and everyone doing his level best. We discovered that both our flanks were well in the air, and getting forward was out of the question until matters righted themselves on the flanks. By this time we had lost the barrage for our second objective, and it had become a question of holding on to what we had until the position cleared up. Being shot at from three sides is never a very pleasant experience but the men stuck it out wonderfully. I saw that we should need every single available man to hold on, so I went down the line a bit to collect any oddments I could find. It is surprising the number one comes across in a big show like this. There were Bedfords and Fusiliers who were beginning to come along in large batches. They were all gathered into parties and sent up straight away. The Fusiliers had a pretty rough time trekking about all night, and had just arrived in time to go over with the Canadians, where they were soon doing their share 'good and hard' as the Brigadier, who had spent his time cheering up the men, would say. I found the Signallers fixing up communications to the Companies and we got news of the poor Bedfords too who had a very rough crossing, but had come through all right. We knew then that our right flank was in touch, though it was thrown back very considerably, and we seemed to catch the whole attention of the Boche.

Presently orders came through that the attack, preceded by heavy barrage on one or two selected places, a sugar factory on the Bapaume-Cambrai Road being one, would be resumed at 2.15.

Everything up the line was as good as we could hope for and the 188th Brigade was getting ready to carry on. They were to go through us, and on to Anneux, and as much further as they could get. We then returned to Brigade H.Q. where we found Prentice and his transport – all safe and sound, and rather surprised to be so near the battle. Thoughts of hot food for the men seemed to be within the range of possibility provided the resumed attack went off all right. I saw the Brigadier again, told him that we were all ready for our original third objective, but he said we need not move at all, as the 188th were going through us, where we were, to their objective. The rest had been cut out and was being dealt with by the Artillery alone, so I went back post-haste, but was not in time to stop many men getting on, especially those at the front, who had numerous scores to pay off by this time.

The 2.15 show was a complete success, so much so that the 188th were able to move right up to Anneux without any trouble; then they bumped into plenty, I believe, but that is outside the story of the Artists. Shortly afterwards the divisional general came round our line, thanking the men for the splendid victory and still more for the magnificent resistance they had made when checked. I had been told beforehand that if we got the crest of the hill, which was our first objective, and stuck to it, we should have won the day whatever happened. As it was we got beyond and held on, against Machine-Gun fire, Trench Mortars, and Bombing, for hours, until the whole situation cleared all along line; a hard enough test for any troops and an achievement in itself that would have made any battalion's reputation.

Late in the evening we got orders to spend the night on our battle positions. Besch and I took a look round the places where we had been held up earlier in the day and in every case there was no lack of evidence of the supreme courage of our men. Before settling down we buried all our dead: there seemed to be a lot, but in comparison to the total casualties of the day, and in relation to the value of the work accomplished, there were really few. So ended one of the greatest days of the War and my first experience of the Artists in action. I, for one, shall never forget the 27th September 1918, and I can only pray to be forgiven if I in any way failed them during that day, or subsequently; they never failed me once.[1]

Order of Battle of the 1st Artists, 27 September 1918

'C' Company (Captain Young) – 'A' Company (Captain Goacher)
'D' Company (Lieutenant Elliott) – 'B' Company (Lieutenant Ashford)
Hd Qrs Company (Lieutenant Morris)

The Artists were detailed to follow the front-line troops and then swing with the Artillery on to the Hindenburg Line.

The remaining stages of the battle for Cambrai to Maubeuge gave every opportunity for the RN Division to show their training and organization. On 30 September the Artists were on the right of the attack on the line Pronville-Fog de Paris, on the outskirts of Cambrai. On 1 October the division was relieved by the 52nd. In four days the RN Division had advanced, fighting the whole way, over seven miles, capturing 63 officers and 2,138 men (unwounded), 5 big guns, 51 field-guns, 90 trench-mortars and 400 machine guns, one of the most successful of the division's innumerable engagements. On 5 October the division was about to entrain for St Pol, but was recalled in order to capture Niergnies. This operation was started on the 8th and Niergnies was soon again in British hands. The fall of Cambrai on 8 October was the direct result of the Artists' work. After a rest around St Pol the division was again in the fighting line on 6 November west of Bois d'Audregnies. On 8 November Audregnies and Witheries were taken, and in the afternoon the line was just west of Blaugies. By 9-10 November (on the 9th the Artists actually advanced 15,000 yards through woods and open country being the first British troops to enter Blaugies), the 190th Brigade had got as far as the Mons-Maubeuge road, running north-east from Quévy-le-Petit, which was their utmost limit, the 188th and 189th Brigades going on through Givry. The Artists were at Harvengt on the 10th and at Harmignies, which they entered twenty minutes after the Germans left, on the following day. The end came at 11 a.m. on the 11th.

We return to the words of Colonel Goldthorp for his description of the last day of the war in the Artists' camp:

> November 11th. At daybreak I started off up the line, having received information that the battalion had commenced to move and that the Boche had 'hooked it'. Reaching Harmignies, I found that our men had been in within less than half an hour of the departure of the Germans, and our patrols reported that at two of

the villages in front there were no signs of the enemy. We had orders to take up our position and remain at Harmignies, and that the 188th Brigade would go through us early in the morning. I went round, saw everybody, and waited until the other Brigade had started to move forward and then set off to return. On my way back I met a whole lot of Lancers, all formed up ready to go through. It was a fine sight seeing them all on their horses anxious to be off. On getting back I was met by a Doctor who said that he owed me some money (he had made a bet with me that there would be no armistice or peace this year). For a moment I could not quite work out what he meant, until I noticed that everybody around seemed pleased and then I learned the news of the Armistice which had come through a few minutes previously. I saw the Brigadier, got confirmation of the Armistice news, sent it up to the Companies, scrounged around making arrangements for baths for the men, got them all back again, and they had their baths and went to bed.

In the following afternoon the Band arrived, after a somewhat chequered journey from England, very sorry for themselves. Also British prisoners, who had been left behind by the enemy began to trickle through; they were in a most pitiable state. And so came the Armistice to the Artists – in the line to the very last. It will always be a satisfaction to us when we come to look back on things that we were there when the end came and that the efforts of our Division contributed in no small degree to the final collapse of the Boche.

The Artists took part, on 15 November, in the official entry of the British First Army into Mons. They then went back to Harmignies and Athis, where educational classes and recreational activities were formed. Christmas was spent at Blaugies. There was a subsequent move to St Ghislain, where Colonel Goldthorp left the Corps. He was succeeded by Lieutenant Colonel A. W. Hall, MC, an Artist, who took over the cadre until return to England in 1919 with its subsequent demobilization.

Note
1. Colonel Goldthorp omits to mention that he was awarded the DSO for this day's work.

ARTISTS RIFLES
BATTLE HONOURS

SOUTH AFRICA
1900-01

Passchendaele '18   Somme '18

Bapaume '18   Ancre '18

Drocourt-Quéant

Canal du Nord

Hindenburg Line

Cambrai

Pursuit to Mons

France & Flanders

1914-1918

SUMMARY OF WAR HONOURS
1914-1918

Victoria Cross	8
C.B.	1
C.M.G.	1
M.V.O.	3
Order of the British Empire	K.B.E., l; C.B.E., 2
	O.B.E., 43; M.B.E., 17
Distinguished Service Order	52; Bars, 4
Distinguished Service Cross	4; Bars, 1
Military Cross	822; Bars, 63; 2nd Bars, 6
Distinguished Flying Cross	23; Bars, 3
Air Force Cross	15
Royal Victorian Medal	4
Distinguished Conduct Medal	6
Military Medal	15
Meritorious Service Medal	14
Foreign Decorations	90
Mentioned in Despatches	564
Brought to notice of Secretary of State	70

STRENGTH

Numbers on Mobilization	621
Recruits during the War (including past members rejoined)	<u>14,401</u>
Total of Muster Roll	<u>15,022</u>
Gazetted to Commissions (so far as ascertained)	10,256

CASUALTIES

Nature	As Officers	As Rank and File	Total
Killed in action, or died	1,614	389	2,003
Wounded or gassed	2,816	434	3,250
Missing	418	114	532
Prisoners of War	256	30	<u>286</u>
			6,071

Chapter 14

The Great War

1914-1918

Oh, Oh, Oh, What a Lovely War
 An anonymous parody of a military march

The purpose of this chapter is to fill in the gaps which have occurred in the foregoing chapters on the Great War, not so much in the development of military events as in background information on organization with special reference to some of the outstanding figures below colonel level in the Regiment and to the volunteers, particularly from the arts community, who were to become well-known to the public at large between two World Wars and after.

The VAD

On 31 January 1911, at the suggestion of Colonel Walter Horsley, then commanding the Artists Rifles, a small provisional committee was formed with a view to raising a Voluntary Aid Detachment to provide a nursing service for the battalion. The result was the formation of the 104th (Artists Rifles) VAD, the original members of which were all wives, other relatives or friends of members of the Regiment. Thus, at the outbreak of war, there was immediately available a well-trained nursing unit, all of whom at once volunteered for service at home or abroad. The primary idea on which the envisaged role of the VAD in war was based was to nurse the sick and wounded of the Territorial Army in the field hospitals, which were to be situated in close proximity to the front line. But owing to the Territorials being merged into other fighting units the VADs were not required for the purpose for which they were originally intended. Thereupon the 104th offered to equip and staff an Auxiliary Military Hospital. Their offer was accepted by the War Office and the hospital was opened on 28 April 1915 at

Egremont, Lyndhurst Gardens, Hampstead, in north London, as an auxiliary to the Hampstead Military Hospital. The new hospital was equipped with twenty-three beds, soon to be increased to twenty-five, and after a year to thirty-two. The entire work of the hospital – superintending, nursing, cooking and cleaning – was performed by members of the Detachment. Before the hospital was closed on 31 May 1919 nearly 1,000 patients had passed through its four wards, only a few of whom were actually Artists.

Altogether there were sixty-two staff, who worked under the supervision of:

Dr Lewis Glover	Medical Officer
Miss A.S. Goodall MBE	Commandant
Mrs de Segundo	Lady Superintendent
Mrs Herbert Shirley	Lady Superintendent
Mrs Ethel Allbutt	Matron (from April 1918)
Miss Janet Venables	Quartermaster
Miss A. Sawtell	Quartermaster
Miss M.Goodall MBE	Secretary & Treasurer

Major Arthur Davidson VD was appointed Chairman of the Committee from 20 October 1916.

List of Honours and Awards 1914-18

Order of the British Empire – Miss A S Goodall MBE
Order of St. John of Jerusalem – Mrs de Segundo,
'Honorary Serving Sister'

Brought to Notice (Secretary of State's Mentions)

Dr Lewis Glover	Mrs de Segundo
Miss A.S. Goodall OBE	Miss O.M. Selfe
Miss M.Goodall MBE	Mrs Herbert Shirley
Miss D. Grinling	Miss W.Turton
Miss M. Neame	Miss Janet Venables
Miss A. Sawtell	Miss M.Wilson

The Drummers at War

The Artists were always justly proud of the Drums. It would have been difficult for any Artists to imagine an Easter march, summer camp or ceremonial parade without them. It was always assumed that if ever the battalion went on active service the Drums would at once cease to be drummers and become stretcher-bearers. But with one exception, and that was shortly after the battalion reached France in 1914, they did no practical stretcher-bearing for the rest of the war, but they did do something of everything else. Among the many tasks that fell to the Drums were those of officers' batmen, runners, man-handling stores, ration and water-carrying parties, and burial parties. However laborious and distasteful these assignments could be and for which they were unlikely to win any medals the drummers performed them well and without complaint.

When the battalion sailed for France, the Drums celebrated their landing by playing the national anthems of the Allies while waiting for the troop-train. On their arrival at their first French quarters at Bailleul, all musical instruments were at once to be returned to Ordnance, but Colonel May put up a great fight for their retention and he was allowed to keep them for the time being. It was not however until May of 1915 that the Drums gave their first performance in France. After that they were in frequent demand for the guards of honour that were to be found by the battalion, for playing off the units at Bailleul going back to the trenches, and for performances in the *Places* at St Omer and Hesdin. On 21 May 1917 bugle-calls were sounded for the first time since the battalion had landed in France, two-and-a-half years before. In the meantime, the personnel of the Drums had changed to some extent. Drafts from home had brought many drummers with them who had been used to replace men invalided home, sent to the Machine Gun school or into the line with other battalions. The drummers were also employed filling in with trade jobs, the sergeant drummer duplicating his job with that of shoemaker sergeant. One drummer was sent to St Omer to look after regimental records.

The Drums went with the battalion in 1917 when it was driven in buses from the barracks at Hesdin to Bajus, and thence on the march to Arras, to take their place in the line with the 63rd Division. Their instruments went with them, only to be played on infrequent occasions, which would occur when the battalion was out of the line at rest providing also entertainment for the French villagers. It may be mentioned here that all the drums, the original ones painted by Colonel Horsley, lived to go home again, with the exception of the big bass drum. A lot of Regimental stores had on several occasions to be left behind for the benefit of the enemy, but no drums ever fell into their hands. The bass drum was busted early in the campaign and, as it was of an 'outside' size, it was not possible to get new heads for it, and a new bass drum had to be requisitioned. The old frame was carried about for a long time, but it went west with a consignment of officers' baggage with the explosion of the ammunition dump at Barrastre caused by German shelling.

Some of the drummers were selected as officers' servants and runners, and joined the battalion in the line at Gavrelle and Oppy Wood, but the bulk of them were assigned to the QM's staff (unkindly described as the 'duds and dunnage') and stores were put into a shell of a house and shop at the foot of St Catherine's Hill on the Lens Road. Some of the men were accommodated in tents, but gradually a few shanties were built. There was plenty of work to be done. All the 'trades' were located here in the Arras sector. Those who remained available for work were formed into the ration-carrying and fatigue parties, which duties the Drums continued to carry out until the end of the war. As other units of the division were to remark with envy, the Artists were better fed and watered than they were, entirely due to the excellent work of the Drums.

The duties of these fatigue parties did not begin and end with the carrying of rations and water to the men in the line. The first task was to find receptacles to carry them in. The tin cases in which the shells were issued were used to carry cooked meat, and nothing was ever found to better petrol-tins for the water. These receptacles had to be burned out, and then scalded and washed before filling them. At Arras it was not too difficult to get tins in sufficient quantities. Later on when the battalion was constantly moving it was a continual struggle. In the Arras sector there was a light railway which ran from the outskirts of the town right up to the front line. The delivery work had to be carried out under cover of darkness, so in the early evening the fatigue party would fall in to carry the rations, water and mail to the railhead, where they would be loaded on to little trolleys, three being allotted to a battalion. A light engine was then attached and the train would commence its journey up a steep incline at about two miles an hour.

It was not unusual for the engine to jib on the incline and the fatigue parties perched on the trolleys would have to climb down and push, mounting again when the gradient got less steep. When the top of the hill was reached, the train ran past Chanticlere Cemetery where the drummers were often to be seen burying the dead. At the Bailleul Cutting, the Puffing Billy was taken off, as the train was now in open country and sparks flying from the engine could be seen from the enemy lines. From this point the trolleys had to be manhandled again, but when the railhead was reached the fatigue men had to be absolutely certain it was dark before carrying their loads to the trenches. On the return journey the trolleys would again have to be manhandled back to the Bailleul Cutting, where the engine would be attached again to carry the men and trolleys back to Arras.

With the spring came better times, some of them most enjoyable. Few of the men who were there quickly forgot the camp at Toutencourt Woods. Later came a delightful stay in the Louvencourt Wood, with perfect weather and the battalion near at hand. There was no trouble from the Germans. A certain amount of road-making had to be done, but no one was overworked. The only casualty at this time was the sacrifice of Martin, the pseudo-Regimental mascot. He had started his soldiering with the Artists as a sucking-pig and had travelled with the Drums over a good deal of country. With the luxurious life of the woods he waxed fat and became too big for his travelling crate. The CO decided that Martin would have to be converted to rations. Lots were cast for him by company, the lot falling to 'A' Company. Whether Blackmore, Martin's keeper and trainer (and, of course, a drummer), was genuinely grieved by his charge's demise is doubtful, for he was a bit of a handful at times!

In the advance to the Hindenburg Line in the autumn of 1918, the Drums moved to the front and in sight of Cambrai, where they made themselves as comfortable as they could in one of the Hindenburg trenches, whilst the Artists with the rest of the division and the Canadians stormed the Line. The battalion was never in the trenches without some of the Drums being with it. For all the principal engagements additional runners were always provided, many of these being found by the Drums. And in whatever capacity they served, all who soldiered with them agreed that their dedication to duty was beyond praise. Although several drummers were wounded, only one – Ray Collins – was killed, but all gave ungrudgingly of the best that was in them.

Space does not permit the listing of biographical details of all the outstanding officers and men who served in the 1st and 2nd Battalions in the Great War, but although a choice of some of them may appear invidious, a selection of a few of such men is given here to typify the spirit of the dedication given unflinchingly by all ranks to the Regiment, abroad and at home.

Major Alfred Blundell joined the Artists Rifles as a private on 9 December 1890 and retired on 3 April 1901 with the rank of second lieutenant. On the outbreak of war he rejoined as a second lieutenant, and was posted to the 2nd Battalion, then in process of formation, and within two months was promoted to captain. Blundell was posted as an instructor to the Artists Rifles School of Instruction for Territorial Force officers on 1 November 1915, and remained with it on its conversion into the Artists Rifles Officer Cadet Battalion on 2 March 1916 but returned to the 2nd or OTC Battalion, when he was appointed major and second in command in June 1916. About this time it became a condition precedent to a commission to receive a training at an OCB and upon Major Blundell devolved the task of organizing the Commissions Department. Men were drafted daily to every school in the country, entailing the onerous work of individual interviews, amounting at times to as many as 200 a day. A solicitor by profession, he was appointed in 1916 as honorary solicitor to the Artists Rifles Regimental Association and was responsible for drawing up the Articles of Association. In addition his service on many committees was of the greatest value to the Regiment. He was a many-sided friend to all members of the 2nd Battalion. Amiable, boyish, he was always ready for a rag. If anyone suffered or sorrowed, or was in trouble of any kind, it was immediately a case of 'Father' to the fore. Even those who had offended were assured of a fair hearing. Entirely selfless, frank and impulsive by nature, his training as a solicitor had taught him reticence and restraint; and if at times over-lenient in character, his duty often required him to be stern. A brilliant second in command to two COs, his relationship with others inevitably developed into conflict over the vindication of discipline. Then the smile would disappear from his face and he became an enigma to his friends. For all that, 'Father' was greatly admired and respected for his exemplary contribution to life at Gidea Park.

Captain R. F. Turnbull, otherwise known as 'Monkey', joined the Artists Rifles in 1900 and was posted to 'D' Company, later serving in 'K' and 'E' Companies, in the latter of which he was a sergeant at the outbreak of war. He was immediately transferred to the 2nd Battalion and at Christmas 1914 went to the newly-formed 3rd Battalion as quartermaster but it was as QM when the 3rd was re-titled the 2nd Battalion that he is best remembered. Throughout his career as an Artist, 'Monkey' Turnbull enjoyed a great success as an entertainer. He was a superb organizer of smoking concerts and children's parties but his great strength as an entertainer was his ability to compose and parody popular songs, which he delivered with great gusto at smokers' and children's parties at Duke's Road or the canteen marquee at camp, and with the assistance of the Drums on route marches. 'Monkey' had a great repertoire of songs and verses, but his favourite was 'Away in a Corner', which originating from the Royal Marines was for ever associated with his name.

> Away in a corner
> Under the tree
> The Sergeant-Major
> Sez to me:
> 'Now wot is your name, me lad?
> I want to know
> And mind you answer every time
> You hear 'Defaulters' go.'

'Monkey' Turnbull came from Border stock, was a chartered accountant by profession and the father of twins. No one would have called him 'Monkey' to his face. At Gidea Park he was respectfully known as Captain Turnbull, the quartermaster, where he was a familiar figure issuing and inspecting kit, supervising garden plots, encouraging vegetable cultivation and food economy, ensuring cleanliness of quarters; and bestowing 'brief, bright and brotherly chats on cookhouse chores and sanitary science'. As a quartermaster Turnbull was in his element and there was no doubt of his success at 'Q' work. There would not on the face of it be much scope for a merry quip or prank in the quartermaster's stores, but this did not impede his sense of fun. He posted a notice on his door which read 'TAILORS WILL BE SHOT ON SIGHT'. This would have appeared to be an unnecessarily offensive warning to a harmless and useful branch of the service, but it was his way of protesting against a War Office decision to clothe cadets *comme officiers* – a pointless exercise in Monkey's opinion, which would involve his stores in a good deal of unnecessary work.

Turnbull took a great interest in the VAD Hospital in Hampstead and there was a motto among the staff – 'If in doubt, ask Captain Turnbull'. The VAD came to rely on him for entertaining at hospital concerts, ordering the Christmas turkeys (not forgetting the sausage meat) and collecting the donations so desperately needed to bolster hospital funds. An incident cherished by several members of his QM staff occurred on the night before they were due to leave in the early morning on a draft for France. The farewell concert in the canteen for the draft was over but Turnbull had been unable to attend on this occasion due to one of his multifarious duties which required him to be away from camp. He returned late at night – cold, wet and hungry – but he immediately went to shake hands with his men and to wish them 'Good luck and safe return'. It was a gesture well remembered 'on the other side', as well as many other instances of Captain Turnbull's happy nature and friendliness.

RSM Peter Emslie, a Scotsman, was apprenticed at an early age to marine engineering and subsequently joined the Submarine Miners Volunteers. Being of a military inclination he enlisted in the 3rd Battalion, the Scots Guards. Promotion was rapid for him – at least by Guards standards – and he was made a colour sergeant drill instructor in the record time of ten years. He was seconded to the Artists Rifles as a Regular in the latter part of Colonel Horsley's tour as commanding officer and at the outbreak of war was a staff sergeant. In this capacity he assisted Colonel May in the selection and organization of the working parties for 'London Duties'. He was shortly appointed regimental sergeant major and although it was at first thought that as a 'Regular attached' he would, with the onset of war, have to return to the Scots Guards, it was only at the very last minute when the 1st Battalion was embarking on the *Australind* at Southampton that he was given permission to go with them. (The Artists were actually already on board ship when Peter Emslie walked up the gangplank only seconds before it was withdrawn.)

Soon after the Artists' arrival in France the task fell to RSM Emslie to assist Colonel May to fit the battalion for the unexpected role of providing the British Expeditionary Force with junior officers. It may be that owing to the vast number of officers that were to graduate from the Artists' School at Gidea Park that those who went from the 1st Battalion in France seem but small in number; but it must be remembered that the foundations on which the home school was built were firstly the reputation earned by the Corps (now the 1st Battalion) in the days of peace, and, secondly the name it so speedily won for itself in France. Most of the credit for the latter is due to Colonel May and RSM Emslie. But perhaps Emslie's apotheosis was the guard-mounting on the old cobbled square at St Omer and later at Hesdin where his wonderful powers as a drill instructor won the Corps such unstinted praise from GHQ for its efficiency. Emslie also mounted some memorable guards of honour for His Majesty King George V (twice), foreign royalty, generals and politicians. Hundreds of cadets, both Artists and Attached, passed through his hands for drill while in the colonel's class, and they had every reason to be grateful to him for his thorough instruction and for his patience.

Later when, in 1917, the Artists took their place in the line, he was absolutely without fear, and always cheerful under the most exacting conditions. It should be recorded that on every occasion the battalion was in the line Peter Emslie was with it, with the solitary exception when he chafed at the transport lines for four days with a crocked knee. Even so he went back up to the trenches before he should have done. It was his complete disregard for personal safety that led to his death in action. On 8 August 1918 the division was ordered north to the Montigny area, south of the Albert-Amiens road, marching only at night between 15 and 19 August. On the 23rd when the fighting was intense, Peter Emslie went out into no man's land to assist a wounded man. He was struck in the head by a piece of shell fragment and died in a field hospital without regaining consciousness. RSM Peter Emslie, Scots Guards, who had been awarded the Distinguished Conduct Medal, 1914 Star, Long Service Medal and the Médaille Militaire, was buried at Bucquoy, but it would be true to say that he cherished none of these decorations so much as the love and esteem in which he was held by all ranks of the 1st

Battalion, the Artists Rifles.

Colour Sergeant William Hammond, always known as 'Bill', was born in 1872 and joined the Artists in 1888. At that time he had a father, four brothers and two uncles all serving in the Corps. He later produced a son who played football for Fulham. Bill Hammond was an outstanding athlete but was best remembered in the Regiment as a champion bayonet fighter. In 1890 the battalion went to camp at Walmer and it was there that an incident occurred of which he was justly proud. News got around that an Army champion runner was in camp and was open to run against all comers. Bill was called for in haste: a match was arranged and in a very few minutes there was an ex-champion in the Walmer Camp. In later years his fleetness of foot led to the capture of an expert West End thief, whose activities had for a long time baffled the police. This rascal made an attempt at burglary at the Hammond business premises in Vigo Street, off Piccadilly Circus. What the thief did not know was that Bill was sleeping on the ground floor and when aroused by the break-in he gave chase clad only in pyjamas and slippers along Regent Street and into Glasshouse Street where his quarry was run to earth and handed over to a grateful 'C' Division.

In 1893 the Matabele War broke out and he went out to join the Cape Mounted Rifles. Finding on arrival in South Africa that the war was over, he was determined to carry out his intention as far as possible. He therefore enlisted in the CMR and stayed with that distinguished force until 1896. During this period Hammond was mobilized on account of the Jameson Raid and took part in the Pondo Land Expedition of 1894. At that time Cecil Rhodes had an escort of twenty-four men of whom Bill Hammond was one. While he was in South Africa he also found time to skipper the Cape Mounted Rifles soccer and cricket teams.

From 1904 he was a member of the School of Arms. A brilliant instructor, he distinguished himself as a combatant with bayonet, sabre and as a fencer. He took part in the old Military Tournaments at the Royal Agricultural Hall in Islington and later at Olympia. He was selected for the England Sabre team for the Stockholm Olympics of 1912 and after the war in 1920 fenced for England at the Olympic Games in Antwerp. At the outbreak of war Colour Sergeant Bill Hammond became bayonet and physical drill instructor to the 2nd Battalion at Gidea Park. He then took a commission in the RAOC and served until 1919. During this time he came across something quicker than himself, being struck by lightning while on duty. Happily, the accident left no ill effects. During the course of a long career with the Artists, he won in bayonet, sabre and foil competitions alone fifty-five prizes – thirty-nine first, ten second, four third and two fourth. Colour

Sergeant Bill Hammond was the finest bayonet and sabre fighter on record, but at the same he was modest and entirely without self-advertisement.

Captain J. W. Marshall was born at Lamberhurst in Sussex and educated at Cranbrook and Eastbourne. He joined the Artists in 1892 and was promoted to lance corporal in 1898; corporal in 1899; sergeant in 1901 and colour sergeant later in 1901. He was transferred to the TF Reserve in 1912 and, returning to the battalion, was mobilized as a sergeant on 5 August 1914. Jack Marshall was said to be the personification of the true Artist. During his many years of service his knowledge of the Corps, wisdom and advice were much sought after especially by new recruits. Available records do not reveal Marshall's profession but the following story will give a clue as to his status in society. As a private he attended the first Easter training at Eastbourne, where the battalion was quartered in the town hall. Private Marshall, who wore a monocle, was detailed to show a party of visitors around. After the tour was over the conversation between Marshall and one of the visitors went like this:

> Visitor: 'Well, thanks very much, my good man. Here's something for you to get a drink with,' pressing sixpence into Jack's hand.
> Marshall: 'Many thanks. I won't if you don't mind, but next time you are in Pall Mall drop into my club and ask for me; there's my card, and we will have a drink together.'

From 1904 onwards Jack Marshall took an interest in the *Daily Telegraph* Cup Competition, which was a road race carrying full kit, rifles and machine guns followed by a range-firing competition.[1] As a sergeant he led the Artists' team on four occasions. He was always ready for a rag. In 1908 when the Territorial Force came into being, only one set of khaki uniforms was issued per man, so a battalion order was published announcing that civilian clothes might be taken to camp. Jack squeezed an old top hat into his kitbag, Buggins had a waiter's waistcoat and tweed cap, others took tailcoats, straw hats and other items of casual attire. At a pre-arranged signal these improperly dressed miscreants appeared 'on parade' on the Sunday afternoon but were sent flying back to their tents with some strong language from the RSM, 'Tottie' Payton. The 'irregular' items of dress were not seen again.

After the outbreak of war it took some persuasion for Jack Marshall to take a commission but he was promoted to lieutenant on 16 October 1914 and posted to the 2nd Battalion. On 16 June 1916 he rose to captain and appointed to command 'A' Company. On demobilization he was transferred again to the TF Reserve but rejoined the Artists when in 1921 the battalion was resuscitated under Colonel May. After outstanding service as an officer he made the surprising decision to resign his commission, preferring to serve as company sergeant major of 'A' Company. Not many men would have taken such a plunge in rank, but he considered that a good CSM was vital to the success and well-being of any company, and he felt this was the best way in which he could serve the Corps. Some Artists were of the opinion that in the next war he would rise to colonel, and when it was all over he would re-join the Regiment ('Not to stay, old thing but just to start 'em again') as a cook!

Jack Smith, whose full name was John Ambrose Smith and was affectionately known by all as 'Jacko' was an Artist for nearly forty years. He was personally known to every pre-war member of the Regiment and was among those who devoted practically all their spare time to the Corps. He joined in 1880, became a lance corporal in 1893, corporal in 1896, sergeant in 1898, battalion sergeant Instructor in Musketry in 1900, quartermaster sergeant in 1903, and was appointed quartermaster just before the war. Although by now he was fifty years of age, he went as quartermaster to France with the 1st Battalion. Jack Smith before the war had always been associated with 'D' Company, that nursery from which came some of the most famous men in the Regiment, and to which company the Regiment owed its great reputation for bayonet fighting at the old Agricultural Hall and at Olympia. Jacko was one of the 'D' Company crowd and his name appeared with almost monotonous regularity in the lists of bayonet teams in the early days. His name was also closely associated with 'Philhurst' and other Corps institutions.

He made an indelible mark on the Regiment as Colonel May's quartermaster in France. He was essentially broadminded and full of initiative in his methods of carrying out his duties. He was equally determined to carry through his schemes for helping others – in the orthodox way if practicable, if not, in some original way of his own. Jacko was somewhat inclined to ignore regulations, but only when they interfered with what he honestly thought was a better way of doing his job. He was never frightened by difficulties and had a wonderful way of overcoming them – making friends wherever he went. It seemed impossible to get to the bottom of his resources, and when no solution to one of his problems seemed apparent he would discover an extra resource, or a friend to help save the situation.

It is doubtful if any battalion in France was better fed or clothed than the Artists, or had better facilities provided for bedding, fires, washing, baths, drying clothes, washing underclothing, or other creature comforts generally. No drafts from England received a better welcome than the

46. The Artists Rifles VAD in the Great War.

47. Captain A.W. Byrne TD.

48. Lieutenant Colonel H.J. Shirley CMG, TD.

49. The King's Review 1913

50. Sidney 'George' Strube.

51. Lieutenant Colonel S.W. Neighbour OBE, TD.

52. Lieutenant Colonel W.H. Ramsbotham.

53. Colonel Harry Willans DSO, MC, TD.

54. Lieutenant Colonel R.R. Cripps TD.

55. Pony Moore.

56. Private R.E. Robotham and Lance Corporal C.S. Goulding, 'C' Company, winners of the 1937 Dodd and Cyclists Lewis Gun Trophy after completing in the LMG shoots that day.

57. 'C' Company, 163 OCTU, Shorncliffe barracks, 1939.

Artists; Jacko made sure they got a hot meal on arrival. It was not only the Artists that benefited from his constant energy. When the battalion was based at Bailleul, the remnants of the old Regular regiments would return to the town to receive new drafts, to refit and to reorganize before returning to the trenches. Hospital trains daily left Bailleul railway station crammed with sick and wounded. Jack Smith led the work of organizing parties of Artists to help the Tommies to find billets and supply their needs during their rest periods. He also arranged for the collection of grapes, which would have been otherwise wasted, from the large grape-houses in Bailleul. The bunches of grapes were placed in hampers and put aboard the hospital trains for the consumption of the afflicted men. When the hampers were returned to Bailleul, they were filled with newspapers, cigarettes, tobacco and chocolates which, with the agreement of Colonel May, were shared between the Artists and other battalions. In addition, he organized farewell dinners and concerts before the troops returned to the trenches.

At Christmas 1914 the Q store was inundated with sixty-two sacks of letters and parcels, including 1,000 briar pipes from 'Lloyds' – one for each of the Artists – and more cigarettes, tobacco, chocolates and other luxuries from relatives and friends in England than the Artists could possibly consume themselves. It was Jacko who organized the voluntary donation of these supplies for the use of the visiting Tommies and French soldiers. An ingenious feature of life at Bailleul was the construction of a bathhouse, the first of its kind on the Western Front, in which the whole of the battalion could get a bath twice a week in one day. Building the bathhouse was the work of Captain Neighbour, the assistant adjutant and an architect by profession, who rose to command the Regiment, (1925-29). Jacko issued invitations to other Regiments to use the bathhouse on the remaining days of the week. He it was who also made arrangements for the Artists' underclothing to be washed by French refugees under the supervision of nuns.

Captain Jack Smith was invalided home early in 1916 and after a spell of sick leave, worked at the Tower of London and elsewhere with the Ordnance Corps (but retained his Artists badge) until the end of the war. Afterwards as a result of the war his health broke down again. In 1922 he wrote to Colonel May: 'I am better, but am not the 'Jacko' you recollect. I go to bed at eight every night, and have only been to work in the City twice since 1919. His health got worse and he died on 14 November 1924, aged sixty-three, leaving a son and a daughter.

Captain S.W. Neighbour OBE TD joined the Corps in November 1898 serving in the old 'D' Company for five years before being commissioned as a second lieutenant. As described above he was an architect by profession. Early in 1914 he took over command of 'G' Company and on mobilization was appointed as assistant adjutant, rising to adjutant (August 1915 – June 1916). Thereafter he served in staff appointments at brigade, division and Third Army (including one with the New Zealand contingent). In 1917 he went to the 1/7th Middlesex as a company commander and was wounded at Arras in April. He returned to the Artists in 1918. Between January and September 1919 he was brigade major Dvina Force, North Russian Campaign and was awarded the Order of St Anne, Russia. He commanded 'A' Company when the Artists were re-constituted after the war.

Captain Alan Byrne joined the Corps in November 1900 and was shortly commissioned. He went to France with the 1st Battalion and was attached in May 1915 to the 1st East Lancs and wounded the following month. Returning to the 1st East Lancs after his discharge from hospital he became second in command and was again hit in August 1916. Captain Byrne devoted his long career with the Artists both before the Great War and after between the two World Wars to the School of Arms, in the annals of which his name is indelibly recorded. At Olympia he served as a judge and steward of the press box.

Major H. K. Eaton Ostle MC joined the Artists Corps in 1900 and was quickly commissioned. He went to France with the 1st Battalion and in 1915 became a company commander and then second in command. He spent 1916 in hospitals and in 1917 was appointed commanding officer of the 10th York and Lancs in which capacity he served until they were disbanded in 1918. He then went briefly as second in command to the 8th Somerset Light Infantry before being transferred to command the 2nd Artists at Gidea Park. Although he wanted to return to France he was turned down for any further active service by a medical board. In addition to being awarded the Military Cross during the war he was twice Mentioned in Despatches. He went on to serve with the Artists after the war as OC 'C' Company.

Captain Austin A. Tyer MVO, who was educated at Charterhouse and King's, Cambridge, joined the Artists in 1907 and went to France as an officer with the 1st Battalion in 1914. He was attached to the Special Brigade for the Battle of Loos, 1915 and went on to the RFA, 50th Brigade, 9th Division, in which he served until April 1919. He was awarded the Croix de Guerre and was three times Mentioned in Despatches. Returning to the Artists after the war he was appointed OC 'D' Company.

Of the artists who served as Artists in the Great War, their number is given prominence by the catalogue of the 'Exhibition of Paintings and

Etchings by Members of the Artists Rifles' mounted at a gallery in Leicester Square, January-February 1916, which appears in Chapter 11. There were no summer exhibitions at the Royal Academy during the war but many of the exhibitors later became distinguished ARAs and RAs. Biographical details of John and Paul Nash, A. Egerton Cooper, Charles J. Blomfield and Sidney Strube, the cartoonist, have already been given but another cartoonist worthy of mention is Alfred Leete. Leete, who hailed from the West Country, was a company clerk with the 2nd Battalion at Gidea Park. Self-taught as a cartoonist and illustrator, his most noteworthy work was the famous Kitchener recruiting poster, which is frequently imitated today for compelling advertising purposes. A contributor to *Punch*, he was often in demand by the Regiment after the war to illustrate dinner menus and memorabilia for other Regimental occasions. Fred Buchanan and Bert Thomas should also be mentioned as talented cartoonists who served at Gidea Park during the war.

Of the sculptors who commemorated the Great War with their work Charles Sargeant Jagger, who knew from his own experience the horror and suffering of war, made more war memorials than any other. He was born in 1885, the son of a pit manager at Kilnworth in Yorkshire. An apprenticeship as a silversmith with Mappin and Webb taught him attention to detail. He studied at Sheffield and the Royal College of Arts. In 1914 he was awarded the Rome Prize for study in Rome but gave this up to join the Artists Rifles and was posted to the 2nd Battalion. On 23 September 1915, as a second lieutenant with the Royal Worcesters, he sailed from Plymouth to the Mediterranean, landing at Suvla Bay as part of the Gallipoli expedition. He was wounded and evacuated to Malta. He returned to England in January 1916, was promoted lieutenant and eighteen months later was sent with the 2nd Battalion the Worcestershire Regiment to France, where he was wounded three times, once at the Battle of Arras in April 1918, after which he was awarded the Military Cross.

While he was convalescing the war came to an end. Naturally, Jagger wanted to return to sculpture as soon as possible. The British School in Rome gave him a year's grant in lieu of the scholarship he had been unable to take up in 1914, which then enabled him to complete for the Tate Gallery what he considered to be his finest work, 'No Man's Land'. Between 1921 and 1923, Jagger made six war memorials. Two, which he seems to have done reluctantly, show purely symbolic figures, but the others all represent soldiers: men like the miners among whom he grew up resolute, tough, suffering, enduring. Although he served in the trenches in France, it was the conditions at Suvla Bay that Jagger remembered with particular horror and which made him resolve to record his experiences in sculpture. He often spoke of his aim to 'show the Tommy as I knew him in the trenches'. He once wrote: 'Any emotional subject, teeming with drama and human tragedy, can only be expressed by grim realism controlled and directed by the artist.'

His work included the British War Memorial to Belgium, in Brussels, the Royal Artillery Memorial at Hyde Park Corner and the Great Western Railway War Memorial at Paddington station. But perhaps his most moving work, and one that seems to be undervalued, is a smaller one, the pair of bas-reliefs on the Tank Memorial at Louvreval in northern France. This stands beside the Cambrai-Bapaume Road and records the names of the men who died in the Battle of Cambrai (1917). When he was working on his memorials Jagger borrowed guns and uniforms from the Imperial War Museum to ensure accuracy. The detail is not obtrusive, it is subordinate to the overall design; but his work meant a great deal to those survivors of the war who saw and admired it. Charles Jagger was elected to the Royal Academy and twice won the gold medal of the Royal Society of British Sculptors, the first time for the Royal Artillery Memorial. He died in November 1934.

Edward Thomas was an established literary figure when at thirty-seven years of age he joined the Artists Rifles in the autumn of 1915. Born in London of Welsh parents in 1878, Philip Edward Thomas was educated at Battersea Grammar School, St Paul's School and Lincoln College, Oxford. From an early age he developed a passionate interest in all aspects of the countryside. As a boy he wandered across London's common land collecting botanical specimens and from teenage onwards spent endless hours studying the life of the natural world in the West Country and in Wales. He married young and moved to Kent, where he and his wife Helen raised a family; there were two daughters Myfanwy and Megan, and a son Mervyn. He supported the family by writing many volumes of prose, as well as newspaper and magazine articles, much of his work being topographical and biographical, including a biography of Richard Jefferies, the writer and naturalist (1909). In 1913 Edward Thomas was introduced by the poet Ralph Hodgson, who shared his interest in country matters, to Robert Frost, the New England poet, whose poetry was also devoted to nature and the countryside. Then living and working in England, Frost persuaded Thomas to try his hand as a poet. Thereafter, poems about the countryside flowed from his pen.

In 1915 Robert Frost returned with his family to America and Edward Thomas was sorely tempted to emigrate with his family to join the Frosts in New England. But with a war going on patriotism prevailed and after some consideration as to how best he could serve his country, he enlisted as a soldier with the Artists at Duke's Road. For a man of his age it was a big decision, more so as he had for some time suffered from ill health inclining towards neurosis, which might well have explained his vacillating income as an author, journalist and poet. As an expert on the countryside, Thomas was quickly picked out at Duke's Road as a map-reading instructor and he spent his early weeks in the Regiment teaching recruits on Hampstead Heath how to read maps.

Before the end of 1915 he was transferred to High Beech, Loughton, to the 2nd Battalion as a lance corporal and member of 'A' Company, later moving to Hut 15 at Hare Hall at Gidea Park. In 1916 he was appointed sergeant Map-Reading Instructor to 'D' Company. All the time he was in the Army Edward Thomas wrote his poetry on odd pieces of paper which he sent to Eleanor Farjeon, who was to become a well-known writer of stories, songs and verse for children, and with whom he had formed a close platonic relationship. Eleanor would give him advice on any revision she thought necessary, then type up his work and send it to publishers on his behalf.

As 1916 progressed Edward Thomas was uncertain as to whether or not he should apply for a commission, but he was eager to go to France and decided he would not do so without one. In August he was posted as Officer Cadet P.E. Thomas to the Royal Artillery School, Handel Street, London, WC, where he was at first inhibited by his lack of proficiency in mathematics. However, he studied hard, going for firing practice at the Royal Artillery Barracks at Trowbridge in Wiltshire. He was then posted still as a cadet to the Royal Garrison Artillery at Wanstow in Somerset. He spent his weekends at a house he had rented for his family and himself at High Beech and visiting his wide circle of friends. His son Mervyn was now also in the Army. Edward was commissioned as a second lieutenant in December 1916 in 244th Siege Battery, Royal Garrison Artillery, located at Lydd in Kent, the camp otherwise known as 'Tintown'. After a brief spell of firing practice at Codford, Salisbury, he volunteered to go with his Siege Battery to France, where he arrived in January 1917. In a letter to Eleanor Farjeon dated 11 January he mentions:

> We await orders to go up country. The place [un-named] is just a clearing house or junction and all there is to do (apart from completing our stores) is to go on route-marches. If we stay for more than a day or so, I am sure to meet somebody. Yesterday, I met an old Artist, whom I had known moderately well.

In the Battle of Arras, April 1917, he volunteered to act as a forward observation officer. On the last day of the battle when victory was in sight he was killed by the blast from a German shell that exploded close at hand while he was filling his clay pipe outside his lookout post. When his body was recovered there was no sign of wound marks on his corpse. In a letter to Helen after his death Franklin Lushington (Major Commanding, 244 Siege Battery RGA) said:

> You will have heard from Mr. Thorburn of the death of your husband. I asked him to write immediately we knew about it yesterday but delayed writing myself until the funeral, from which I have just returned.
>
> He was always the same quietly cheerful, and ready to do any job that was going. The day before his death we were rather heavily shelled and he had a very narrow shave. But he went about his work quite quietly and ordinarily as if nothing was happening. I wish I could convey to you the picture of him, a picture we had all learned to love of the old clay pipe, gum boots, oilskin coat and steel helmet ... His was the gallant death of a very true gallant gentleman.

He was buried in a little military cemetery a few hundred yards from the battery site on the Arras sector.

Wrongly labelled a 'war poet', Edward Thomas unlike Wilfred Owen and Siegfried Sassoon did not write poetry about the terror of the trenches but he did manage to capture the mood of the war in poems like *Lights Out, The Trumpet, As the Team's Top-Brass* and *Rain* without mentioning the trenches. His subjects were the soldiers' thoughts, images of home and the emotions of men at war, reverberating in the minds, not on the battlefield itself.

Apart from Wilfred Owen and Edward Thomas there were other poets and writers who enlisted in the Artists Rifles in the Great War. Joining in 1916 (John) Edgell Rickwood was awarded the Military Cross in 1918 while serving in France as an officer with the 5/Royal Berkshire Regiment. Many of his poems were published in periodicals in the 1920s. See *Collected Poems* (1947), *Up the Line to Death – The War Poets* (1964) and *Edgell Rickwood, A Poet at War* (1969).

Martin Donisthorpe Armstrong, poet, novelist and biographer, was educated at Charterhouse and Pembroke College, Cambridge. He joined the Artists in September 1914 and in August 1915 went as a lieutenant to the 8/Middlesex serving in France until 1919. His first collection of poems was published in 1912. See also *The Buzzards and Other Poems* (1921). Armstrong was associate literary editor of *The Spectator*, 1922-4.

Cyril Herbert Emmanuel Bretherton, who also wrote under the nom de plume ALGOL, enlisted with the Artists in February 1916 and was commissioned in the RAOC as a lieutenant in 1917. A writer of light and humorous verse, Mr. Punch wrote 'long ago as 1903 he began writing for Mr. Punch.' Bretherton had a deep knowledge of politics and history. He was for many years on the staff of *The Morning Post* (eventually as 'Peter Simple') and leader-writer of the *Evening News*. His poems were published in 1945 by his son Paul. See also *In Winter, In Innocent Merriment: An Anthology of Light Verse*, compiled by Franklin P. Adams (c.1942).

Edward Shanks (Richard Buxton), poet and biographer, joined the 2nd Battalion in September 1914 and in December was commissioned in the 8/South Lancs serving in France. He was invalided home in 1915 and worked in the War Office for the rest of the war. Educated at the Merchant Taylors and Trinity College, Cambridge, where he was senior scholar in history and editor of *Granta*; he graduated as BA in 1913. He was the first winner of the Hawthornden Prize for Poetry (1919), lecturer in poetry at the University of Liverpool (1926) and a journalist on the *Evening Standard* (1928-35). His publications include *76 Poems* (1916), *Poems 1912-32* (1933), *Collected Poems 1909-1925* (1926) and *The Man from Flanders and Other Poems* (1950). We quote here his poem *Drilling in Russell Square* from *Collected Poems 1909-1925* (1926):

> 'The withered leaves that drift in Russell Square
> Will turn to mud and dust and moulder there.
> And we shall moulder in the plains of France
> Before these leaves have ceased from their last dance.'

Rugby football was seen as an important part of the training of the 2nd Battalion at Gidea Park. In the 1914-15 season matches were played against the mighty New Zealanders (New Zealand Expeditionary Force), the HAC and other London District units, London hospitals and various public schools. In March 1915 the Artists played their first match against St Bartholomew's Hospital and won 10:0. The team had taken part in a ten-mile march before the game was played at St Paul's School, Wormwood Scrubs. In the same month the 2nd Artists lost 34:3 to the 3rd HAC.

The game was played at Richmond where a charge was made at the gate with the proceeds going to the Prince of Wales' National Relief Fund and the Richmond Emergency Fund. In April 1915 the Artists beat the Sportsman's Battalion 20:6, the Bank of England 3:0 and Whitgiftians 3:0. At all rugby fixtures notices were posted inviting 'professional men whether or not they want commissions to become members' of the Artists Rifles. The Artists wore narrow, horizontal, striped shirts or plain white shirts.

There was a series of four games at the end of December 1915 and in January 1916 for the 2nd Battalion against public schools XVs. There were 500 spectators and the Artists' band at the first match, which the Artists won 23:3. The Artists also won the three other fixtures 9:6, 26:6 and 17:3. In February 1916 they lost against Guy's Hospital 15:6 and then took on the New Zealanders. This match was played at the Queen's Club, West Kensington, and 3,000 spectators watched the game. A collection was made on behalf of the Red Cross Fund. The All Blacks, all of whom had fought at Gallipoli, turned out in their famous black jerseys adorned with the silver fern inscribed NZEF. In a close-fought game the New Zealanders won 11:0. At the end of the 1915-16 season the Artists beat Christ's Hospital 22:0.

The 1st Battalion during the 1916-17 season played both Rugby Union and Association Football games in France but the locations and sometimes the names of the opponents were censored. The first rugger match was played against the Army School which the Artists lost 15:6. Tries for the Artists were scored by Lieutenant John Scrutton and Sergeant Jeffries. Lieutenant Carter captained the side. There were three Scrutton brothers, two of whom, John and Alan, both served in the Artists Rifles. Alan followed his brother John into the Regiment in 1909 and during the Somme Campaign in 1916 was ADC to Generals Kiggell and Haig. Although Haig tried to persuade Alan Scrutton against it, he went into the Tank Corps and was awarded the Military Cross.

The 2nd Battalion results for the season 1916-17 were:

Played	24
Won	22
Lost	2
Drawn	0
Points for	405
Points against	139

The only defeats were against the New Zealanders (NZEF) again 18:5, played at the NZ camp at Hornchurch and a public schools XV 19:6. Fixtures included St Bartholomew's, St Thomas's and Guy's hospitals, and various public schools including Tonbridge, Radley College, Christ's Hospital, King's School, Wimbledon, and other units, including the Royal Engineers ASC, the Canadians and Inns of Court OTC. The *Illustrated Sporting and Dramatic News* of 11 March 1917 included a two-page illustrated article on the 2nd Battalion Artists Rifles 1916-17 rugby season. The introduction reported that the 'powers-that-be' in command of the Artists Rifles OTC 'have recognized to the full the value of games as a training for war. Amongst players today there is a saying that "insane bravery" is the norm – anything less than that is too despicable to mention.'

The team captain was CSM G. F. Grundy of the Customs Sports Club and a Surrey County Player. Private T. Williams, who played for Swansea, had won six caps for Wales in 1912-14 in the Welsh 'Terrible 8' but played in several positions for the Artists. Lance Corporal Ivor Walters and Private R. Williams had both played for the Dunvant Club near Swansea. R. Williams captained Swansea 2nd XV and played two seasons for Swansea 1st XV. Ivor Walters was a leading tenor in the Royal Choral Society at the Royal Albert Hall Ballad Concerts. Lance Corporal A. L. Venables, on the right wing, played for Sale and Cheshire; he was described as 'fairly fast, a strong runner and fearless tackler'. Second Lieutenant H.K. Evans had played for Bristol; he was an 'extremely dangerous player with his short legs and gallop'. Cadet A. N. Widdop, on the left wing, had played for Lancashire in 1911-12 he was 'a fast, straight-running wing, and a very strong tackler.' Mention has already been made of Colour Sergeant Greenwood, who joined the 1st Battalion in 1914 and was commissioned in the East Surrey Regiment, before transferring to the Grenadier Guards. Greenwood played rugby for Cambridge in the University match five times, being captain of the side in 1912 and 1919. He played for England thirteen times, captaining the team in all the international matches in 1920. He was president of the Rugby Union and a senior trustee of the RFU, 1935-39.

Cricket was not as well reported as rugby in the Great War, but we do know that the Artists' star performer on the cricket field was the Oxford Blue and Surrey County batsman (who played for England after the war), D. J. ('Dolly') Knight. Apart from 'Dolly', notable Artists players included C.C. Page (Cambridge and Middlesex), C.T.A. Wilkinson (Cambridge and Surrey), C.D. MacIver, J.N. Thorpe and G.L. Hebden. The captain of the 1916 team was Lieutenant Lubbock. The first match took place in August 1916 against the Scots Guards at the Oval, the Artists winning by an innings and 120 runs. Three matches were played against public school XIs at the Oval, one against Hampstead, one against Eastbourne at Eastbourne, one against the Guards' Depot at Caterham, one against a reserve battalion of the Rifle Brigade at Winchester and one against the Grenadier Guards at the Oval. The Artists won all but two of these matches. D.J. Knight was the leading batsman, scoring 1,474 runs (highest innings 203), average 67. Somewhere in France the 1st Battalion played four matches versus the HAC, Royal Engineers (twice) and an Army School of Instruction, winning all of them. There is no record available of cricket matches played in 1917 and 1918, either in England or France. Several Artists competed in the Olympic Games in London (1908), Stockholm (1912) and Antwerp (1920). In 1908 BSIM A.C. Murray and Lieutenant A.V. Keene were representatives for the United Kingdom in Sabres. In 1912 Colour Sergeant W. Hammond and Captain A.V. Keene were selected for the Individual Sabre Competitions at Stockholm and Hammond was again in the British Sabre team at Antwerp. As a fencer Bill Hammond took part in International Fencing Tournaments at Ostend in 1911 and at Earl's Court in London in 1913. The spotlight was on Hammond again, as captain of the British Sabre team in their match against America (in America) in 1921 and again against America (in Great Britain) in 1922. Jack Beresford, Jr., a champion oarsman, participated in the Antwerp Olympics and went on to represent Great Britain in a record number of four Olympiads. He rowed in Paris (1924), Amsterdam (1928), Los Angeles (1932) and at the Kiel Regatta during the Berlin Olympics of 1936 when he was nearly forty years of age. At Kiel he was bow in the double skulls winning after a gruelling race. Moreover, Beresford won the Diamonds at Henley in three consecutive years, and the amateur championship seven times.

In the world of entertainment, the smoking concerts, which dated from the earliest days of the Artists Rifles at Duke's Road, played an important role in the social activities of the 1st and 2nd Battalions. An orchestra and choir were also formed at Gidea Park, many of its members being recruited from the Royal College of Music, both staff and students. The concert parties revelled in names like 'The Star Shells' and 'The Artistics'. A star performer at Gidea Park was Sergeant (later CSM) Clay-Thomas, a professional baritone, who performed during the course of a long career as a singer on the stage and in concert halls in London and in the provinces. (The present writer vividly remembers the Christmas Candlelight concerts Clay organized for the Artists Rifles Association in the 1950s at Duke's Road.) He was also the 2nd Battalion's champion swimmer performing in events taken most seriously by the battalion at Romford Baths. Another regular and talented performer at Duke's Road and Gidea Park was Sergeant H.J. ('erb) Collings, a professional prestidigitator, who actually founded 'The Magic Circle'. He was also an excellent compère.

In 1918 a full-scale concert was mounted by the Artists at the Alhambra Theatre in London's West End, raising £700 for the Soldiers Free Buffet at Charing Cross. The performers included Nelson Keys, Carrie Tubbs, Marie Löhr and Lilian Braithwaite. Clay-Thomas sang an aria from *Pagliacci* and 'erb Collings performed his conjuring tricks. Another Artist who played at the Alhambra on this occasion was Thomas C. Sterndale-Bennett, gazetted in the Royal Flying Corps in

1917. Sterndale-Bennett was a composer and entertainer, who twice toured the world with concert parties before the Great War. He published over 300 popular songs. Another concert also took place in 1918, funded by the United Arts Rifles – the breakaway Artists group based at the Royal Academy. The show was put on at the New Theatre (now the Albery) in St Martin's Lane in aid of the 1st Battalion's Comforts Fund. Again a star-studded cast freely gave their services in the cause of charity and the evening was a great success.

There were a number of Artists serving in the Great War who later became well-known and indeed rich and famous for their work in the theatre and cinema. Pride of place at the top of the list of this select band of celebrities must go to the playwright, novelist and film script writer R. C. Sherriff (1896-1975). Until Robert Sherriff wrote his play *Journey's End*, apart from the poetry of Wilfred Owen, Siegfried Sassoon and Robert Graves, no British writer had tackled the monstrous theme of the Great War. *Journey's End* had a shattering impact on the theatre-going public. As well as reminding its survivors of the horrors of the war, the play served to introduce the four years of conflict to a new generation too young to have experienced it. Born in the London area, Sherriff was educated at Kingston Grammar School and New College, Oxford. A keen oarsman, while at Oxford he had every prospect of getting a Blue but volunteered to join the Artists Rifles in 1916. Commissioned the same year into the East Surrey Regiment, he was wounded in France in 1917.

After the war Sherriff worked as an insurance assessor and the only writing he did in the early 1920s were a few light entertainments for his rowing club, Kingston. In fact when *Journey's End* was first produced at the Savoy Theatre in London in 1929, he considered its success to be a bit of a fluke. The play was first produced on a Sunday evening by The Stage Society in 1928 and was transferred to the West End by Maurice Browne, the actor and dramatist, who had taken over the management of the Savoy Theatre earlier in 1929. Set in a company commander's command post in the trenches at the start of Ludendorff's great offensive in March 1918, the play deals with the inter-relationships of the company officers and the broader aspects of the war. The part of Lieutenant Raleigh was played by Maurice Browne and that of Captain Stanhope, the company commander, who, after three years in the trenches, was on the verge of a breakdown, by Laurence Olivier; also in the all-male cast were Robert Speaight and Jack Hawkins. The play ends with the destruction of the command post and the death of all its occupants in the initial German bombardment.

Journey's End opened in New York in 1929 enjoying great acclaim and Hollywood made a film of it starring Colin Clive, which was released in 1930. The play has since been seen (in English and in translation) in theatres throughout the world and has been revived on the West End stage on several occasions since the Second World War, as well as being played frequently in repertory theatres throughout the country. Robert Sherriff went on as a playwright to write *Badger's Green*, a story of village cricket (1930); *St Helena*, about Napoleon's last years (1935); *Miss Mabel* starring Mary Jerrold (1948); *Home at Seven* (1950) and *The Long Sunset* (1955), the latter two plays both starring Ralph Richardson. He published his autobiography, *No Leading Lady*, in 1968. As a film script writer he wrote the screen plays for *The Invisible Man* (1933); *Goodbye Mr Chips* (1939); *Lady Hamilton* (1941); *Odd Man Out* (1947); *Quartet* (1948); *No Highway* (1950) and *The Dam Busters* (1955). A staunch supporter of ARRA and ARA reunions, he wrote a short story entitled *A Ghost of Vimy Ridge*, which appeared in a *Mars and Minerva* issue in 1970.

Clive Brook (1887-1974), the British leading man of stage and screen for over forty years, was more often than not seen as the perfect gentleman, although very occasionally he risked his reputation in social circles by playing caddish parts. He joined the Artists Rifles in 1914, was commissioned in the Machine Gun Corps, was wounded, shell-shocked and invalided out of the Army as a major in 1917. Clive Brook began his stage career in 1919 and first acted in British silent movies in 1920. In 1924 he went to America as yet still in the era of silent films, making his first appearances in talkies in 1929, in *Interference, A Dangerous Woman* and *The Four Feathers*. He was one of the first actors to introduce the English accent to American films. At one time between his arrival in Hollywood and the mid-1930s he was reported to be the world's highest paid actor. He made over 100 films, among them *Shanghai Express* with Marlene Dietrich (1932) and *Cavalcade* (1933). He abandoned Hollywood before the Second World War, returning to Britain to appear in such films as *Action for Slander* (1937) and *Convoy* (1940). He was also seen again on the West End stage and after the war on TV. In 1933 he was quoted as saying, 'Hollywood is a chain gang and we lose the will to escape. The links of the chain are forged not with cruelties but with luxuries.'

Another well-known actor who joined the Artists Rifles in 1914 was Wilfrid Lawson, a character actor, who will be remembered for playing eccentric parts and for his gravelly voice. Unfortunately there does not appear to be an extant record of his service with the Artists. On stage since 1916, he played a variety of parts, including Shakespearean roles and starting in 1931, appeared in fifty films, the best-known being *Pygmalion* (1938); *The Farmer's Wife* (1941), *Fanny by Gaslight* (1944) and *Room at the Top* (1959).

On the humorous side the Artists Rifles could boast a comic actor of the calibre of Eric Blore (1887-1959), who served in the Regiment in 1915-16. Born in London, he began his career as an insurance agent but was on the stage from 1908. He went to Hollywood where from 1931 until 1954 he appeared in ninety films. He was usually seen as the unctuous and insulting English butler, whose by-line was 'If you will excuse the liberty, Sir'. His films included *Flying Down to Reno* (1933), *The Gay Divorcee* (1934), *Top Hat* (with Fred Astaire and Ginger Rogers) (1935) and *Piccadilly Jim* (1936). He did return home from time to time to appear in British films usually as a butler.

Another actor who served with the 1st Battalion in France was Arthur Margetson (1897-1951). A former stockbroker's clerk, he went on the stage after the war, and in 1937 he played with Clive Brook in the film *Action for Slander*. In 1940 he went to Hollywood playing supporting roles. His films included *Random Harvest* (1943) and *Sherlock Holmes Faces Death* (1944). Yet another actor who served as an Artist during the war was Reginald Denny (1891-1967). Denny had been on the stage since childhood and in 1919 went to Hollywood where he played in action films and comedies. When sound came he took to playing amiable, stiff upper lip Britishers. His talkies included *Private Lives* (1932), *Of Human Bondage* (1934), several Bulldog Drummond films (as Algy) (1937-8), *Rebecca* (1940), and *Around the World in Eighty Days* (1956).

A familiar figure in the 1st Battalion was Captain L.G. Abbott Anderson MBE, who acted in the name of Louis Goodrich. He frequently appeared on the West End stage after the war, and was particularly complimented for his performance in *Clive of India* at the Savoy Theatre.

The thespian contribution to the Artists Rifles ends however on a slightly unhappy note. The young Noel Coward, who enlisted in the Corps in January 1918, when posted to Gidea Park had a habit of falling off his bicycle. After eight months service he was diagnosed as suffering from neurasthenia and discharged. After the war the ARRA watched Noel Coward's progress in the theatre with keen interest obviously proud to have once, if briefly, owned him. The outstanding personality certainly in the theatre of the last century thus enjoys an important place in the annals of the Artists Rifles!

Note
1. A full history of the *Daily Telegraph* Cup competition is given in Chapter 15

Chapter 15

Between the Wars

1919-1929

It is far easier to make war than peace.
                                    Georges Clemenceau, 18 July 1919

On 24 May 1919, the 1st Battalion arrived home from France and the Artists Rifles as a regiment was demobilized. There followed a brief period during which although the Artists Rifles Regimental Association remained in place the 28th Battalion London Regiment (Artists Rifles) as a military unit ceased to exist. Of prime concern to the ARRA was the resettlement of its officers and men returning to civilian life. Indeed the association had been first founded at Gidea Park in 1916 with this main objective. However, on demobilization the work of finding post-war employment for Artists' veterans, if assistance was required, was taken over by the Ministry of Labour (Appointments Department), Artists Rifles Adjutancy, whose temporary address was 90 Queen's Gate, London, SW7. (The office was later moved to Earl's Court.) The department was set up to help ex-officers, warrant officers, NCOs and men with professional and business qualifications to find suitable employment. The scheme also dealt with officers and men who were in Category ll (unfit G.S. 3 months), who desired training during their period of unfitness as would enable them to obtain lucrative appointments. The Adjutancy for the Artists Rifles was administered by Captain C.E. Newton.

The Artists Memorial Service for the fallen took place at St Pancras Church on Saturday 31 May 1919. The church located only a few paces away from the Regimental HQ in Duke's Road is one of the largest in London but it was packed to capacity on this sad and moving occasion. Women in black formed by far the larger part of the congregation, which also included khaki-clad men who had returned from France and other theatres of war. Before the service began, Major Higham, who had often played the organ in the church before, with the aid of a small Regimental orchestra, gave beautiful renderings of Mendelssohn's *Adagio*, Arthur Somervell's elegy *Killed in Action*, and other music by Beethoven, Tchaikovsky and Handel. Major Higham was also assisted by a hastily improvised choir, which included such well-known singers from the Regiment as Glyn Walters, Tom Kinniburgh, Falkner Lee and Stanley Newman.

The service was conducted by the Bishop of London, assisted by the Revd. G. L. Metcalfe, vicar of St Pancras, and the Artists' own VC padre, the Revd. E. Noel Mellish. After *For All the Saints* came the sentences that begin the burial service and the 23rd Psalm. The lesson (Wisdom iii, 1-9) was read by Colonel May. 'Let us remember with thanksgiving and with all honour before God and men,' said the vicar, 'the officers and men who have been enrolled in or attached to the Artists Rifles, who have died giving their lives in the service of their country'. The whole congregation then knelt in silence for several minutes, probably the most sacred moment of the afternoon. And then there was another hymn and the special prayers.

The Bishop of London took for his text Matthew vi, 21, 'For where your treasure is, there will your heart be also'. Before his sermon he gave a short history of the Corps, alluding to a speech by the Prince of Wales at the Guildhall a few days before, in which His Royal Highness had congratulated London on its Territorials and their achievements in the war. The Bishop also made special mention of his connection with the Corps and of the service he had conducted for the Artists in France on Good Friday, 1915. He had with him in the pulpit the stick which Colonel May had cut down from a tree and presented him with on behalf of the 1st Battalion at Bailleul to commemorate the occasion of the service. In an eloquent address his Lordship spoke of that most glorious of all causes, for which the fallen Artists had laid down their lives. The last hymn with Watts' wonderful words, which seem so fully in accord with any service, *O God our help in ages past* was followed by the bishop's benediction, and then it was all standing for *The Last Post*. The service ended on a new note of hope for the future with the sounding of reveille, far away in the gallery, and the National Anthem. Some 1,500 people were present, including Colonels Edis and Horsley.

The Victory March through London took place on Saturday 5 July 1919. The Artists contingent, quite small when compared with many of the other units taking part, was led by Major Edlemann, and included Captain Barnett, adjutant, Captain Hewitt, standard bearer, Captain Coleman, Lieutenant Silcock and twenty-eight 'old boy' officers, who wore the cap badges of the regiments into which they had been commissioned, thirty-three Artists' other ranks and thirty-six drums led by Sergeant Drummer Caslake. The Artists assembled at 10 a.m. opposite the Royal Chelsea Hospital around a banner bearing simply the one word 'Artists'. The march commenced at 0000 precisely and reached His Majesty King George V's saluting base at the scheduled time. Marching in double columns of four, the parade went past Buckingham Palace, up the Mall, through Admiralty Arch, Trafalgar Square, the Strand, Fleet Street and into the City, where another salute was given this time by the Lord Mayor in uniform. Then on to the Tower of London, the scene of the Artists' 'London Duties' in 1914, and the welcome order to dismiss.

The London crowd was justly in a celebratory mood but the loudest cheers came from the London County Council schoolchildren on Constitution Hill, and those who recognized the Artists en route also gave them rousing cheers. The Artists had every reason to be proud of Sergeant Drummer Caslake and his drummers, who were easily the finest on parade. There had been no rain during the day and it was quite hot when the Artists reached their dispersal point in Fenchurch Street, where Major Edlemann dismissed them appropriately outside the London Tavern. The original plan to fall out at Duke's Road was cancelled, but most of the marchers went on to the club at 17 Craven Street where they had a party of their own. Colonels Edis and May were entertained at Buckingham Palace.

Earlier in 1919 (on 22 January) a very large number of past and present Artists met at the Drill Hall in Duke's Road to consider the advisability of establishing a fund whereby the services of the Artists who had fallen in the Great War would be suitably commemorated. At the meeting, chaired by the Honorary Colonel of the Regiment, Colonel Robert W. Edis CB,VD, it was resolved that:

> An Executive Committee be appointed to issue an appeal and collect subscriptions for a memorial to all past members of the Artists Rifles who had fallen in the Great War. Such memorial to take the form of a fund to assist past and present enrolled members who have been permanently disabled and are otherwise in need of financial assistance.
>
> Also to the erection of some suitable memorial in the Drill Hall or elsewhere as the Executive Committee may decide.

It was further resolved unanimously that the Committee to obtain and administer the funds should be composed of the following:

Col. Robert W. Edis, CB,VD	Capt. A.C. Goulder
Col. H.A.R. May, CB,VD	Capt. C.S. Peach

Col. W.C. Horsley, VD	Capt. J.E. Prentis
Lieut. Col. H.K. Eaton Ostle, MC	Capt. A.F. Royds
Lieut. Col. R.H. Goldthorp, DSO	Capt. R.F. Turnbull
Maj. T.D. Dudley-Cocke, OBE	Capt. W.G. West
Maj. H.E. Edlemann	Col-Sgt A.S. Drewry
Maj. S.S. Higham	A.G. Cowell, Esq.
Maj. A.J. Neame	G.F. Freund, Esq.
Capt. A.W. Byrne	M.S. Hack, Esq.

A meeting of the above Committee was held at headquarters on 27 January and the following were co-opted as additional members of the Committee -

Maj. Gen. C.F. Romer, CB, CMG, ADC	Capt. M.B. Hewitt
Sir Thomas Brock, RA	RSM Fox
Sir Arthur Cope, RA	CSM Bluhm
Sir J. Forbes-Robertson	CSM A.W. Clay-Thomas
Lieut.Col. S. Chatfeild-Clarke, VD	QMS F.J. Curzons
Lieut. Col. Herbert J. Shirley, CMG	CQMS K.S. Grant
Maj. L.H.M. Dick	CQMS S.H.H. Heppenstall
Maj. J.J Gover	CSM H.W. Bolingbroke
Capt. C.J. Blomfield	E.W. Boot Esq.
Capt. D.L. Davey, CF	Frederick Litchfield, Esq
Arthur Wagg, Esq.	

Colonel Edis consented to act as chairman; Colonel May was appointed deputy chairman; Captain A.F. Royds was appointed honorary secretary; Captain A.C. Goulder was appointed assistant honorary secretary and Majors T.D. Dudley-Cocke and H.E. Edlemann were appointed joint honorary treasurers.

In October 1919 a concert was organized at the Alhambra Theatre in aid of the Artists Rifles Memorial Fund, which had been extended to include the widows and orphans left by the Artists who had fallen in the War. Those taking part, including a number of the reigning stars of the West End stage and music halls and a strong contingent from the Regiment itself, all of whom gave freely of their services, were as follows:

Miss Katherine Arkandy	Mr George Grossmith
Miss Yvonne Arnaud	Mr Fred Grove
Miss Fay Compton	Mr Leslie Henson
Miss Phyllis Dare	Mr Tom Kinniburgh
Miss Gina Palerme	(Artists Rifles)

Miss Ivy Shilling
Miss Gladys Voyle
Mr Rex Burchell
   (Artists Rifles)

Mr H.J. Collings
   (Artists Rifles)
Mr Edgar Coyle
Mr C.V. France
Mr Walter Glynne
   (Artists Rifles)

Mr Fred Norton
Mr H. Ralph
   (Artists Rifles)
Mr Arnold Smith, Mus
Bac.Oxon (Artists Rifles)
Mr C.F. Smyly
   (Artists Rifles)
Mr T.C. Sterndale-Bennett
   (Artists Rifles)
Mr A.W. Clay-Thomas
   (Artists Rifles)

Colonel May, although still not entirely fit, had by the end of 1919 settled down again to his job as an attorney in his London office. On relinquishing his command of the Officers' School at Tidworth, and his responsibilities for the Australian officers' and Chaplains' courses, he had held the substantive rank of lieutenant colonel since 1903. At fifty-six he was four years older than the extreme limit that War Office regulations permitted an officer to hold that rank. He had found his business affairs in a state of disarray, but although it took a considerable amount of effort on his part to put matters right, he still harboured the hope that with the end of the war his military career was not at an end.

Then quite suddenly in 1920 he received an invitation from the War Office to 'resuscitate' the Artists as their commanding officer for a period which in any event was not to exceed twelve months. May was more than happy to take over the reins of CO again but at first he encountered certain difficulties in bringing the Regiment to life again. Although there was no shortage of members of the ARRA, there was no rampant mood among past members of the Regiment to shoulder arms once more. To make matters worse, Duke's Road headquarters had been very much run down, administration was in a mess and the building badly in need of refurbishment. With the help of his old adjutant, Captain R. Coleman, May started by sorting out a mass of papers. Captain Mansbridge at the County of London TF Association was instrumental in putting up money to help in the redecoration and the supply of new furniture and fittings, including kitchen equipment, for the premises. Above all, Colonel May used all his considerable powers of persuasion to encourage old members to sign on again and to attract new recruits to the Regiment.

The chief difficulty faced by Colonel May however was with regard to the kind of Corps that was to be re-created. The authorities were anxious to re-start the Artists as a Senior Officers' Training Corps, which May well knew, in spite of its spell as an OCTU during the war, was contrary to the views and traditions of the Regiment. The Artists were essentially an elite infantry battalion, in which future amateur officers were given a long and hard training as privates and NCOs before they were awarded their commissions. Colonel May, who placed emphasis on recruiting only the elite, had always seen the Artists as a public school battalion, and his recruiting campaign as launched in 1920 was directed at public schoolboys, especially those educated at the leading public schools. He placed posters in these schools and arranged for committees to be formed among the masters to encourage their scholars to join the Artists. The scheme did not always work to the Regiment's advantage however as many of the young men who went to work in London and who were armed with their Cert As from their OTCs, on learning that it might take seven years or more to get a commission in the Artists Rifles, joined other Territorial units in which commissions were readily obtainable. So far as the present writer can ascertain, the majority of recruits to the Artists Rifles, 1920-39, were in fact public schoolboys, although a significant number of grammar school boys were also enrolled, many of whom rendered distinguished service to the Regiment.

Fortunately for the Regiment the War Office accepted Colonel May's arguments for the reconstitution of the battalion and on 1 February 1921 Battalion Orders No. 1, 28th (County of London) Battalion, The London Regiment (Artists Rifles) was published at Duke's Road. Sir Robert Edis (he had been knighted after the war) was to continue as honorary colonel, but he resigned on 16 April and was succeeded in the post by Colonel Walter Horsley. Major H.J. Shirley, CMG, TD, was May's second in command and Captain J.C.H. Brunt (Duke of Cornwall's Light Infantry) his adjutant. The regimental sergeant major was to be RSM E. Walwyk, MM, Rifle Brigade, who was a champion shot. The first of the Battalion Orders was a lengthy document, in which Colonel May thanked the successive generations of Artists who since 1859 had contributed to the success of Artists, especially to those who had served in the Great War.

In the reconstruction, the eight companies which had been formed in 1914 to bring the Artists into line with other Territorial units, which actually took effect in September 1920, were to be reduced to four companies – 'A' and 'B' to form the new 'A', 'C' and 'D' to form the new 'B', 'E' and 'F' to form the new 'C' and 'G' and 'F' to form the new 'D' company. The traditions and customs of the 'old' companies were to be combined in the 'new' companies. The canteen, School of Arms, the officers' mess and the Drums and Fife Band were to be re-instated in their old form and the ARRA, ARRA Club, Regimental Journal, War Memorial Fund, Roll of Honour and other institutions created before, during and after the war were to continue with their work.

A new syllabus of training was decided upon. The conditions of service were to be the same as for any other battalion of the new Territorial Army (the TF had now been retitled the TA), which in effect were a) to attend drills, forty a year for recruits, ten for trained men; b) to shoot a musketry course; and c) to attend annual camp. Past members not exceeding thirty-eight years of age, who had served for not less than six months in the war and who enrolled before 31 July 1921, were allowed to join as trained men. All past members of whatever age could re-join as honorary members and would thereby incur no liability for military service whatever. The strength of the new battalion later in 1921 reached twenty-seven officers, twenty-three NCOs, one hundred and fifteen privates and fifty-two honorary members. The first annual camp was planned for Shorncliffe from 23 July to 6 August, which included the August Bank holiday.

On 16 February 1921 Colonel May's job was done and he was succeeded in command of the Regiment by Major H.J. Shirley, his second in command. Herbert Shirley's second in command was Major S.W. Neighbour, OBE, TD, and his adjutant Captain and Brevet Major W.H. Ramsbotham, West Yorkshire Regiment. Herbert Shirley had joined the Artists Corps in 1885 and commanded a battalion of the Lancashire Fusiliers in the Great War, then reverted to his civilian profession as a doctor, at the same time holding an appointment as a colonel in the RAMC. From his earliest days as an Artist Shirley showed unmistakable signs of the gift of leadership and was promoted to colour sergeant at an early age. His search for knowledge of the soldier's trade was as marked as his work among the intricacies of medical science. In those days before the South African War Shirley was one of a group of Artists who were attached to the Flying Column marching out of Aldershot for the annual Army manoeuvres. He always went with an array of soothing potions for both feet and stomach. His tent was daily surrounded by Tommies seeking treatment from Shirley, another ranker, in preference to seeing their own medical officers! In 1899 he was among the early volunteers for the South African War and went out on the medical staff of the Langman Hospital, which had been equipped at the expense of a rich American.

For his services in the war he was awarded the CMG. After his return from South Africa he was commissioned by the Artists and rose to command 'D', which at that time had the enviable reputation of being the best company in the Regiment, and he in turn was considered one of the best company commanders the Artists had ever produced. During his tour as commanding officer (1921-5), after a lot of hard work, Shirley took the battalion back to its pre-war strength. He was incidentally the brother of Colonel William Shirley who raised the 3rd Battalion and commanded the 2nd at Gidea Park.

The War Memorial Committee at first considered a statue to commemorate their dead but finally chose oak panels containing in gold painted letters the names of the 2,003 of their fallen comrades. The oak panels lined one of the walls of the Drill Hall at Duke's Road. They were unveiled on 12 July 1921 by Lord French and dedicated by the Bishop of London, both staunch friends of the Regiment. A guard of honour was present outside the Drill Hall to receive Lord French and inside, posted in front of the memorial, was a small guard who all had distinguished records as officers during the war, and after the war had re-enlisted as privates. (It was not unusual in the post-war years to see other ranks wearing officers' medals with their uniforms on parade.) When Lord French unveiled the memorial the guard presented arms and buglers sounded *The Last Post*. Colonel Shirley laid a wreath on behalf of the Regiment. The centre piece of the memorial read -

ARTISTS RIFLES
In memory of our comrades who gave
Their lives for their country, 1914-1919

On Sunday 24 July the Regiment entrained for its first post-war summer camp at Shorncliffe. The men were accommodated in huts and the officers in tents. Platoon and company drills were carried out in camp but range practice took place on several days in each week at Rainham. RSM Walwyk was pleased to report that all range tests had been successfully completed before camp ended on 6 August. There was a NAAFI and YMCA at Shorncliffe and leisure hours could also be spent in Folkestone.

Misfortune struck on the second Thursday when a gale blew down the officers' ante-room and YMCA tents and scattered most of the accommodation tents. In spite of this, all agreed that the camp had been a great success.

On 21October of that year Colonel Horsley, the honorary colonel, presided over the third post-war reunion dinner, attended by 400 guests at the Connaught Rooms. The opportunity was taken to make a presentation to Colonel May to mark his retirement after very nearly forty years with the Regiment. The actual presentation, which took the form of a silver casket, was made by Captain E. Paul Bennett, one of the Artists' eight VCs, who had won the award while serving as a lieutenant in the 2/Worcesters near Le Transloy, France, on 5 November 1916. The elaborately designed casket, which featured the Regimental badge, motto and CB decoration was executed in hand-wrought repoussé and chiselled silver, encasing wrought bronze. The inside was gilt. The inscription read:

> I was wrought by Alwyn Carr for his comrades of the Artists Rifles, and presented by them to Col. H.A.R. May, C.B., V.D., who earned and enjoyed the affection and high esteem of all who served with him, by his single-minded devotion to the Regiment and its welfare. Enrolled in 1882. Served in all ranks. Commanded in 1913 to 1921

The first edition of the *Regimental Roll of Honour* was published on 4 August 1915, one year after mobilization. It was chiefly a list of every Regular Infantry Regiment in the British Army (including four of the five Regiments of Foot Guards) and it showed to which regiments the upwards of 1,500 young men had been sent from the Artists Rifles as officers up to that date. The casualties and promotions were also noted against each officer's name, but there was no separate 'Roll of Honour' of the men killed; afterwards they appeared in later editions. It was then intended to bring out a new edition of this book as it developed each year, up to each succeeding 4 August in each year, and a new second edition was prepared and printed (up to 4 August 1916) but its publication and circulation were forbidden by the censor until after the termination of hostilities.

It was not, therefore, until 1922 that the third and final and much enlarged edition of the *Regimental Roll of Honour* was published. After a complete 'Roll of Honour' proper, listing in chronological order with dates and other particulars the 2,003 men of the Artists Rifles whose lives had been sacrificed in the Great War, the book continued with a complete list with citations of the VCs, DSOs, DSCs, MCs, DFCs, AFCs, DCMs, and MMs, holders of foreign decorations and those 'Mentioned in Despatches', amounting in all to 1,852 honours. There followed a full list, by regiment, of more than 10,000 Artists who were commissioned. This list demonstrated that officers had been sent from the Artists Rifles to every single regiment, including the Royal Artillery and support and service units, in the British Army – Regular, Territorial and New Army.

The book also contained the names of about 5,000 men who served and fought in the ranks of the Artists throughout the war and a list of past members who re-joined the Corps at the outbreak of war. There was in addition a very full preface setting out the work of the Regiment, 1914-19, and there was a comprehensive index listing the names of all the men who served. The book, which included many interesting illustrations, was the work of Major S.S. Higham, assisted by a small staff supervised by him. It was printed in London by Howlett & Son, 10 Frith Street, Soho Square, W.1., the head of which firm was the veteran Artists Transport-Sergeant and bayonet fighter, A.G. 'Sammy' Cowell.

The *Daily Telegraph* Cup competition had been a fixture in the Artists Rifles calendar since long before the Great War but when it resumed after the war years in 1922, the Regiment decided to make a special effort to train a squad that stood a chance of winning the cup. The competition was open to all units of the London District, both Territorial and Regular, which included each of the five regiments of Foot Guards. The *Daily Telegraph* Cup was offered annually to the squad of about platoon strength that earned the highest points for an 11-mile route march followed by deployment on the range and hitting their targets in the quickest time. Points were also awarded for marching and range discipline and turn-out. The course extended along good roads and bad from the Woking area to the range at the Guards Depot at Pirbright. Each man wore his khaki uniform with well-oiled boots, carried a full pack and personal equipment, was armed with rifle, bayonet and ammunition, and two Lewis machine guns were to be carried with each squad. Marching in column of fours, the time allowed for the march was two and three-quarter hours.

At the beginning of each year the Artists selected twenty-six men from the companies, who trained exclusively as a 'star squad'. Practice marches were made at weekends in the London area and in the suburbs and firing practice took place on the range at Pirbright and later when the club house was opened at Bisley. It was left to each man to get as fit as he could and special instruction was given by the medical experts on the care of the feet. Eleven teams were entered in 1922, four of which were Territorial and seven from the Brigade of Guards. The H.A.C. were the winners and the Artists came ninth. The following year they were seventh out of fifteen, and in 1924 seventh out of seventeen. In 1925 they went up to third, in 1926 to second, the leading TA team, the winners that year being the 1st Scots Guards. There was a lapse in 1927 (down to ninth); in 1928 the Artists were third; in 1929 they won the competition; in both 1931 and 1932 they were second to a Regular battalion. The *Daily Telegraph* Cup was thereafter phased out as it was no longer considered to be an appropriate exercise, infantry in future being lifted to the firing line in trucks. The high standard of training of the Artists *Daily Telegraph* squad had a significant effect on company training, which increased in efficiency as a result of it.

In 1922 the main camp was at Aldershot (Rushmoor), which took place during the last week of July and the first week of August. The camp was set up in a clearing on the top of a hill overlooking the Long

Valley. The brigade canteen tent was already in place and the advance party ate a good meal before accommodation tents for officers and men, marquees, and miscellaneous tools and equipment were installed. A busy programme was drawn up embracing company and platoon drill, night operations, route marches and sports. There was no requirement this year for the Annual Musketry Course and only one day was spent at the Caesar's Camp range, which was devoted to inter-company shooting matches. Aldershot town did not offer as many leisure activities as Folkestone had done the previous year, but in spite of the rain on the first week, Rushmoor was an enjoyable camp and the time was well spent.

There were no major developments in the Regimental story over the next two years, although inter-company rivalry in the musketry and sporting fields reigned. There were two rugby teams but the Artists met with only mixed success in this field. One significant development on the social side however was the rebirth of The Mars and Minerva Ball, which was resurrected after a long sleep. The Ball, which was organized by a committee headed by Captain Byrne, took place after the Christmas festivities were over in February 1923. Dinner for two was arranged at the Carlton, the Ball beginning at 9.30 p.m. on a Saturday night and continuing until midnight. A first-rate dance band was laid on and a revue and pageant provided extra entertainment for the guests. Light refreshments were dispensed at 11 p.m. with breakfast at midnight, buses being laid on to take the revellers home afterwards. The Mars and Minerva Ball was to be a popular annual event during the rest of the Artists' time as an active regiment.

Camp 1923 (29 July-12 August) took place at Sandling Camp, Hythe. There were strenuous parades and route marches during the first week and the Hythe School of Musketry gave an interesting demonstration of a platoon in action as a fire unit. In the second week there was a Brigade Field Day and a divisional inspection by Major General Sir William Thwaites, CB, CDG 47th (2nd London) Division. Leisure hours were spent in Folkestone and there were two splendid smoking concerts in camp. At the end of 1923 donations to The Artists Rifles War Memorial fund, the target for which was £20,000 had reached £12,311 1s 6d.

In 1924 Camp was again in Aldershot (Rushmoor) where the Corps took part in the 47th Division annual manoeuvres. Battalion and company parade grounds were adequate, while the Messing Tent, which was Captain Byrne's idea, was a triumph of organization. Hot and cold showers were provided as was for the first time a corporals' ante-room. The battalion arrived, as in 1922, on a wet afternoon during the last week of July, but this did not dampen spirits and everybody was full of beans and raring to go on the Monday morning. The first week as usual was spent on company training in areas which were near at hand, which meant that the men did not get much practice in road-marching. On Wednesday night there were company night-ops and on the following day was held the first annual Platoon Tactical Competition, which was won by a team from 'A' Company under Captain Hewitt and Sergeant Fox. On the Friday there was a Grand Benefit performance by the Aldershot Amalgamated Circus – quite a brilliant spectacle. After a run across the Long Valley on the Saturday, pay was followed in the evening by a first-rate smoking concert, attended by Major General Thwaites.

The second week starting on the Sunday saw the investiture by the divisional commander of several Artists with Territorial decorations and efficiency medals, the ceremony taking place after Church parade. On Tuesday the Artists first made the acquaintance of the Bedfordshire and Hertfordshire Regiment, a platoon of whom had arrived in camp to show how things were done in the Regular Army. The Artists watched them give a demonstration from the top of a hill, and after it was over they had to admit that they had some way to go to attain the Regulars' proficiency. On Wednesday the battalion was drenched by a cloudburst at Cove Common and within ten minutes there was a danger of the camp being flooded. The incumbents turned out in their bathing costumes to dig trenches to divert the course of the rivers running through the tents, and it was not until the rain had stopped and half-a-dozen tents had been rendered uninhabitable that matters returned to normal.

Tanks were on view on the Thursday morning, and all who saw them were impressed by their speed and climbing powers. After this demonstration 'A' Company led by Captain Harry Willans and the Beds and Herts Platoon put in a flank attack supported by four tanks across the Long Valley, and 'B' Company, who formed the enemy, had to retire hurriedly after putting up a stiff defence. The tanks were probably the Vickers Light Infantry or No. 1 Tank, which carried a crew of four and moved at 30 mph, a considerable advance on the three previous marques, whose maximum speeds were 6, 8 and 25 mph respectively. This exercise was followed in the afternoon by a demonstration attack by the Beds and Herts, who kept 'A' Company on the run for some time while the divisional train ran round and round in small circles – quite an independent stunt!

The last big event of the camp was an attack by a composite battalion at war strength, each company being found by one of the battalions serving in the camp. It was quite an impressive sight to see the battalion move off across the Long Valley with its transport, and it was also instructive in showing how a battalion looked when committed to the attack. The camp inevitably ended with a grand smoking concert, in which even the divisional commander took part. Items from 'Cum Marte Minerva' were very much in evidence and the revised version of 'Packing up your Limbers' was received with terrific applause and cries of 'author', which eventually brought Captain Harry Willans on to the platform, where he delighted the audience with one of his inimitable yarns, and so it was back to London to complete the training programme for the current year in November.

In 1925 Lieutenant Colonel H.J. Shirley, CMG, TD was succeeded in command of the Artists Rifles by his second in command, Major S.W. Neighbour, OBE, TD. Colonel Neighbour's second in command was Major W.H. Ramsbotham, West Yorkshire Regiment, and his adjutant Captain T.J.B. Webber, OBE, The Royal Marines. The title of the Corps (since 1924) had been changed from 28th Battalion London Regiment (Artists Rifles) to 28th London Regiment (Artists Rifles). Camp for 1925 was based on Swingate Camp, Guston, Dover. Unfortunately there does not appear to be an official record of the camp, although Colonel Neighbour was later to remark that in his opinion the Regiment was not provided with adequate training grounds this year. We are indebted therefore to Private X for a subjective view of Dover 1925, as revealed in 'Letters of a Recruit to his Uncle, Camp, 1925', from the Regimental Journal, 1925 -

> The Camp of my actual experience differed from that of my dreams (inspired by your descriptions [Private X's uncle was an 'Old Artist'] in two particulars – we did less work, and had better food than I was led to suppose from my recollections of your reminiscences of the Spartan Age). In fact, however, I suspect that conditions are much the same as when you fought in '64 you – old liar! Be that as it may, you can have no happier memories of the Grey Goose Shaft than those that I cherish of Dover in 1925. 'Omnia Gallia' observed the sage, 'in tres partes divisa est,' which may be interpreted roughly, as meaning, 'Camp is divided into three parts' – work, play and the business of existence (known to the ultra-militarist school as 'Interior Economy'.) From the view-point of a Recruit, each of those was eminently satisfactory, as I will try to explain.
>
> Our labours, as I have already remarked, were light and often amusing. In the opinion of the authorities, the business of the T.A. is to concentrate upon essentials, cutting out much that was once held to be all-important, and teaching a little about warfare as it may be expected to be. The result, looked at from the ranks, is excellent, for almost all the evolutions practiced appear to have some bearing upon preparations for actual war, and are, therefore, not devoid of interest, even to the partly uninitiated, whilst the

eclipse of the Drill Book – once regarded as a second Gospel, and still openly lamented by the survivors of the Bow and Arrow era – provokes no protest on the part of the modern student of arms. The bulk of our efforts was directed towards inculcating the understanding of the theory of the 'Attack' and I gather from gossip ('heard on the mahogany' as the old army saying goes – you see I am fast becoming militarized!) that our final exposition of this operation found favour with the critics.

On 4 May 1926 the country was paralysed for nine days by a general strike called for by the Trades Union Congress in support of the coal miners. It began following a TUC pledge in 1925 to back the miners in their dispute with the coal owners, if necessary by calling a general strike. Following the lockout of the miners on 30 April and a breakdown of negotiations with the Baldwin government over continuation of a subsidy to the mining industry, the TUC called the General Strike on 4 May. The first workers called out were in transport, construction, printing, and iron and steel, with an almost 100 per cent response. The government, however, was well prepared. Declaring the strike unconstitutional, it utilized plans for the emergency movement of supplies and mobilized middle-class volunteers to maintain skeleton services, which included forming the Civil Constabulary Reserve, of which Company No. 1 was enrolled at Duke's Road.

The first job for the volunteers was to fill palliasses with straw so that they could bed down on the floor of the Drill Hall. As the cafés nearby were on strike they had to rely on the canteen but food and beer supplies were soon exhausted. Among the volunteers at Duke's Road was a bizarre group of men who were not actually members of the Regiment but who considered the Artists would be a good mob to join – 'for the duration'. A move was made to the University College Hospital where the volunteers were billeted in comfortable beds, well fed and cared for by hospital staff. The whole of the battalion's motor transport was assembled and based at Olympia to lift supplies as needed. It cannot be said that the reservists were overworked during the General Strike and some even regarded it as a holiday. The TUC surrendered on 12 May without obtaining any worthwhile concessions for the miners. The miners, under their leader, A.J. Cook, refused to compromise and remained out on strike until forced to return to work in November.

Colonel Neighbour, who joined the Corps in 1898 – his biographical details and war record are given in Chapter 14 – will be chiefly remembered for his work as the architect, assisted by a Mr Bax (also a member of the Regiment), who designed and built the clubhouse at Bisley. In

1924 it was decided that club facilities at Bisley, providing accommodation and meals and a well-stocked bar would attract members to spend the weekend there and thus stimulate an interest in musketry. The Bisley Hut, which was opened on 29 May 1926 by Mrs Horsley, wife of the honorary colonel, was built at a cost of £1,850 which was raised by members of the Regiment. Standing near the south-eastern end of Club Row next to the HAC Hut, the Artists' Hut followed the established Bisley theme with dormer windows set into a large tiled roof. At the front two large bay windows sat under the roof and flanked the entrance doors. The small areas of wall under the roof were mainly clad with dark timber boarding with a little face brickwork, which faced on to Club Row. On the ground floor the space between two wings was occupied by a dining hall, and there was a lounge, bar, kitchen, officers' room, a small armoury and blanket and kit stores. The attic contained the caretaker's quarters and dormitory-style sleeping accommodation.

In front of the Artists' Hut, the Club Row site was once appropriately named the Bazaar Lines. A gun and allied trades fair was once an annual feature of the camp, the equivalent of the present-day American gun show. The tradesmen erected their marquees in two lines to form a street running from the corner of the old National Association offices (Sutton's) to the later gap between the Artists' Hut and the British Commonwealth Club. The line was later marked by an avenue of trees and is still an important route for shooters passing to and from the Century Range. The Bazaar Lines appeared not unlike the trade show of the later Game Fair pre-dating the successful trade tents of the National Pistol Association. At the time of writing the Artists' Hut is no longer the property of the Artists Rifles Association, but the Bisley Hut has been preserved in the name of the Artists Rifle Club, which is independently run under private management. Visitors to the clubhouse today will find an interesting archive of Artists' memorabilia.

Camp 1926 was spent at Ovingdean, Brighton, but there do not appear to be any reminiscences of camp activities on record. In 1927 the Regiment went for annual camp to Middlewick, Colchester. Again no individual memories have survived and, in the absence of news of the progress of Private X, we give a brief report by Colonel Neighbour.

CAMP

Training must be judged by results, and the culmination of our year's training is Camp. This year (possibly because the areas, though cramped, were more suitable for the training of small units than those at Brighton or Dover the work in the field showed marked improvement on last year. The section leading was better, and movement was quicker and more decided. There is still, however, much to be learned. Too much attention cannot be paid to getting the elementary part of Field training – the movement and control of the section – absolutely right in the early stages, otherwise training will be hampered all through. The Platoon, Tactical Competition forms a useful part of the year's training, because of the work put in by the Companies preparing for it, the opportunity it affords of testing the degree of progress achieved, and the lessons to be learned from the comparison of the methods adopted by the various platoons in dealing with the situations encountered. The Competition this year was designed to test the work of the whole platoon, giving the weight to that of the subordinate commanders and of the men themselves. Looked at from that point of view it can be regarded as one of the most successful and instructive that we have had. One platoon was very unlucky in having to work in heavy rain, but it came through satisfactorily, the interest and keenness being well maintained.

Work began in 1927 under the supervision of Colonel Neighbour on extending the facilities at Duke's Road for training, administration and recreation. A scheme was approved which by adding a storey to the Drill Hall would give the Regiment a new Drill Hall, the same size as the existing one, but raised to the level of the gallery, and underneath at the lower level where the old Drill Hall had been there was room to build a miniature range, five company offices, a lecture room and a harness room. A stairway was built from the canteen at first floor level to the new sergeants' mess which was in the attic.

In 1927 RSM E. Van Walwyk, MBE, MM, was promoted lieutenant and quartermaster. During 1927 the honorary members were formed into the 'Veterans' Company'. Designed to strengthen the social side of the Regiment, it was in no sense a military organization, except in so far as matters affecting it would be subject to the approval of the commanding officer of the serving battalion. Its commandant was Colonel Walter C. Horsley, VD, JP and assistant commandant Colonel H.A.R. May, CB VD.

Summer camp in 1928 took place in the Aldershot area from 29 July to 12 August but again there is no record of camp events. In February 1929 Colonel Neighbour was succeeded in command of the Regiment by Lieutenant Colonel W.H. Ramsbotham from the Reserve of Officers. His second in command was Major W. Campbell Smith, MC, and his adjutant Captain T.J.B. Bosville,MC, (Rifle Brigade), who had taken over from Captain Webber in 1927. Colonel Ramsbotham, as a Regular officer was the first non-Artist to command the Regiment, but having first joined as adjutant in 1923, he was thoroughly conversant with

Regimental traditions. He was educated at Uppingham (where he was head of games) and Clare College, Cambridge. Commissioned in 1912 in the West Yorkshire Regiment, he served in France and Germany during and after the Great War. Ramsbotham was a talented cricketer, playing for the Free Foresters, Cambridge and Sussex. In the words of the long-serving Artist P.L. Leigh-Breese: 'In my view he was the best Adjutant we ever had and one of the best COs later.' Summer camp 1929 (again unrecorded) took place at Seaford (East Blatchington).

The Artists in the 1920s, it should be mentioned, were once more back in the 'Grey Brigade', consisting of the Kensingtons, the London Scottish, the Queen's Westminsters and the Artists. (Before the war there had been two more battalions – the Inns of Court and the Civil Service Rifles. The Inns of Court became an OTC and the Civil Service Rifles were amalgamated with the Queen's Westminsters.) The Grey Brigade was now officially mustered as 140th Brigade of 47th (2nd London) Division. The Easter and Summer camps were the main out-of-town events of the year, Easter camps being held from 1922-26 with the Royal Marines, thus keeping up the association formed during the war when the Artists were serving in the Royal Naval Division.

Extra-military pursuits also grew in strength during the 1920s, notably, of course, the School of Arms and the Assault-at-Arms, which burgeoned from the mere display of skill-at-arms it had been before the war into a full-blown theatrical production. When the Royal Tournament was resumed in its 38th year after the war in 1921, Captain A.W. Byrne came second in the Bayonet v. Bayonet Competition but went on to gain a first five times during the decade. The first of the stage shows entitled *Cum Marte Minerva* came from the pen of Harry Willans, a private who held the DSO and MC. Harry Willans provided, or partly provided, eight more of these entertainments before his elevation to the command of the Regiment in the early 1930s put him above that kind of frivolity. Harry Willans' plays produced at The Annual Prize Distribution, 1923-29 were as follows -

   1923 *Cum Marte Minerva*
   1924 *Youth Will be Served*
   1925 *Ye Crooked Crusader* (with R. Filmore)
   1926 *Wild Oats*
   1926 *Wild Oats* (Second Crop)
   1927 *Cannibal Nights Entertainment*
   1928 -
   1929 *Contraband*

Also resumed in 1921 was the Royal Academy Guard, which with the exception of the war years, had taken place every year since the earliest days of the Regiment's association with Burlington House. The occasion each year was the dinner on the evening preceding the opening of the Summer Exhibition when about 100 men formed up in four files and led by a guard commander and two other officers would assemble in the forecourt of the Royal Academy to honour the guests arriving for the dinner. The guard always put on a splendid display of marching headed by the Drums from Duke's Road, into the Euston Road, along Tottenham Court Road, down Shaftesbury Avenue and into Piccadilly. The Artists were allotted the rare privilege of marching through London with fixed bayonets. The guard would be inspected by the principal guest, usually royalty or the Prime Minister, and the guard commander was privileged to accompany him into the dinner. At the first guard after the war the Prince of Wales expressed surprise to see so many of the men on parade wearing officers' medals. On 12 May 1922 a War Memorial in the form of a small plaque was placed in the forecourt of the Royal Academy to honour the members of the Corps who had lost their lives in the war. The unveiling ceremony was conducted by the Earl of Cavan, CIGS, and the dedication by the Dean of Westminster.

In 1928 the War Office decided in its inscrutable wisdom to affiliate the Artists to the Rifle Brigade. No one in the Corps could have any objection to association with so distinguished a regiment, but it meant re-learning all the drill to conform with Rifle Regiment usages but even then the conversion only went half-way and the Artists were mercifully spared the need to march with that short, fast pace adopted by the Light Infantry. From that time on until the outbreak of war in 1939 the permanent staff were all supplied from the Rifle Brigade and the links between the regiments grew steadily firmer. During the 1930s conscious efforts were made to draw them closer still, but more of that in Chapter 16.

Chapter 16

Between the Wars

1930-35

*I KNOW 3 TRADES
I SPEAK 3 LANGUAGES
FOUGHT 3 YEARS
HAVE 3 CHILDREN
AND NO WORK FOR 3 MONTHS
BUT I ONLY WANT
ONE JOB*
Placard worn by unemployed man, London, 1930

The post-war depression which had begun in the 1920s was accelerated by the Wall Street crash of 1929, which affected the whole of the Western world. In the United Kingdom unemployment doubled to 2 million between 1929 and 1930; it hit a peak of 3.1 million (18 per cent of the work force) at the end of 1932. Whilst the Fascist dictatorship of Benito Mussolini consolidated itself in Italy, dire economic conditions in the Weimar Republic caused by Germany's defeat in the Great War and the heavy cost of reparations to the Allies, had given rise to the power of Adolf Hitler in 1933, and in both Italy and Germany militaristic nationalism led to the pursuit of more territory. While millions of unemployed Americans in the early 1930s responded with gratitude to President Franklin D. Roosevelt's 'New Deal', in Britain the piecemeal attempts of a coalition government, notionally led by a Labour Prime Minister, Ramsay Macdonald, to ameliorate the effects of the depression led to the defection of a Labour politician, Oswald Mosley, and the formation of the British Union of Fascists. Britain's political leaders viewed the ascendancy of Fascist dictatorship in Europe with approval, or at least with complacency. It was regarded as a bulwark against Communism; and in the second half of the decade Britain and France pursued a policy of appeasement of Adolf Hitler's Third Reich in the hope of sparing their people the horrors of another major war.

The world trade slump and in particular the sharp decline in Anglo-American trade of the early 1930s, at a time when Britain should have been re-arming, led to cuts in military spending. In 1930 an Artists' Easter camp took place with the Royal Marines at Eastney Barracks, Portsmouth, but the summer camp attached to a guards battalion at Aldershot (Rushmoor) was restricted to seven days only. The biggest problem faced by the Regiment in the first half of the decade was its decline in numbers. The solid body of officers and men who had enlisted both before and during the Great War and who had been the instructors of the 1920s was breaking up, having reached the retirement limit for service with the Territorial Army. The Artists was fast becoming a young battalion, the majority of its members having had no direct experience of war.

So it must have been with some satisfaction that in September 1930, the commanding officer, Lieutenant Colonel W.H. Ramsbotham, was able to report:

> The outstanding feature of the year happened at the Royal Tournament at Olympia, where the battalion won both the Army and Inter-Services Bayonet Team Championships and a member of the Regiment, Sergeant M.J. Carter, ['H.Q.' Wing] became Champion of the Services as well as of the Army.
>
> This is a wonderful result of constant training and hard work.
>
> One feels that the Bayonet is a weapon of 'Morale' and that this success shows that the 'spirit' of the Battalion is as sound and as keen as ever.
>
> But we must ever be on our guard. We know that the Battalion is getting younger, old members who have borne the heat and burden of the day are gradually dropping out, but our training and tactical knowledge must not deteriorate.

Again in 1931 Colonel Ramsbotham reported:

> The training year 1930-31 has been satisfactory ... Improvement has been made in the intercommunication within the battalion, and the Machine Gun Company is growing daily more efficient. But with the greatly enhanced firepower of the modern infantry battalion, the rifle is still the weapon of the infantry soldier and there must be no decrease in the knowledge and use of that weapon, in spite of machine guns and light automatics.
>
> The 'spirit of the bayonet' has flourished; our successes at Olympia this year, as well as last, tell their own story.

As regards leadership in the field, the battalion ever needs good leaders and I ask all serving members to concentrate with all their might on courses, lectures and the study of all military subjects, so that the efficiency of the battalion will remain at a level which cannot be belittled.

At Olympia on 10 June 1931 the winner of the Army Championship was Lance Corporal W. Horton, 'B' Company, and the Artists Bayonet Team won the Inter-Services Championship, Gold Medal and Challenge Cup as well as the Army Championship and Silver Medals.

Easter camp in 1931 was spent at Bisley and summer camp at Wannock (Eastbourne). There was no Easter camp in 1932 but summer camp took place at Aldershot (Barrossa Barracks). No records of the camps 1930-32 appear to have survived. One interesting participant in these camps however was Private Leslie O'Brien, who served in 'C' Company, 1928-32. Later as Sir Leslie and raised to the peerage as Lord O'Brien of Lothbury, PC, GBE, he was Governor of the Bank of England 1966-73. He was reputed to have said that, although he was not a member of the Regiment for very long, he was always proud to be an Artist. Company commanders serving under Colonel Ramsbotham in the early 1930s were:

'A' Company: Lieutenant R.R. Cripps (Captain 1931)
'B' Company: Captain R.A. Barnett, MC, TD
'C' (M.G.) Company: Major (Junior Major) H. Willans, DSO,MC
'D' Company: Captain C.M. Rait, MC.

C.R. Cormack, MC and P.G.R. Burford also served as captains in the battalion at this time. The adjutant, Captain A.W. Allan, Rifle Brigade, was succeeded in 1931 by Captain T.J.B. Bosville, MC, Rifle Brigade, who held the post until 1934. The quartermaster continued to be Captain E.J.M. Van Walwyk, MBE, MM and the RSM was E. Partridge.

In 1933 Colonel Ramsbotham was succeeded as commanding officer by Lieutenant Colonel H. Willans, DSO, MC and Bar. Born in 1897, Harry Willans was educated at Aldenham School, Hertfordshire, and enlisted in the Corps shortly before the outbreak of the Great War. He sailed to France in the *Australind* and was one of the famous 'First Fifty' to be commissioned at Bailleul by Colonel May. Willans went as a second lieutenant to the 2nd Battalion, the Bedfordshire and Hertfordshire Regiment. He served with the Beds and Herts between 1914-18 with a spell in Italy in 1917. Wounded in 1916, he won two MCs, one in 1917 and the other in 1918, and as captain and adjutant of his battalion he was awarded the DSO in the same year. Captain Willans was twice Mentioned in Despatches (once by Haig and once by

Plumer) during the war. When Colonel May revived the Regiment in 1920 Harry Willans, resigning his commission, re-joined the Artists as a private and served as a ranker for six years. On being commissioned again he quickly rose to the command of 'C' (MG) Company and junior major. Harry Willans, a senior executive with Joe Lyons, the well-known catering firm, had always been a popular personality in the battalion as a performer and writer of sketches for smokers' and musical entertainments and plays for performance at camps and at Duke's Road. Major Walter Campbell Smith MC continued as second in command; he was promoted brevet lieutenant colonel in 1935.

The following announcement from Colonel Willans dated May 1933 appeared in the first issue (published in June) of *The Artists Rifles Gazette*, which published in a new format, replaced the year books of the mid-1920s to early 1930s. Willans was as conscious as Ramsbotham had been of the declining numbers on the nominal roll, the average yearly strength bordering on 400, the battalion establishment being 500:

> By the time the first number of the *Gazette* appears, the Territorial Year will be more than half over and Camp will be almost in sight. It is gratifying to observe that, in spite of every difficulty, real and imagined, much excellent work has been and is being done; a first-class Bayonet Team and keen D.T. and Dewar Teams maintain the old tradition (the fact that they were unsuccessful this year in no way lessens the value of their efforts); the Academy Guard was well up to the standard of its predecessors; Easter Training at the Rifle Brigade Depot, Winchester, was, I think, remarkable for the revival of the Easter March, on a small scale, it is true, but a real step in the right direction; the Regimental Prize Meeting at Bisley was well attended and well-run; company training has been energetically and capably conducted; a large number of officers and N.C.Os attended a T.E.W.T. at Whitchurch.
>
> The firing of Weapons Training Courses began with fairly good results, but there is still a large number of men who have not completed their courses. It should be clearly understood, however desirable our other activities, such as competitions, the performance of the complementary exercises – Drills, Weapon Training and Camp – which a man undertakes on enlistment are of paramount importance and every man in the Artists Rifles is expected to perform these duties punctually, as a matter of course and without persuasion. In particular, I hope that every member of the Corps will make an effort to attend Camp for 15 days. The value of Camp, both from the point-of-view of training and of enjoyment, largely

depends upon numbers, and, with our reduced strength, it is of vital importance that every available man should be there throughout.

I need not say that the King's Parade in Hyde Park on June 24th [it was cancelled on the day as a downpour turned the park into a sea of mud] demands the attendance of all ranks. I am confident that the Regiment will be at full strength and will live up to the high standard set by itself on previous occasions on which His Majesty has done us the honour of Commanding our presence.

We have always set more store upon quality than quantity; but our strength at present is dangerously low – lower than it has been for years past. Whatever the cause, the result is bad; without adequate numbers we can neither maintain the amenities of the Corps, nor be in a position to fulfil our peculiar responsibilities in the event of war. I appeal strongly to all Serving and Veteran Members to do their utmost to introduce suitable recruits, and to men whose time is nearly up to extend their service for a little longer. There is no better way of helping the Regiment and the country. Recruiting is our most urgent problem – far more important than success in competitions, more pressing than training. Given adequate numbers and the enthusiasm of all ranks, military efficiency will follow automatically.

In May 1933 a recruiting committee was appointed by the commanding officer to consider the recruiting problem in all its aspects and to take such steps as would in due course promote a steady flow of suitable recruits. The committee was given no brief to employ 'stunt' methods but rather to institute a long-range policy which would in time produce good and permanent results. Letters were written to over 100 of the Public School Cadet Corps and they were forwarded a booklet on the Regiment. The committee received many encouraging replies. Colonel Willans himself visited Felsted School and Brighton College, in each case addressing members of the OTC. Visits by a representative of the Regiment to other schools were also arranged. The recruiting campaign did not, however, meet with a dramatically significant result.

Camp 1933 was held in July/August at Myrtle Grove, West Sussex. Myrtle Grove was a lone farmhouse and there was a notable lack of myrtles on the site! The Brigade camp lay on the South Downs just over four miles north-west of Worthing and five miles north-east of Arundel, the nearest railway station being Goring-by-Sea. The position of the camp (150 feet above sea level) lay in a fold in the Downs, overshadowed to the south-east by a rim of a down, under which ran the Findon-Clapham road. Every inch of the steep northern escarpment of the South Downs commands a magnificent view of the Weald, and between the ridge and the camp lay the training areas on an undulating plateau, with the twin humps Blackpatch and Harrow Hills. Three miles to the east of Myrtle Grove lies Cissbury Hill, which in ancient times was considered to be the centre of the flint industry, where Palaeolithic man made his tools for domestic and warlike use. Cissbury has been called the 'Palaeolithic Sheffield' but this title must be shared by Blackpatch and Harrow Hills, a few miles to the north and north-west.

Perfect weather contributed greatly to the success of the Myrtle Grove camp, which was voted by those present to be the best within living memory. The Marching Detachment consisting of six officers and seventy men led by Major Campbell Smith detrained at Horsham late afternoon on the Saturday and covered seven miles, Colonel Willans, joining in for the last three miles, a gesture much appreciated by the marchers. At Cookham some time was spent in sleep, the acquisition of food, blankets and floor space in a local hall occupying most of the attention; nor did the local publican complain of neglect. The ascent of Shillington Hill next day was accomplished in the grand manner and was long remembered; this brought the marches to the last stage over Blackpatch Hill, and hence to Myrtle Grove.

As Colonel Willans later wrote:

> Many things contribute to a successful Camp; in particular, good food and comfortable conditions, interesting training and conveniently arranged amusements. For these blessings we are indebted to a number of people to whom I take this opportunity of tendering the thanks of the battalion: the Regular personnel, both officers and O.R.s who helped to make the training interesting and instructive; the Cooks, Quartermaster and Staff and Transport, who were responsible for providing the best food and most comfortable arrangements in many years; Captain Turnbull, who at a moment's notice took over the duties of Quartermaster when Captain Walwyk fell ill; Major Bax, Captain Jerwood and others, who arranged the amusement programme, including the 'buses' which took many parties to the sea to bathe, and the ice-creams which were welcome in the training areas.

The canteen smoking concert which was held on the Friday evening of the first week of camp was a great success. Two companies provided acts. In addition 'B' Company with their band and entertainers started the programme with about twenty minutes of song and dance. As for the concerted items, 'D' Company presented a pageant entitled *The Pageant of Myrtle Grove* with 'Mother' Oakley in the leading role. It was exceedingly well constructed and excellently performed by members of the company. Congratulations were especially due to Sergeants Moody and Naimaster for such a brilliant entertainment. 'A' Company staged an excellent piece of buffoonery, being a running commentary on camp life, with particular reference to bugle horns, socks and boots stuffed with newspaper. Among the veterans attending annual camp that year were Colonel Ramsbotham, Major Tyer, Captain Byrne, Captain Goodbody, Captain Jerwood, Arthur Drewry, 'Woggie' Groom, R.F. Hartley, H. Mills, F.N.J. Moody, E.G. Nye, Bill Smalley, H. Solomon, R.F. Store and E.F. Williams, all of whom participated in the lighter side of camp life.

The annual Assault-at-Arms and pantomime took place at headquarters on the evenings of Monday and Tuesday, 20-21 November 1933, and the occasion was attended on both nights by large gatherings of serving and veteran members, their relatives and friends. As in former years the pantomime was preceded by a display of physical training, boxing, bayonet fighting and fencing, of a serious and comic nature by members of the School of Arms, entitled *Fencing, Fun and Frolic* in seven acts. The participants in the display *inter alios* were R.R. Cripps, L.K. Sweet, W.G.T. Burne, E.H. Owen, E.J. Barrenger, J.W. Leslie, R.L. Norris, J.L. Naimaster, G.G. Darley Bentley, J.M. Fuller, G.L.G. Harry and F. Deltzi. This was followed by *El Bevah*, a pantomime written by John Lee, music by C.F. Smyly and John Lee, and produced by Spurgeon Parker, which provided a blazing spectacle of the mode and manners of life in the glamorous and gorgeous East. All the female parts were of course performed by male members of the Regiment.

The author offers no apology for describing the plot of *El Bevah* in some detail, as it would have appeared to have been a masterpiece of tomfoolery induced no doubt by the high degree of neurosis which had descended on all concerned during the arduous training year! The story concerns the fortunes of Fatuma (M.J. Carter), the beautiful daughter of Scherezade (W. Horton), who is greatly desired by a wicked Sultan, El Bevah, a veritable Blue Beard with a murky past (B.S. Cave-Chinn), who commissions a wealthy merchant (E.B. Howard Rice) to purchase Fatuma for 2,000 sequins and bring her to his palace. Fortunately for Fatuma with the help of an obliging fairy, Bint El Phripet (B.A.C. Hills), she discovers the secret of 'Chamber No. 9', in which the murdered bodies of the Sultan's former wives are hidden away. Now the secret is out, the Sultan resolves to cut off Fatuma's head but she is rescued by the valiant captain of the Sultan's bodyguard, the inappropriately named Nasti Fellah (E. Margetson), into whose arms she falls in the gripping finale. Others taking part in the entertainment were M.B. Hewitt, L.R.C. Cornford, P.L. Leigh-Breese, E.A. Abrahams, B.A.

Rotger, J.A.D. Lansdell and T.W.C. Robinson, but the honours for the evening were carried off by the chorus for their splendid appearance and most professional dancing.

By naming their latest type of passenger locomotives after famous British fighting units, the London, Midland and Scottish Railway made what was probably the most popular decision in the history of railway engine nomenclature. The system of bestowing names on railway engines was as old as the railway engine itself. Actually, the early locomotives carried names only, a system of numeration being brought into use only when railways had made such progress that it became essential for their efficient operation. An amazing variety of nomenclature was to be found in the list of named locomotives on the LMS Railway, and of the seventy of the Royal Scot type, which were used on long-distance express services where high average speeds over long stretches of track were maintained, many were named after famous regiments, the type itself being named after one of the oldest units in the British Army.

In the early 1930s the names of several London Territorial Regiments were given to Royal Scot-type locomotives and in 1934 it was announced that *The Artists Rifleman* was to be one of them. No. 6164 was the number and the engine pulled mainline express passenger trains running between Preston and Carlisle, occasionally working the Royal Scot express into Euston from Carlisle, and in the reverse direction, namely the 11 p.m. night Scottish express from Euston to the North. The naming of the new engine did not entirely meet with the approval of the Regiment: there was no such person as an 'Artists Rifleman', the term used for the lowest rank in the Regiment being 'Private'; and it was generally felt that 'The Artists Rifles' would have been a more appropriate name-plate for the engine.

London/104 (Artists Rifles) VAD, which had been revived after the Great War with its headquarters at Duke's Road, flourished throughout the 1920s and 1930s and was always ready for an emergency. The unit was never hard up for a job, as there were many ways in which it could be used in peace, as in war. Such members as could spare the time did voluntary work in hospitals, clinics, infant welfare centres, and helped to run canteens. For the training of the detachment at Duke's Road there were meetings every other Monday from 5 p.m. to 6.15 p.m., when there were courses of lectures on First Aid, Home Nursing, Hygiene and Sanitation, as well as Child Welfare, with examinations; or there were practical classes at which every member was taught to do bandaging, dressings, blanket baths, and to make beds and fomentations etc.; in fact all kinds of useful knowledge necessary for nursing. The commandant during this period was Miss Marjorie Pilcher, who always welcomed new recruits, particularly those who were related to members of the Regiment.

On 22 April 1934 the honorary colonel, Colonel Walter C. Horsley, CB, VD, TD (in 1932 he had been created CB in recognition of his services to the Volunteer and Territorial Forces), having reached the limit of his extended period of service as honorary colonel, finally retired after more than sixty years' service in the Corps. It was a matter of deep sorrow when the Regiment learned that he had died on 18 May, less than four weeks after his retirement. The new honorary colonel was the Most Honourable the Marquis of Londonderry, KG, PC, MVO, Secretary of State for Air, who took up his appointment on 23 April. Lord Londonderry was the first honorary colonel who had not served as an Artist and risen to command the Regiment. (Colonel May, who was Colonel Horsley's true successor, had died in April 1929, but Colonel Chatfeild-Clarke must have also been a candidate.) His Lordship was a busy politician, his star sparkled brightly in the social world and he was known irreverently in the mess as 'Good-Time-Charlie'; it would be idle to pretend that he made any great mark on the Regiment during his tenure of office, but he went to camp and attended a modicum of regimental functions. Nevertheless, it was a good thing so far as the Regiment was concerned to have an honorary colonel who was a member of the House of Lords and a cabinet minister as a member of the officers' mess.

The first night of the Easter march, 1934, was spent at the depot of the Royal Berkshire Regiment at Reading. Friday's march took the participants in fifty-minute stages via Tilehurst to Streatley, where lunch was had at The Swan. At Wallingford the local platoon of the 4th Battalion, the Royal Berkshire Regiment TA spared no pains to make the marchers comfortable; the officers were put up at The Lamb, the sergeants at the Drill Hall, the troops at the Masonic Hall and the QM staff had a cosy billet at The George. On Saturday the marchers tramped via Shillingford and Dorchester to Nuneham Courtenay, where they lunched hard by the Harcourt Arms; then on by Littlemore to Cowley Barracks, the depot of the Oxfordshire and Buckinghamshire Light Infantry, where the Artists were again made very comfortable. A large parade fell in and marched to church at Cowley on Sunday morning. In the afternoon Captain Burford arranged for a party to visit Christ Church, Oxford, while others went sightseeing at other colleges, some journeying further afield to such pleasant places as Burford, Stratford-on-Avon and over the Cotswolds. On Monday morning the Artists visited the Ox. & Bucks. Regimental museum and after a short march over Shotover Hill and through Wheatley to Tiddington, where after lunch the detachment, which numbered in similar strength to previous years entrained for Paddington. The drummers had played the marchers on their way in an excellent manner, arousing much interest and contentment in the cattle grazing in the fields.

The Royal Academy guard of honour, which was commanded by Captain Burford, on 3 May 1934 was inspected by three eminent personages in the space of one hour. Responding to the RSM's 'Hints on Deportment in Piccadilly' on arrival in the forecourt of the Royal Academy, the guard was inspected by the Prince of Wales and on its return to Duke's Road by General Sir Cecil Romer, the Artists' adjutant in 1905 and now adjutant general to the Forces. As the occasion coincided with an officers' mess dinner, the guard was also inspected by Lord Londonderry, paying his first official visit to headquarters. At the School of Arms the season 1933-34 may quite fairly have been called successful for, after winning the London Territorial School of Arms Association Bayonet Team Combats for the fourteenth year in succession, the Regimental contingent went on to fight at Olympia in the Royal Tournament where the Artists won first the Army and then the Inter-Services Championships Bayonet Team Combats.

ARMY CHAMPIONSHIP
Final: Artists beat Cameron Highlanders – 10 wins to 9
INTER-SERVICES CHAMPIONSHIP
Final (Army v. Royal Marines): Artists won 11 wins to 7

Congratulations were due also to the Artists on winning the Divisional Challenge Cup at the Divisional Rifle Meeting at Bisley. Although 'B' Company was the only team to actually win a first prize, the Artists won the Aggregate Cup for extremely consistent shooting throughout the competition. In July 1934 a new double-breasted blue flannel blazer was available in a large variety of fittings at Duke's Road. The commanding officer expressed the hope that as many men as possible would provide themselves with these blazers for walking out at camp and for general informal use. The blazer with Artists buttons was priced at 32s. 6d.

The practice of enlisting as privates in the Regiment and a long period of assessment in the ranks before being considered for a commission will be well known to the reader by now. In 1934 Colonel Willans broke that tradition by commissioning three young men, two straight from Harrow School and a third from Haileybury. Naturally there was a certain amount of protest from within the ranks of the Corps, but the complaint was levelled more at the principle than the individuals concerned. The young second lieutenant from Haileybury was C.J.M.

Alport, a good boxer, who rose quickly to command a company and was very popular with his men. 'Cub' Alport, the Conservative MP for Colchester from 1950, was made Minister of State at the Commonwealth Relations Office in 1959 and a life peer in 1961, when he negotiated the break-up of the Rhodesian Federation. (Fuller biographical details of Alport's career as a soldier, politician and administrator are given in Chapter 18.)

Colonel Willans had several reasons for his controversial decision to take on officers directly from the Public School OTCs. Firstly, he was acutely conscious that the Regiment was under strength and consequently there was a shortage of good leaders. This was partly because of the young men's reluctance, having obtained their Cert. As from their OTCs, to join the Artists because of the lengthy time it might take them to win their commissions, always with the risk that they might not obtain one at all. It was also partly because the 'right type' of other rank, who had enlisted in the Artists, often preferred to shine as privates, corporals or sergeants, always with the mental reservation that they would, of course, take commissions if a war emergency arose. Colonel Willans' move was recognized in the Territorial Army as a sign that he was determined to put efficiency above any other consideration.

Summer camp at Colchester in 1934 was as successful and enjoyable as the previous year at Myrtle Grove had been. The site, weather and the training carried out with the help of the Bedfordshire and Hertfordshire Regiment (Colonel Willans' old regiment in the Great War), the Rifle Brigade and the Welsh Guards were all useful and the food excellent. An enthusiastic marching detachment, a really good advance party, interesting and unusually instructive schemes, a gymkhana and many other events contributed to the comfort and entertainment of all ranks, whose enthusiasm ensured the success of the Colchester camp. 'B' Company won the Tactical Competition, Transport captured the Brigade Transport Competition and 'A' Company won the Glee Competition at the Smoker.

The third march to camp, now an integral feature of annual training, began at Witham on the Saturday afternoon. The party numbered over seventy and was organized into two platoons by Lieutenant P.B. Greenway. After tea at the Spread Eagle the Detachment started off in good style over a course of six miles, including a long, uphill climb to Great Braxted, where a fine meal was prepared at the Du Cane Arms. During the course of a convivial evening the CO and several veterans visited the party. Troops were quartered in a large barn with a lavish supply of straw. 'Rouse' was sounded by the local cock and, after a good breakfast, the Detachment took up the march in dull weather. A good pace was kept up throughout the whole day and after two halts the

Fox at Layer de la Haye was reached for lunch. Moving on the Detachment, making its last halt at Berechurch, marched into camp in very good order and well up to schedule.

On the Thursday afternoon of the second week a new departure in camp entertainment was made by an informal shoot arranged by the Weapon Training officer, Lieutenant N.R. Brown. The event that aroused most interest was 'The Empire's Delight' for which twenty-four teams entered. This was a knock-out tile shoot and was won by 'C' Company (Corporal D.V.G. Brock). The individual, five rounds deliberate, was won by Corporal J.F.W. Fennell, and the Inter-Mess Match (best eight scores) was won by the privates (124) with the officers (111) as runners-up. A sports meeting and gymkhana were held on the Bank Holiday. After a miserable morning, which threatened to wash out the whole proceedings, a start was made about 3.30 p.m. with the Boat Race, which opened up an interest in the event which was sustained throughout the afternoon. The results were:

Boat Race (with poles)	Major C.M. Rait and crew
Sergeants' Wheelbarrow Race	Sergeants R.G. Garton & W.B. Jones ('B' Company)
Inter-Battalion Relay Race	Artists Rifles
Officers' Race	Major C.M. Rait
Four-legged Race	Privates G.F. Hall, A. Kelly and B.H. Rotger ('A' Company)
Inter Team (Four) Wrestling on Horseback	London Scottish
Inter-Company Tug-of-War	'B' Company
Horse, Bicycle, Running Race	Private G.F. Hall ('A' Company)
Inter-Company Tent-Pitching	'A' Company
Drummer's Race	Drummer Miller

At the smoking concert RQMS 'Smithy' occupied the chair and managed the turns and the assembled audience in his usual masterly way. The 'B' Company band opened the programme, followed by a few song items and John Lee's 'Musical Treat'. This in turn was followed by an act written and performed by Lance Corporal B.A.C. Hills, being a running commentary on an imaginary contest between a team of WOs and sergeants and a team of other ranks. As for the concerted items, 'B' Company's contribution was a mannequin parade, mounted by the most insanitary-looking members of the company, in which the audience was shown the latest articles of male attire suitable for wear in camp and all the purely masculine occasions. 'D' Company entertained the audience with another Naimaster Production entitled *A Pageant of Colchester, or*

Cockwatch in an Oyster Shell. 'A' Company staged a musical comedy, all about Mrs Grundy at Clacton-on-Sea – lyrics and dialogue by Corporal Chomley. Music which a few of those present may have heard before was alleged to be specially written for the occasion by Sir Arthur Sullivan. At the termination of the concert the CO made the presentation of the new Regimental Colours, the names of the recipients read out by CQMS Lee.

It had been decided to introduce a new tie for civilian wear, to be awarded for outstanding achievements by any member of the Regiment. The tie was coloured in the Rifle Brigade green and bore the same black and white diagonal stripes as the grey tie, which all members of the Regiment were entitled to wear from the date of enlistment. The new 'green tie', as it was to be known, was awarded by the commanding officer, on the recommendation of the second in command, company commanders, chairman of the Musketry Committee, leader of the School of Arms, leader of the *Daily Telegraph* Cup and Dewar teams, captain of the Rugby Football Club, captains of other sporting clubs, and president of the messes, for meritorious performance of any kind, whether military, sporting or of general value to the Corps. It was a little-known privilege of a bearer of the green tie when entering a room at headquarters or the Bisley Hut for the door to be held open for him by one of the assembled company.

The following constituted the first list of green tie awards:

Captain R.R. Cripps	Leader of the Bayonet Team
Private W. Horton	Bayonet Team (and entertainer)
Lance Corporal G.G. Darley-Bentley	Bayonet Team
Sergeant J.L. Naimaster	Editor of the *Artists Rifles Gazette*
Lance Corporal V.M. Marshall	Corporal Cook
Lance Corporal C.A. Fox	Sports
Corporal G.H. Macadam	Cricket Club
Corporal P.G. Barker	Rugby Football Club
Corporal H.S. Lashbrook	Rugby Football Club
RQMS H.R. Smith, MC	Chairman of the Bisley Hut
Lieutenant N.R. Brown	Weapon Training Officer
Lance Sergeant H.A. Abram	Shooting
Corporal G.W. Smith	Shooting
Private R.W. Bellamy	Shooting
Private S.G.E. Willis	Shooting
Private D.C. Baynes	Shooting
Lance Sergeant G.H. Shearer	Shooting
Lance Corporal B.S. Lush	'A' Company (and entertainer)

Private M.A. Causbrook	For stopping a runaway horse at the Colchester Camp on 2 August.
Captain E.J.M. Van Walwyk	Quartermaster

The final major event of the Artists' training year was a second helping of *Cannibal Nights*, written and produced by the same team that had staged the first version in 1927. The show was preceded by Part One of a film, *Let's Join the Artists*, written and directed by Maurice Hart and F.A. Stocken, both members of the Regiment, commissioned no doubt to assist the recruitment campaign. Narrated by Captain Burford, the all-talking movie told the story of how the Artists lived and trained. Although the screening was reported to be a great success, it is sad to record that to the best of the author's knowledge, no copy of the footage has survived.

When the curtain went up on *Cannibal Nights* it revealed a multitude of repulsive cannibals, beauteous cannibelles, magicians, medicine men and a chief, all promising a terrible fate in the cook-pot for a shy, white missionary and his grown-up, Parisian-gowned daughter. When the party was joined by the unexpected arrival of two members of the Artists Air-Arm, unfortunately crashed on the way to camp in Australia, the promise of a really jolly feast for the natives became all the more inviting, and it was only the fact that the three leading cannibelles fell for the three white faces that delayed the meal until the timely arrival of the air commodore with reinforcements to save the situation. B.S. Lush played the dual role of Gumboots, the Prime Minister and Snerge, the Queen Mother, D.H. Flint was Gladeye, the Chief of Harem, W. Horton took the part of Cuthbert, the Missionary, and H.A.C. Hills his charming daughter.

As a result of a great deal of criticism of the lack of accuracy and stability of the standard issue SMLE rifle as a target weapon, which had been going on for several years, the Council of the National Rifle Association decided to permit the use of the Rifle Pattern 14 in all SR(b) competitions in the year 1935. Good as a service weapon, the SMLE had been found inadequate for competitive target work, in spite of packing, broad foresight and various gadgets. The Pattern 14 was in an experimental stage when the Great War broke out and was issued to Home Defence troops. Because of its great accuracy it was used in France and on other fronts as a sniper's rifle. Individuals could purchase the new rifle from the NRA for £3, but without aperture sight and other accessories and it could be hired for the season for £1 for the first year (5s. returnable), and 10s. a year subsequently; if hired by the day the charge was 1s.

The year 1935's Easter march was chiefly remembered for the extremely varied weather. It did not rain – it poured; the sun was not warm – it was hot; and the wind was not so much breezy – it was a hurricane. Under the command of Bt Lieutenant Colonel W. Campbell Smith, the marchers embussed on the Thursday evening at Duke's Road for the 4th Divisional Signals Barracks at Canterbury. Friday's march took the men by way of Nackington, Street End and the Hardres to Bossingham where they lunched at The Star; thence by a somewhat circuitous route via Lynsore Bottom and Kingston to Barham. There they were divided into two parties, one occupying the village school and the other the Memorial Hall. On Saturday the route took the marchers to Tilmanstone and they lunched at The Plough and Harrow, before making their way to the Royal Marine Barracks at Walmer, where they were greeted by the Artists' former adjutant, Major Webber, RM. The evening was spent at leisure in Deal. On Sunday morning the Detachment attended morning service at the Royal Marine Chapel, the afternoon and evening being spent in Deal and other towns nearby. Monday's short march took the men via Kingsdown, Ringwould and Sutton, where they lunched at The Boot, and on to Martin Hill, where they entrained for the return journey to London, which was made in brilliant sunshine.

Monday, 6 May 1935, was Jubilee Day, marking the celebration of twenty-five years of the reign of King George V. The Regiment mustered 19 officers and 342 other ranks for the occasion. The glories of the pre-war full-dress uniforms were absent, but even so from such vantage points as the church of St Mary-le-Strand, the long avenue of khaki-clad figures, with the sun twinkling and flashing on polished brass, must have provided a fitting background for the Royal Procession to St Paul's Cathedral. Parade was at 7.45 a.m. at the Drill Hall. Four markers per company were sent in advance to mark out the distances on the route to be covered. The Regiment led by the Drums then marched by way of Upper Woburn Place, Kingsway and the eastern arm of Aldwych to the Strand, where their limits were inclusive of Burleigh Street and exclusive of the door of Somerset House. There the men were drawn up in single ranks on either side of the street, less than two paces between each man. Behind them was a row of 'Bobbies' and behind them the packed, good-humoured crowd, ready to cheer anything and anybody. It took two hours for the long procession of cars to make its way to the cathedral and when their Majesties passed by the cheering was so loud that the assembled troops had to lip-read their orders. On their return to Duke's Road the marchers were treated to a cold lunch. Colonel Willans took the chair and reminded those present that this was the first time the Regiment had dined together since the Great War. Congratulating the

Regiment on its numbers and turn-out, he stated that the Artists were the strongest unit on parade that day.

In the summer of 1935 the Regiment returned to Myrtle Grove for annual camp. The marching detachment mustered at Victoria Station on Saturday 27 July, to entrain for Horsham, before alighting for the march to camp. The men were smartly turned out with shining equipment and square packs. Arriving at Horsham, the Detachment led by Colonel Campbell Smith marched along the road and were glad to reach Cookham, where they made their 'bivvy'. Those who slept under the stars, as many did, rose to a Scotch mist, which continued into the morning. Sunday's march was eventful if only because of that colossal hill forming the edge of the Downs, an hour's marching then taking the Detachment within sight of camp. At camp, 'A' Company was to be congratulated on winning the tactical competition, as were the transport, the advance party and especially the messing staff and cooks who, with the support of the NAAFI, brought the messing arrangements within sight of perfection.

The gymkhana held on Bank Holiday Monday was again a great success. The first event, the Boat Race was won by a section of 'A' Company. This was followed by the Four-Legged Race, won by Private Ayres' 'A' Company team. The Invitation Mile Relay was between the London Rifle Brigade, the London Scottish, the Queen's Westminster Rifles and the Artists. The Artists won the event. Wrestling on Horseback with eight teams taking part was won by the London Scottish 'A' team. The Sergeants' Wheelbarrow Race was won by Sergeants Fennell and Taylor of 'C' Company. The Horse, Bicycle, Running Race was pleasanter to watch than to take part in, being somewhat strenuous; this was won by Private K.C. Molyneux ('C' Company); H.P. Kitcat won the Veterans' Egg and Spoon Race. The drummers, who had been playing in their own small corner for most of the afternoon emerged to run a handicap, which was won by Drummer Lamerton.

The Mystery Event, a super-barging match in sacks, was very popular; it was won by Corporal N.E. Saunders ('A' Company). The Mounted Apple-Bobbing Competition was won in good form by Private B.C. Laws ('H.Q.'). The final event, the Tug-of-War, was very keenly contested, and 'B' Company thoroughly deserved their win, as they had to tug hard every inch of the way.

On the first Friday the annual camp smoker was held in the dining tent, which was crowded out. For the concerted items this year, 'A' Company produced a Russian ballet with Cossacks and attendant sylphs (with hairy legs); 'B' Company's band did good work at the opening of the show and turned themselves into an excellent minstrel troop. At the last moment 'D' Company put on an impromptu skit on the rulers of Europe and Africa, the principal target being Adolf Hitler, which brought the house down.

As a mark of the high esteem in which the late Colonel Walter Horsley was held by the Regiment, a fund was set up after his death in 1934 to provide a fitting memorial at headquarters to mark his sixty years' service with the Corps. As a result a clock was installed in the canteen and Captain W.L. Lee-Hankey, one of the Regiment's outstanding artists, was commissioned to paint his portrait. The portrait was unveiled on Thursday evening, 18 July 1935, in the presence of Mrs Horsley, in the officers' mess. The portrait, a half-length painting, depicted the late honorary colonel in khaki uniform as he had appeared in the 1920s. Colonel Chatfeild-Clarke (CO 1915-17), in presenting the portrait to the Regiment on behalf of Old Artists, gave a brief sketch of Colonel Horsley's Regimental career, saying that all Artists owed him a debt in his having saved the Regiment from ultimate extinction in 1908, at the transition between the Volunteer and the Territorial eras. In reply, on behalf of the Regiment, Colonel Willans said: 'We shall treasure it, not only as a memorial to the greatest and best commanding officer we have ever had, but as one to a gallant and loyal friend.' There was a balance in hand from the fund, which had been subscribed to in small amounts, so it was proposed to provide a cabinet, with reading desk, for the scrap-books then being compiled of the Regiment's history. After the ceremony was over the older Artists took the opportunity to walk around the building to see the various structural alterations that had been made in recent years.

The thespian element was to the fore again at the end of the training year in November with the staging at Duke's Road of *A Midsummer Night's Nonsense*. Once again the 'female' members of the cast were at their best as chorus girls, dames – or what you will. The show, which was produced by Spurgeon Parker, was written by John Lee, who also wrote the music, with additional numbers by Cecil Smyly, F. Mendelssohn-Bartholdy and others. The story presented in two acts was about Hermia (R.G.J. White), the daughter of Theseus Longbottom (W. Horton), who is led astray by a dashing young corporal, Lysander Lember of the Dentists' Rifles (M.J. Carter), and how Demetrius Hoppit (E. Margetson), Hermia's timid fiancé, is miraculously made even more dashing than his rival and wins back his true love. As Hippolyta Hoppit, the angular and refined boarding house keeper, B.S. Cave-Chinn dominated the stage. R.C.B. Horsley played a depressed and adenoidal maidservant. D. Glyn Owen was a very Welsh Puck; R.G. Bailey was an elegant fairy and J.D. Foxall was Oberon, King of the Fairies. The ballet was gracefully performed. The production was enhanced by beautiful scenery and splendid lighting. A special word of praise was due to Arthur Drewry, who took over as chairman from RQMS H.R. Smith ('Smithy'), who was indisposed, and did the job supremely well. A.G. Betts was responsible for the scenery and lighting and H.J. Willans for a clever programme design.

On a more serious note, reports that appeared in the press at the end of the year about the reorganization of the Territorial Army in London led to some speculation in the Regiment as to what the Artists' future was likely to be. The 2nd (London) Division was disbanded and the Grey Brigade went with it. The former two London Infantry Divisions were sacrificed to the expansion of the London anti-aircraft defences, but out of the rump of them a new London Division arose consisting of the 1st, 2nd and 3rd (London) Infantry Brigades. The Artists were not actually incorporated in any of these formations, but were attached for administration and training to the 2nd (London) Brigade, along with the HAC, the London Rifle Brigade, the Kensingtons and the London Scottish. In order to quash speculation that arose in the Regiment, Colonel Willans issued the following announcement dated 10 December 1935:

> The Regiment's function and responsibility will be the same as it always has been; it will be, by reason of the type of personnel it enlists, an officer-finding unit. In the event of war it will again become our duty to find officers for the Army and other Services. To do so has always been our main object and desire, and it is unnecessary for me to recall that during the last war the Artists found 10,256 officers for every Regiment and branch of the Army, besides many for the Royal Navy and Royal Air Force.
>
> IT IS DESIRABLE TO MAKE IT CLEAR THAT THERE IS NO INTENTION TO MAKE THE ARTISTS INTO AN O.T.C., or to alter its methods, conditions, or length of service; indeed there is no reason to fear any change which will adversely affect any member of the Regiment. We shall – as always – be one of the main reserves of officer material, and we shall continue to be a Regiment of the T.A.
>
> I hope that nobody will be misled by uninformed statements in the Press or elsewhere into fearing that our fundamental status or traditional aims are in any jeopardy.

Already the war clouds were gathering and, although there were those in the nation who doubted the prospect of conflict, the course was set for war.

Chapter 17

Between the Wars

Crisis at Duke's Road
1936-1938

Peace for our time.
                    Neville Chamberlain, on his return from Munich, 1938

One of Adolf Hitler's first steps on coming to power in 1933 had been to withdraw his newly established Third Reich from the League of Nations. In March 1936 Germany re-occupied the Rhineland, mandated to France under the Locarno Pact of 1925. The overthrow in civil war (1936-39) of Spain's elected government by the Fascist dictator General Francisco Franco, with German help, was applauded in Parliament with few vocal dissenters. In 1938 Germany annexed Austria, adding 6 million German speakers to the Third Reich and later in the year Hitler seized the Sudetenland bringing 2 million Sudeten Germans under his control. This caused the meeting at Munich when, on 30 September, Chamberlain and Daladier, the French Prime Minister, agreed that Hitler should retain the Sudetenland. Britain had, however, in 1937 begun to re-arm: the Royal Navy and Royal Air Force were considerably strengthened but little extra money was spent on the Army.

On 20 January 1936 His Majesty King George V died, eight months after he had celebrated his Silver Jubilee. Eight days later, after most of the men had spent the night in the Drill Hall, 24 officers and 401 other ranks (90 per cent of current strength) of the Artists Rifles at 6 a.m. filed out by company into the rain to practise the movements of 'Rest on your arms reversed'. Shortly afterwards, the parade embussed for Hyde Park where the Artists were to be stationed in Park Lane for the funeral procession on its way to Paddington station for the conveyance of the King's coffin by rail for burial at Windsor. As recalled by A.D. Marsh: 'The coffin fell off the gun carriage at Marble Arch and the procession was brought to a halt. Queen Mary's carriage was stopped immediately in front of the Artists' rank and we were held at the "Present Arms" for 45 minutes.' Even greater crowds had assembled than for the Silver Jubilee. In spite of the unfortunate mishap at Marble Arch, the spectacle was impressive. The slow pacing of spurred feet, the Dead March and the gun carriage bearing the King's coffin had a distinctly emotional effect on the spectators. Behind the gun carriage came King Edward VIII and his brothers and behind them the carriage bearing the dignified figure of Queen Mary. By 1.30 p.m. the Artists had returned to Duke's Road where, before dismissal, they observed two minutes' silence in honour of the late King.

At a meeting of the London Territorial School of Arms Association Committee it was decided that the Monro Shield should not be competed for this year (1936), there no longer being a 47th Division, but that the Byrne Shield should be fought for instead by all units of the LTSAA. The bayonet competition was held on Tuesday, 11 February, at the London Rifle Brigade headquarters, and was well attended by supporters. Altogether nine London teams competed, namely the 1st, 2nd, 3rd, 10th, 13th and 16th London, the London Scottish, the London Rifle Brigade and the Artists Rifles. The competition was won by the Artists, after beating the 10th and 16th London and in the final the London Rifle Brigade by seven wins to one. The Artists' team was supplied by 'B' Company.

In the reorganization of the Infantry (1936), although the Artists did not at first enjoy its effects, each Regular and Territorial division now had a machine-gun link. An Infantry brigade now consisted of three Rifle battalions and a Machine-Gun battalion. The constitution of the Rifle battalion remained the same (four heterogeneous companies), each company now having a Mortar platoon. Each platoon was to be equipped with a hand-operated 0.5-inch anti-tank rifle, weighing 35lbs, which was to be carried in company transport. It was not regarded as a specialist weapon and no special team was to be provided to handle it. The Bren light machine gun was introduced. This weapon, which was to see over thirty years' service in the British Army, weighed 21½lbs, fired a 0.303 bullet and was mounted on a light tripod for defensive fire or conversion to an anti-aircraft mounting. Although the Artists retained some horses for transport purposes, officers' chargers were to be replaced by motor cars. In the Rifle battalion the commanding officer was to ride in a four-seater and there would be fourteen 2-seaters, eleven motor cycles and forty-four bicycles.

Easter camp, 1936, which was based on Hyderabad Barracks, Colchester, was marred by icy blasts and violent downpours of rain and hail. Some 170 all ranks, commanded by Captain P.G.R. Burford with Second Lieutenant D.H. Flint as acting adjutant took part. On the Friday morning the Artists went to Middlewick Ranges to see a demonstration by the 61st Field Battery RA, equipped with four 4.5-inch howitzers, and a cavalry regiment, the 5th Inniskilling Dragoon Guards. In the afternoon the Artists moved to Martlesham Heath aerodrome where they were introduced to a large transport and supply aircraft. On Saturday morning they marched to an emergency landing strip where the lucky few were given joy rides in Hawker fighter planes, and in the afternoon a soccer match was played against the Ox. and Bucks Light Infantry, who won 1:0. Divine service was attended in Colchester and this was followed by a march-past, the salute being taken by Major General C.G. Liddell, commanding 4th Division, Colchester, who had been the last commander of the 47th Division; the rest of the day was devoted to leisure pursuits.

On the Monday a mortar demonstration was given by Regulars and this was followed by a pleasant march to Blackheath where a demonstration was given on the practical use of smoke by a platoon of the 2nd Battalion, the Somerset Light Infantry. After lunch the Artists embussed for London and thence home.

The commanding officer, Lieutenant Colonel Harry Willans, was in 1936 granted a two-year extension of office. In consequence of the death of King George V there was no Summer Exhibition at the Royal Academy Dinner this year and therefore no Royal Academy Guard. Once again the Regimental Bayonet Team was successful in winning the Army Championship at the Royal Tournament at Olympia. This year, however, the Artists were unable to emulate their success in previous years in the Inter-Services Championship, being beaten in the first round by the Royal Navy by 11 wins to 7. In the Army Championship the Artists beat the 1st Battalion, the Leicestershire Regiment in the first round, in the semi-final the 2nd Battalion, the East Surrey Regiment, and in the final the 1st Battalion, the Royal Sussex Regiment.

Camp 1936 was spent with the 2nd (London) Brigade at Lavant, the eastern part of the training area adjoining Goodwood Park, near Chichester, Sussex. The marching detachment paraded at Victoria Station on Friday 10 July. On alighting from the train at Pulborough, the Detachment marched four miles to Watersfield, where they spent the night after eating and drinking at The Three Crowns. The following day they marched about ten miles via Duncton Hill, Singleton and the Trundle before arriving in camp in the late afternoon. For the first time in recent years the good weather deserted the campers, an unpleasant experience, especially for the new recruits. The site was a new one for a TA camp. The training areas were generally the best the Regiment had encountered in a dozen years. There were limitations, however, in calling for the skilful use of ground on the Downs, and the many fields of standing crops were a handicap to deployment.

Attendance this year was very good. The high strength registered on the middle Saturday was 23 officers and 433 other ranks, not far short of the establishment. Innovations were introduced to make the training more interesting for the rank-and-file. During the first week there was an unfortunate motor accident in mid-Lavant involving five members of 'D' Company, resulting in the death of Private H. Thackwell and in one of his companions being seriously injured. Altogether there were about eighty motor vehicles at camp during the first week, plus two motor-cycles, slightly less in numbers in the second week. In spite of the fact that the Transport Section was now motorized, there were still a few of the four-legged beasts around. Whilst riding a mile or so away from camp, Colonel Willans was pitched from his saddle when his mount shied. His right elbow was dislocated with a complicating fracture. Despite his obvious pain, the Colonel stuck to his duties, carrying on as much as he was able. With the foul weather conditions, much of the time was spent digging ditches to divert the surface water. There is no necessity to say any more about the weather except that it was so wet that one afternoon a young porpoise found its way into 'B' Company lines.

Held as usual in the dining tent on the first Friday evening, the annual camp smoker was again a great success. The chair was taken by RQMS 'Smithy', who handled the audience with his usual skill. Choruses performed by Private R.A. Boxall opened the show, followed by songs from Corporal T.W.C. Robinson, Corporal R.D. Connery and Captain Guy Chater, while Privates Leigh-Breese and W. Horton clowned. 'A' Company produced an extravaganza concerning a full-dress prize giving at Narkover College. 'B' Company put on a sketch entitled *Somewhere in Sussex*. 'C' Company erected a blanket screen and produced surreal-istic charades. 'D' Company managed a spontaneous effort that was extremely topical – very much up to the minute.

At the end of the 1936 training year C.S. Goulding, Spurgeon Parker and John Lee put on a show called *New Blood* at Duke's Road that portrayed Spain as a land of romance and villainy in equal measure. Great credit was also due to R.H. Young for the lyrics, and for the music by S. Killick, R.A. Lee, C.F. Smyly and E. Van Walwyk. The play told of how George Smith (A.W. Cook), an Englishman, who woos Carmen (R.G. White), the fair daughter of mine host (R.C.B. Horsley) of 'La Bassa Bitte', triumphs with the aid of Theo Q. Pink (John Platt) from Pittsburgh, USA, over the intrigues of Pedro (E. Margetson), the wicked toreador. The second act opened with George Smith being thrown into prison charged with stealing the jewellery of Mrs Golightly (L.D.L. Browne), a wealthy widow and a most striking soprano. Sam Small (W. Horton) appears on the scene to interrupt the proceedings armed with two bottles of beer, much of which he had consumed before coming on stage. B.S. Cave-Chinn played a cockney-born sentry. In the final scene the hero's name is cleared, Pedro being forced to confess that he 'planted' the jewellery, and Carmen with a most moving fit of weeping pleads forgiveness for having doubted her George. The innkeeper's wife Dolones (J.A. Bullivant) might more aptly have been named 'La Passionaria'. Praise must be said for the lighting by S.E. Hamilton, F.A. Stocken and D.H. Lightfoot for the scenery. The commanding officer was pleased to present a 'green tie' to C.S. Goulding, who was mainly the inspiration behind *New Blood*.

In March 1937 Major F.H. Hawksford retired after ten years' service as the Artists' first Regimental secretary. His connection with the Regiment dated back forty-two years to February 1895, when he was appointed a sergeant instructor from the Rifle Brigade. In a very short time he was promoted regimental sergeant major and served in that capacity to 8 November 1901. He was an enthusiastic supporter of the School of Arms, both while RSM and during the years after when he was a voluntary instructor. Again on the re-formation of the battalion after the Great War Hawksford started the cult of the bayonet in the Regiment and trained such experts as A.C. Murray, the first Gold Medallist, W. Hammond and A.W. Byrne, who each in their turn gained fame for the Artists' bayonet teams. At the outbreak of the Great War he enlisted as a private in the 3rd Battalion of the Artists and was shortly appointed RSM. From there he gained a commission in the Royal Flying Corps, ultimately becoming major on the staff in Canada and receiving the OBE for his services. Given the new appointment of Regimental secretary, in 1929 he was mainly responsible for the enrolment of 500 members of the Veterans' Company, which was formed from the nucleus of the honorary members. A presentation was made to Major Hawksford on 22 April 1937 at the Annual Dinner of the Veterans' Company.

In April 1937 Lieutenant Colonel Harry Willans made an important announcement about the Regimental uniform, which is reprinted here in full:

> For some time it has been apparent to me that we should, sooner or later, be faced with the necessity for reconsidering our attitude towards our grey uniform. The Grey dates from the time when the Artists were first formed and were part of what was known as 'The

Grey Brigade', all the regiments of which were clothed in this colour. When the Territorials were formed in 1908, khaki was issued as Service Dress and the Grey was retained as Full Dress and for Mess Dress, etc. When the battalion paraded publicly for reviews and other events, Full Dress was worn, and the Grey, of course, conferred a distinction upon the Regiment, which, in course of time, was identified in the public mind with that colour.

Since the War there has been no Full Dress and the Grey Brigade has finally been disbanded. Grey is now only used for Officers' Mess Dress, Officers' Patrols or Undress, Sergeants' Patrols and for the Drums' Full Dress. The colour is not satisfactory for practical purposes and there has frequently been difficulty in matching.

So long as there was no important object in reconsidering the question, it is probable that we should have continued indefinitely to use grey for the purposes named, even though the fact that we are now a part of the Corps of the Rifle Brigade and very much closer identified with that Regiment than in the past suggested that, sooner or later, circumstances would probably demand a change.

I had, however, no immediate intention of making such a change and when it was announced that a walking-out dress would be issued to troops taking part in the Coronation, I immediately applied for authority to wear Grey for that occasion, at the same time taking such steps as appeared necessary to secure a supply of suitable cloth. The War Office approval for the wearing of Grey at the Coronation has now been received, but only after so long a delay that it is impossible to secure a grey cloth to match that which we wear, and it is extremely doubtful whether buttons and badges could be obtained in time for the Coronation. Quite apart from the difficulty in obtaining this cloth, it has been ruled that the cost of supplying the grey uniforms would have to fall upon the Regiment and not upon public funds. This would mean an expenditure from Regimental funds of approximately £100. Of greater importance is that there is on foot a tentative proposal to issue a walking-out dress to all Territorial troops. The free issue of walking-out dress will, however, be Green or Blue as the case may be. If authority were given for Grey it would again be at the Regimental expense and would mean an initial expenditure of something like £2,000. Such an outlay is quite out of the question and this fact, taken in conjunction with the other circumstances set out above, has determined me to make out the change set out below, which I am convinced will be in the best interests of the Regiment in the long run:

For the Coronation our troops will wear Green walking-out dress, similar to that worn by the Rifle regiments. The Officers on parade will wear green Patrol uniforms, similar to those worn by the Rifle Brigade officers.

After the Coronation, Officers' Patrols or Undress uniform will be changed to Green, Officers being permitted to retain their present uniform until the new one is needed. Sergeants' Mess Dress will be green, sergeants being permitted to retain their existing uniforms until they have occasion to purchase new ones or until the free issue is made.

As a natural corollary to this change, Officers' and Other Ranks' khaki tunics will carry black buttons instead of brass, and silver cap badges, instead of brass, all of Artists' Regimental pattern. When the walking-out dress is issued it will be green. Officers' Mess Dress and the Drums' Full Dress will continue to be grey as at present. Grey will continue to be used for flags, ties, blazers and other Regimental equipment, other than Officers and Sergeants who purchase new uniforms in the course of events, which will certainly not be more costly than the present ones. If expense is entailed in the initial issue of black buttons, silver badges, etc., it will be borne by Regimental funds. Further issues of buttons will be made on payment, but are unlikely to cost more than the present Regimental buttons, which every man buys on enlistment.

For the Easter weekend that year nine officers, sixteen warrant officers and sergeants and 180 men under the command of Captain P.G.R. Burford embussed for Canterbury where they were billeted at the depot of the Buffs (Royal East Kent Regiment). On the Friday morning snow was falling as the marchers took to the Sandwich road, going by way of Patrixbourne ford passing over open downland to a halt for lunch at Adisham. In the afternoon twelve miles were completed to Barham where a river was in flood. The Detachment was accommodated in a school, memorial hall and in a barn, and on the Saturday marched via Tilmanstone, where lunch was taken at The Plough and Harrow, to the Royal Marine Depot at Deal, a distance of thirteen miles. The Sunday church parade was commanded by Captain F.R. Beausire, a veteran Artists from pre-Great War days, who had retired from the active list the previous day. On the Monday the Detachment marched out of Deal at 10.30 going by way of Kingsdown and Ringwould to Martin Hill, where they entrained for London in a hail storm.

The Royal Academy parade in 1937 fell on Saturday 1 May, which, apart from being a dull and chilly day, was May Day, Labour Day, Cup Final Day and the first day of the London bus strike. The absence of the buses on the streets gave the guard more room to manoeuvre on its march from Duke's Road to Piccadilly, whilst the Drums and words of command were for once audible to the last men in the column. At the south end of Shaftesbury Avenue, as if to give a flourish to their entry to Piccadilly Circus, the Drums forsook their usual music for bugle calls, which coincidentally heralded their approach to those waiting to receive the guard in the forecourt of the Royal Academy. The guard was commanded by Captain R.R. Cripps, who brought the ranks to attention for several important personages, including Lord Londonderry, the honorary colonel, and the principal guest this year, HRH the Duke of Kent, who was accorded the royal salute. The return to headquarters did not take long. Everyone had done their best and it was encouraging to reflect on the expressions of appreciation from the Duke of Kent and Lord Londonderry.

Edward, Prince of Wales, who succeeded his father George V as Edward VIII, ruled the nation and empire as uncrowned king only until December 1936 when he chose abdication in order to marry the American divorcée, Wallis Simpson. In his place his brother Albert was crowned at Westminster Abbey as King George VI on Wednesday, 12 May 1937. The great Imperial event for the individuals taking part fell into two distinct parts – firstly the assembly during two days in the Royal parks of Regular British, Dominion and Colonial servicemen and Territorials, as well as representatives of the nursing services, and the procession on the great day itself. A small Artists contingent took part in the procession; another lined the route on the Victoria Embankment, while individual members of the Regiment volunteered to act as special constables. Several weeks before the coronation the Artists were fitted out with their new green uniforms. There were those who regretted the passing of the grey but the mood among most of the Artists was that they were glad now to be more closely associated with the great Corps of Riflemen.

The Artists, who were billeted in tents in Hyde Park on the day, fell in with the other Territorial units at the Serpentine before moving in four files in the rear of the band of the 1st Battalion, the Highland Light Infantry, through the gates at Hyde Park Corner, past the British Legion standards, around the Artillery Memorial, then swinging to the left through the arch on to Constitution Hill, where a halt was called. The timing of the halt coincided exactly with the broadcast of the ceremony of the Anointing , the Robing, the Girding with the Sword and the central and supreme act of the Crowning. On again, between the grandstands around the Victoria Memorial, and down the Mall, which was lined on both sides by guardsmen in their scarlet tunics. Passing Big Ben at 1.09 p.m., the procession turned in a great sweep on to the Embankment where 37,000 loudly-cheering London school children were stationed. Trafalgar Square was reached, then along Pall Mall and up the hill of St James's Street and into Piccadilly. A long halt was called in Regent Street before the procession moved along Oxford Street and back to Hyde Park.

The Artists contingent, which was to take its place in lining the route, left Duke's Road at 6.40 a.m., marching through the as yet deserted streets. After a short pause under Hungerford Bridge, they took up their position in extended order opposite the RAF Memorial on the Victoria Embankment, in order to test the spacing arrangements. The Artists then left for Whitehall Court and fell out until midday when they took up their position again on the Embankment, which by now was lined with thousands of school children. The head of the procession arrived on time but there was a long wait before the Abbey guests and the state coach appeared bearing Their Majesties on their long drive to the Palace. Finally, the Artists marched back to headquarters, each mindful of a day well spent.

In company with other London Territorial units, the Regiment again had the privilege of lining the streets on the occasion of His Majesty the King's drive to the Guildhall to be received by the Lord Mayor of London on 19 May. It was, unfortunately, a wet, dull morning and groundsheets were issued for protection against the rain. The Regiment was allotted the area from the Savoy Courtyard to the Aldwych, and was in position before 11 a.m. The rain did not appear to dampen the enthusiasm of the crowd, who began lining the street an hour before the King was due to pass by. Disappointment was felt that the royal drive would have to be in closed cars without a cavalry escort, but the cheering grew quite loud as the royal car containing Their Majesties drove slowly past, preceded by cars with other members of the royal family on board. The return route was also to be lined, but as the rain showed no sign of abatement, all troops were withdrawn. An excellent cold lunch was laid on at headquarters, during which the Colonel proposed the health of the King.

In June 1937 the Regiment ceased to be known as the 28th London Regiment (Artists Rifles) and not before time, was called simply 'The Artists Rifles'. Further the word 'Artists' in the title was shorn of its apostrophe, which so many people had in any case put in the wrong place. The Artists Rifles was detached from the 2nd (London) Brigade and posted to a new formation with the title of the Officer Producing Group, disrespectfully referred to as the OGPU of Soviet affiliations. This meant that the Regiment was now an Officers' Training Corps in all essentials bar one; and that one was very important; the potential officers on the successful conclusion of their course were not immediately required to take commissions. Instead they were invested with a new distinction called an Officers' Qualification Certificate to become officers if and when the individual so wished. The men could continue to be other ranks in the Artists until a national emergency or the workings of their consciences drove them to higher things. The Officers' Qualification Certificate was not compulsory, but for those whose time was not taken up with fulfilling some administrative function it was the obvious goal of their training.

There was more reorganization later that year. 'C' Company ceased to be 'C' (Support) Company armed with MMGs and became an ordinary Rifle company. The MMGs were forced to find a new home in HQ Wing, which now became HQ Company and an altogether ambitious set-up. The Drums after many years of faithful service were disbanded in the cause of efficiency (a move that hardly seemed particularly clever when one looks back at it, for Regimental Bands and Drums were high up in the Army's morale-building scale). The Drums made their last appearance with the Royal Academy guard in the spring of 1938. Thereafter they became anti-aircraft Lewis gunners as a platoon in HQ Company.

At the Royal Tournament in 1937 the Artists Bayonet Team emerged from the Services Bayonet Combats as Army Champions for the seventh time in eight years, and as runners-up in the Inter-Services Championship after taking the fight to 11:7 before losing to the Portsmouth Division of the Royal Marines. The fighting this year was close, as shown by the results, and in one round the 1st Battalion the Scots Guards, in particular, gave the Artists many qualms. At one stage the Artists were 7:3 down, and it seemed impossible that they could ever fight back, but some magnificent fighting brought them to 9:8 down, when R.G. Garton plunged into the fray and with great ferocity brought the fight to nine all. Captain Cripps then defeated the leader of the opposing team, while the spectators held their breath. The final was in the nature of an anti-climax, the Artists beating the 2nd Battalion, the Seaforth Highlanders, 13:5.

Lympne, Kent, was chosen as the Artists first camp as an officer producing unit, and it was generally considered to be a very successful one. Taking place in July/August 1937, the Marching Detachment comprising forty-five all ranks entrained for Ashford, then covering four miles to The Sparrows' Arms at Mersham, where they spent the night. Next morning, after sleeping on a hard floor, the more hardy ones in the party took a plunge in a stream near the mill. The pretty, winding roads of Kent seemed to lead the Detachment in a semi-circle towards camp, but after eight miles and none too soon for some of the men they arrived at the pub in Ruckinge. Six more miles to Lympne along the ridge of hills gave the marchers a glorious view over the Romney marshes to the sea. Except for two or three who were obliged to get on good terms with transport, the Detachment arrived in camp on the Saturday just as the rain was beginning to fall at 4.30 p.m.

The situation, in the lovely countryside, close to the Kent border with Sussex was ideal; the weather, particularly in the second week could hardly have been better and amenities available to the troops were more numerous than ever before. The numbers present gave the Regiment great credit. During the first week 513 officers and other ranks were present in camp; in the second week this declined by sixty or so. There was a larger contingent of Regular officers and NCOs attached for training than hitherto, and they laid a special emphasis on drill and spit-and-polish. Also present at camp in the second week was Major Kirschmann, the German Assistant Military Attaché; what impressions he may have conveyed to Adolf Hitler of the Artists in training was not disclosed by the German High Command!

Once again cooperation with the Air Arm was an integral part of the training, for which the Regiment was indebted to No. 2 (AC) Squadron at Hawkinge, and the hope was expressed that the Territorial Army and Auxiliary Air Force would continue to train side-by-side. Transport was the branch of the Corps that prospered most from the demon progress. While the Signals continued to employ the wartime pattern D3 telephone, while the Bren gun was still largely a matter of the imagination, while mortars and anti-tank protection were more imaginary still, the Transport rejoiced in the prettiest of modern equipment. This year the few occupants of the horse-lines were scarcely to be seen, except in the gymkhana, the programme for which does not appear to have survived, as also seems to be the case with the smoker.

On 31 July 1937 Captain E. Van Walwyk, MBE, MM died; had he lived until October he would have been fifty-eight years of age. No man could have acquired the spirit and tradition of the Artists better than he did. Coming to the Artists from the Rifle Brigade in 1920 as regimental sergeant major, it did not take the Regiment long to appreciate what manner of man he was. Wally enlisted in the Rifle Brigade on 13 January 1897, and after four months at the depot in Winchester he was posted to the 4th Battalion. He served in South Africa, Malta and Egypt, and the outbreak of the Great War saw him with the 3rd Battalion in Ireland. He proceeded to France on 8 September as colour sergeant in the 3rd Battalion, was promoted to CSM on 13 October and taken prisoner at the Battle of the Aisne on 21 October. He was interned at Doebritz camp until 1916, when as an exchanged prisoner of war he was sent to Holland, where he remained until the Armistice. While at Doebritz he organized and became bandmaster of the Allied Prisoners of War band. Wally was a good musician and up to the time when he became too ill to carry on he supplemented his income by playing and teaching music.

Shortly after he came to the Artists he reached the age for compulsory retirement from the Regular Army but there was a vacancy for a quartermaster and he applied for and got the job. He was a magnificent quartermaster, many of his counterparts in other London TA units seeking his advice on 'Q' matters. He was also a great entertainer at smoking concerts, his best remembered songs being *The Old Chapeau*, *The Musketry Song* and *The Four Italians – Pizzicato, Rallentando, Agitato and me*. He was an expert with rifle and revolver. For a number of years he trained and captained the Artists officers' and sergeants' team for the London District Spring Meeting. He was very proud of his Military Medal, which was awarded in recognition of gallant conduct and determination in attempting to escape from captivity, and for gallant conduct in the field.

Towards the end of 1937 A.R. Moore retired after five years service as RSM. Few knew his Christian names and he was known throughout the Regiment as 'Pony'. He had been recruited by the Artists from the Rifle Brigade in 1932 and became a worthy scion of a line of RSMs from the Greenjackets, which had included Frank Hawksford and Van Walwyk. A Rifleman to the core, he had enlisted at the depot in Winchester prior to and served throughout the Great War, and continued to serve with it at home and abroad until posted to the Artists. Under 'Pony Moore', the orderly room, then conducted by three ORs only, became a model of efficiency and tidiness. His recruit courses were immensely successful and in the last three competitions for the *Daily Telegraph* Cup his advice and practical help were much appreciated. When at the end of 1937, his time in the Army expired simultaneously with his term with the Artists he was succeeded as RSM by 'Buck' Norton of the Rifle Brigade. But he remained with the Artists as assistant Regimental secretary, becoming a Territorial sergeant attached to the quartermaster, who was also Regimental secretary. 'Pony' Moore did not suffer fools gladly but he was greatly liked; his ability was unquestionable; he was a true Artist in every sense of the word.

In November 1937 Captain R.R. Cripps was appointed second in command, although he was not appointed major until the following April, when Captain P.G.R. Burford was promoted junior major. Also in November Captain R.A. MacGeorge's tour of office as adjutant drew to an end and he was followed by Captain W.P.S. Curtis, also of the Rifle Brigade. The company commanders at the end of the year were Captain A.J. Godrich ('A), Captain A.N. Browning ('B'), Captain P.G.R. Burford ('C') and Lieutenant J.L. Baucher ('D'). Pressure of affairs at this time having compelled the Marquis of Londonderry to tender his resignation, the appointment as honorary colonel was offered to and accepted by the

Lord Stathcona and Mount Royal, Under-Secretary of State for War. Strathcona, the third Baron in line, was the grandson of the first holder of the title, born a Scot as Donald Alexander Smith, who was a Canadian fur trader, and became governor of the Hudson's Bay Company, a prominent Canadian financier, railway promoter and statesman. Knighted in 1886, he was appointed High Commissioner for Canada in London and, in 1897, granted a peerage as Lord Strathcona and Mount Royal (of Mount Royal and Glencoe). On his death in 1914, his peerage passed to his only daughter, Margaret Charlotte Howard.

The 3rd Baron, born Donald Stanley Palmer Howard in 1891, was the son of R.J.B. Howard, F.R.C.S. and the (later) Baroness Strathcona and Mount Royal. Educated at Eton and Trinity College, Cambridge (BA Honours Historical Tripos), he joined the Regular Army (3rd Hussars) in 1913. He served throughout the Great War in the same Regiment: he was awarded the Belgian Croix de Guerre and retired as a captain in 1919. Elected a Member of Parliament in 1922 for North Cumberland, he was Private Secretary to the First Lord of the Admiralty, 1925-26; a member of the Indian Statutory Commission, 1928-30; Captain of the King's Body Guard of the Yeomen of the Guard, 1931-34, and, after his elevation to the peerage, Parliamentary Under-Secretary of State for War. At the time of his appointment as honorary colonel of the Artists Rifles he was chairman of a committee that was set up to enquire into conditions in the Territorial Army.

The show put on at the end of the training year for 1937 was entitled *Alias John Brown*, a romantic melodrama with music, set in the Foreign Legion based at Sidi-bel-Abbes and at Fort Ste Juste, a 'hard station' in the middle of the desert. The plot concerned a bunch of English toffs who after joining the Foreign Legion plan to murder the infamous Sergeant Briac and intrigue at the Café Bleu in Sidi-bel-Abbes where Briac makes known his doubtful intentions towards Simoni, the dusky proprietress. The commandant discovers the plot to kill Briac and the Englishmen are sent out on patrol into the desert, where they drop dead one by one at the hands of the hostile Bedouins. The cast was as follows:

Lady Cynthia	Dudley S. Matthews	Brown	William Cook
Leroux	Patrick K. Burkitt	Hagen	Robert Hughes
Müller	Alfred H.J. Palmer	Briac	Arthur R. Kempson
'erbert	William Horton	Simoni	Eric E. Sanderson
Clarke	John A.B. Mumford	Frou-Frou	George Reddick
Hawkins	John H. Lloyd	Marie	Tom Danes

Book by C.S. Goulding..Lyrics by R.A.B. Chomley.
Music by John Ivimey.

For Easter training, Thursday 14 April to Monday 18 April, 1938, the Regiment was attached to the Rifle Brigade depot at Winchester. Cold winds made it a weekend for lingering in pubs and canteens. Yet it was excellent weather for training, save on the Chilcomb Range, where the recruits were shooting their weapon-training course. The rest of the Detachment spent Friday and Saturday doing either a TEWT or a skeleton exercise by double companies. The TEWT was good and very interesting, but the skeleton exercise was good only in parts. What with The George, the New Forest and the South Coast, Sunday was a good day. Church Parade was suitably impressive and the sermon inspiring; then the Detachment dispersed over the south of England, some reaching as far afield as Hayling Island. On the Monday, after a nine-mile march to New Alresford, lunch was taken at The Running Horse; and so ended the Easter weekend happy in spirit and pleasant in execution. This year's Royal Academy guard was commanded by Captain Browning. Parading 105 strong on 30 April, the guard marched through streets abnormally crowded as it was Cup Final Day and reached Burlington House shortly after 6 p.m. The inspection this year was carried out by the Earl of Athlone.

Every year since the Regiment was revived after the Great War, the artists, architects, sculptors and designers, both former and serving Artists, continued to make a significant contribution to the Summer Exhibition. As a typical example, the list of Artists who showed their work at the Summer Exhibition for 1938 is given here in full.

THE SUMMER EXHIBITION 1938

This year's Summer Exhibition included an exhibit by a serving Artist a small self-portrait in tempera of Hubert Williams ('H.Q.' Company), evidently in a stern frame of mind. It was unpretentious and undeniably attractive, and deserved to have been better hung.

Other work by Artists was as copious as usual:

JAMES BATEMAN, ARA was this year's most prolific in output. His best picture on display, *Cattle Market* had been bought under the terms of the Chantry Bequest. Cattle also appeared in No. 227 *Farm Yard*. His remaining exhibits were a Westmorland landscape, and two water-colours of the Sussex countryside.

JAMES GUNN this year showed only two pictures, portraits of his wife and H.J. Scrymgeour-Wedderburn in Scottish uniform. They were well up to the usual standard of the painter's work.

MEREDITH FRAMPTON, A.RA. showed what was in most viewer's opinion the portrait of the year, a picture of Sir Frederick Gowland Hopkins, OM, depicted amongst the paraphernalia of his science. The meticulous attention to detail of this artist was something to marvel at. 'You almost expect him to walk out of the frame' was a comment actually heard more than once during the exhibition.

W. LEE-HANKEY's two bluff portraits (Nos., 164 and 458) were in marked contrast and in their way very effective; though the first of Charles Stanley Jarvis caught the eye awkwardly wherever one stood.

FRANCIS HODGE, ADRIAN CHORLEY and ALFRED HAYWARD completed the Artists' tally in the oil-painting rooms.

Artists were also strongly represented in the architecture room with work by MAXWELL AYRTON, E. VINCENT HARRIS, OBE, ARA, WILLIAM G. NEWTON, HAROLD D. SUGDEN and PERCY THOMAS, OBE.

Percy Thomas also appeared in another role: No. 285 was a portrait of him by Harold Knight, RA.

Among the water-colourists, GERALD ACKERMANN was outstanding with an attractive composition of buildings at Wells-next-the-Sea, and with a lively *The Fair Blakeney.*

ERNEST BLAIKLEY'S *The Neglected Barn* was a study in dark brown. The Regiment's representatives in the black-and-white room were WILLIAM P. ROBINS, who exhibited a dry-point of *Mantles Farm* and a very distinguished mezzotint, *The Artist's Mother*, and C.W. CAIN, with a dry-point, *The Burmese Paddy Boat.*

WILLIAM McMILLAN, RA, was the Artists' only sculptor. His model for the bronze statue of King George V to be erected in Calcutta was a truly noble conception. His bust of *Sylvia* was also worth noting.

G. KRUGER GRAY's design for King George VI's Great Seal revealed once more how decided was his aptitude for this type of stylized work.
Finally, there were three designs for stained glass windows by REGINALD BELL.

Of the other personalities from the arts world who flourished between the wars and after perhaps the most prominent was the writer and broadcaster, S.P.B. Mais. Stuart Mais' enlistment in the Corps can be traced back to 1904 and his literary career to 1916. He was a versatile

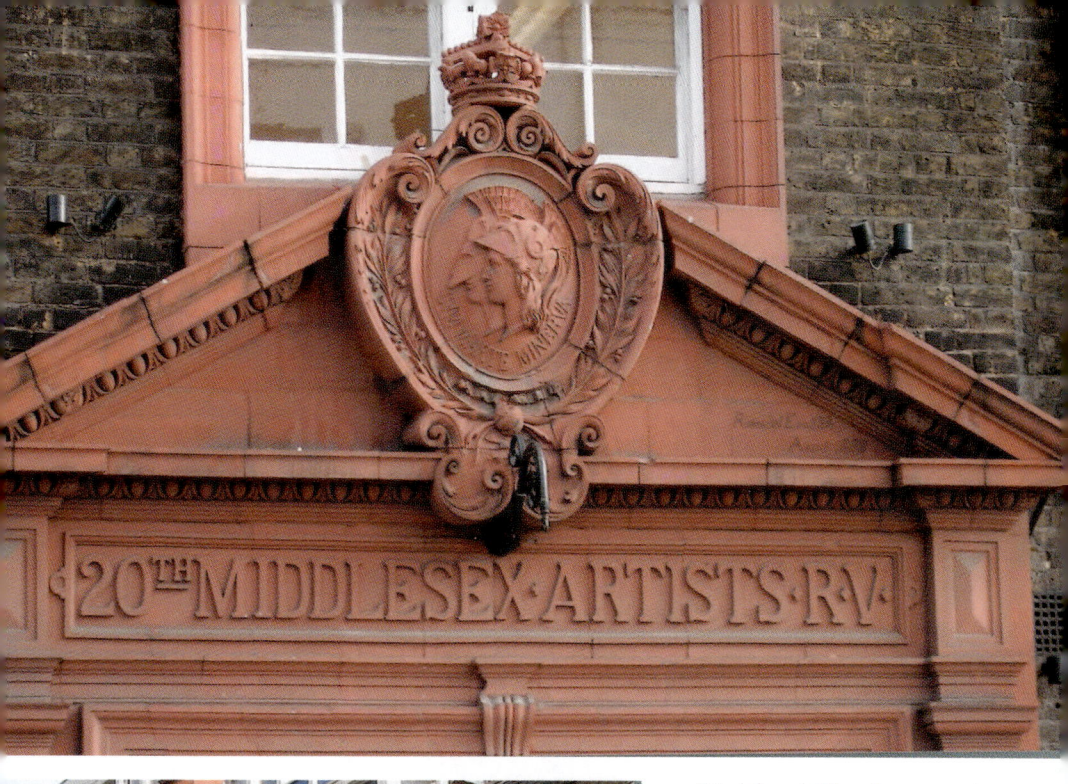

58. *(above)* The doorway to No. 17 Duke's Road.

59. *(left)* No. 17 Duke's Road, Euston. Principal home of the Artists Rifles, a freehold property purchased by private subscription from within the Regimental circle in 1868. Sold by the MOD for £132,000 in 1970 and the proceeds claimed by the Ministry! Now 'The Place', home of the internationally renowned London Contemporary Dance School and others, teaching up to post graduate level. The theatre (formerly the drill hall) has hosted more than 2,500 public performances in the past thirty year.

60. (left) *A Centenary of Artists Uniforms 1859 to 1960.* A. E. Haswell's water colour drawings of the Artists Rifles' uniforms was commissioned for the 21st Special Air Service Regiment (Artists) TA Centenary Celebration in 1960 and includes three SAS soldiers from 1941.

61. *(below)* Artists Rifles Uniforms 1859 - 1913 by Lieutenant A. Egerton Cooper.

62. (above) *The Artists Rifles in Camp 1884* from an oil on canvas by Godfrey Merry.

63. (left) *The 20th Middlesex (Artists) Volunteers* by G.H. Giles in 1907 showing Artists' uniforms in the Boer War.

65. *(left)* Artists Rifles Roll of Honour and Victoria Crosses, Leighton House, Regent's Park Barracks.

66. *(below)* Artists and SAS Battle Honours 1860 to 1960, Leighton House, Regent's Park Barracks.

21ST S.A.S. REGIMENT
–ARTISTS– T.A.
Battle Honours
1860–1960

SOUTH AFRICA 1900-01 – YPRES 1917 – PASSCHENDAELE
SOMME 1918 – ST QUENTIN – BAPAUME 1918 – ARRAS 1918
ANCRE 1918 – ALBERT 1918 – DROCOURT-QUEANT
HINDENBURG LINE – CANAL DU NORD – CAMBRAI 1918
PURSUIT TO MONS – FRANCE AND FLANDERS 1914-18
N.W. EUROPE 1944-45 – BENGHAZI RAID – TOBRUK 1941
N. AFRICA 1940-43 – LANDING IN SICILY – SICILY 1943
TERMOLI – VALLI DI COMACCHIO – ITALY 1943-45
GREECE 1944-45 – ADRIATIC – MIDDLE EAST 1943-44

64. *Early One Morning*. Post war artist David Jenner depicts the Artists Rifles in battle 1916-18. (Note the blue flash on the Artists' tunics.)

TO THE GLORIOUS MEMORY
OF THE 2003 MEMBERS OF THE
ARTISTS RIFLES. 28TH BATTALION
THE LONDON REGIMENT, WHO
GAVE THEIR LIVES FOR KING
AND COUNTRY IN THE GREAT
WAR ANNIS DOMINI 1914-1919.
THEIR NAME LIVETH FOR EVERMORE

AND OF THOSE WHO GAVE THEIR
LIVES IN THE WORLD WAR
ANNIS DOMINI 1939-1945

(*Left page*) The Artists Rifles War Memorial located at the Royal Academy, Burlington House, Piccadilly, the early home of the Corps of Artists.

68. (*Above*) The 63rd Royal Naval Division Great War Memorial recently restored to Horse Guards Parade, includes the 1st Battalion Artists Rifles, who replaced the Honourable Artillery Company on 24 June 1917.

69. (*Left*) Bust of Sir Barnes Wallis CBE, FRS located in front of a painting depicting some of his many aeronautical achievements. *By kind permission of the Royal Air Force Club, Piccadilly*

70. *(right)* The Artists' Drummer, part of the Artists' display.
By kind permission of the Airborne Forces Museum, Aldershot and the Trustees of the SAS/Artists Rifles Regimental Collection

71. *(below)* Selection of Artists' Memorabilia.
By kind permission of the Airborne Forces Museum, Aldershot and the Trustees of the SAS/Artists Rifles Regimental Collection

writer, being a novelist and author of many books on travel and the countryside. (His works occupied a complete column of *Who's Who.*) He was also well-known for his talks on radio and later as a TV personality. Educated at Denstone and Christ Church, Oxford, he was awarded a Blue for track and cross-country running. A school teacher for forty years, S.P.B. Mais' last post was at Radley in 1945.

The Corps could also boast two top executives of the BBC, namely Charles Brewer and Lance Sieveking. Charles Brewer, a producer of musical comedy and revue programmes and a future director of the Light Programme, joined the Artists in 1913 and was one of the famous 'First Fifty' officers to be commissioned at Bailleul. Posted to the 2nd Bedfords, he was present at the fraternization with German troops in the trenches at Fleurbaix in Christmas 1914; he later served with distinction in the Royal Flying Corps. Lance Sieveking, who joined in 1914 and who was said to be one of the most originally-minded of BBC producers, was also celebrated as a novelist, playwright and actor. Jan van der Gucht was a talented, professional singer who performed at concert halls, including several Promenade concerts, and broadcast frequently on the radio. He was much admired in the Regiment for his rendering at smoking concerts of seventeenth and eighteenth century songs.

Among the actors performing on stage and in films, on radio and TV, in addition to the galaxy of professional talent already mentioned, Michael Goodliffe, Howard Marion-Crawford and Desmond Llewelyn, who all joined the Artists in the late 1930s, are to be noted.

Educated in Liverpool and at Keble College, Oxford, Michael Goodliffe played his first walking-on part on the stage at the Playhouse in 1936. Commissioned from No.163 OCTU early in 1940 into the Royal Warwickshire Regiment, he was taken prisoner in France later in the same year. After the war he played Shakespearean roles for three years at Stratford before appearing in London in *Antony and Cleopatra* and *Macbeth* (as Banquo). His films, in which he usually played an officer or a diplomat included *The Small Back Room* (1948), *The Wooden Horse* (1950), *The Battle of the River Plate* (1956), and *The Man with the Golden Gun* (1975). He died in 1976.

Howard Marion-Crawford was known in films for his jovial, beefy and sporting roles. He first appeared in a movie *Forever England* in 1932; his later films included *The Rake's Progress* (1945), *The Hasty Heart* (1949) and *Where's Charley?* (1952), but he is best remembered as the second Paul Temple on BBC radio. He served with the Irish Guards in the Second World War and died in 1969.

The Welshman Desmond Llewelyn, best known for playing 'Q' in the James Bond movies, also appeared in many other films, including *They Were Not Divided* (1950), *The Lavender Hill Mob* (1950), *A Night to*

Remember (1955) and *Dr Jekyll and Mr Hyde* (1980). Commissioned in the Royal Welch Fusiliers in 1939, he spent five years as a POW. He died in a car crash in 1999, aged eighty-five.

Sport in the 1930s continued to be an important aspect of training in the Artists Rifles. After its post-Great War resuscitation in 1923/24 the Rugby Football Club, which eventually grew to four XVs, for many years played at the UCS Old Boys club, at Syon Park, and at the London Scottish RFC at Eden Park. There were quite a few Artists who played for various Old Boys clubs, the banks and insurance sides, as well as the London Welsh, Harlequins and Wasps, but they only turned out for the Artists' most important matches. Apart from John Greenwood, who won thirteen England caps and was the 35th President of the RFU, there was one other rugby international in the Regiment. He was W.E. Tucker, who was a one-time medical officer in the Regiment, and who played for England many times. Association Football played a comparatively minor role in Regimental sporting activities, but in the 1930s the Artists in J.C.D. Tetley could boast the captain of the England Amateur Association Football team.

Cricket (two teams), hockey, badminton, golf and boxing remained a strong feature of the sporting programme. Between the wars the Artists were also very active in the athletics and cross-country fields. The Inter-Company Annual Sports held at the Duke of York's, Chelsea, was invariably the occasion for the first display of individual talent, and usually 'B' Company were the star performers, tug-of-war and tent-pitching being included in the events. One year Dr Henry Stallard, the Cambridge Blue, AAA and Olympic middle-distance runner, who was medical officer in the Regiment, showed how to run a last leg half-mile with over sixty yards to catch up in the relay race, which he won for the Artists in truly professional style. In boxing A.W. Hewson, a Cambridge Blue, was twice the TA Lightweight Boxing Champion in the 1930s. Another boxer, Ron House, a member of the Drums, reached the final of the TA Welterweight Championship in 1929 but lost. He was also for several years an enthusiastic member of the *Daily Telegraph* Cup team. But all this was not quite exciting enough for Ron House, who in the mid-1930s joined the Foreign Legion. He kept the Regiment well posted with his progress as a legionnaire, expressing the regret that there were no post offices to be found in the desert, the Bedouins managing to carry all their messages on camels.

In May 1938, Lieutenant Colonel Harry Willans, DSO, MC and Bar, TD completed his very successful tour of duty as commanding officer and was succeeded by Lieutenant Colonel R.R. Cripps, with effect from 30 May. On the termination of his appointment as CO Harry Willans was first promoted colonel and then brigadier becoming the first Territorial to command a TA brigade – the 2nd London. Dick Cripps was the eldest of four brothers who served together in the Regiment between 1936/39. Dick joined in April 1924 and was commissioned and posted to 'C' Company in 1927. He soon became a prominent member of the School of Arms and was in the all-powerful Royal Tournament Bayonet team in 1929, and thence until the outbreak of war in 1939. He was TA Officers' Champion for ten years and also qualified in fencing (epée). In rifle shooting also he soon became outstanding, was a Silver Jewellist and leader of several competitive shooting teams, in particular the winning *Daily Telegraph* Cup team for 1929. In 1935 he was appointed Transport officer, standing out as an expert driver and mechanic. When he took over as CO at thirty-three years of age he was by far the youngest colonel to command the Regiment. His second in command was Major P.G.R. Burford.

The School of Arms season was brought to a successful conclusion with part triumph in the Royal Tournament. The Artists retained the Army Bayonet Trophy but suffered defeat by the Royal Marines in the Inter-Services Final. In the first round of the Army Bayonet Championship the Artists beat the Lincolnshires fairly easily if not convincingly. In the semi-final the Scots Guards were leading 5:0 but were gradually pegged back and the Artists won by the slender margin of 10:8. Encouraged by this success, the Artists routed the Seaforths in the final by 15:3. Then there was a long wait in the Inter-Services Championship competition, while the Artists, who had won their way through to the final, awaited the outcome of the semi-final between the Royal Air Force and the Royal Marines, which was won by the latter. In the final, the Royal Marines went on to beat the Artists 11:7.

Annual summer camp held at Farringdon July/August 1938 was otherwise known as the Alton Camp. After it was over, in September Colonel Cripps made the following observations:

> Annual Training at Kitcombe House will long be remembered by all as a most successful camp; and this is a particularly happy thought in view of the fact that such a large number of officers and NCOs were new to their commands.
>
> The largest strength since the War, new comforts, excellent weather, and above all interesting training combined to impress us. For all these we owe thanks – to the Regular assistance for an excellent job of work, to the War Office for additional comforts, which included hot shower-baths, and to our own cooks for work mightily well done.
>
> The appearance of a separate training squad of recruits,

amounting this year to more than a full-strength company, was an innovation, which was an unqualified success. While on the subject of recruits, let me stress how very important it is for me to continue recruiting, in view of the very large wastage that occurs annually in the Artists.

We were very fortunate to be visited by so many members of the Veterans' Company, whose assistance with the pioneers, the loud-speakers, the Smoker and above all Major Bax's work with the messing, was invaluable. This assistance is more than appreciated, and on behalf of the Serving battalion, I offer all my sincerest thanks.

Kitcombe was a rather more self-contained camp than usual; but there were not so many facilities for entertainment close at hand and as a result campers were compelled to entertain themselves to a greater degree than they had been accustomed to in recent years. The camp was pleasantly situated on a wooded slope: the site was excellent from many points-of-view, but lacking in space. To reach the canteen it was necessary to cross Mary Lane into the adjoining field where the HAC held sway; and there was no real room for a battalion parade. The surrounding country was picturesque, but from the tactical point-of-view a little devoid of small features. One thing was short-sighted and that was that no time was allocated to cooperation with the RAF. Three squadrons of AC aircraft were conveniently located at Odiham, five or six miles away, but the Artists were not given the opportunity to work with them. One sign of technical progress, however, was the presence of some 150 motors in the park by The Horse and Groom, but it would be apt to remark how really odd some of them were!

The experiment of training recruits in a separate company proved a considerable bone of contention. The argument against it, advanced almost without exception by the older soldiers, was that by being segregated in this way, Recruits were debarred from free-and-easy intercourse with older men that made for good comradeship; but against this it could be held that, shielded from the somewhat blasé tendencies of the old soldiers in the field, the recruits achieved a degree of keenness and efficiency that was quite astonishing to see. The smoker on 5 August was a good evening's entertainment but there was no outstanding talent on display this year and hence no permanent record of the programme was bequeathed to posterity.

The night operations of 10-11 August were blighted by rain from the start. Generally speaking the exercise was uneventful and the umpire was obliged to adopt the mask of the enemy to hot things up. When the war was won (or was it?), after a sharp action at daybreak, hot bangers were distributed to the clamouring troops, the gut feeling being that it was worth the sacrifice of a few sausages to get back to camp for a decent breakfast. The camp messing arrangements under the capable direction of Major Bax and Major Burford were admirable. The Regiment was delighted to receive a visit from Brigadier Willans and Lord Strathcona, who travelled all the way down from Scotland for camp, and returned to Scotland immediately afterwards.

It was on Tuesday, 27 September 1938 that the Artists at last realized that their training was going to culminate in something more serious than a fortnight's camp. Three anti-aircraft batteries had been called up; gas-masks were being issued to the civil population; trenches were being dug in the public parks. On the Monday Herr Hitler had declared in his speech in the Berlin Sportspalast that 'his patience was at an end'. 'It is evident,' said Mr Chamberlain, 'that the Chancellor has no faith that the promises to him will be carried out.' Germany, in fact, was determined on war. On the Tuesday the British Fleet was mobilized. That evening at headquarters the Premier's speech was relayed in the Drill Hall. He spoke of the situation as 'horrible, fantastic, incredible' and, though he declared that he had not yet given up hope of a peaceful solution, there were few of those in the Regiment that heard him but doubted that war was inevitable.

Next day at headquarters activity began. The two vital interests were 'ARP', or 'Passive Air Defence', to give it its Army name, and the problems of embodiment and recruitment. PAD occupied most of the Regiment's attention. Lieutenant Greenway scoured London for sand and sandbags; the price had gone up almost overnight by 200 or 300 per cent. Respirators were neatly docketed in alphabetical order, under the energetic eye of Sergeant Dawkins; work was begun on the transformation of the iniature range into a gas-proof chamber and the creation in the washrooms of a casualty clearing station; a splinter-proof barricade of sandbags was in due course erected before the windows of the orderly room and the officers' mess; Lieutenant Tanner's working party in St Pancras churchyard laboured like Trojans shovelling sand into sandbags; and when the sand ran short earth was substituted.

Fortunately the sandbags were not after all asked to withstand anything more lethal than the attacks of small boys, who discovered that Passive Air Defence was the best game they had played for years. Though periodically chased away by officers armed with soda-water siphons, one or more of the boys was generally to be found on top of the sandbags. 'It's strong enough, ain't it?' replied one boy when requested to get the hell out of it – 'It ought to be – you made it!'

Meanwhile a steady stream of enquiries was coming in both from old Artists and intending recruits. A reception unit was formed under

Major Rait (TARO) to deal with these. At the beginning of the emergency the Artists were at full strength and no recruits could be accepted; two lists were kept, however, one of the people offering to serve in the event of war and one of those who would be willing to join under ordinary peacetime conditions. A list was also kept of veterans wishing to rejoin. On Thursday the 29th a signal was received authorizing the Artists to recruit another 10 per cent of establishment, in effect, creating another sixty vacancies. Notices were sent out to men on the waiting-list and on Friday afternoon a grand recruiting-party was held. From 3 p.m. to 7 p.m. seven recruits trickled in, reported to the reception unit, passed on to Captain Baucher's department, where they filled in their papers and were allocated to a company; they then proceeded to medical examination under Colonel Shirley and Lieutenants Stallard and Tucker, finally reporting to the quartermaster's store where, since uniforms and equipment had not yet been provided for them, they drew a blue armband as a 'token issue'.

By Friday morning, however, the political skies albeit for the time being had cleared; on that day the agreement promising 'peace for our time' was signed in Munich. In spite of this, it was decided to go on with the mobilization scheme, the practice being timed for Tuesday evening. Everything went according to plan and, though some of the zest had gone out of the proceedings with the realization that the Artists on the face of it were not, after all, preparing to fight in earnest, but the lessons learned were to prove of very great value.

The following serving members and officers of the Reserve took part in the preparations at headquarters on Wednesday, Thursday and Friday, 27, 28 and 29 September:

Majors Burford, Browning, Hubble, Rait; Captains Baucher, Beausire; Messrs Bance, Greenway, Flint, Tanner, Russell, Johnson, Hopper, Noel-Johnson, Muirhead, Passmore and Johnston.

RQMS Smith; Sergeants Brock, Kitcat, Eager; Corporals Lobb, Young; Lance-Corporals Christmas, de Berry, Page; Privates Bird, Birnage, Bignell, Chapman, Davie, Donnelly, Dettmer, Dubarry, Denny, Fell, Foskett, Francis, Germaine, Goodwin, Hall, Hutchins, Horton, Pritchard, Pringle, Royds, Sanders, Smith (W.), Simmons, Taylor, Van Maurik, Whittingham, Willis, Archbutt, Beverley, Moore, Collins.

In December 1938 it was announced that the Auxiliary Territorial Service (ATS) was to be formed from the women of the United Kingdom with the object of their performing non-combatant military duties in the event of national emergency. As part of peacetime training, they would perform these duties wherever it was practical to do so. The Artists Rifles was to have an ATS company affiliated to it of fifty-five members for general duties with a separate company of twenty-four members for clerical duties. The enrolment of these companies commenced on Monday, 5 December and training was scheduled at headquarters for every Monday from 7 p.m. to 9 p.m. It was expected that in 1939 the ATS would attend annual camp with the Artists. Details of service, pay, training, etc. were obtainable from the adjutant, Captain Curtis. The company commander covering the two companies was Mrs Collett-Wadge, the deputy commander Mrs P.G.R. Burford, and the assistant commander Miss H. Williamson.

As 1938 drew to a close the Regiment must indeed have been very busy: by order of Colonel Cripps the annual stage production at Duke's Road was cancelled; as it happened it would never take place again.

Chapter 18

The Second World War

1939-1945

The Artists spread their wings.
We can only do the right as we see the right,
and reverently commit our cause to God.
King George VI, BBC broadcast, September 1939

Hitler's breach of the Munich Agreement by occupying northern Czechoslovakia in March 1939 marked the final collapse of the policy of appeasement pursued by Britain and France. Both countries accelerated preparations for war with Germany and Britain introduced peacetime conscription for the first time in its history. In August Britain and France offered security guarantees to Poland as Germany's likely next victim. Germany signed a surprise Non-Aggression Pact (the Molotov-Ribbentrop Pact) with its arch-enemy, the Soviet Union, secretly agreeing to partition Poland, which was invaded on 1 September. Two days later Britain and France declared war on Germany. Although Hitler did not expect the Anglo-French declaration, Germany is widely accepted as being responsible for the outbreak of war.

By January 1939 the strength of the Artists Rifles had risen, less HQ staff, to 661 effectives – 26 officers, 5 WOs, 24 sergeants, 33 corporals, 33 lance corporals, and 540 privates. There were in addition 3 drummers. Colonel Cripps ordered a strenuous training programme: the Drill Hall was open on four week nights and at weekends. First year men (recruits) were with few exceptions called upon to fire both rifles and Bren light machine guns and qualify on either. Second and subsequent year men were required also to fire the rifle and Bren, and to qualify on the latter. Times were allocated and ranges up to September, including field firing at company weekends. Members were warned that those not completing the annual classification would be liable to summary discharge. There were initially only two Bren guns in the Regiment but a further ten were borrowed from the 1st Battalion the Welsh Guards, which were held on loan until 28 February 1940. Running the weapons training programme was in the hands of RSM Norton.

Sport continued to play its part in the Regimental scheme of things. In February the Artists participated in a bayonet competition for the London Divisional Byrne Shield with the Queen's Westminsters, 5th Royal Berks, 8th Royal Fusiliers, the London Scottish and the London Rifle Brigade, the Artists Rifles beating the LRB in the final 7-1. The annual sports event was held at the Polytechnic Harriers' ground at Chiswick on 22 April with a very full programme commencing at 2.30 p.m. and ending at 5.50 p.m. At hockey on 15 January the Regiment beat the Chartered Bank of India 15-0; on 4 March it lost to Harpenden 17-6; on 11 March beat Nore Command 10-3 and, on 18 March, lost to the London Rifle Brigade 3-0. In February and March the Association Football Club 1st XI won twelve and lost eight matches and the 2nd XI won three and lost fifteen matches. On 31 December 1938 the Rugby Football Club beat Chiltern 3-0; on 7 January the RFC lost to Tonbridge 11-0; and on 14 January the game against Blackheath 'A' was lost 3-0.

A guard of honour was found by the Regiment for HM The King on the occasion of his opening of the new wing of Westminster Hospital on 20 April. The guard, under the command of Major Browning, was ninety-five strong. Headed by the band of the Grenadier Guards, the guard marched to the hospital from Wellington Barracks, conflicting ideas as to the rate of pace ended in a compromise decidedly in favour of the Artists. The King and Queen arrived at 3 p.m. After giving the royal salute and being inspected by the King, the guard formed a passage between the reception tent and the hospital entrance. At this stage of the proceedings the Queen was heard to say, 'Don't they look awfully smart!' After such praise a long wait was lightly endured. Their Majesties returned about 5 p.m. and a final royal salute was given before the guard retired for tea in the pleasant surroundings, both architectural and human, of the Nurses' Home.

The training at Easter this year (6-10 April), based on the Rifle Brigade depot at Winchester, was both interesting and instructive, and it was a pity that not more than 100 men were there to take advantage of it. The main body arrived on the Thursday evening and had a hot meal before going to bed. On Friday the party was split up into three, two sections doing TEWTs, and the third, made up of recruits, mastered the new drill, among other things, under the instruction of the permanent staff. Both TEWTs dealt with defence – the first emphasized particularly the digging and wiring of section posts. The second TEWT introduced cooperation with other arms and brought in interesting points arising from the use of the Carrier Platoon and administrative details such as dealing with casualties and feeding the troops. On Saturday the OQC candidates managed to deceive the examiners with some success. On Sunday the Detachment attended church parade at Winchester Cathedral and on Monday a 6½-mile march was the prelude for embussing for home.

The Royal Tournament at Olympia, which took place on 2 June 1939, marked another great success for the Artists Rifles, their team consisting of the CO, Dick Cripps, two officers, two sergeants, two corporals, two lance corporals and nine privates, who were all young soldiers. Each man fought once in each match, to be decided by three hits. Captain Byrne lead an Artists' team into the arena for a 10-minute display before the day's programme commenced. On 3 June the *Daily Telegraph* reported as follows:

FENCING
BAYONET TEAM TITLE
ARTISTS RIFLES ROB MARINES
OF CHAMPIONSHIP
By M. Pollock Smith

Yesterday at the Royal Tournament, Olympia, was 'Bayonet Day', when the last of this year's Services and Inter-Services' fencing titles, the bayonet team championships, was decided.

The fighting certainly was hard. I have watched bayonet fencing for years and never seen tougher. In making gigantic efforts rifles were dropped, men sometimes fell, and hard knocks were exchanged with great good humour. And, despite the all-in fighting element there was no rough play, but a great deal of highly skilled fencing.

The Service championships were decided first, the winner of each contesting the Inter-Services' title. Teams are 18 a side, all ranks, each man fighting his opposite number, and the leader only taking part in the event of a tie. For the Army title, six regiments competed. Details:

Round 1. 1st Bn the Q.O. Cameron H. bt 2nd Bn Lincolnshire Regt on fight-off between leaders after a tie of 9 wins all. 2nd Bn Seaforth H. bt 2nd Bn Lancashire Fus., 11-7. Semi-finals Artists Rifles bt 1st Q.O. Cameron H, 14-4, two fights on each side being on the odd hit. 2nd Seaforths bt 1st Scots Gds, 12-6, one of the latter's and 3 of the Seaforths on odd hits. Final Artists R. bt Seaforth H., 11-7.

Thus the Artists Rifles won the Army title for the ninth time in 10 years, and scored their sixth successive victory. This is the third time running that the Seaforths have been their opponents in the final, and this year the Highlanders gave them a tougher fight than ever before. Five of the Artists' and six of the Scots' wins were scored on the odd hit.

HENLOW'S SUCCESS

The Royal Air Force teams were: Henlow bt Linton-on-Ouse, 13-3 and Tangmere bt Felixstowe, 12-2, with two to go. In the final Henlow, champions in 1936, and runners-up to Abingdon last year, regained the title by beating Tangmere, 14-4.

The Royal Marines' championship was retained for the twelfth successive year by Portsmouth, who had been Inter-Services' champions 11 times, when they bt Plymouth, 14-4. The Royal Navy title went to the R.N. Barracks, Portsmouth, who won it in 1926, 1928 and 1929, without fighting the other finalist, H.M.S. Ganges.

The four champion teams were paired by lot in the Inter-Services' title, the victors contesting the final. This time the Royal Marines, holders for the last four years and winners 11 times out of 19, drew the Army, who have won six times between 1921-28. A terrific battle, in which seven bouts, five of them the Army's were won on the odd hit, resulted in a 10-8 victory for the army team.

ROYAL NAVY BEATEN

In the other match the Royal Air Force reached the final for the first time by beating the 1933 champions, the Royal Navy, 11-7. In this eight fights ran to 2-all, five of these being won by the R.A.F. and three by the Royal Navy.

The final was a foregone conclusion, for having disposed of the RM, there could be no doubt about the Army's ultimate victory over the youngest Service. That the R.A.F. scored six wins against the Army's 12 was to their credit, for these Artists Rifles are a great bayonet team.'

In May 1939 the *Artists Rifles Gazette* ceased publication, so there was no official account published of the summer camp which took place at Warminster from 29 July to 12 August. We are therefore indebted to Private E.H. Van Maurik, a Lancing schoolboy who worked for a City firm of tea merchants, for his brief impressions of the camp:

From now on [after the Munich crisis] the Artists Rifles had no difficulty in attracting recruits but by the time our next annual camp had come round in July 1939, the situation was again precarious. After obtaining large frontier areas of Czechoslovakia under the terms of the Munich Pact, Hitler was eyeing Poland. That year our brigade – the Artists, the H.A.C. and the Inns of Court – was encamped at Warminster in Wiltshire; at least we were encamped until torrential rain flooded our tents and we were found accommodation in nearby Warminster barracks.

Whilst some were prepared to take bets that we would be mobilized even before camp ended, no-one let this spoil the usual fun. We may have route-marched a bit further and taken some aspects of training a bit more seriously but basically things were unchanged: the camp concert; the evening sorties into town to dine on giant-sized mixed grills and pints of ale (it all got sweated out the next day!); the good-natured rivalry between the Artists and the H.A.C.; and attempts usually unsuccessful to persuade any new recruit to report to the company office, where he was wanted for a fatigue to whitewash the Last Post.

A less carefree and somewhat patronizing overview of the Warminster camp is provided by *The Times* special correspondent in his report published on 2 August:

This quiet little Wiltshire town is at present enjoying a night life suggestive in its well-bred exuberance and its early abandonment of Oxford during Eights week. This is caused by presence in camp about half a mile away of the units of the Officer Producing Group. If they enjoy themselves a little noisily in the evening it is welcome evidence that the depressing weather, which has made their camp a quagmire, has failed to damp their spirits.

The group is commanded by Colonel W.A.L. Fox-Pitt. It consists of two battalions of infantry, the H.A.C. commanded by Lieutenant Colonel W.B. Farrar, and the Artists Rifles commanded by Lieutenant Colonel R.R. Cripps; the Inns of Court Regiment, commanded by Lieutenant Colonel G.H. Newson, and composed of two mechanized and one horsed squadrons; and the 22nd Battalion, the Royal Tank Regiment, better known as the Westminster Dragoons, commanded by Lieutenant Colonel E. Munt. These units are now in camp, but the H.A.C., of course, also includes gunners, who, having received their training at Whitsun, are not under canvas now.

DESPERATE NEED

The units of the Officer Producing Group are quite dissimilar in their character from any other units in the Army, Regular or Territorial. They are, in a sense, analogous with the R.M.C. Sandhurst, or with the O.T.C. contingents. The military authorities take them much more seriously than the latter – which, in a year when perhaps the Army's most desperate need is for junior officers for the doubled Territorial Field Force have not been sent to Camp – but, for some reason, not very easily comprehensible, much less seriously than the former. It is an axiom of military policy that they are not to be employed as units in the field and the fundamental question to ask concerning them must necessarily be, how far are they succeeding in producing officers? It can be answered in two ways: the historical method of inquiring how many officers have been produced, and the method of estimating from inquiry and observation, how many officers will be produced in the future and how good will they be.

The present is not the best occasion for pursuing the historical method. It would be a matter for research at the London headquarters of the respective units, though incidentally it seems a little odd that group headquarters have not, in the past, shown their interest in the fruits of their work by collating the relevant statistics. One is told that some 60 or 70 commissions have been granted to members of the O.P.G. units during the past year. Assuming the latter to be the correct figure, it is still one that seems a wholly inadequate response to the demands of the current year.

KEEN AND INTELLIGENT

The reason is not far to seek. The men themselves are keen on the whole; the Regular officers in command attached to them appear to be excellent, though one doubtless admirable officer attached to one of the units seemed not to have the right mentality or personality for a post which essentially requires the teacher rather than the leader. The training programme is sensible if rather strenuous.

The failure in so far as it is a failure lies at the door of the War Office. If men are to be trained as officers they must be treated as officers and equipped as officers. They should be put on the same footing as the gentleman cadets at Sandhurst in receiving field-glasses, compasses, and so forth, whereas, at present, they are treated just as other Territorials; hence repetition and loss of time. Further there should be a far more generous allowance of Regular instructors.

This morning watching the various units at work, one was able to see examples of the waste of time – and of fine human material. A company of the H.A.C. was carrying out an elementary tactical scheme as a drill for the benefit of recruits. It was carried out, quite rightly, section by section, but, quite wrongly, under the supervision of the company commander, not of the platoon commanders. The work was protracted into an hour, and those not actively engaged derived what comfort they could from sitting on the wet grass. But who is to blame the company commander? The average Territorial platoon commander in this year of rapid expansion and quick promotion, has naturally too much to learn himself to be able readily to give instruction. The place for him to learn is not in the officer-producing unit; the officer there should be able to teach.

APPRECIATION OF GROUND

Instruction is naturally based on the officer's qualifying, or 'Q' certificate. Those taking the practical part of the examination at the end of the camp period spend most of their time in tactical exercises without troops; those who plan to take it next year gain experience of platoon and section leading with their companies. Major General A.F.A.N. Thorne, commanding the London District, who visited the camp yesterday morning, saw both types of training in progress. The point which he most emphasized in his comments was the importance of basing all tactical orders on appreciation of the ground. Each commander down to the section leader should explain what he regards as the difficulties of the situation confronting him in such a way that his direct subordinates understand the reasoning behind his orders and can carry out his plan intelligently should he become a casualty.

A scene which was entertaining and significant of the spirit of the new Army was enacted when the general discussed a plan formulated by a corporal of the Artists Rifles, and a lengthy debate between the two ensued. The corporal thought the enemy more likely to attack over dry ground with little cover, while the general considered an infiltration over marshy ground with good cover from view more probable, on the ground that the enemy would prefer to be delayed and soaked rather than be killed. It perhaps spoils the story to say that the general's arguments carried the more conviction but the real point is that he gave an inspiring example of how an officer-producing unit should be taught.

However useful or not *The Times* correspondent's assessment of the OPG actually was, there was little time left to give it serious consideration because from 23 August a series of code-words were received at Duke's Road from the War Office to set in motion preparations for war. A children's holiday camp located at St Mary's Bay near Dymchurch, Kent, had already been allocated and reconnoitred as the site for the Artists' OCTU. On the morning of Thursday 31 August Major Burford, the second in command, Major H. Hubble ('Bubbly'), the quartermaster, Captain Tom Robb, one of the MOs, another officer and some thirty Artists other ranks left London to spend the day at St Mary's Bay to assess the available facilities. On the morning of Friday 1 September the Army Reserve was called up and the brigade major telephoned to say that someone was to go to St Mary's Bay at once in case any reservists, who were to form a large part of the staff, arrived there first. The holiday camp, which was for underprivileged children was fairly primitive and none too clean but the reservists from the Royal Sussex Regiment who arrived during the weekend were put to work to clean it up. Four Guards NCOs under CSM Lambert and Major Hubble's stores also arrived during the weekend. The main body of the Regiment, which was due to arrive on the following Monday, was scheduled to detrain at Sandling Junction, some nine miles from St Mary's Bay and Tom Robb arranged with the manager of the Romney, Hythe and Dymchurch Light Railway to convey the Artists from Hythe in two lifts to the camp. Officers were to be accommodated at the Sands Hotel.

We now turn again to E.H. Van Maurik for his memories of mobilization and the setting up of what was to be known as No. 163 OCTU at St Mary's Bay:

Peace did outlast our Warminster Camp, but not by very much. Hitler's onslaught on Poland commenced on 1 September 1939 and we were mobilized the following day which was a Saturday.

Dressed in uniform, our personal kit stuffed into our kitbags, we reported to Duke's Road. Here we were submitted to a fairly thorough medical examination, we signed documents, were issued with identity discs which we slung around our necks with cord which became dirtier and greasier as the war progressed and finally we had to report to the paymaster. Here to our astonishment we were handed five pounds against signature, the equivalent of accepting the King's shilling and instructed to report again two day's later on the Monday morning.

My friend Peter Stephenson and I finished signing on about the same time and he asked me what I intended to do until the day after tomorrow. When I said I would have to return home to Tunbridge Wells, he volunteered to accompany me as far as Charing Cross station where we could have a quick drink. With five pounds in our pockets we felt remarkably rich. Either in the Underground or in Charing Cross station we fell in with three of four more Artists and we all repaired to the station bar. Someone said that port and rum was the appropriate tipple and although neither Peter nor I had ever heard of it, we readily agreed. We all, of course, had to stand a round and in between more than one City Gent insisted on pushing out the boat to the 'boys in uniform'.

We all ended up pretty drunk but just sensible enough to realize that a train journey was not immediately advisable. First Peter said he would accompany me to see I got home safely but as he, if anything, was drunker than I, this had its disadvantages. But when he suggested I spend the night in London in the flat he shared with his sister, this was agreed upon. It had the advantage, he suggested, we could have further drinks when we got there. My memory as to how we got to the flat and how much we imbibed thereafter is blurred – by the passage of time no doubt – but I do remember being woken up by his sister around eleven o'clock on the Sunday morning and being told we should have some breakfast before the prime minister made an important announcement on the radio at noon, which was when the Allies' ultimatum to Germany expired. Getting up, except for a slight unsteadiness, presented no difficulty, since both Peter and I discovered to our surprise that we were already fully dressed even down to our army boots.

We listened to Chamberlain's short announcement that since Germany had failed to cease hostilities with Poland, Britain and France were now at war with her.

As the prime minister stopped speaking the air-raid sirens began to wail, followed by whistle-blowing and shouting from down on the street as London's A.R.P. went into action for the first time in earnest. We had little doubt we were about to experience an air attack of the sort that the Luftwaffe had just let loose on Warsaw. Betty filled the bath with water, explaining that this was one of the requirements demanded of householders in instructions they had received; if water mains were disrupted we should at least have something to drink and to cook with, assuming of course we had gas or electricity. This precaution taken, we sat down to wait but the all-clear soon sounded. This was the first time but not the last of the false alarms of the early war years.

The following morning Peter and I reported to Duke's Road in more or less good shape. All we were told was that we should don full battle order and would shortly march off but no-one knew where to. Wartime secrecy had already descended on us. Our march through the streets of London took us to Charing Cross station, where we boarded a special train. Once under way, we followed my daily commuting route as far as Tonbridge but then branched off to Folkestone and Dover. By this time we were all convinced our officer producing status had gone by the board and that, as in 1914, we were bound for France to fight as a unit. But as we neared the Channel Ports our train halted at Sandling Junction and we were ordered to detrain. We formed up by companies and were marched off down small lanes but still no word of our destination. As we approached the outskirts of Hythe the terrain became familiar from past camps spent in the neighbourhood.

'I'll tell you what,' declared one wag, 'we're going to war on the Romney, Hythe and Dymchurch Railway.' This was a miniature railway, a tourist attraction, which ran along the flat coastal strip between Hythe and Dungeness.

We laughed but when we came alongside the toytown railway station we halted. We were ushered down the platform and embarked four to a carriage. Each with his rifle, side arm, water bottle, back pack, gas mask and rolled gas cape, together with webbing belt and ammunition pouches, it was a tight squeeze. The engine-driver perched behind his chest-high steam locomotive, we puffed along level with the coast.

Our destination, we discovered only on arrival, was St Mary's Bay Holiday Camp. Judging from appearances it had been unoccupied for a while and the bleakness of the barrack-like huts indicated it had never been in the luxury class. The beds were wooden frames a foot or so off the ground with canvas stretched across. Once we had exchanged a couple with split canvas for others from a nearby hut, whose inhabitants had not yet trained in, we set about making ourselves as comfortable as circumstances permitted.

On morning parade we were informed that the Artists Rifles had been transformed into 163 Officer Cadet Training Unit (OCTU) and that we ourselves were now cadet officers and that the training course to turn us into officers would be of three months duration, although those with sufficient length of service in the Artists would pass out in six weeks. Meanwhile the only other parade of the day would be for medical inoculation.

We stood in long lines for the jab and the first inkling that this might be somewhat more than a mere pinprick was when a man two or three in front of me passed clean out at our feet. He was indeed an exception but slowly and surely we all discovered that we had developed swollen and painful arms and many felt ill enough to writhe and groan on their bunks. We realized later that not only had the army combined all necessary inoculations into one bumper shot but as none of us had been through the treatment before the effect was all the greater.

We paraded next day looking rather bedraggled and were then put through half-an-hour's arms drill with our heavy old Lee-Enfield rifles. This was an unpleasant experience for everyone but agonizing for those worst affected, the theory being that the exercise worked the serum more quickly through the body and one thus recovered all the sooner. We did recover quickly but no-one was prepared to give any credit to the arms drill!!!

We were kitted out afresh. Our old-fashioned Artists uniform with its button-up neck, reminiscent of the Tommy's 1914 wear, was exchanged for the new-fangled battledress. We were sorry to lose our Mars and Minerva buttons and badges but we came to appreciate the comfort and easiness of the new everyday uniform. No buttons to clean, no puttees to threaten to unravel on the march and in their place gaiters one could buckle on in a third of the time. And into the bargain it made a pleasant 'walking-out' attire for now we remained in uniform all the time, not as in the days of pre-war camp changing into civvies as soon as the day's work was done. In our exalted capacity of officer cadets we wore a forage cap with a white band round it and the battledress unbuttoned at the neck with a khaki shirt and tie showing through; gaiters were only worn on parade and civilian shoes, off duty, took the place of army boots.

Peter and I remained together as we were both in a squad aiming to pass out within the six weeks limit. The weeks passed quickly but not unpleasantly as a fair proportion of the training was revision rather than new to us. The Romney, Hythe and Dymchurch Railway, which ran to a regular schedule, was a blessing as it enabled us to get to Hythe and thence to Folkestone, where food rationing as yet had had no time to have any effect on the restaurants.

We were now given forms on which we could express a first and second choice of regiment to which we would prefer to be posted as officers. After passing out we would be sent home on some two weeks leave, during which time the War Office would inform us of the regiment we had in fact been commissioned into. This would enable the appropriate insignia to be affixed to the officer's uniform which we would have to acquire during this period of time.

This inspired Peter to put a proposition to me. He was sure he would be posted to the Wiltshire Regiment. One of his brothers was adjutant at the Regimental depot at Devizes and he was arranging it all with the War Office. Would I not like to come to the 'Wilts' with him? I thought hard and finally replied that as I had lived in Kent all my life and was attached to the place, I felt I would like to apply for my local regiment, the Royal West Kents. I would put the latter down as my first choice but put the Wilts down as my second. I felt slightly mean about this as in many ways I would have liked to continue to serve alongside Peter, but I reckoned, in any case, that I was just as likely to get my second choice as I was my first.

Passing-out day came: no peace-time Sandhurst affair this; just a few handshakes and a few beers. I wished Peter good luck, promised to keep in touch but thought it quite likely that we would meet up again in two week's time – I did go to the Wilts but Peter was sent to the King's Liverpool!

By the end of September 168 Artists had left St Mary's Bay to become officers and No.163 OCTU (commanded by Colonel Cripps) in October moved to Shorncliffe barracks, where much improved training facilities were in place. 'Pony' Moore incidentally was recalled into active service with the Artists as RQMS. A second Artists OCTU, No.164, under the command of now Lieutenant Colonel Burford, was formed at Colchester but by the end of 1939 the battalion as a battalion was no more than a memory. In 1941 Nos.163, 164 and 167 OCTUs were merged with No.168, which somewhat confusingly changed its name to No.163 at the same time. The designation may have been the same but by that time there were no Artists officers and men on strength. Later on the War Office introduced the Artists' name as a subtitle for the Reconnaissance Regiment of the 56th Division. The idea was quickly dropped and no badges or insignia reflecting the name of the Artists were ever designed. So there was no cohesive Artists Rifles during the Second World War. On the other hand, there were Artists wherever you chose to look in the services, especially, of course, the Army, leavening, one would like to think, the whole of the Forces with the Artists.

Choosing a select group of those who served in the Artists Rifles in both World Wars is an invidious task but the following names have been chosen because with a few exceptions they reached the highest ranks in the Army or Royal Air Force or in government in the Second World War or after.

A.V. ALEXANDER OF HILLSBOROUGH, who was born in Weston-super-Mare in 1885, joined the Artists in 1914. He was promoted to corporal and later commissioned; he was discharged in 1918 and gazetted out in the honorary rank of captain. Elected a Labour Member of Parliament for the Hillsborough Division of Sheffield in 1922, A.V. Alexander was appointed Parliamentary Secretary to the Board of Trade in Ramsay Macdonald's Labour government of 1924 and First Lord of the Admiralty in the Coalition government of 1929-35, again serving in that post in Winston Churchill's wartime cabinet of 1940-45. He was made Minister of Defence 1947-50 and Chancellor of the Duchy of Lancaster 1950-51, in Clement Atlee's post-war Labour government. A.V. Alexander was created 1st Viscount of Hillsborough, Sheffield, in 1950, 1st Baron in 1963, and Earl in the same year. An Elder Member of Trinity House from 1941, in 1955 he was appointed Deputy Leader of the Labour peers in the House of Lords. A Baptist lay preacher, he died in 1965.

LORD ALPORT, PC, TD, born in Kenya in 1912, was educated at Haileybury and Pembroke College, Cambridge, where he read History and Law and was President of the Cambridge Union in 1935. Subsequently he was called to the Bar in the Middle Temple. Joining the Artists Rifles in 1934, he was one of the few Artists to receive a direct commission without serving in the ranks. 'Cub' Alport rose quickly to command 'A' Company and was mobilized at the outbreak of war in 1939. He commanded a company of the Royal Fusiliers and later went to Africa to command a battalion of the King's African Rifles in the rank of lieutenant colonel. In 1950 Alport entered Parliament as Conservative MP for Colchester and in 1955 he was made Assistant Postmaster General in Anthony Eden's Conservative government. In 1957 he was appointed by Harold Macmillan as Parliamentary Under-Secretary and two years later, Minister of State at the Commonwealth Office.

In Rhodesia in 1961, Alport's task was to negotiate the break-up of the Federation. It was a thankless task, with few plaudits to be gained at home. To most white Rhodesians he was an instrument of British betrayal. The task completed, he returned to England hoping to renew his political career. In his parting message he pleaded with the white population not to ignore the gathering forces of African nationalism and to realize that 'adjustment, compromise and change were the price of survival'. His plea went unheeded and Rhodesia slithered to UDI. His experience had made him bitterly critical of the dominant Rhodesian Front, which he described as 'a party ruled by emotion, prejudice and narrow self-interest'.

In 1967 with the return of another Labour government, to his and everyone else's astonishment, Alport was asked by Harold Wilson to return to Salisbury as his special envoy, following the collapse of talks on board *Tiger*, to see if negotiations could be resumed. He was denounced by Ian Smith as a 'listed enemy of Rhodesia' but Alport persisted and he found no shortage of people at all levels anxious to help him to find a solution. His report to Wilson led to fresh talks aboard

Fearless but these proved as abortive as the *Tiger* talks and confirmed Alport's view that there was no hope of a settlement with Ian Smith. After the return of the Conservative government in 1970 Alport made an unofficial visit to Rhodesia, but Smith refused to see him. However, his private report on the visit led Sir Alec Douglas-Home, then Foreign Secretary, to begin fresh talks, which again proved abortive. Rhodesia became Zimbabwe in 1980.

'Cub' Alport was sworn as a Privy Councillor in 1960 and created a life peer as Lord Alport of Colchester in the following year. He was High Steward of Colchester from 1967 and a Deputy Lieutenant for Essex from 1974. He was Master of the Skinner's Company in 1969-70. When Margaret Thatcher became Conservative Prime Minister in 1979 he became increasingly critical of her policies. Matters came to a head when after a number of rebellions in the House of Lords he voted Labour after a debate on unemployment. It provoked the usually tolerant Chief Whip, Lord Denham, to take the rare step among Tory MPs of withdrawing the Whip from him, so he became an Independent Conservative. He wrote three books: *Kingdoms in Partnership* (1937), *Hope in Africa* (1952) and *The Sudden Assignment* (1965). He died in 1998, aged eighty-five.

AIR CHIEF MARSHAL SIR JOHN BARRACLOUGH KCB, CBE, DFC, AFC, FRAeS, Mentioned in Despatches (twice), was born in 1918 and educated at Cranbrook.

He joined the Regiment in 1935 as a private in 'D' Company and remained as such until 1938 when he was commissioned into the Royal Air Force. He flew as a pilot throughout the war from the Arctic to the Mediterranean, and the Indian Ocean where he took part in the Madagascar campaign and went on to command the captured airfield at Mogadishu in Italian Somaliland. After the war he served as a chief instructor at the Central Flying School and then commanded two fighter stations (Biggin Hill and Middleton St George) in the early days of the Cold War.

An early exponent of jet flying, he made the first single-engined jet flight to South Africa in 1951. After wide overseas service he was to hold several senior posts in NATO and UK commands from the Atlantic to the Far East before taking up the post of Vice Chief of Defence Staff in 1970. His final appointment on the active list was as Commandant of the Royal College of Defence Studies in 1974-76. Among his many subsequent activities, he was Vice Chairman of the Commonwealth War Graves Commission and later Honorary Inspector General of the Royal Auxiliary Air Force which was to reconnect him with the infantry role and the subtleties of volunteer service. In the literary field he was editor-in-chief of an international defence magazine for several years and was a co-author of the best selling book *The Third World War*. He lives in Bath where he is President of the Royal Crescent Society.

REVD. CANON DANIEL V.G. BROCK, DD, VD was born in 1908 and educated at Brentwood School, Essex. He enlisted in the Artists Rifles in 1930 while working for the Tote in London. During the 1930s he helped train the Lewis gun and rifle teams for the*Daily Telegraph* cup and the Vickers machine gun teams for the Dewar Trophy competitions. During this period he volunteered to be a Special Constable. A sergeant in the Artists in 1939, he was commissioned into the 2/7th Middlesex Regiment in which he was promoted to captain as a company commander and then major, serving as second in command. In May 1942 Daniel Brock was appointed lieutenant colonel commanding a battalion of the Kensington Regiment and served in that capacity in Iceland, in Normandy in June 1940 and throughout the campaign in North-West Europe.

In 1946 he took up farming in Devon but in 1954 he entered Bishop's College, Cheshunt, to study for the priesthood. In 1956 he was made Deacon of Trinity at Exeter Cathedral, which was followed by service as a priest at St Mark's and All Angels at Princetown. During 1959 and 1962 he was Deputy Chaplain of Dartmoor Prison. In 1962 he resigned and joined the Melanesian Mission and was appointed chaplain and teacher in Maramova School. Between 1964 and 1967 he was made headmaster of Alangaula School and then director of all Melanesian Anglican Schools, numbering about 130 at that time. In 1967 Brock employed a local man, Moffat Maleikuli, as a house boy. Moffat Maleikuli, who was the proud father of six children, became a local Councillor, and Daniel Brock adopted his eldest son, as was the custom out there.

Between 1967 and 1969 Brock concentrated on the training of teachers and as education administrator before being appointed Archdeacon of the Eastern Outer Isles in 1970. Whilst Archdeacon he consolidated the scattered churches of the Eastern Outer Isles into an organized and viable Archdeaconry for the first Assistant Bishop. When Independence was granted to the Solomon Islands in 1978 this area was renamed Temotu Province. In 1984 he was voted Premier of Temotu Province. As he wrote, 'I have had a wonderful and happy life ever since I came out here in 1962'. He died in 1993.

Ralph Robotham has written:

> He and I agreed that some of the most memorable things about King George V's Silver Jubilee were the enormous roar given up by the

crowd when he lifted little Princess Margaret Rose up so that she could see over the balcony of Buckingham Palace; the red, white and blue circular waxed paper chains strung from lamp posts along the route from Buckingham Palace to St Paul's and, of course, Princess Marina's white cart-wheel hat. Walking through the masses of knee-high newspapers used by people to sleep out on the previous night was quite like getting through surf.

Due to arrive in France during the Normandy invasion on D-day, Lt.Col. Brock, C.O. 2nd Bn. Kensington Regiment, found himself involved in the much hushed-up dockers' strike at Southampton and was unable to get his unit's kit and equipment loaded on to the designated ship. Although it was carefully explained to the dockers it was all to help the chaps who were going over to France, the dockers in turn explained that they were most sorry but they could not get the rate they wanted.

In the end the troops had to load the stuff themselves under guidance from a docker. As a result a lot of Bren carriers got broken.

GENERAL SIR JOHN CROCKER, GCB, KBE, DSO, MC, joined the Artists Rifles in 1914 and was commissioned in the Machine-Gun Corps, later attached to the Royal Tank Corps. In 1929 Crocker joined the Middlesex Regiment. Returning to tanks, in 1940 he commanded an armoured brigade in France, a corps in Tunisia (1942-3) and was commander of I Corps throughout the campaign in North-West Europe (1944-5). After the war he was GOC Southern Command (1945-7), C.-in-C. Middle East Land Forces (1947-50), Adjutant-General to the Forces (1960-63) and ADC General to the King (1948-5). His other awards included the Legion of Honour (Commander, 1943) Virtuti Militari (Poland, 1943), the Order of Orange-Nassau (Grand Officer), 1945 and the Croix de Guerre (1946). In 1953 Sir John Crocker was appointed chairman of the Artists Rifles Association, in which capacity he served for several years. He died in 1963.

GROUP CAPTAIN KENNETH DORAN, DFC served in 'C' Company, the Artists Rifles, from 1932-36 when he was in the *Daily Telegraph* Cup teams of 1934-5, in the Bayonets team, which was third in the Army Bayonets competition at Olympia in 1935, and later gained a Fencing Blue after joining the RAF in 1937. Ken Doran will be long remembered as the first to be awarded the DFC in the Second World War following his air attack on the German pocket battleship *Scheer* at Wilhelmshaven in September 1939. (On hailing his bravery the newspapers claimed he should have been awarded the Victoria Cross.) He also had the unique distinction as the first recipient of a Bar to his DFC. He was taken prisoner after being shot down over Stavanger during the Norway operations in 1940. After the war Ken Doran became an Air Attaché in Tel Aviv and at the Hague. He retired from the RAF in 1961 and then travelled widely as Advisor to the Ministry of Overseas Development on National Youth Services.

CHARLES FOX, who was educated at the University College School (Hampstead), joined the Artists Rifles in 1928. A bank clerk, he was keen on athletics, hockey and cricket. He was a member of the London Athletics Club and usually won the mile race in the annual Artists sports meetings, which were held at the Duke of York's Chelsea ground. He played hockey regularly and formed the Artists' team for the annual match at Armoury House against the HAC and was an all-round cricketer playing for the Artists' eleven. He was commissioned in 1939 and posted to the 2nd Battalion the King's Own Yorkshire Light Infantry and in 1940 went with his battalion to Burma where he contracted polio and had to wear a caliper for the rest of his life. After the retreat from Burma he was stationed in India. After the evacuation of Maymyo his battalion had reached Shwebo on the west side of the Irrawaddy and Captain Fox tried to organize the evacuation of the Regimental silver in boxes strapped to elephants but he was unable to obtain permission from GHQ for an escort party to be formed, so he supervised the burial of the silver in the jungle. However, when advancing British forces reached Shwebo in early 1945, Fox following closely behind found that the silver had disappeared, obviously looted by Burmese villagers. An appeal to the locals resulted in 101 pieces of silver being returned for safe keeping by the KOYLI.

Charles Fox retired in 1965. The Regiment had by then became 21st SAS (Artists) and he set about exploring and digging out piles of old records and rallying surviving Artists to the Artists Rifles Association (ARA), which he successfully accomplished bringing the membership up to over 1,000. He was also appointed Editor of the *Mars and Minerva* Regimental Magazine. His last contribution to the Regiment was to hand over a file of photographs, captioned and classified, providing an unique record of Artists Rifles history from beyond the turn of the century, and essential display material for the Regimental Museum then being set up. He died in 1983.

LIEUTENANT GENERAL SIR HUMPHREY GALE, KBE, CB, CVO, MC, who was educated at St Paul's School, joined the Artists in 1909 and became Signals Sergeant before entering the RMA, Sandhurst, in 1911. He served throughout the Great War. He was G2 Staff College

1934-7, Major General 1941, and in 1943 Lieutenant General Allied Chief Admin. Officer Allied Forces in North Africa. Knighted in 1943, Sir Humprey Gale in 1944 was appointed Deputy Chief-of-Staff, SHAEF, under General Eisenhower, and after the war he became Personal Representative in Europe of the Director-General UNRRA. He retired in 1947. Colonel Commandant RASC 1944-54 and the Army Catering Corps 1946-8, he received foreign decorations from the USA, Panama, France and Morocco. He died in 1981.

AIR MARSHAL SIR VICTOR E. GROOM, KCVO, KBE, CB, DFC, joined the Artists in 1915 and went to No. 2 OCB at Queen's College, Cambridge, from Gidea Park. He was commissioned in early 1917 to the West Yorkshire Regiment. He later transferred to the Royal Flying Corps in France and won his award of the DFC with No. 20 Squadron in 1918. Sir Victor Groom was Head of Staff Planning for the Normandy invasion under the Chief-of-Staff Supreme Allied Commander, 1942-3, SASO, 2nd Tactical Air Force, 1943-5 and AOA Flying Training Command, 1945-6. After the war, following various high appointments, Sir Victor became AOC.-in-C. Technical Training Command in 1952. He retired in 1955.

AIR CHIEF MARSHAL SIR DONALD HARDMAN, GBE, KCB, DFC, who was educated at Malvern, was with the Artists at Gidea Park, 1916-17. He was then commissioned in the Royal Air Force and shot down eight German planes. After the war he went up to Hertford College, Oxford, and re-joining the RAF in the 1920s, he served in various overseas campaigns. During the Second World War he finished up commanding No. 232 Transport Group in Burma, being Deputy to the US Commanding General. Since 1945 Sir Donald had been i/c Admin. Air Command, SE Asia; Assistant Chief of Air Staff (Ops); Commandant of the RAF Staff College; AOC.-in-C. Home Command; Chief of Air Staff, RAAF, and on the Air Council (AMSO) from 1954. He retired in 1958 and died in 1982.

MAURICE DE JONQUIÈRES, who was born in 1904, having a French father, spoke fluent French. He worked between 1923 and 1928 for a bank in London and Paris, and was also an evening lecturer in London on the French language at an advanced level. He then changed his job, working in London as a copywriter for various advertising agencies until 1937 becoming a director of commercial and photographic studios. He joined the Artists Rifles in 1931, serving as a lance corporal in 'B' Company, transferring to the Horse Transport Section until 1938. 'Jonx', as he was known throughout the Regiment, was then commissioned in the RAFVR Equipment Branch and promoted to wing commander in 1944 having served with Staff Duties Flying Command as the Equipment Member of the Air Ministry Establishment Committee in North Africa. Whilst in Algiers he was sitting on a beach when an ammunition ship blew up, the blast causing him serious injuries, permanently affecting his hearing. Invalided home in 1944, he served with RAF HQ Maintenance Command until his release in late 1945; he received the Air Efficiency Award in 1943.

After the war he went on to become the chairman and managing director of an advertising agency from 1948 until his retirement. 'Jonx' was made vice president of the Artists Rifles Association in his 94th year in 1997. He had been a great supporter of the association since the war, being a founder member in 1946 of the first post-war ARRA Council, devoting much of his time to the General Purposes Committee (now the Management Committee). More recently he assisted in the formulation of the new constitution to ensure it safeguarded the principles of the Artists. Late in life he suffered from cancer of the larynx which affected his speech but he continued to be a staunch supporter of Regimental reunions. A regular contributor to the *Mars and Minerva* Regimental magazine, he wrote recruiting leaflets for 21st SAS (Artists) and provided information for the museum. As a serving Artist, 'Jonx' is best remembered as a horseman of renown when he and Blake Duddington and Dennis de Berry were the first Artists team to win the Inter-Regimental jumping event at the Inns of Court Regiment's Gymkhana in 1935. Maurice de Jonquières died in 2001; he was in his 96th year.

SIR DAVID MUIRHEAD, KCMG, CVO, was born of a British father and Mexican mother in 1918. He was educated at Cranbrook School and was commissioned into the Artists Rifles in 1937, serving in 'D' and 'B' Companies. With the outbreak of war in 1939, he passed out of Sandhurst and was commissioned into the Bedfordshire and Hertfordshire Regiment, seeing service in Belgium and France in 1940. Seconded to the Special Operations Executive (SOE) as he spoke fluent Spanish learned from his mother, he was sent to Spain acting in the guise of Honorary Attaché at the British Embassy in Madrid, where he was secretly involved with MI9, playing a key role in the exfiltration of escaping British forces from German-occupied Europe. Following a parachute course in 1944, SOE sent Muirhead in the rank of lieutenant colonel to south-east Asia, where he was a member of Force 136 in India, Burma, Siam and Malaya.

He passed the Foreign Office examination in 1946 and held posts in La Paz, Bolivia, in 1948; Buenos Aires, Argentina, in 1949; and Brussels, Belgium, in 1950. After two years in London, in 1955 he was sent to Washington DC, where he played an important part in planning the

Queen's state visit of 1957. He then served as Head of Personnel at the Foreign Office for seven years before being promoted to Under-Secretary. His mastery of Spanish helped to secure him his first ambassadorial post in Peru at the then unusually early age of forty-eight. He went on to serve as HM Ambassador in Portugal and Belgium. In retirement, Sir David Muirhead was Commissioner of the Commonwealth War Graves Commission. He also served for some years as a senior representative of the Secretary of State for Commonwealth and Foreign Affairs, carrying out the largely ceremonial duties with dignity and grace. He was appointed CVO in 1957, CMG in 1964, and advanced to KCMG in 1976.

An active supporter of the Artists Rifles Association in the post-war years, he was senior vice president of the association and chairman of the Museum Committee at the time of his death in 1999. It was his wish that mourners at his funeral instead of giving flowers should make financial donations to the association. After his funeral service at St Mary Abbot's, Kensington, Sir David's daughter, Mary Gore-Booth, wrote to Air Chief Marshal Sir John Barraclough as the Artists' representative: 'His attachment to the Artists Rifles was life-long and he would have been so proud to have such good companions to see him go – the Artists' wreath was lovely and went with him at the committal.'

RALPH ROBOTHAM, MC, TD, who joined the Artists Rifles in 1934, was sponsored by his friend C.S. Goulding (always called Peter), who joined in 1933. Private Robotham and Lance Corporal Goulding, as members of 'C' Support Company, trained together on the Lewis machine gun and in 1937 were winners of the Dodd and Cyclists Lewis Gun Trophy competed for by TA units, with the best score among all the British Army and RM teams competing in LMG shoots that day. With the onset of war, 'Robum', as he was known to his friends, was commissioned into the 2/7th (Machine Gun) Battalion, the Middlesex Regiment, and went on to win the Military Cross at Anzio in the Italian campaign.

He returned to Duke's Road in 1947 and, giving up his commission, he helped to form 21st SAS Regiment (Artists), in which he served as RQMS. A year later he was asked by two Army brigadiers to be Assistant Commandant of the Middlesex Army Cadet force in the rank of lieutenant colonel, but, due to business pressures, he had to stand down after a time, returning to 21st SAS (Artists) as a private soldier, serving for another three years. A vice president of the Artists Rifles Association he led a campaign from 1985 to 1996 to have the Artists Rifles' War Memorial at the Royal Academy cleaned and restored. 'Robum' has recorded his memories of characters, great and small, spanning his generation of service to the Artists Rifles from time to time in *Mars and Minerva,* the Regimental journal, and was a vice president of the Artists Rifles Association until his death in 2006.

SIR BARNES WALLIS, CBE, FRS of 'Dambuster' fame. Details of his career are given in a previous chapter.

SIR BRUCE WHITE, KBE, MBE, FICE, F.I.Mech.E, F.I.E.E. was born in 1885 and joined the Artists Rifles in 1902 as a result of a recruiting drive at his school, Marlborough. He was posted to 'M' Company, which was equipped with two horse-drawn limbers and Maxim guns, presented to the Regiment by the brothers Wagg. After passing out from the recruit's squad he attended a course at the Vickers Crayford works, thereafter acting as an instructor for the weapon, for which he produced a simplified instruction manual published at 6d. 'M' Company had a large contingent of old Marlburians, among whom was Harold R. Smith, known as 'Smithy', who throughout the inter-war years acted as RQMS, and who was feared but highly respected and loved by all. In 1912 White resigned in the rank of sergeant but was recalled at the outbreak of war in 1914 and posted to the 2nd Battalion at Gidea Park where he was invited by Colonel Shirley to be RSM of the school for officers who had obtained commissions without previous training. An engineer by profession, later in the war he was sent to the USA to join the British Purchasing Commission, crossing the Atlantic in the *Rotterdam,* in which he shared a cabin with the future Lord Reith. After the contract was handed over to the Russians, White returned to England to be commissioned as a second lieutenant in the Royal Engineers and posted to Sandwich where the mystery port of Richborough was set up to supply the Armies in France.

Demobilized in the rank of major in 1919, he went back to work in London as a partner in White, Wolfe and Partners, Civil and Consulting Engineers. On the reserve, he was recalled in May 1940 and posted to the Transportation Directorate at the War Office to head the branch concerning ports. Attaining the rank of brigadier, his responsibilities embraced all maritime work for the Army including provision for re-entry to Europe and the equipping of ports in the UK for military use and the building of military ports in Scotland, built and operated by Royal Engineers. His tasks culminated in the preparation of the two floating Mulberry harbours, including all designs and the raising and training of specialist RE troops, to facilitate the landing of supplies on the Normandy coast. Thanks to Winston Churchill, whose support he had been given throughout, White received the Order of the KBE, an honour normally reserved for general officers.

Thus in all, Sir Bruce White completed over sixteen years of service, of which over nine years were spent in the Volunteers and Territorials and over seven years on active service. As he himself wrote: 'That I was, in two wars, able to integrate civil engineering practice with military requirements was due to the sound military training obtained in the Artists.' He died in 1983.

MAJOR GENERAL HARRY WILLANS, CBE, DSO, MC, TD, whose career details up to and including his service as commanding officer, 1933-8, have already been given, was, in 1938, promoted to command the 2nd (London) Infantry Brigade. He was the first Territorial officer to hold the rank of brigadier. He was made Director-General, Army Welfare and Education, in the rank of major general. He died in February 1943 when a plane in which he was travelling from the UK to North Africa was lost without trace.

During the Second World War decorations and awards conferred on members of the Artists Rifles numbered approximately: CH 1, KBE 3, CB 1, CBE 7, OBE 9, MBE 5, DSO and Bar 3, DSO 6, AFC 2, DSC 1, MC and Bar 8, MC 55, DFC and Bar 1, DFC 7, TD 1, Croix de Guerre 1, Mentions 12.

Casualties (as far as can be ascertained) were: Killed 119, Missing 23, Wounded 156, Prisoners of War 91.

Chapter 19

Postscript

1945-1947

I wish peace to the world.
　　　　　　The last words of Hitler's Foreign Minister, Joachim von Ribbentrop, executed at 1.11 a.m. on 16 October 1946, after being sentenced at Nuremberg.

The Second World War in the West ended on 4 May, 1945 with the surrender of all German forces in north-west Germany, Holland and Denmark, followed three days later by all the remaining German armed forces in the West. The war against Japan ended after the dropping of the atom bombs on Hiroshima on 6 August and Nagasaki on 9 August 1945. With the peace signatures, the wartime alliance between the Soviet Union and the Western Allies came to an end and, with the establishment of the North Atlantic Treaty Organization (NATO), relations between West and East cooled rapidly. The prevailing mood in Britain in 1945 to 1947, was that there would soon be another war, this time with Russia, and veteran Artists hoped that the Regiment would be restored to its former status as an elite Infantry battalion of the Territorial Army, or as an OCTU for training potential TA officers.

A general meeting of the Artists Rifles Veterans' Company was held at Winchester House, Old Broad Street, on Wednesday, 5 December 1945, at which 150 members were present. In opening the meeting H.R. Smith referred to the great loss sustained by the Veterans' Company, through the recent death of R.A. Barnett. The following officers were elected: Chairman C.M. Rait; Honorary Secretary P.B. Cowell; Honorary Treasurer E.H. Owen. C.M. Rait then took the chair and conducted the proceedings. The chairman made the following proposals, which were adopted:

1. The name to be the Artists Rifles Regimental Association. (In June 1947 'Regimental' was dropped from the title.)
2. The Governing Body to be a Council of twenty-one members consisting of the Chairman, Honorary Secretary and Honorary Treasurer, and eighteen others. The following were then elected: S.C. Hall, J.L. Boucher, E.G. Bax, A.W. Byrne, R.R. Cripps, M. de Jonquières, G.C.L. Fry, J.A. Jackson, E.N. Kitcat, J.L. Naimaster, R.O. Nash, S.W. Neighbour, D. Glyn Owen, A.J. Samson, H.G. Scotcher, A.E. Scrutton, A.R. Smith and W. Lacy Smith.
3. The Council to co-opt a General Purposes Committee and Sub-Committees to deal with other activities of the Association.
4. Subscription to be 10s. per annum as a nominal subscription fee, until such time as better facilities can be offered. Those members who have joined since September 1945 will be considered as covered for 1946.

Members of the General Purposes and Sub-Committee as appointed were as follows:

1. General Purposes: Chairman, Honorary Secretary, Honorary Treasurer (all ex-officio) and R.R. Cripps, J.L. Naimaster, S.W. Neighbour, H.J. Samson, H.R. Smith and W. Lacy Smith.
2. Sub-Committees: Artists Rifles Club, H.R. Smith; Rifle Club, H.R. Smith; School of Arms, A.W. Byrne; Golfing Society; A.E. Scrutton; Other Sports, R.O. Nash; Social Events, E.N. Kitcat; Employment Bureau, D.Glyn Owen; Chronicle, J.L. Naimaster.

As a result of this meeting a new journal was launched under the title of *The Artists Rifles Regimental Association Chronicle*. The editor was Jack Naimaster, an antiquarian bookseller, later managing director of The Fine Arts Society in Old Bond Street and an acknowledged authority on the Fine Arts. One of his early editorial tasks was to report on the Victory Parade, which took place in London on 8 June 1946. On the Friday, the Detachment was assembled by RSM Buck Norton at the Duke of York's HQ in Chelsea and issued with uniforms and then marched to Kensington Palace Gardens, where the Artists were billeted in tented accommodation. In Jack Naimaster's words:

> The move to the Kensington Gardens Belsen on the Friday evening was simplicity itself, but the removal of a complete band of pipers from the four tents allocated to our Detachment was no mean task, and Hercules himself would have found it hard to extract from the sergeants' mess more than one bottle of very light ale. Small beer was, however, found not far away, and here a CQMS was

approached by a young lady and heard to say: 'What ees this Artists Rifles? Ees it for artists? I am a model, and perhaps I ...?' A type of appeal that had no attraction for a CQMS.

Reveille brought a dull day and our Detachment ate a hearty breakfast, parade time approaching with little fuss. It must be said that a lamentable absence of panic was everywhere apparent, and brought up as every Artist has been by some of the finest exponents of frenzy the Army has ever known, this aspect was a little disappointing. There was a small shuffle when it became clear that some would have to take the active part in a drill designed to transform six men walking in one file. Not by any means, dear reader, an easy task as it sounds and requiring both explanation and demonstration.

And from then on there remain a number of impressions, momentarily overcoming the noise and the growing discomfort of carrying a rifle through London on a wet Saturday morning. A halt in Charing Cross Road, with apples and cigarettes supplied; blue-streamered fountains in Trafalgar Square; saluting at the Cenotaph; through Smithy's Arch to the Mall, Guardees at the present; the King and Queen looking to coin a phrase 'fresh as paint'; a glimpse of El Supremo, Alexs, Alanbrooke and Smuts, and thence to Palace Buckingham where the worst was over with only Constitution Hill to climb. And then we came to a halt in Hyde Park with Meteors flying overhead, and early parts of the procession already being whisked away in buses.

Just one bottle of beer in the sergeants' mess, an unanimous expression that we were not so young as we had been at Warminster, and then a rather tired-looking lot moved off to Duke's Road to re-assume the civilian exterior which today covers so many martial bosoms. And so to bed, dear reader, fireworks or no fireworks.

On Wednesday, 14 December 1946 at 12.30 p.m. a memorial service was held at St Pancras Church for those members of the Artists Rifles who fell in the Second World War. About 450 people, among them many relatives of the fallen, filled the nave. The service was conducted by the Reverend A.E. Wilkinson, OBE, MC, TD, assisted by the Reverend Frank E. Jones, the vicar of St Pancras. In the dim Regency splendours of the galleried church, the order of service had an appropriate, simple dignity. The hymn *For all the saints who from their labours rest* and the twenty-third Psalm, *The Lord is my Shepherd*, were followed by a short lesson from the *Book of Wisdom*, read by Colonel R.R. Cripps, TD. An anthem, *O Loyal Hearts*, sung by the choir, preceded Laurence Binyon's *They shall not grow old as we that are left grow old*, and a short silence of remembrance.

After another hymn, prayers for the fallen and the commendatory, Mr Wilkinson ascended the beautiful curving stairs of the old Fairlop oak pulpit, high above the heads of the congregation. In quiet, almost conversational tones, he invited those present to think of this service of remembrance in the three parts of a new Armistice Service – Remembrance, Thanksgiving and Dedication. Those who had fallen in the service of their country should not be regarded as young lives cut off in their prime, but as passing through an open door into another room, better lighted than that from which they had come. At the same time they should not be regarded as heroes, perfect and without reproach but as sons, brothers and friends, who had lived their lives as normal human beings and who had left memories of themselves, as it were 'scattered about the house'. He then drew attention to the fact that the *Last Post* and *Reveille*, shortly to be sounded, were composed in 1759 by Haydn for King George III; the *Last Post* was not a sad call, but one rising in its final notes to a pitch of hope and expectancy leading to the rousing notes of the *Reveille*. Mr Wilkinson concluded his sermon by asking the elders amongst his listeners to dedicate themselves to the help of younger people by advising them on how to surmount the difficulties in life they themselves had already overcome.

After *O God our help in ages past*, Mr Wilkinson pronounced a valediction from *The Pilgrim's Progress*. As he spoke, three drummers in their familiar grey full-dress uniforms appeared between the columns over the altar. On the words 'And so he passed over all the trumpets for him on the other side,' they raised their bugles, and the notes of the *Last Post* rang over the standing congregation. The *Last Post* was followed by the *Reveille* and the service was concluded with the singing of the National Anthem. The thanks of all Artists, their families and friends attending were due to those arranging the memorable service of remembrance, to those who acted as ushers in the church, and to all those who assisted in the provision of light refreshments, only a stone's throw away at headquarters.

In July 1946 Mr J.J. Lawson, Minister of State at the War Office, announced in the House of Commons that Britain's military needs could only be met in the long run by a professional, long-service Army. He also said that he was determined in view of the great services performed by the old Territorial Army to see the return of most, if not all, first-line Territorial units. He was also anxious to fully support the Army Cadet Corps. In November of the same year Mr F.J. Bellenger, Secretary of State for War, announced officially that the Territorial Army was to be reconstituted to provide anti-aircraft defences for Great Britain. In addition the TA would comprise not only infantry but armoured units, an airborne division, and all the necessary support troops. A month later it was announced that the TA was to consist of six infantry divisions, two armoured divisions and one airborne division, besides independent infantry and armoured formations, and support units.

Voluntary recruiting for the new Territorial Army was to commence on 1 April 1947 and it was hoped during the period 1947-8 to recruit 8,000 officers and 144,380 other ranks, who could be persuaded to give up some of their spare time for military training. The National Service Act to call up eighteen year old male youths, initially for a period of one year, received the Royal Assent on 18 July 1946, the period of service being extended in 1948 to eighteen months, and then, with the start of the Korean War in 1950, to two years. National Servicemen on completion of their service were at first posted to the Army Reserve Class Z (T), but by 1950 National Service included the commitment to serve for four years in the Territorial Army. Clearly the TA was to rely heavily on National Servicemen to make up their numbers.

After taking up his post as Director, Territorial Army and Army Cadet Force (ACF), Major General R.E. Urquart, CB, DSO, the former commander of 1st Airborne Division, on 26 October 1946, attended the 22nd Annual Dinner of the Artists Rifles, held under the chairmanship of Lord Strathcona, at the Connaught Rooms in Holborn. In his after dinner speech as guest of honour, General Urquart outlined his hopes and plans for the future of the TA. Although he gave no clear idea of how he proposed to achieve his recruitment goals, he good-heartedly foresaw the Territorials as the 'tail that wagged the dog', conveying the CIGS's concern that the TA should remain alive and well, if only to 'act as a sort of Home Guard'. The General had first met the Artists the previous July at Duke's Road and was well aware of the Regiment's proud history. Now in a state of 'suspended animation', many old Artists were content to use Duke's Road as a social club but there were others who were confident that the reconstituted Regiment was destined for more 'sterner stuff', as it had been in two world wars.

In 1946 General Urquart made several visits to Duke's Road during which time he suggested that the Regiment should be reformed as an SAS unit. What discussions took place at Duke's Road is not on record but it is thought that Urquart offered the command to either of two Artists, Daniel Brock and David Davidson – but both declined. Clearly it was more appropriate for an experienced SAS commander to be the new colonel. However, little was known in those days, even in the Army, about the SAS, which had been founded in 1941 in Egypt and which had fought behind the lines in the Western Desert, Sicily, Italy and north-west Europe.

Who would command the new Regiment? The founder, David

Stirling, himself naturally mindful for the future of his Regiment, was turning in interest to the part he could play in the 'Winds of Change' that were about to blow across the African sub-continent. Paddy Mayne, who had taken over command of 1st SAS after David Stirling's capture in early 1943, after the war had first tried the life of a crew member on a South Atlantic survey voyage but he found it rather boring and returned to the legal profession in Belfast. There was really only one choice, Lieutenant Colonel B.M.F. Franks, DSO, MC who, in 1944, had taken over the command of 2nd SAS from Bill Stirling (David's brother) for operations behind the lines in north-west Europe. Brian Franks was conveniently domiciled in London where he had taken up his career as managing director of the Hyde Park Hotel.

21 SAS (Artists) was officially established on 8 July, 1947, although the historic occasion elicited no comment from the media. The birth was certificated with the following announcement from the Court of St James, authorized in the name of King George VI, by the Secretary for War, F.J. Bellenger, and which is to be found as a handwritten document held by the National Archives.

SRO/1947/No.1593 A.O. 78/1947
20/Miscellaneous/2497
Reconstitution of the Special Air Service and the Artists Rifles.
George RI

Whereas we deem it expedient that the Special Air Service Regiment shall be reconstituted and that the Artists Rifles (Territorial Army) shall cease to be a component body of 'P' Corps of Infantry and shall become part of the Special Air Service Regiment, Army Air Corps.

Our Will and Pleasure is that the Special Air Service Regiment shall be reconstituted and be a component of our Army Air Corps.

Our further Will and Pleasure is that the Artists Rifles (Territorial Army) shall henceforth be entitled the 21st Battalion Special Air Service Regiment (Artists Rifles) (Territorial Army).

Lastly our Will and Pleasure is that the Schedule (attached to the Warrant of His late Majesty King George V) dated 27th February 1926, declaring what bodies of our Military Forces shall be Corps for the purpose of the Army Act, the Reserve Forces, 1882, and the Territorial and Reserve Forces Act 1907, should be amended as follows:-

Under 'Infantry' against Corps 'P' delete 'and the Artists Rifles (Territorial Army).'

Given at our Court of Saint James's this 8th Day of July, 1947, in the eleventh year of our reign.

By His Majesty's Command, F.J. Bellenger.
National Archives (Kew): WO 380/15: 1919 – c.1953: Infantry Regiments and other units. F. 900 over.

21 SAS was first named the 21st Regiment Special Air Service (Artists) TA, the authorized abbreviation being 21 Regt SAS (Artists) TA, but the Regiment was shortly re-titled 21st Special Air Service Regiment (Artists) TA, for which there was no authorized abbreviation. '21' represented 1st and 2nd SAS in the reverse order. In mid-September the association launched an appeal for Artists to join the new Regiment. By the end of October 1947 ninety applications to join 21 SAS had been received at Duke's Road, of which fifty had been accepted. This number included eighteen Artists: C.G. Johnston, P.B. Greenway, D.F. de Berry, A.W. Horner, A.R. Moore, N. Rogers, C.S. Colbeck, R.E. Robotham, E.D. McClure, F.T. Russell, R.O. Nash, D.G. Newton, J.P. Crickmay, C.H. Owen, G.P. Hall, P. Webber and W. Lacy Smith.

Ralph Robotham, MC, who had reverted to the rank of trooper on enlistment in 21 SAS but was promoted corporal and then appointed RQMS, and two other Artists, C.S. Colbeck, MBE, and H.W. Newton were appointed to HQ Squadron as SSM and CQMS respectively. Two more Artists, R.O. Nash, MC and D.G. Newton were made SSM and SQMS of 'A' Squadron respectively. The Artists joining the new Regiment were not required to take parachute courses, which were mandatory for those men who were recruited directly into the Regiment. The SAS adopted the Artists' tradition that all new recruits who had held commissions or NCO rank should, on enlistment, start as troopers. The SAS also adopted the Artists' grey tie and green award tie for distinguished service to the Regiment.

In concluding *A History of the Artists Rifles, 1859-1947* we must look forward in time to 1 April 1967 when the Territorial Army was replaced by the Territorial and Army Volunteer Reserve. Early 1967 saw the disappearance of TA Divisions and of TA Armoured and Infantry Brigades, which had seemed so necessary to the Labour Government in 1946. (The only survivor was the Para Brigade.) These disbandments of headquarters and the sad sale of mess properties, not omitting the furniture and the oil paintings that proudly adorned the walls, led to protest. Although the future of Britain's new T & AVR seemed assured on paper, its usefulness as a reserve force of such modest strength was a matter for speculation. It was refreshing news therefore that both 21 SAS (Artists) and 23 SAS, the latter having been set up in 1959 and based in Birmingham, would be unaffected by troop reductions, and indeed provision was made for adding new squadrons, which would give the

TA SAS wide regional coverage, with '23' extending its network from the Midlands with squadrons in the north of England and Scotland.

The one casualty of the dissolution of the Territorial Army, so far as 21 SAS (Artists) was concerned, was its red brick Victorian Drill Hall at 17 Duke's Road, St Pancras. During 1966 it had been announced, without giving reasons, that in April 1967 the Regiment would be moving to the Duke of York's HQ, King's Road, Chelsea. What some may have considered in moving to the King's Road as a fitting gesture in the climate of the 'Swinging Sixties' was taken by others as an urgent need for more room and the extra facilities that the Duke of York's could undoubtedly supply. But there were those mindful of the history and traditions of the Artists who deplored the move.

Although the Artists Rifles Association obviously had cause to regret the passing of an institution built on freehold land and purchased in 1868 with money raised by private subscription from within the Regimental circle, the ARA was reconciled to the demise of 17 Duke's Road and even looked forward with some relish to banking the proceeds of the sale of the property which, although Bloomsbury was not what it was, were likely to be substantial. This was not to be. Although the premises was owned by the Artists, the building was classified as WD property, with a nominal rent payable by the incumbent Regiment of £1 per annum. When it was discovered by the MOD that '21' was in default of payment of the rent, the Regiment was given notice to quit.

When No. 17 was sold by the MOD in 1970, the sale realized £132,000, a vast increase on the £500 the Artists had paid for it. The premises was bought by an experimental dance company, who turned it into a theatre with a seating capacity for an audience of 450 people.

In 1972 the four trustees of the Regimental Aid Fund took the case to the High Court to obtain a ruling on the Regiment's entitlement in the matter. On 13 March the Judge decreed that the proceeds of the sale of the Artists Rifles' property belonged to the Crown. The explanation was that in 1967 a new unit, the 21st Special Air Service Regiment (Artists) (Volunteers), had been formed. But new units formed in 1967 could not be legally identified with their predecessors, as earlier units had been expressly disbanded. It would seem that in time of upheaval and turmoil in the Territorial Army the carpet-baggers from the Ministry had made a smart move!

Epilogue

As the current commanding officer of 21 Special Air Service (Artists) (Reserves) I was delighted when asked to provide the epilogue for the Artists Rifles History. It is a great honour to be in command of such a prestigious Regiment and in making this contribution I feel especially proud and privileged. I am aware that a huge amount of time and effort, over many years, has gone into this project. The resulting book is impressive and a credit to all those involved but most especially to Barry Gregory, the author.

I am conscious that as the British Army's Regimental Order of Battle is changing again, well diminishing actually, it is even more important that we preserve our military history and regimental heritage. The title and spirit of the Artists Rifles lives on within its modern day successor 21 Special Air Service. I can also tell you that the Regiment of today is immensely proud of its formidable and hugely successful predecessor. Having said that, I am not convinced that many of the serving soldiers fully understand or appreciate who the original Artists were, what they symbolized or indeed what they achieved over their eighty-eight years' history. I believe that this book leaves no stone unturned and provides a unique, and unrivalled, insight into the Artists Rifles Regiment. The book contains a fascinating amount of interesting material on the art of soldering in days gone by. From the carefully chronicled biographies of all the Artists' commanding officers down to the detailed recollections of annual camps, memoirs of mobilization and active service as well as covering the Regiment's well renowned sporting prowess.

As I reflected on 'past and present' there were a number of details that struck me as being worthy of mention. It is perhaps no coincidence that the Artists and the SAS have become entwined. The Artists were formed within a contemporary atmosphere of nationalistic fervour and entre-preneurial spirit under the watchful eye of Edward Sterling. The SAS was formed under similar conditions, albeit some eighty-two years later, but also under a man called Sterling (different spelling of course). The Artists supplied officers and men to all arms which was a fairly groundbreaking, if not a unique, policy in its day. Paradoxically, the modern day SAS is drawn from all arms, in fact all three services, so there appears to be another coincident twist in the seemingly random pairing. Both regiments have also borne an impressive list of gallantry awards in British Army campaigns spanning over a century. I suspect that historians and military analysts will conclude that there was a certain amount of inevitability that these two unique regiments would be become merged or inextricably linked together at some stage.

I have attended many functions over the last two years in my capacity as commanding officer whereupon I was privileged to meet a number of former Artists including pre-Second World War Artists. I felt quite humbled when I listened to their recollections of military service including active service in a number of campaigns. I was particularly struck by their modesty and their unassuming approach to the rigours of military service at that time an example to us all.

Of course the legacy of the Artists Rifles endures to a degree through the existence of the Artists Rifles Association (ARA). But I also sense that many of the values and characteristics of our predecessors in the Artists live on within the modern day Regiment. The volunteer ethos as well as the selfless devotion to Queen and country is still very much at the heart of the Reservist's philosophy in 2006.

The Association and the modern Regiment maintain very close links and we are very appreciative of all the support that we receive from former members of both the Artists and 21 SAS Regiment. It is my great pleasure to wholeheartedly commend this book to you and hope that it will keep the Artists' spirit alive – Once an Artist always an Artist!

Lt Col D
Commanding Officer
21 SAS (Artists)(Reserves)

Appendix I

Art in the Artists

Brief lives of most well-known artists in Regimental history are given below. These cover painters, sculptors and engravers who have passed through the Artists Corps since its formation in 1859.

Official abbreviations used are as follows – A: Associate, ARA: Associate of Royal Academy, BI: British Institution, BWS: British Water Colour Society, F: Fellow, H: Honorary Member, NEAC: New English Art Club, NS: National Society of Painters, Sculptors and Engravers, NWCS: New Water Colour Society, OWCS: Old Water Colour Society, P: President, RA: Royal Academy, Royal Academician, RBA: Royal Society of British Artists, RBS: Royal Society of British Sculptors, RCA: Royal College of Arts, RE: Royal Society of Painters, Etchers and Engravers, RELG: Regimental Exhibition, Leicester Galleries, London, 1916, RI: Royal Institute of Painters in Water Colours, ROI: Royal Institute of Oil Painters, RSA: Royal Scottish Academy, RWS: Royal Society of Painters in Water Colours, SGA: Society of Graphic Arts.

ACKERMANN, Gerald. Landscape painter Ex. mainly about 1892, RELG. Joined 1915, Corporal. Commissioned 1917 to Army Education Corps.

ANDREWS, Felix Emile. (B 1883). Trained RA schools. Ex. RA and RI. J. 1915, Private.

BATEMAN, A. James. (1893/1959). RA, ARWS, RE. Studied at the Slade. J. 1916, CRFC 1917. Seriously wounded then dropped sculpture for painting.

BIRCH, Charles Bell. (1852/93). RA Sculptor, Ex. London and Berlin. 'F' Coy 1876/84.

BLAIKLEY, Ernest. (B 1885). SGA. Painter and etcher of figures, landscapes and portraits. Ex. RARI, RSA. J. 1914, Sergeant. Awarded MSM.

BROMLEY, John Mallord. Landscape painter. Ex. 1876/1904. RA,RI. 'F' Coy 1876/99.

BURGESS, John B. Ex. 1850/93 RA. Figure painter. No.2 Coy 1876/99.

BURNE-JONES, Sir Edward. (1833/98). Painter and leader of the 2nd phase of the Pre-Raphaelite Brotherhood. Friend of William Morris and Rossetti. Created Baronet 1894, Legion of Honour and other European decorations. A great-uncle of Robin Howard, director of the Contemporary Ballet Trust, 'The Place', 17 Duke's Road – the old Artists' HQ. Entry in Enrolment Registers not traced.

CALKIN, G. Lance. RA. Portraits. Ex. 1881/93 London. 'B' Coy 1876/80.

CALDERON, W.F. ROI. Landscapes. Ex. 1882/1921. RA, Suffolk St & ors. Founder of the School of Animal Painting. His *Feeding the Hungry* was purchased by Queen Victoria. 'H' Coy 1881/86.

CARY, F.S. Elwes. Ex. 1834/76. RA, BI and ors. 'C' Coy 1892/97.

CHANDLER, W. Frank. Paintings and sketches of 1st War Scenes in France. RELG. J. 1914, C 1919, Artists.

CLARK, Philip Lindsey. DSO. FRBS. Ex. RA and Paris 1919/21. Sculpted the Cameronians and Belgian Soldiers' War Memorials. J. 1915, CR Sussex 1916.

COKE, Alfred S. Painter of historical subjects. Ex. RA, Suffolk St and ors between 1869/92. No.1 Coy 1870/74.

COLE, A. Ernest. Widely exhibited sculptor. Professor of Sculpture RCA 1924/26. J 1915. C 1916 York & Lancasters.

COLE, George Vicat. RA. Landscapes. Ex. 1852/92. RA, BI and ors. No.2 Coy 1861. Struck off.

COOPER, A. Egerton. A leading Chelsea artist, died 1974. Ex. RA and Paris. His most famous picture was of Sir Winston Churchill, copies being distributed worldwide. Close friend of Sir Barnes Wallis and Annigoni. Official artist to the RAF.

COPE, Sir Arthur. KCVO, RA. Portraits and landscapes. Ex. RA from 1876. Knighted 1917. 'A' Coy 1873/81.

DE LA BERE, Stephen B. 1st War paintings and sketches. RELG. J, 1916. Lance Corporal. C 1917 RGA.

DEVEY, Georges. Ex. RA 1841/48. J. 1860. Hon Member No.2 Coy.

DICKSEE, Herbert Thomas, 1882.

DOBSON, Frank, CBE. RA. Professor of Sculpture RCA up to 1953. Many official purchases. J. 1915. C Border Regiment.

DOLLMAN. RWS, ROI, RBS. Painter and sculptor. Ex. From 1871 RA, Suffolk St and ors. 'A' Coy 1881/88.

DUFFIELD, William. Mainly still life painter. Ex. From 1838 at RA and ors. No. 1 Coy 1871.

EARLES, Chester. Portraits. Ex. RA, BI and ors 1842/63. Went abroad 1864. No. 2 Coy 1860/64.

FOLKARD, Charles J. Book Illustrator, on staff of *Daily Mail*. Invented 'Teddy Tail' 1915. J. 1917. Private.

'FOUGASSE' (Cyril Kenneth Bird), CBE, BSC, FSIA. Famous cartoonist. Art Editor *Punch* 1937/44. Editor 1949/53. Many publications, signs 'Fougasse'. J. 'M' Coy 1906.

FRAMPTON, G.V. Meredith. RA (1942). Ex. RA from 1920. J 1916. Private.

FRIPP, Charles E. ARWS. Water colours of figures and military subjects. War correspondent in Kaffir, Zulu and Boer Wars. Ex. RWA and RA. 'F' Coy 1876/89.

GASCOIGNE, George. Painter mainly of domestic scenes. Ex. RA and ors from 1882. 'H' Coy 1881/86.

GETHIN, Percy F. 1st War sketches and paintings. RELG. J 1914. C Devons 1915. Killed in action 1916.

GOW, Andrew C. RA (1891), RI (1868). Military subjects. Keeper of the RA from 1911. 'H' Coy 1879/82.

GRAY, George E. Kruger. (1880/1943) ARCA. Portraits and landscapes in watercolours, also heraldic and stained glass. Ex. RA, war cartoons in AR Journal 1917/19. J. 1917. Corporal.

GUNN, Sir Herbert. RA, PRP, NS. Portraits and landscapes. Gold

Medal Paris. Painted HM The Queen 1953. J. 1915, C 1917, Cameronians. Mention.

HAAG, Carl. (1820/1915). RWS. Ex. Between 1849/88 at RA, OWCS, Suffolk St and ors. Mainly portraits. Also member of Society of British Artists. No. 2 Coy 1860/67.

HANDLEY-READ, Edward. MBE. (1869/1935). Oils and water colours. Illustrator for *Graphic* and *Illustrated London News*. Painted widely in Holland, Belgium and France. RELG. J. 1915. Sgt. C. MG Corps.

HANKEY, William Lee. RBA, RI. Landscapes and sketches. Ex. from 1893. Member NWCS. J 1914, C Artists (15 OCB). RELG.

HAYWARD, Alfred. RP. ARWS. Portraits and landscapes. Official war artist 1916. Ex. Tate, Imp War Museum, S. Africa, NZ and Venice. C. RGA 1917.

HODGE, Francis E. RI, RP, RBA, ROI. Ex. RA, NEAC. Hon Mention Paris 1927. Silver Medal 1938. J. 1915. C 1917 RHA, wounded 1917.

HODGSON, John E. RA. Domestic scenes. Ex. From 1856 RA, BI and ors. Librarian and Professor of Painting at RA. Member of St John's Wood Clique No. 1 Coy 1861/73.

HORSLEY, Colonel Walter C., VD, ps. Mainly domestic subjects. Ex. RA, NWCS and ors. J 'F' Coy 1874. Rejoined 1914. Became OC 2/Artists and Hon Colonel 1928. Died 1934.

HUGGILL, Henry P., A CAM A. ARE (1917), ARCA. Painter, etcher and engraver. Ex. RA. J. 1914, C. 1915 Cheshires, wounded 1918.

HUNT, William Holman. (1827/1910). First ex. 1846 and in 1848 helped to found the Pre-Raphaelite Brotherhood. Specialized in painting biblical subjects. His most famous picture *Light of the World* is in Keble Coll, Oxford, and a copy of it is in St Paul's Cathedral. J. No. 2 Coy 1860.

JAGGER, Charles S, MC. ARA (1926), FRBS. Sculptor and official War Artist. Recorded some war experiences in bronze relief in *No Man's Land* at the Tate and did the R. Artillery War Memorial, Hyde Park Corner. RBS. Gold Medals 1926 and 1933. J. 1914, C. 1915 Worcesters with whom he won his MC.

KING, J. Yeend. RBA, RI, ROI. Ex. between 1874/1924. Domestic scenes at RA, NWCS and ors. 'F' Coy 1886/92.

LARA, Percy L. Landscape painter. Ex. RI, ROI, Paris. J. 1915. Sergeant, Artists 15 OCB.

LEETE, Alfred. (1882/1933). Illustrator and cartoonist. Designed the famous Lord Kitchener poster, *Your King and Country Needs YOU*. J. 1917. Med. unfit for comm. Coy Clerk Artists (15 OCB).

LEIGHTON, Lord (Frederick) PRA, RWS, HRCA, HRSW. Baron Leighton of Stretton. Painter of historical and mythological subjects. Leader of the Victorian neo-classical painters. Ex. 1855/96 RA, Suffolk St and ors. Elected PRA 1878 and knighted. Baronet 1886. Raised to the Peerage 1896. He was the first English artist to achieve this honour. J. 1860 (No. 9 enrolment), CO 1869/84. Died 1896. Service and burial at St Paul's Cathedral.

LEWIS, Arthur James, Landscapes and Portraits. J. 1860.

LONG, Edwin. RA (1829/91). Historical and biblical genre. Ex. RA, BI and ors 1855/91. His painting *Babylonian Marriage Market* caused a sensation in 1875 when it sold for 7,000 guineas. J. No. 1 Coy 1860. Struck off.

LUCAS, J. Seymour. RA, RI, FSA. Ex. 1867/93, mainly historical pictures. 'H' Coy 1879/81.

LYNDON, Herbert. Mainly landscapes. Ex. From 1867/9 at RA, NWCS and ors. 'A' Coy 1881/7.

McMILLAN, William. CVO, RA, Hon FRBS, Hon LLD. (B. 1887). Sculptor of figure subjects and designer of medals. Master of the RA School of Sculpture. Elected RA 1933. Worked in Tate – many public commissions. J. 1915, comm. Oxford & Bucks LI.

MARKS, H. Stacy. RA, RWS, HRCA, HRPE. (1829/98). Ex. RA 1878/96. His early paintings were on mediaeval subjects, later specializing in bird panels. A close friend of Ruskin and a member of the St John's Wood clique. No. 1 Coy 1862/79.

MASON, Arnold H. RA, RP. (1885/1963). A painter of landscapes who worked almost exclusively in Provence. J. 1915, comm. 1917 to 4/KSLI. Elected RA 1951.

MAUD, W.T. (1865/1903). War illustrator and artist for the *Graphic*. Ex. 1890 only. Travelled widely. 'F' Coy 1886/88.

MERRY, Godfrey. Ex. in London from 1883, mainly domestic scenes at RA, Suffolk Street, etc. 'B' Coy 1880/83.

MILLAIS, Sir John. PRA,HRI, HRCA. (1829/96). A founder member in 1848 with Holman Hunt and Rossetti of the Pre-Raphaelite Brotherhood. Achieved great popularity with his story-pictures, portraits and sentimental child studies e.g. *Bubbles*. Created a baronet in 1885 and elected PRA in 1896. Hon. Member. No. 2 Coy 1860.

MOODY, F.N.J. A commercial and landscape artist in watercolour. Served in 'D' Coy and HQ from 1921/32, becoming Pioneer Sergeant. In First War served in RNVR & RA and in the last war became a camouflage expert with REs in Iceland. Died in March 1975, aged eighty-two.

MOORE, Charles E. Stained glass artist. Fellow of the Society of Master Glass Painters. His works are in many churches. J. 1902, rejoined 1916. Lance Corporal.

MORRALL, John B. Did a number of First World War sketches in France. J. 1916, comm 1917 R. Warwicks. Killed in action.

MORRIS, Philip R. Was encouraged to study art by W. Holman Hunt. Ex. RA mainly scriptural subjects. Rome prize winner. No. 2 Coy 1868/.

MORRIS, William. Poet and painter. A close friend of Burne-Jones, his art was influenced by Ruskin and Rossetti. He did much to raise the standards of craftsmanship, manufacturing furniture, wallpapers, church decorations, etc. Founder of the Socialist League. No. 1 Coy 1860/67.

MUFF-FORD, John W. D. Has exhibited paintings in S Africa for some years. Lived at Port Elizabeth. J. 1915, comm. 1916 to 19 London Regiment.

NASH, John. CBE, RA, NEAC, LG, SWE. (1893/1978). Painter in oils and watercolour. Was commissioned in 1918 to paint pictures for the Imperial War Museum. His painting, *Over The Top*, depicting the Artists advancing in the snow, is well known. In 1940 he became an official war artist to the Admiralty. Also a wood engraver. Served with 1 Artists in France from 1916/18. Died in 1978, aged eighty-one.

NASH, Paul. NEAC, LG, SWE. (1889/1946). Elder brother of John Nash. Painter, engraver, illustrator and theatrical designer. Became an official war artist in 1917. J. 1914, 'D' Coy, L/Cpl, commissioned to 3

Hampshires in 1916. Died in 1946, aged fifty-seven.

NEWTON, W.G. MC. Architectural drawings mainly. Designed a burlesque coat-of-arms for Colonel May. J. 1909, comm 1914, becoming ADC to the CGS, twice wounded. Believed to have died about 1947.

NICOL, J. Watson. (1876/1924). Painter of historical scenes. Ex. RA and other galleries. 'A' Coy 1873/75.

OSBORNE, Malcolm. CBE, RA, PRE, RBC, ARCA. (1880/1963). Painter and engraver. Professor of Engraving at RC Arts. J. 1915, comm 1917 to 17 London Regiment.

OULESS, W.W. Gold and Silver Medallist. Lived in Berlin, Munich, Vienna and Paris. No. 1 Coy 1871.

OUTRAM, R.L. Member of the Herkomer School of Art, Bushey. 'F' Coy 1893/95.

PAGET, H.M. (1856/1936). Ex. in London from 1874. Painter of sporting pictures, at RA, Suffolk Street, etc. Also painted classical and historical subjects. No entry in Enrolment Register traced.

PARKS, Murray T. Ex. landscape at RA. 1949. A quiet but popular member who served in 'C' and 'A' Coys from 1926/39. Died about 1952.

PATTISON, Edgar L. (B 1872). Painter in oil and water colour of landscapes. Ex. RA and ROI. J. 1915, Sergeant, comm 1917 RGA.

PEARCE, Charles Maresco. (1874/1964). NEAC, LG. Studied painting under Sir William Orpen and Walter Sickert. Painter in oils and water colour. Had also studied architecture. J. 1914, Sergeant.

PERUGINI, Charles E. Painter of figures. Ex. London, RA, Brit Inst, Suffolk St and ors from 1863. Married Kate Dickens, daughter of Charles Dickens. No. 3 Coy, 1860/64.

PHILLIPS, Henry Wyndham. (1820/68). Ex. in London from 1863, mainly portraits at the RA and Brit Inst. J. 1860, No. 1 Coy. No. 6 in the Enrolment Registers. Succeeded Lord Bury, afterwards the Duke of Albemarle, the first Commandant. On his death in 1868 he was followed as CO by Lord Leighton.

POTT, Charles L. Ex. in London from 1888 at Suffolk St and ors.

Landscape painter. Was a Capt in the Artists and his far-seeing cartoon (page 95 of Colonel May's *Memories of the Artists Rifles*) drawn in 1907 depicts hilariously airdrops of the future.

POYNTER, Sir Edward. PRA, RE, RWS, HFRPE. (1836/1919). Painter of mainly historical subjects. Ex. in London from 1859 at RA, BI, OWCS. No. 1 Coy, 1860. Struck off.

PRINSEP, Val. RA. (1839/1904). Painter of domestic scenes. Ex. 1862 onwards at RA, Suffolk St and Grosvenor Gallery. No. 1 Coy, 1860/85.

RICHMOND, Sir William B. RA, FSA, MA. (1842/1921). Ex. London from 1861, mainly portraits at RA, Brit Inst, Grosvenor Galleries and ors. Knighted in 1897. Corporal in No. 1 Coy. Resigned 1869.

ROBERTS, Thomas. RBA. (1820/1901). Ex. From 1850 at RA, Suffolk Street and ors. Mainly domestic scenes.

ROBINS, William P. RWS, RE, NS. (1882/1959). Landscape painter and etcher. Studied architecture at King's Coll. Silver Medallist, also at St Martin's and Goldsmith's Schools. Member of Printmakers of California and Chicago Soc. of Etchers. Joined 1915. Became a sergeant.

ROGERS, J.E. ARHA. (1838/1896). Ex. 1876 onwards-landscapes at RA, NWCS and ors. Joined 'F' Coy 1877.

ROSSETTI, Dante Gabriel. Founder of the Pre-Raphaelite Brotherhood. J. 1860.

RUSKIN, John. Honorary Member. J. 1860.

SEVERN, Arthur. RI. (1842/1931). Ex. 1863/93. Landscapes at RA, NWCS, Grosvenor Galleries and ors. Studied art in Rome. Founder of the Lake District Artists Soc. 1904. Married Joan Agnew, a cousin and ward of John Ruskin. No. 2 Coy 1866.

SEVERN, Walter. RCA. (1830/1904). Ex. 1853/89 at RA, Suffolk Street and ors. Fifty of his paintings were sold by the Agnews in 1874. No. 2 Coy 1860.

SKEATS, Leonard F. (1874/1943). Painter of portraits and figures. Ex. RA, RI, ROI, RWA. Joined 1915, comm. to RA 1917.

SMYTH, Montague. RBA. (1863/1965). Ex. From 1890 – landscapes at Suffolk Street and ors. Trained for a career in the Army which he abandoned for painting. Ex. also at RA, ROI. Joined 1915, became a sergeant, comm. 1917 to the RNVR. Died at 101. Member of London Sketch Club with Clay-Thomas, a close friend. Played golf at Hampstead in his late nineties.

STALEY, David C. ('B' Coy 1935/37). Was known in 'B' Coy mainly for his drawings and cartoons. Re-trained after the war at the Plymouth College of Art and Design. Member of the Society of Industrial Artists and Designers. Spent many years in Kenya in general trading. During the war he served with the Kenya RNVR. A keen supporter of the SW reunions and a friend of Peter Thursby, artist and sculptor of Pinhoe, Exeter.

STERLING, Edward C. RA. To him is attributed the original proposal for the founding of the Artists Corps in 1859. He was a ward of Thomas Carlyle and had served in the Cornish Militia. He started this project in the life class at Cary's Art School in Chelsea. After an unenthusiastic response he and two others, Field Talfourd and John Milner Allen, undertook to find recruits. This resulted in the enrolment of 119 members on 10 May 1860, which included a number of Pre-Raphaelites of great fame. Edward Sterling exhibited in London from 1867/77, mainly portraits at RA and other galleries.

STOCKS, Arthur. RI. (1846/89). RA in London 1866/89. Domestic scenes at RA, Suffolk Street, NWCS and ors. No. 1 Coy 1871. Res. 1886.

STOKES, Adrian. (1854/1935). RA, VPRWS. Ex. domestic scenes from 1871/1935 at RA. Suffolk Street, PWCS, NWCS. Medal winner at Paris Exhibition 1889 and Chicago World Fair. Represented in many collections. Author of 'Landscape Painting' 1925. Joined in 1884, aged seventeen.

STRUBE, Sidney C. The famous cartoonist for the *Daily Express* and other papers. Joined in 1915 and became a sergeant-instructor in 15 OCB (Artists). A member of the London Sketch Club and The Savage Club.

TALFOURD, Field. (1815/74). See under Edward Sterling. Ex. In London from 1845. Painter of portraits, landscapes and genre. Ex. at RA, BI. Obtained a considerable reputation. No. 2 Coy 1860.

THACKERAY, Lance. (-/1916). Painter and illustrator. One-man shows at Leicester Galleries 1908, Fine Art Soc. 1910 and ors. Published *The Light Side of Egypt* 1908, and *The People of Egypt* 1910.

Joined 1915. Lance Corporal. Killed in action 1916.

THOMAS, Bert. PS, OBE. Illustrator of humorous work, contributor to *Punch. The Sketch* and ors. Joined in 1917.

THORNYCROFT, Sir Hamo. RA. (1850/1925). A prolific exhibitor of sculpture at the RA, NWCS, Grosvenor Gallery and ors. No. 1 Coy 1871/82.

WALKER, Frederick. ARA. Genre painter and water colours. Elected ARWS 1864, ARA 1871. No. 2 Coy 1860, resigned 1874. Died of consumption 1875.

WATERHOUSE, John William, FIRA, 1885. RA, 1893.

WATERLOW, Sir Ernest. RA, PRWS. (1850/1919). Landscape painting at RA, Suffolk Street, OWCS, NWCS, Grosvenor Gallery and ors. Studied in Lausanne and Heidelberg, also RA Schools. Knighted 1902. Joined No. 1 Coy 1871. Resigned 1874.

WATTS, George Frederick. (1817/1904). OM, RA, HRCA, DCL. Ex. prolifically in London from 1837 historical pictures at RA, BI, Suffolk Street and ors. Joined No. 3 Coy 1860.

WAY, Thomas R. (1862/1913). Ex. landscape paintings at RA, Suffolk Street, NWCS and ors from 1883. 'H' Coy 1880/93.

WEBB, Sir Aston. PRA. (1849/1930). Was president of the RA 1919/24 as well as president of various architectural bodies. Knighted in 1904. No entry in Enrolment Registers traced.

WHALL, Christopher W. Ex. Portraits at RA, Suffolk Street and ors. No. 1 Coy 1864. Res 1874.

WHEATLEY, John. ARA, RWS, NEAC. (1892/1955). Etcher and engraver of genre subjects. Studied under Stanhope Forbes and Walter Sickert. Official War Artist, 1918/20. Taught at the Slade School. Director of the Nat Gallery of S Africa. Professor of Fine Art at Cape Town. Joined 1915. Sergeant.

WIGMAN, Theodore B. Portraits. No. 1 Coy, 1870/74.

WILDASH, John. Became member RSA in 1940 and has had a number of his works exhibited by art societies in London and Paris. Comm from 163 OCTU (Artists) in 1940 to QR West Surrey Regiment.

WILLIAMS, Hubert S. PS, SGA. Trained at RA Schools. Landseer prize winner. Works in many public collections including Imperial War Museum. Also an illustrator for the *Observer* and other newspapers. 'D' Coy 1931/36.

WIRGMAN, Theodore B. (1848/1925). Painter of portraits from 1867 at RA, NWCS, Suffolk Street and ors. No. 1 Coy 1870/74.

WOLLEN, William B. (1857/1936) Ex. paintings mostly domestic scenes from 1879 at RA, NWCS and ors. Also painted genre and military subjects. Trained at the Slade. In 1900 went to S Africa as an artist for *Sphere*. 'H' Coy 1879/88.

WOOD, Wilfred R. (1888/-). Painter, lithographer and poster artist. Ex. at RA, RI, NEAC. Joined in 1916, comm. 1917 to Machine Gun Corps.

WOODS, Henry. RA. (1846/91). Brother-in-law of Sir Luke Fildes, RA. Settled in Venice in 1881, devoting himself to Venetian subjects. Started as a magazine illustrator in Warrington. Joined ?, left in 1881.

WYNFIELD, David W. (1837/87). Ex. from 1857 at RA, RI, Suffolk Street and ors. Domestic scenes. No. 1 Coy 1860/66. Founder of the St John's Wood clique.

WYON, Alfred B. Sculptor, mainly medals. Ex. from 1857 at RA, BI, Suffolk Street. Joined No. 2 Coy 1860. Hon Member.

YEAMES, W.F. RA (1835/1918). Born in Russia, lived in Odessa and Dresden. Ex. in London from 1859, mainly historical paintings at RA, BI, Suffolk Street and ors. Elected ARA 1866, RA 1878. Member of St John's Wood clique. No. 1 Coy 1863/74.

Appendix II

Eight Artists Rifles VCs in the Great War and Why

The following citations are taken from the *Artists Rifles 1914-1919 Roll of Honour* published by Howlett & Son, 1922.

HALLOWES, 2/Lt Rupert Price, MC. 4/Middlesex

Hooge, Belgium, between 25th September and 1st October, 1915 for most conspicuous bravery and devotion to duty. 2/Lt Hallowes displayed throughout these days the greatest bravery and untiring energy and set a magnificent example to his men during the four heavy and prolonged bombardments. On more than one occasion he climbed up on the parapet, entirely regardless of danger, in order to put fresh heart into his men. He made daring reconnaissances of the German positions in our lines. When the supply of bombs was running short he went back under heavy shell fire and brought up a fresh supply. Even after he was mortally wounded he continued to cheer his men to inspire them with fresh courage.

(Reg. No.1422. Gazetted 5th April. Killed in action 30th September 1915)

FLEMING-SANDES, 2/Lt. Arthur James Terence 2/East Surrey

Hohenzollern Redoubt, France, September 29th 1915 for most conspicuous bravery. 2/Lt Fleming-Sandes was sent to command a company which at the time was in a very critical position. The troops on his right were retiring and his own men, who were much shaken by continual bombing and machine-gun fire, were also beginning to retire owing to shortage of bombs. Taking in the situation at a glance, he collected a few bombs, jumped on the parapet in full view of the Germans, who were only twenty yards away, and threw them. Although very severely wounded almost at once by a bomb, he struggled to his feet and continued to advance and throw bombs until he was again severely wounded. The most gallant act put new heart into his men, rallied them, and saved the situation.

(Reg. No. 1482, Gazetted 9th May, 1915)

MELLISH, Capt, the Rev. Edward Noel, Chaplain to the Forces (R.A.C.D.)

St. Eloi, France, 27th to 29th March 1916 for most conspicuous bravery. During heavy fighting for three consecutive days he repeatedly went backwards and forwards under continuous heavy shell and machine-gun fire, between our original trenches and those captured from the enemy, in order to tend and rescue wounded men. He brought in ten badly wounded men on the first day from ground swept by machine-gun fire and three were actually killed while he was dressing their wounds. The battalion to which he was attached was relieved on the second day but he went back and brought in twelve more wounded men. On the night of the third day he took charge of a party of volunteers and once more returned to the trenches to rescue the remaining wounded. This splendid work was quite voluntary on his part and outside the scope of his ordinary duties.

(Gazetted 5th May, 1915)

CATHER, Lieut. Geoffrey St.George Shillington. Adjutant 9/Royal Irish Fusiliers

Near Hamel, France, 1st July, 1916. For most conspicuous bravery. From 7 p.m. till midnight he searched 'No Man's Land' and brought in three wounded men. Next morning at 8 a.m. he continued his search, brought in another wounded man and gave water to others, arranging for their rescue later. Finally, at 10.30 a.m. he took out water to another man and was proceeding further on when he was himself killed. All this was carried out in full view of the enemy and under direct machine-gun fire and intermittent artillery fire. He set a splendid example of courage and self-sacrifice.

(Reg. No. 685 Gazetted 22nd May 1915 Killed 2nd July, 1916)

BENNETT, Lieut. Eugene Paul, M.C. 2nd Worcester

Near Le Transloy, France, 5th November 1916. For most conspicuous bravery in action when in command of the second wave of the attack. Finding that the first wave had suffered heavy casualties, its commander killed and the line wavering, Lieut. Bennett advanced at the head of the second wave and by his personal example of valour and resolution reached his objective with but sixty men.

Isolated with his small party, he at once took steps to consolidate flanks and, although wounded, he remained in command directing and controlling. He set an example of cheerfulness and resolution beyond all praise and there is little doubt that, but for his personal example of courage, the attack would have been checked at the outset.

(Reg. No. 1253. Gazetted 1st January 1915)

CATES, 2/Lt. George Edward 2/Rifle Brigade

E. of Bouchavesnes, France, 8th March, 1917. For most conspicuous bravery and self-sacrifice. When engaged with some other men in deepening a captured trench, this officer struck with his spade a buried bomb, which immediately started to burn. 2/Lt. Cates, in order to save the lives of his comrades, placed his foot on the bomb, which immediately exploded. He showed the most conspicuous gallantry and devotion to duty in performing the act which cost him his life but saved the lives of others.

(Reg. No. 3035. Gazetted 27th February, killed 9th March 1917)

DEAN, Lieut. Donald John 8/Royal West Kent (T.F.)

N.W. of Lens, France, 24th to 26th September, 1918. For most conspicuous bravery, skilful command and devotion to duty when holding, with his platoon, an advanced post, when taking over on the night of September 24th, was ill-prepared for defence. Shortly after the post was occupied, the enemy attempted, without success, to recapture it. Under heavy machine-gun fire consolidation was continued and shortly after midnight another determined enemy attack was driven off. Throughout the night Lt. Dean worked unceasingly with his men and about 6 a.m. on September 25th a resolute enemy attack, supported by heavy shell and mortar fire developed. Again, owing to the masterly handling of his command, Lieut. Dean repulsed the attack, causing heavy enemy casualties. Throughout the 25th and the night of the 25th-26th consolidation was continued under heavy fire which culminated in intense artillery fire on the morning of the 26th, when the enemy again attacked and was finally repulsed with loss. Five times in all (thrice heavily) was this post attacked and on each occasion the attack was driven back. Throughout the period, Lieut. Dean inspired his command with his own contempt of danger and all fought with the greatest bravery. He set an example of valour, leadership and devotion to duty of the very highest order.

(Reg. No. 3692. Gazetted 4th October 1916)

VANN, Lieut. Col. Bernard William, M.C, and Bar, Croix de Guerre, 8 Notts & Derby (T.F.) Bellenglise, France, 29th September, 1818. For most conspicuous bravery, devotion to duty and fine leadership during the attack on Bellenglise and Lehaucourt. He led his battalion with great skill across the Canal du Nord through a very thick fog and under heavy fire from field and machine guns. On reaching the high ground above Bellenglise the whole attack was held up by fire of all descriptions from the front and right flank. Realizing that everything depended on the advance going forward with the barrage, Lt. Col. Vann rushed up to the firing line and with the greatest gallantry led the line forward. By his prompt action and absolute contempt for danger, the whole situation was changed, the men encouraged and the line swept forward. Later he rushed a field gun single-handed and knocked out three of the detachment. The success of the day was, in no small degree, due to the splendid gallantry and fine leadership displayed by this officer. Lt. Col. Vann, who had on all occasions set the highest example of valour, was killed near Ramicourt four days later, when leading his battalion in attack.

(Reg. No.1800 Gazetted 2nd Sept., 1914. Killed in action 3rd Oct., 1918)

(Editorial note: eleven times a casualty)

Appendix III

The Artists Rifles Conditions of Service and Notes (1920)

I
Summary of Conditions of Service in the TERRITORIAL ARMY.

RECRUITS.

AGE, Etc. – Must be subjects of His Majesty the King, physically fit, and between the ages of 18-38 years (inclusive).

TERM. – Join for four years.

OBLIGATIONS (during the first year of service):
a). To do forty Drills of one hour each (twenty before Camp).
b). To shoot Recruits; Musketry Course.
c). To attend the Annual Camp (usually held the beginning of August) with the Unit he joins for not less than eight or more than fifteen days (as may be prescribed for his Unit), unless excused for illness or other sufficient reason.

TRAINED MEN
(i.e., those who have served for not less than six months during the war, and Recruits after their first year of service).

AGE, Etc – As for Recruits (an extension of age is allowed for Sergeants and Bandsmen).

TERM. – Can join for either one, two, or three years (as man may elect).

OBLIGATIONS (each year):
a). To do ten Drills of one hour each.
b). To shoot prescribed Musketry Course.
c). To attend Annual Camp (as above).

NOTES.
(a) In Time of Peace.

(i) All Arms, Uniform, and Equipment are issued free.
(ii) Pay and Allowances are given (at Army Rates) during

Annual Camp, and additional bounties for drills, etc. can be earned up to £4 per annum.
(iii) There is no liability to be called out in aid of the Civil Power.
(iv) Exemption can be claimed from serving on a Jury.
(v) Discharge can be claimed (before the expiration of term of enlistment) on (a) giving three months' notice, (b) delivering up Arms, Uniform, and Equipment, and (c) paying a sum not exceeding £5; may be less according to the service completed, and payment may be remitted altogether for sufficient reason.

(b) In Time of War.

(i) Can only be embodied in case of great emergency after Army Reserves have been called up by Royal Proclamation.
(ii) On embodiment each man receives a Bonus of £5 and Pay and Allowances at Army Rates.
(iii) Can be sent Overseas only after an Act of Parliament has been passed authorizing the dispatch of the Territorial Army – and will then be used as Regimental Units, and not for supplying drafts to the Regular Army.

II

Additional Conditions of Service in the ARTISTS RIFLES.

1. Recruits must be nominated by a past or present member of the Corps, who will be responsible to the Corps for the introduction.
Note – Nomination forms can be obtained at headquarters. Candidates for Enlistment who do not happen to know a member should apply to the Adjutant at headquarters.
2. Recruits must be Approved by the Captain of the company the Candidate wishes to join, and this approval must be subsequently confirmed by the commanding officer.
3. The Annual Subscription to the Corps is £1 5s, payable on joining, and again on each 1st November (for the year from 1st November to the following 31st October).
Recruits joining on or after 1st May in any year pay 12s 6d. only for that year.
4. NOTE – Opportunities will be given to every man to fit himself for the duties of Commissioned Rank, of which he will be expected to take advantage, and he will be encouraged to take a Commission in the Territorial he desires it, to either attend or pass advanced Courses or to take a Commission in any Unit.

III
NOTES ON THE ARTISTS RIFLES

THE HEADQUARTERS of the Corps are situated in Duke's Road, Euston Road, W.C. (immediately behind St. Pancras Church), about five minutes walk from Euston, St. Pancras, King's Cross, and Euston Square Stations. They comprise a large Drill Hall, officers' and Sergeants' Messes, a Canteen (where a good plain meal can be obtained at a reasonable cost), dressing and ablution rooms, etc.
Telephone number: 6741 Museum.
Telegraphic address: "Painterly," London.

UNIFORM – Khaki Service dress issued free to Men, and an allowance towards cost made to officers.

DRILLS are of one hour each, in Plain Clothes at headquarters (usually Tuesdays and Fridays from 6.30 to 8.30 p.m., two drills each night), also various parades in Uniform on Saturdays and weekends at various parts of the country.

RANGE not yet allotted.

THE SCHOOL OF ARMS, founded in 1877 with a view to the improvement of the physique of the Corps, and to provide opportunities for its members to acquire skill at arms. It has an exceptionally large number of Amateur Championships and Prizes for important open events standing to its credit. Classes are held twice a week in the evenings during the winter months. The very best instruction is given in Bayonet, Fighting, Physical Training, Gymnastics, Boxing, Fencing (both Sabres and Foils), Wrestling, and other subjects.
Subscription about £1 per season. Rent of a locker at headquarters (if required), 2s 6d per season. Apply Hon. Sec., School of Arms, at headquarters.

THE ARTISTS RIFLES REGIMENTAL ASSOCIATION (A.R.R.A.) AND THE A.R.R.A. CLUB. The A.R.R.A. is an Old Comrades Association – all past and present Members are eligible for membership – connected with which is a Club with club rooms at 17-19 Craven Street, Strand, W.C.2 (close to Charing Cross Station), where lunch and tea (daily) and dinner (weekly) can be obtained at club prices.
Subscription to the A.R.R.A. If any subscription has ever been paid to the Corps, nil. If no subscription has ever been paid, £1

1s. entrance fee (and life membership).

Subscription to Club. – £1 annually for London members; 10s. for country members (which subscription includes the free issue of the Journal mentioned below).

All inquiries, personally or by letter, to Secretary, A.R.R.A., 19 Craven Street, Strand, W.C.2.

THE ARTISTS RIFLES JOURNAL. Published four times a year (usually March, June, September, and December), contains all Regimental news.

Subscription, 4s. per annum post free. (Note. – The subscription to the A.R.R.A. Club will include subscription to the Journal).

Apply Secretary, A.R.R.A., 19 Craven Street, Strand, W.C.2.

THE SWIMMING CLUB, GOLF CLUB, PHOTOGRAPHIC CLUB, AND RIVER CLUBS – at various small Subscriptions. It is hoped that these Clubs will soon be renewed as in pre-war days. All interested in any of them, and wishing to become members or willing to serve on the Committee of any of them, should apply to the Adjutant at headquarters.

HONORARY MEMBERS OF THE CORPS. – Past members of the Corps may become honorary members (subject to the approval of the C.O.) on payment of the annual subscription of £1.5s, due 1st November of each year, and thereupon will be entitled, in common with the other members, to the use of the headquarters and to such other privileges as the C.O. shall from time to time determine. Apply to the Adjutant at headquarters.

THE REGIMENTAL ROLL OF HONOUR which has been prepared and is about to be printed will contain not only a Chronological Roll of those who fell (about 2,000 of all ranks, with date and place of death), but also of all honours and decorations awarded to members of the Corps (about 1,400), commissions obtained by men of the Corps (about 10,000 – by regiments and with promotions, casualties, etc.), and a roll of men who did not take commissions (about 4,000), and other information, the whole book – of about 700 pages – forming a very complete and wonderful record of the Corps and of the past and present members thereof during the war.

The enormous increase in the cost of printing and producing makes it imperative that the price must be increased and that only a few copies can be printed beyond those actually ordered, and past and present members requiring copies for themselves or their friends are requested and advised to send in an order for copies required to the publishers (Messrs. Howlett & Sons, 10 Frith Street, Soho, London, W.1), as soon as possible. Price not to exceed 20s each copy, but please do not remit any cash at present.

A BOOKLET OF THE CONDITIONS OF SERVICE in the Corps (with reproductions of a few pre-war photographs) is being prepared, and a limited number of copies will be printed, and, when ready, will be issued or forwarded, on application at headquarters, to past and present members who are bona fide desirous of rejoining or introducing recruits.

FINAL NOTE – It is the earnest desire of the C.O. and of everyone connected with the Regiment to give help and assistance of every kind to young men of the Public School type who are living in or near London, all of whom are cordially invited to visit the Headquarters and to communicate with an old member of the Corps, or with the Adjutant at headquarters (Duke's Road, Euston Road, W.C.), or with the Secretary of the A.R.R.A. (19 Craven Street, Strand, W.C.2.)

Appendix IV

Cum Marte Minerva

(Original Regimental Chorus.)

Words by George Cayley. Air by Salvator Rosa.

Sons of Art, our voices raising,
Onward we march with step so free.
Sons of Art, our voices raising,
United thus in Harmony.

Peaceful or warlike our song shall be
'Cum Marte Minerva'
Thus sing we as onward we march,
As onward we march in Harmony.
'Cum Marte Minerva' our song shall be.

Peaceful Arts new vigour gaining,
Whilst we guard our liberty;
Art and freedom thus obtaining
Strength increased by unity.

Peaceful or warlike, etc.

Danger and hardship ne'er can alarm us,
Ready at England's call are we;
The arts of peace themselves shall aid us,
We fight for King and liberty

Peaceful or warlike, etc.

Appendix V

The Elfin Oak

Frank Innes, always known as Ivor, joined the Artists Rifles in 1917. After the Great War, Ivor turned his hand to painting landscapes in oils; His unique skill however was in transforming the gnarled roots of gorse bushes which he harvested on the South Downs, into carved depictions of the fairy folk, in which he earnestly believed!

His many artistic skills came to the attention of Lady Winifred Fortesque who responding to the Lansbury Appeal, funded Ivor's transformation of an 800 year old hollow oak tree trunk in Richmond Park between 1928 and 1930, into a playground for the Little People. The tree depicts the world of Wookey the Witch with her three jars of health, wealth and happiness; of Huckleberry the gnome, carrying a bag of berries up the Gnomes' Stairway to the banquet within Bark Hall, of Grumbles and Groodles the elves being woken up by Brownie, Dinkie, Rumplestocks and Hereandthere stealing eggs from the crows' nest. Some of the Little People are carved into the wood while other magical figures are constructed in plaster and each painted in bright colours.

Permanently installed in Kensington Gardens in 1930, the Elfin Oak complements the statue of Peter Pan, which Barrie erected in 1912. Together, the two sculptures make Kensington Gardens very much the world capital of fairies, gnomes and elves. Ivor illustrated the children's book written by his wife Elsie in which she describes how 'for centuries now it has been the home of fairies, gnomes, elves, imps and pixies. In the nooks and crannies they lurk, or peer out of holes and crevices, their natural windows and doorways. It is their hiding place by day, their revelry place by night and where the great moon tops the bare branchless tree, the Elfin Clans come out to play and frolic in the moonlight.' (Elsie Innes, *The Elfin Oak of Kensington Gardens*, Frederick Warne & Co, 1930).

Ivor with the help of friends maintained the Elfin Oak for over forty years, but following his death in New Zealand, the Elfin Oak deteriorated. Its sad state caught the attention of the comedian Spike Milligan, who personally funded restoration work in the mid sixties and thirty years later came to its rescue again by launching a successful fundraising campaign. The restored Elfin Oak was once more a place of wonder to young visitors when HRH The Prince of Wales, with Spike Milligan, formally reopened it on 12 June 1997.

What is less well known is that Ivor also prepared and presented a miniature 'Elfin Oak' to his benefactor Lady Fortesque, which she kept in her home in Provence. On 19 December 1997, the then Heritage Minister Tony Banks, announced that the Elfin Oak had been added to a list of 'buildings of special architectural or historic interest'.

The more recent development of the Princess of Wales Memorial Playground close to the Elfin Oak and Peter Pan, reinforces the magical appeal of this corner of Kensington Gardens for children of all ages.

Bibliography

The sources of much of my written material have been the numerous articles in the Regimental journals – *The Artists Rifles Journal* (1916-1927), *The Artists Rifles Year Book* (1926-1932), *The Artists Rifles Gazette* (1935-1939) and *Mars & Minerva/The Special Air Service Regiment* (1947 to the present time).

Gaunt, William, *Victorian Olympus*, Jonathan Cape, London, 1952

Higham, Major S.S.(editor), *The Regimental Roll of Honour and War Record of the Artists Rifles*, Howlett & Son, London, 1922

Hutchinson, Sidney C., *The History of the Royal Academy 1768-1986*, Chapman & Hall, London, 1968

May, Colonel H.A.R., CB, VD, *Memories of the Artists Rifles (1882-1921)*, Howlett & Sons, London, 1931

Spiers, Edward M., *Haldane an Army Reformer*, Edinburgh University Press, Edinburgh, 1980

Stirling, A.M.W.,*The Richmond Papers from the correspondence and manuscripts of George Richmond RA and his son Sir William Richmond RA, KCB*, William Heinemann Ltd., London, 1926

Index

2nd Artists Rifles OTC, 124, 160
2nd London Division (TF), 96, 97, 265
2nd Manchesters, 135, 136, 137
7th Division, 117, 118, 120
20th Middlesex (Artists) Rifle Volunteers, 14, 47, 48, 50, 53, 66, 75, 88, 96
21st SAS (Artists), 286, 288, 289, 296, 297, 298, 299
23 SAS, 298
28th Battalion County of London Regiment (Artists Rifles), 96, 98, 110, 113, 114, 212, 217, 224, 256
38th Middlesex (Artists) Rifle Volunteers, 2, 7, 9, 11, 13, 42, 43, 46
47th (2nd TF) Division, 114
63rd (Royal Naval) Division, 160, 168, 169, 170, 172, 181, 190, 228
104th (Artists Rifles) VAD, 123, 188, 194, 237
190th Brigade, 160, 168, 169, 179, 180, 181, 184

A Dialogue at Waterloo 24
A Midsummer Night's Nonsense, 246
A Pageant of Colchester, or *Cockwatch in an Oyster Shell*, 242
Abbot-Anderson, Captain S.G., 160
Abercorn Rooms, 74
Abrahams, E.A., 236
Abram, Lance Sergeant, H.A., 242
Accademia delle Belle Arti, 41
Acheux, 179
Ackermann, Corporal Gerald, 162, 164, 165, 262, 302
Adams, Franklin P., 205
Adams, Stephen, 12, 49
Aitchison, George, 43
Albemarle, Earl of, 80
Albert, the Prince Consort, xvii, xix, xxiii, 24, 37
Albert Edward, Prince of Wales, xxiii, 68, 73, 155

Aldershot Camp, 218
Alexander, A.V., 281
ALGOL, 204
Alias John Brown, 260
Allan, Captain A.W., 232
Allbutt, Mrs Ethel, 189
Allen, John Milner, 310
Alma-Tadema, Lawrence, 27, 30, 49
Alport (Lord) C.J.M., 240, 282
Amiens, 135, 136, 177, 178, 180, 195
Anderson, Mary, 70
Andrews, Felix Emile, 302
Angel, Captain S., 115
Anglo-Saxon fyrd, xiii
Archbutt, Private, 268
Architectural Association, 13, 32, 49, 72, 88, 146
Argyll Rooms, 2, 44
Arkandy, Katherine, 215
Armistead, W.H., 49
Armitage, 49
Armstead, H.H., 22
Armstrong, M.D., 204
Army Cadets, 96
Arnaud, Yvonne, 215
Arras, 167, 174, 177, 190, 191, 200, 201, 203, 204
Artists Club, 161
Artists Rifleman, 237
Artists Rifles Association (ARA), 161, 208, 226, 285, 286, 288, 289, 299
Artists Rifles Clubhouse, 221, 225, 226, 242
Artists Rifles Journal, 84, 156, 157, 161, 320
Artists Rifles Regimental Association (ARRA), 161, 162, 193, 212, 293, 319
Artists Rifles Regimental Association Chronicle, 293
Artists Rifles Regimental Club, 161
Artists Rifles, 2nd Battalion, 84, 115, 119, 122-66, 122, 123, 124, 146, 160,

326

161, 167, 179, 192, 193, 196, 197,
  201, 203, 205, 206, 208, 290
Artists Rifles, 3rd Battalion, 123, 124,
  193, 219, 252, 258
Artists Volunteer Corps. *See* 38th
  Middlesex (Artists) Rifle Volunteers
Arts Club, 2, 7, 13, 73
Ashford, Lieutenant, 184
Aspinall, Corporal A.J., 64
Assault-at-Arms, 66, 228, 236
Assize of Arms, xiii
Athlete Struggling with a Python, 46
Athlone, Earl of, 261
Auchonvillers, 180
Audregnies, 184
Austin, C.E.W., 106
Austin, C.F., 120
Australind, SS, 115, 155, 195, 232
Auxiliary and Reserve Forces Circular
  (May 1879), xxi
Auxiliary Territorial Service (ATS), 268
Ayres, Private, 245
Ayrton, Maxwell, 262

Bailey, Captain the Hon. J.H., 87
Bailey, R.G., 246
Bailleul, 117, 119, 139, 142, 143, 145,
  147, 149, 165, 190, 191, 199, 213,
  232, 263
Baird, Dorothea, 87
Bajus, 168, 190
Baker, John, 18
Baker, W.H., 15
Baker-Carr, Major C.D'A.B.S., 145
Balfour, A.J., 80, 92
Bance, 268
Bare, Captain A.E., 158, 169, 170
Barff, F.S., 27
Barker, Corporal P.G., 242
Barnett, Captain R.A., 172, 213, 232,
  292
Barraclough, Air Chief Marshal, Sir
  John, 289
Barrastre, 190
Barrenger, E.J., 236
Barrett, George, 18
Barrett, Wilson, 70
Barrington, Rutland, 87
Bartolozzi, Francesco, 18
Bass family, 73
Bate, Revd. Canon H. Rowland, 130,
  132
Bateman, James, 261, 302
Bath, Major F.N., 145

Baucher, Lieutenant J.L., 259, 268
Bavrincourt, 156
Bax, Major, 225, 235, 266, 267
Bax, Private E.G.G., 145, 293
Baynes, Private D.C., 242
Bazentin-le-Petit, 179
Beaumont-Hamel, 180
Beauquesne, 156
Beausire, Captain F.R., 130, 254, 268
Belchamber, Private D.F., 145
Bell, Reginald, 262
Bell, R. Anning, 32
Bellamy, Private R.W., 242
Bellenger, F.J., 295, 297, 298
Bennett, Arnold, 136
Bennett, E. Paul, 219, 314
Bentley, Lance Corporal Darley, 236, 242
Bere, Stephen de la, 304
Beresford, Jack, 208
Bergendal, 85
Berlin Academy, 41
Bertram, Charles, 50
Besch, Intelligence Officer, 180, 183
Betts, A.G., 247
Beverley, Private, 268
Bignell, Private, 268
Birch, Charles Bell, 49, 302
Bird, Private, 268
Birnage, Private, 268
Bishop of London, 82, 149, 213, 219
Bisley, 65, 232, 233, 239
Bismarck, Otto von, xvii
Black Week, 79, 80, 82
Blackwood's, 130
Blaikley, Corporal Ernest, 158, 162, 262,
  302
Blaugies, 184, 185
Blendecques, 143, 152, 156, 160
Bloemfontein, 83, 84
Blomfield, Captain C.J., 64, 126, 127,
  128, 129, 163, 164, 215
Blomfield, Reginald, 32
Blore, Eric, 211
Bluhm, CSM, 215
Blundell, Major Alfred, 192
Boehm, 49
Boer Wars, 75-87
Bolingbroke, CSM H.W., 215
Boot, E.W., 215
Bosville, Captain T.J.B., 227, 232
Botha, Louis, 79, 85
Boucher, Captain J.L., 293
Boughton, 49
Boulogne, 115, 155

327

Bouzaincourt, 179
Boxall, Private R.A., 251
Boyle, Richard, 25
Braithwaite, Lilian, 208
Bretherton, C.H., 162, 204, 205
Brett, 49
Brewer, Charles, 120, 263
Brickett Wood, 115
Brisbane, Sergeant, 104
British South Africa Company, 67, 76
British War Memorial, Brussels, 202
Brock, Captain Arthur, 135
Brock, Revd. Canon Daniel V.G., 241, 284, 296
Brock, Sergeant, 268
Brock, Sir Thomas, 24, 30, 35, 50, 215
Bromley, J.M., 303
Brook, Clive, 210
Brotherhood of St Luke, 41
Brough, Lionel, 50, 51
Brown, Ford Madox, 6, 22
Brown, Lieutenant N.R., 241, 242
Browne, L.D.L., 252
Browne, Maurice, 209
Browning, Captain A.N., 259, 261, 268, 271
Browning, Elizabeth Barrett, 42
Browning, Robert, 42, 44
Brunt, Captain J.C.H., 217
Buchanan, Fred, 162, 201
Bucquoy, 195
Buller, Sir Redvers, 79, 83, 85
Bullivant, J.A., 252
Burchell, Rex, 216
Burden, Jane, 6
Burford, Lieutenant Colonel P.G.R., 232, 238, 239, 243, 250, 254, 259, 265, 267, 268, 269, 277, 281
Burgess, John B., 49, 303
Burgoyne, Field Marshal Sir John, xvi
Burke, Edmund, 18
Burkitt, Patrick K., 260
Burlington House, 2, 13, 24, 25, 26, 27, 30, 35, 36, 44, 45, 47, 229, 261
Burlington, Third Earl of, 25, 26
Burne, W.G.T., 236
Burne-Jones, Sir Edward, 3, 4, 5, 6, 7, 23, 28, 303, 307
Bury, Lord, 2, 3, 7, 43, 49, 72, 308
Busk, Captain E.H., 15
Buxton, Richard, 205
Byles, Corporal W. Hounsom, 166
Byrne, Captain Alan W., 200, 215, 222, 228, 236, 252, 272, 293

Cain, C.W., 262
Calderon, P.H., 28, 29, 49
Calderon, W.F., 303
Caley, George, 12
Calkin, G. Lance, 303
Cambrai, 172, 183, 184, 192, 202
Cambridge, Duke of, xviii, 2, 46, 68
Camp 1920, Shorncliffe, 218, 219
Camp 1921, Folkestone, 222
Camp 1922, Rushmoor, 221
Camp 1923, Hythe, 222
Camp 1924, Rushmoor, 222
Camp 1925, Dover, 224
Camp 1926, Ovingdean, 226
Camp 1927, Colchester, 226
Camp 1928, Aldershot, 227
Camp 1930, Rushmoor, 231
Camp 1931, Wannock, 232
Camp 1932, Aldershot, 232
Camp 1933, Myrtle Grove, 234, 240
Camp 1934, Colchester, 240
Camp 1935, Myrtle Grove, 245
Camp 1936, Lavant, 250, 251
Camp 1937, Lympne, 257
Camp 1938, Farringdon, 265
Camp 1939, Warminster, 273, 274, 277
Campbell, Colin, 26
Campbell, Mrs Patrick, 71
Campbell, Colonel R., 161
Campbell-Bannerman, Henry, 91
Campbell-Smith, Lieutenant Colonel W., 227, 233, 235, 244, 245
Cannibal Nights, 228, 243
Cantor Lectures, 73
Capitation Grant, xxi, 12, 94, 96
Capper, C.A., 50
Carden, Private Alexander, 87
Carden, Private R.H., 120
Cardwell, Edward, xxi
Carlini, Augustino, 18, 20
Carlyle, Thomas, 1, 310
Carr, Alwyn, 220
Carter, Lieutenant, 206
Carter, M.J., 231, 236, 246
Cary, F.S., 303
Cary's School of Art, 1
Caslake, Sergeant Drummer, 214
Castellan, C.E., 124
Castellan, V.E., 124
Cates, Second Lieutenant George Edward, 315
Cather, Lieutenant G. St. G. S., 314
Causbrook, Private M.A., 243
Cavan, Earl of, 229

Cave-Chinn, B.S., 236, 246, 252
Cavell, Nurse, 32
Cavendish, Lord George, 26
Cavendish, William, 26
Cayley, George, 322
Cecil, Arthur, 49
Chamberlain, Joseph, 76, 79
Chamberlain, Mason, 18
Chamberlain, Neville, 248, 267, 278
Chambers, William, 18, 19
Chandler, W. Frank, 303
Chapman, Private, 268
Charley's Aunt, 68
Chartist Disturbances, xvi
Chater, Captain A.D., 120
Chatfeild-Clarke, Lieutenant Colonel S.J., 146, 155, 168, 215, 238, 246
Chemin des Dames, 167
Chetwood, Lieutenant E.S., 169, 170
Cholmondeley, Lieutenant Colonel, 80
Chomley, R.A.B., 242, 260
Chorley, Adrian, 262
Chowne, Captain Gerard, 164, 165
Christian, J. Henry, 3
Christmas, Lance Corporal, 268
Cimabue's celebrated Madonna is carried in procession on the streets of Florence, 43
Cipriani, J.B., 18, 20
City Imperial Volunteers (CIVs), 74, 75, 80, 82, 86
Clark, Philip Lindsey, 303
Clark, Private R.B., 145
Clausen, George, 31, 32
Clay-Thomas, CSM A.W., 208, 215, 216, 310
Clemenceau, Georges, 212
Clive, Colin, 209
Close, Corporal M.A., 120
Coborn, Charles, 50
Cockerell, Frederick P., 2
Coke, Alfred S., 303
Colbeck, C.S., 298
Cole, Ernest A., 163, 164, 166, 303
Cole, George Vicat, 49, 303
Coleman, Captain R., 213, 216
Colenso, 79
Colette, Charles, 50, 51
Collett-Wadge, Mrs., 269
Collier, Hon. John, 50
Collingbourne, Florence, 87
Collings, Sergeant H.J., 208, 216
Collins, Private, 268
Collins, Ray, 192

Collinson, James, 22
Commager, A.D., 51
Commissioners of Musters, xiii
Compton, Fay, 215
Conditions of Service and Notes, 317
Connery, Corporal R.D., 251
Constable, John, 21
Constitutional Club, 73
Contraband, 228
Cook, A.J., 225
Cook, A.W., 251
Cook, William, 260
Coombs, Private W. Fraser, 87
Cooper, Lieutenant A. Egerton, 125, 162, 165, 303
Cope, Sir Arthur, 32, 33, 215, 303
Cormack, Captain C.R., 232
Cornelius, Peter van, 42
Cornford, L.R.C., 236
Cotes, Francis, 18
Couillet Wood, 172
Courcelette, 179
Coward, Noel, 211
Cowell, P.B., 292
Cowell, Sergeant A.G. 'Sammy', 14, 63, 67, 89, 215, 221
Coyle, Edgar, 216
Craiglockhart War Hospital, 135, 136
Crickmay, J.P., 298
Crimean War, xvi
Cripps, Lieutenant Colonel R.R., 232, 236, 242, 255, 257, 259, 264, 265, 269, 270, 272, 274, 281, 293, 294
Crisp, Corporal F.E.F., 120
Crocker, General Sir John, 285
Cronje, Piet, 79, 83
Crosse, Private M.E.B., 120
Cum Marte Minerva, 12, 228, 322
Curtis, Captain W.P.S., 259, 269
Curzons, QMS F.J., 215
Cuthbertson, Private F.T., 120
Cuttle, Private G., 120
Cyclist Section, 61, 63, 64, 110, 126

D'Oyly Carte, Rupert, 49
da Vinci, Leonardo, 23, 31
Dabell, Private N.B., 120
Daily Telegraph Cup, 197, 221, 242, 259, 264, 265, 285
Dalton, Richard, 19
Danes, Tom, 260
Dare, Phyllis, 215
Davey, Captain D.L., 215
Davidson, David, 296

Davidson, Major Arthur, 189
Davie, Private, 268
Dawkins, Sergeant, 267
de Berry, Lance Corporal D.F., 268, 288, 298
de Buriatte, Lance Corporal H., 120
de Grey, Earl, xxii
de Jonquières, Group Captain Maurice, 287, 288, 293
de Segundo, Captain Dr. C.S., 114, 146
de Segundo, Mrs, 189
de Wet, Christian, 83
Dean of Westminster, 229
Dean, Lieutenant D.J., 315
Decoration and Furniture of Town Houses, 73
Defence not Defiance, xix
Deltzi, F., 236
Denbigh, Earl of, 87
Denham, Sir John, 25
Denny, Private, 268
Denny, Reginald, 211
Derby, Lord, xvi, xviii, xx, 24
Dettmer, Private, 268
Deverell, Walter, 23
Devey, Georges, 304
Devonshire, 6th Duke of, 26
Diamond Hill, 85
Dick, Major L.H.M., 106, 155, 215
Dick, Sir William Reid, 35
Dickens, Charles, 7, 23, 133, 308
Dickinson, Revd. Harry, 168, 170
Dicksee, Sir Frank, 27, 29, 32, 33, 34, 50
Dicksee, Private H.J.H., 145
Dicksee, Private H.T., 304
Disraeli, Benjamin, 24
Dixon, Sergeant S.W.H., 64
Dobson, Lance Corporal F., 165, 166, 304
Dodd, Lance Sergeant A.E., 64
Dollman, R.W.S., 304
Donnelly, Private, 268
Doornkop, 68, 78
Doran, Group Captain Kenneth, 285
Douglas, Private A.H., 145
Drake, Sir Francis, 1
Drewry, Colour Sergeant A.S., 161, 215, 236, 247
Drill and Rifle Instruction for Volunteer Rifle Corps, xx
Drum and Fife Band, 15, 108, 134
Drums, 15, 114, 189, 190, 191, 192, 217, 229, 244, 257
Du Maurier, 50

Dubarry, Private, 268
Dudley-Cocke, Major T.D., 215
Duffield, William, 304
Duke's Road, 2, 17, 50, 61, 62, 63, 67, 73, 83, 87, 99, 111, 113, 114, 115, 122, 124, 126, 130, 134, 146, 193, 203, 208, 212, 214, 216, 217, 219, 225, 227, 229, 233, 237, 239, 244, 246, 249, 251, 254, 256, 269, 277, 278, 289, 294, 296, 298, 299, 303, 319, 320
Duncan, J.H. Elder, 162

Eager, Sergeant, 268
Eames, W.F., 27
Earles, Charles, 2
Earles, Chester, 304
Eastlake, Charles Lock, 24
Écoivres, 168
Ecuires, 155
Edis, Colonel Sir Robert, v, 2, 12, 13, 14, 45, 48, 49, 50, 51, 53, 69, 70, 72, 73, 74, 75, 81, 87, 88, 89, 98, 103, 105, 106, 155, 161, 213, 214, 215, 217
Edis, Captain Wilkie, 82
Edlmann, Private F.J., 120
Edlemann, Major H.E., 168, 169, 213, 214, 215
Edward VII, 8, 30, 51, 74, 98
Edward VIII, 34, 35, 249, 255
Edward, Prince of Wales, 146, 158, 213, 229, 255
Edwardes, Major Passmore, 123
El Bevah, 236
Elcho, Lord, xxiii
Elfin Oak, 323
Elliott, Lieutenant, 184
Ellison, Colonel Gerald, 91
Elmhirst, Captain E. Pennell, 14
Emslie, RSM Peter, 113, 118, 140, 144, 159, 173, 180, 195
English, Lieutenant, 173
Enguell, G.J., 15
Eringham, 171
Étaples, 167
Etty, William, 5
Evans, Second Lieutenant H.K., 207
Eves, R.G., 32

Faulkner, Charles, 6
Fell, Private, 268
Fencibles, xvi
Fenn, William W., 3
Fennell, Corporal J.F.W., 241

Fennell, Sergeant, 245
Ferdinand, Archduke, 112
Field Service Pocket Book, 100, 118
Fildes, Sir Luke, 29, 30, 32, 49, 312
Fisher, Melton, 32
Fisher, Private W.H., 166
Fitzroy Square, 36, 2, 50, 73, 102, 155
Flag Signals, 61
Fleming-Sandes, Second Lieutenant A.J.T., 313
Flint, Second Lieutenant D.H., 243, 250, 268
Foch, Marshal, 177, 180
Folkard, Charles J., 304
Forbes, Archibald, 49
Forbes, Stanhope, 27, 311
Forbes-Robertson, Eric, 71
Forbes-Robertson, Ian, 71
Forbes-Robertson, Jean, 71
Forbes-Robertson, Sir Johnston, 70, 71, 215
Forbes-Robertson, Norman, 71
Fortesque, Lady Winifred, 323
Foskett, Private, 145, 268
Foster, Captain, 123
Fougasse, C.K.B., 304
Fox, Captain Charles, 286
Fox, Lance Corporal C.A., 242
Fox, RSM, 180, 215
Fox, Sergeant, 223
Foxall, J.D., 246
Frampton, Sir George, 32
Frampton, G.V. Meredith, 262, 304
France, C.V., 216
Francis, Private, 268
Frank, CSM H.E., 176
Franks, Lieutenant Colonel B.M.F., 297
French, Field Marshal Sir John, 79, 116, 117, 118, 139, 140, 143, 144
Freund, G.F., 215
Fripp, Charles, 304
Frith, W.P., 27, 30, 49
Frost, Corporal K., 120
Fry, G.C.L., 293
Fuller, J.M., 236
Furness, Harry, 50

Gainsborough, Thomas, 18, 35, 37
Gale, Lieutenant General Sir Humphrey, 286, 287
Garrad, Sergeant, 163
Garton, Sergeant R.G., 241, 257
Gascoigne, Colonel, 178
Gascoigne, George, 304

Gatacre, Sir William, 79
Gavrelle, 168, 191
General Strike (1926), 225
George III, 17, 18, 19, 31, 34, 37, 295
George IV, 12, 21, 37
George V, 30, 33, 34, 98, 111, 143, 158, 195, 214, 244, 248, 250, 255, 262, 284, 297
George VI, 35, 125, 255, 262, 270, 297
George, Ernest, 24
George Street, 8, 2, 10
Germaine, Private, 268
German Spring Offensive, 136, 179
Gethin, Percy F., 304
Gibb, Revd. John, 116
Gidea Park, 124, 126, 131, 132, 134, 135, 160, 161, 162, 171, 178, 193, 194, 195, 196, 200, 201, 203, 205, 208, 211, 212, 219, 287, 290
Gilbert, Alfred, 27
Gilbert, Arthur, 3
Gilbert, Sir John, 27
Gillick, E.G., 34
Gipps, Major General, 49
Girlhood of Mary Virgin, 4
Givry, 184
Gladstone, W.E., 5, 27, 76
Glover, Dr. Lewis, 189
Glynne, Walter, 216
Goacher, Captain, 181, 184
Godfrey, Intelligence Officer, 173
Godrich, Captain A.J., 259
Goldthorp, Lieutenant Colonel R.H., 178, 180, 184, 215
Goodall, Miss A.S., 189
Goodall, Miss M., 189
Goodbody, Captain, 236
Goodliffe, Michael, 263
Goodwin, Private, 268
Gore-Brown, Captain H., 104
Gore-Browne, Sir Thomas, 49
Gould, Caruthers, 50
Goulder, Captain A.C., 214, 215
Goulding, C.S., 251, 252, 260, 289
Gover, Major J.J, 215
Gow, Andrew C., 304
Grant, Francis, 24, 27
Grant, CQMS K.S., 215
Grantham, 146
Graves, Robert, 136, 209
Gray, C. Kruger, 35, 363
Gray, Effie, 7
Gray, George E. Kruger, 262, 304
Great Central Hotel, Marylebone, 74

331

Great Trek, 75
Great War, 31, 107, 119, 130, 131, 145, 173, 214, 220
Great Western War Memorial, Paddington Station, 202
Green Point, 82, 83
Green Tie, 242, 252
Greenway, Lieutenant P.B., 240, 267, 268, 298
Greenwood, Colour Sergeant John, 125, 207, 264
Greenwood, Lieutenant Colonel C.F.H., 168
Grey Brigade, 12, 98, 115, 228, 247, 253
Griffiths, Private F.S., 145
Grinling, Miss D., 189
Groom, Air Marshal Sir Victor, 287
Groom, Lieutenant, 173, 236
Grossmith, George, 49, 51, 215
Grosvenor Gallery, 28, 309, 311
Grove, Fred, 215
Grundy, CSM G.F., 207
Gucht, Jan van der, 263
Gunn, Sir Herbert, 304
Gunn, James, 261
Gwyn, John, 18

Haag, Carl, 2, 305
Hack, CSM, 168
Hack, M.S., 215
Haggard, Captain Charles, 103, 104
Haig, Field Marshal Sir Douglas, 131, 143, 154, 155, 156, 171, 177, 206, 232
Haldane Army Reforms, 88, 91
Haldane, Richard Burdon, 91, 92, 93, 94, 95, 96, 325
Hall, Captain A.A., 164
Hall, Captain A.H., 164
Hall, Lieutenant Colonel A.W., 185
Hall, Private, 268
Hall, Private G.F., 241
Hall, Private G.P., 298
Hall, S.C., 293
Hallowes, Second Lieutenant R.P., 313
Hamilton, Bruce, 84
Hamilton, Colour Sergeant, 14
Hamilton, Ian, 84
Hamilton, S.E., 252
Hammond, Colour Sergeant W., 196, 197, 208, 252
Hampton, Sergeant Instructor of Musketry, 103
Hand Lamp, 62
Handley-Read, Sergeant E., 165, 305

Hardman, Air Chief Marshal Sir Donald, 287
Hare Hall Camp, 124, 131, 134
Harington, Lieutenant Colonel John, 171, 178
Harman, Captain King, 13
Harmignies, 184, 185
Harris, E. Vincent, 262
Harry, G.L.G., 236
Hart, Maurice, 243
Hartley, R.F., 236
Harvengt, 184
Haslam, Lieutenant, 170
Havrincourt Wood, 179
Hawkes, Private Clifford, 87
Hawkins, Jack, 209
Hawksford, Major F.H., 252, 259
Hay, John Le, 50, 51
Hayden, Seymour, 50
Hayman, Francis, 18
Hayward, Private Alfred, 163, 164, 165, 262, 305
Head, Sir Francis, xvi
Healthy Furniture and Decoration, 73
Hebden, G.L., 207
Heliograph, 61, 62
Heliostat, 62
Henson, Leslie, 215
Heppenstall, CQMS S.H.H., 215
Herbage, Private P.F.W., 120
Herbert Wagg & Co., 72
Herbert, Sidney, xxiii
Herford, Laura Anne, 24
Herkomer, Sir Hubert von, 30, 31, 308, 363
Hermelin, Captain, 180
Hesdin, 156, 167, 168, 169, 190, 195
Heuchin, 156
Hewitt, Captain M.B., 180, 181, 213, 215, 223, 236
Hewson, A.W., 264
Higginson, Lieutenant General, 49
Higham, Major S.S., 106, 162, 213, 215, 220, 325
Hillas-Drake, Private R.F., 120
Hills, H.A.C., 243
Hills, Lance Corporal B.A.C., 236, 241
Hindenburg Line, 135, 137, 167, 175, 178, 179, 180, 181, 182, 184, 192
Hitler, Adolf, 35, 230, 231, 246, 248, 258, 267, 270, 274, 277, 292
Hobson & Co, 52
Hodge, Francis, 262, 305
Hodgson, G.A., 73

332

Hodgson, John, 49, 305
Hodgson, Ralph, 202
Holland, Second Lieutenant A.L., 173
Hollis, Private H.L., 120
Holman Hunt, William, 3, 4, 10, 11, 22, 23, 43, 305, 307
Honourable Artillery Company (HAC), 80, 168
Hopper, 268
Horner, A.W., 298
Horsley, Gerald, 88
Horsley, John Calcott, 27, 29, 49, 88
Horsley, Private O., 88, 120
Horsley, R.C.B., 246, 251
Horsley, Private S.M., 88, 120
Horsley, Sir Victor, 88
Horsley, Vivian, 88
Horsley, Colonel Walter C., 88-101, 103, 107, 109, 110, 123, 143, 162, 165, 188, 190, 194, 213, 215, 217, 219, 226, 227, 238, 246, 305
Horton, W., 232, 236, 242, 243, 246, 251, 252, 260, 268
House, Drummer Ron, 264
Houtkerque, 169
Howarth, Lieutenant F.S., 106
Howe, Lieutenant, 170
Hubble, Major H., 268, 277
Huggill, Henry P., 305
Huggins, Pioneer Sergeant L.R., 142
Hughes, Arthur, 22, 23
Hughes, Robert, 260
Hughes, Captain T.H., 164
Hull, 49
Hullah, John, 3, 8
Humphreys, Private D.F., 120
Hunter, J.W., 120
Hunter, William, 18
Hutchins, Private, 268
Hutt, H.V., 120

Inchy, 180
Inglis Portable Bridge, 160
Innes, Frank I., 323
Irving, H.B., 87
Irving, Henry, 49, 70, 71
Ivimey, J.W., 70, 260

Jackson, J.A., 293
Jackson, Surgeon Captain, 103
Jagger, Charles S., 201, 202, 305
Jameson Raid, 68, 76, 78, 196
Jameson, Sir Leander Starr, 67, 68, 76, 77, 78

Jeffries, Sergeant, 206
Jenner, Sir William, 49
Jennings, S.H., 156
Jerwood, Captain, 235, 236
Johannesburg, 76, 77, 78, 83, 84
John, Augustus, 37
Johnson, 268
Johnson, Dr., 18
Johnson, Major F.S.B., 178
Johnston, C.G., 268, 298
Jones, Revd. Frank E., 294
Jones, Inigo, 20
Jones, Corporal L., 120
Jones, Sergeant W.B., 241
Journey's End, 209
Judd, Private F.G., 145
Junior Constitutional Club, 73

Kapper, General Sir Thomas, 118
Kauffman, Angelica, 18
Keane, Charles, 50
Keene, Captain A.V., 123, 156, 208
Kelly, Private A., 241
Kelly, Sir Gerald, 37
Kelmscott Press, 5, 6, 7
Kempson, Arthur, 260
Kent, Duke of, 34, 255
Kentish, General R.J., 161
Keys, Nelson, 208
Killick, Private S., 251
Kimberley, 68, 79, 80, 83
King, CSM C.W.W., 169
King, J. Yeend, 305
Kinniburgh, Tom, 213, 215
Kipling, Rudyard, 71, 82, 83, 86, 88
Kirschmann, Major, 258
Kitcat, 268
Kitcat, Private A.J., 120
Kitcat, E.N., 293
Kitcat, H.P., 245
Kitchener, Lord, xviii, 80, 85, 91, 123, 201, 306, 363
Klein, Second Lieutenant Adrian B., 163, 164, 165
Knight, D.J., 126, 207
Knight, Harold, 262
Kruger, Paul, 68, 75, 76, 78, 79, 85
Krugersdorp, 77
Kynoch & Co., 51

Lacy Smith, W., 293, 298
Ladysmith, 79, 80, 83
Laing, Isabel, 42
Lamb, Captain, 65

333

Lamb, Colonel Sir Charles, 161
Lambe, Aaron, 18
Lambert, CSM, 277
Lamerton, Drummer, 245
Landseer, Edwin, 24
Lane, Charles Thomas, 2
Lansdell, J.A.D., 237
Lashbrook, Corporal H.S., 242
Lathom, Major, 178
Lawrence, Sir Thomas, 21, 37
Laws, Private B.C., 245
Lawson, J.J., 295
Lawson, Wilfred, 210
Le Barque, 180
Le Touquet, 146
Le Transloy, 219, 314
Leader, 50
Lear, Edward, 22, 28
Lee Hankey, Second Lieutenant W., 162, 163, 164, 165, 246, 262, 305
Lee, CQMS, 242
Lee, Falkner, 213
Lee, Lance Corporal J., 145
Lee, John, 236, 241, 246, 251
Lee, R.A., 251
Lees, Captain E.H.H., 99
Leete, Alfred, 162, 201, 306
Legge, Lieutenant Colonel J.F., 178
Leigh-Breese, P.L., 228, 236, 251
Leighton House Museum, 363
Leighton, Blair, 50
Leighton, Frederic Septimus, 39
Leighton, Lord Frederick, 2, 4, 7, 10, 13, 27, 28, 29, 38-48, 48, 49, 65, 155, 306, 308
Leighton, Sir James, 39
Leighton, Private N., 145
Leno, Dan, 87
Lepingwell, Captain, 172, 173
Leslie, J.W., 236
Let's Join the Artists, 243
Lewis, Arthur James, 2, 7, 13, 43, 306
Liddell, Major General C.G., 250
Light, Captain F.R., 123
Light, QM 'Freddy', 168, 180
Lightfoot, Lieutenant D.H., 173, 252
Litchfield, Frederick, 215
Little Willie, 159
Llewellyn, Sir William, 32, 33, 35
Llewelyn, Desmond, 263
Lloyd, Edward, 51
Lloyd, Major General Sir Francis, 113
Lloyd, John H., 260
Lloyd-George, David, 167

Lobb, Corporal, 268
Löhr, Marie, 208
London, Bishop of, 213
Londonderry, Marquis of, 238, 239, 255, 259
Long Acre Indignation Meeting, xviii
Long, Edwin, 49, 306
Lord's Cricket Ground, 114, 126, 131
Lords Lieutenant, xiii, xix, xxi, 94
Lotz, Private H.J., 164, 165
Louis Napoleon, Prince Imperial, xviii
Louvencourt Wood, 191
Lubbock, Lieutenant, 207
Lucas, Captain F.A., 14
Lucas, J. Seymour, 27, 306
Ludendorff, General Erich von, 177, 209
Lush, Lance Corporal B.S., 242, 243
Lushington, Major Franklin, 204
Lutyens, Sir Edwin, 35, 36
Lyndon, Herbert, 306
Lyson, Colonel D., xx

Macadam, Corporal G.H., 242
MacGeorge, Captain R.A., 259
MacIver, C.D., 207
Mackinnon, Colonel W.H., 80, 84, 85, 86, 87
Mackinnon's Force, 85
Mackintosh, Corporal H.L., 120
Macpherson, Corporal of Horse, 14
MacWhirter, 50
Mafeking, 77, 79, 80, 83
Mais, S.P.B., 262, 263
Majuba Hill, 75
Mansbridge, Captain, 216
Marcoing, 172, 173, 174, 175
Margetson, Arthur, 211
Margetson, Lieutenant E., 173, 236, 246, 251
Marion-Crawford, Howard, 263
Marks, Stacey, 49, 306
Mars and Minerva Ball, 222
Mars and Minerva Magazine, 210, 286, 288, 290
Marsh, A.D., 248
Marshall, Captain J.W., 197
Marshall, Private O.P.B., 145
Marshall, P.P., 6
Marshall, Lance Corporal V.M., 242
Martinpuich, 179
Mason, Lance Corporal A.H., 18, 163, 164, 166, 306
Mathew, Captain Dr., 170, 172
Matthews, Dudley S., 260

334

Maud, W.T., 306
Maximilian, Archduke, xvii
May, Colonel H.A.R., 53, 74, 97, 98, 101-11, 113, 114, 115, 116, 117, 118, 119, 120, 123, 140, 143, 144, 145, 146, 155, 161, 162, 174, 190, 194, 195, 198, 199, 213, 214, 215, 216, 217, 218, 219, 220, 227, 232, 233, 238, 308, 309, 325
Maybrick, Michael, 12, 49, 50, 51, 81, 155
Mayne, Lieutenant Colonel 'Paddy', 297
McClure, E.D., 298
McMillan, William, 35, 262, 306
Meli, Signor Francesco, 40
Mellish, Revd. E. Noel, 213, 314
Mendelssohn-Bartholdy, F., 8, 213, 246
Merry, Godfrey, 307
Messom, Corporal H., 120
Metcalfe, Revd. G.L., 213
Methuen, Lord, 79, 83
Meyer, Jeremiah, 18
Michaelangelo, 23, 31
Miéville, Captain W.S., 156, 169, 172
Militia, xiii, xiv, xv, xviii, xix, xxii, xxiv, 92, 93, 95, 310
Millais, John Everett, 2, 3, 7, 10, 13, 22, 23, 27, 28, 29, 42, 43, 44, 49, 132, 307
Miller, Drummer, 241
Mills, H., 236
Mills, Private H.J., 145
Milner, Sir Arthur, 78
Mobilization Plan, 98, 109, 111
Modern Painters, 8
Modjeska, 70
Moeuvres, 180
Moller, Private A.A., 120
Molotov-Ribbentrop Pact, 270
Molyneux, Private K.C., 245
Moncrieff, Charles Scott, 136
Moncrieff, Colonel, 49
Monk, Private G.B., 120
Mons, 117, 130, 184, 185
Mont St Eloi, 168
Montreuil, 155
Moody, F.N.J., 236, 307
Moody, Sergeant, 236
Moore, Albert, 24
Moore, RSM A.R. 'Pony', 259, 281, 298
Moore, Bertha, 87
Moore, Charles E., 307
Moore, Private, 268
Moray Minstrels, 7
Morrall, John B., 307

Morris & Co., 4, 5
Morris, Lieutenant, 184
Morris, Marshall, Faulkner & Co, 6
Morris, Philip R., 307
Morris, Signalling Officer, 180, 181
Morris, William, 3, 4, 5, 6, 7, 9, 23, 43, 49, 72, 307
Morrison, Arthur, 163
Moser, G. Michael, 18
Moser, Mary, 18
Mother, 159
Muff-Ford, John W.D., 307
Muirhead, Sir David, 268, 288, 289
Mulberry Harbour, 290
Mulock, Corporal E.R., 120
Mumford, John A.B., 260
Munnings, Sir Alfred James, 37
Murray, BSIM A.C., 208, 252
Murray, Sir David, 35

Naimaster, Sergeant J.L., 236, 241, 242, 293
Napoleon III, xvi, xvii, xviii
Nash, John, 173, 174, 175, 176, 307
Nash, Paul, 165, 173, 174, 175, 307
Nash, R.O., 293, 298
National Gallery, 21, 22, 23, 29, 34, 49
National Rifle Association, xxiii, 12, 65
National Service League, 91
Nazarenes, 41, 42, 44
Neame, Major A.J., 123, 215
Neame, Miss M., 189
Neighbour, Lieutenant Colonel S.W., 199, 218, 224, 225, 226, 227, 293
Nelson, Dr., 180
Newman, F.W., 1
Newman, Stanley, 213
Newman, Private Theodore, 165
Newton, Sir Alfred, 80
Newton, Captain C.E., 212
Newton, D.G., 298
Newton, Francis Milner, 18
Newton, H.W., 298
Newton, Lieutenant W.E., 143
Newton, William G., 262, 308
Nicholson, Alfred, 2, 12, 43
Nicol, J. Watson, 308
Niergnies, 184
Noel-Johnson, 268
Norris, R.L., 236
Norton, RSM 'Buck', 259, 271, 293
Norton, Fred, 216
Nye, E.G., 236

O'Brien, Private Leslie, 232
Officer Cadet Training Unit (OCTU), 98, 136, 143, 145, 155, 160, 216
   No. 163, 277, 279, 281
   No. 164, 281
   No. 167, 281
   No. 168, 281
Officer Producing Group, 256, 274, 275
Officer Training Corps (OTC), 95, 140, 206
Officers Cadet Battalion (OCB) No. 15 (Artists Rifles), 160
Officers' Qualification Certificate, 256
Olivier, Laurence, 209
Once an Artist Always an Artist, 127
Oppy Wood, 168, 174, 191
Orange Free State, 75, 78, 83, 85
Orange River Station, 79, 83
Orchardson, W.Q., 29
Orpen, William, 32, 34, 308
Orsini, xvi
Orton, E.H., 145
Osborne, Lance Corporal Malcolm, 163, 164, 308
Ostle, Lieutenant Colonel H.K. Eaton, 179, 200, 215
Ouless, W.W., 49, 308
Outram, R.L., 308
Overbeck, Friedrich, 41, 42
Owen, C.H., 298
Owen, D. Glyn, 246, 293
Owen, E.H., 236, 292
Owen, Harold, 132
Owen, Susan, 132
Owen, Wilfred, 131, 132, 134, 135, 136, 137, 209

Paddebeeke, 169, 170
Page, C.C., 207
Page, Lance Corporal, 268
Pageant of Myrtle Grove, 235
Paget, H.M., 308
Palerme, Gina, 215
Palmer, Alfred H.J., 260
Palmerston, Lord, xviii
Parker, Spurgeon, 236, 246, 251
Parkes, Lance Corporal H.F., 120
Parks, Murray T., 308
Parsons, Alfred, 32
Partridge, RSM E., 232
Passchendaele, v, 162, 167, 169, 171
Passmore, 268
Pattison, Lance Corporal E.L., 163, 165, 166, 308

Pattison, Sergeant L., 162
Payne, Edmund, 87
Payton, RSM 'Tottie', 197
Peach, Captain C.S., 214
Pearce, Private G.V., 120
Pearce, Sergeant C. Maresco, 163, 164, 165, 308
Pearson, 49
Pellegrini, 49
Penley, W.S., 68
Penny, Edward, 18
Perkes, Henry, 2
Perugini, Charles Edward, 2, 308
Peterloo, xvi
Pettie, John, 27, 49
Pforr, Franz, 41
Philhurst Club, 71
Philip, Major C.A., 71
Phillip, John, 22
Phillips, Captain Henry Wyndham, 1, 2, 7, 13, 43, 45, 308
Physical Energy, 5
Pickup, Private A.J., 120
Pike, Captain C.W., 165, 172, 173
Pilcher, Marjorie, 238
Pingo, T., 20
Pipon, Major General H., 114
Platt, John, 251
Poems and Ballads, 8
Poll, Laslett, 50
Portland, 3rd Duke of, 26
Pott, Captain Charles L., 308
Powers, Hiram, 40
Poynter, Sir Edward, 24, 29, 30, 32, 33, 309, 363
Prentice, Transport Officer, 180, 183
Prentis, Captain J.E., 215
Pre-Raphaelite Brotherhood, 3, 22, 23, 44, 303, 305, 307, 309
Princip, Gavrilo, 112
Pringle, Private, 268
Prinsep, Major Val C., 2, 7, 12, 13, 29, 89, 309
Pritchard, Private, 268
Prize Shooting, 53, 65
Pugin, Augustus, 6
Purvis, Tom, 162

Queen Alexandra, 51, 155
Queen Guenevere, 6
Queen Mary, 33, 249
Queen Victoria, xviii, 15, 21, 24, 30, 43, 47, 68, 74, 78, 80, 86, 88, 91, 303

Rait, Major C.M., 232, 241, 268, 292
Ralph, Mr. H., 216
Ramsay, Captain J.A., 13, 14
Ramsbotham, Lieutenant Colonel W.H., 218, 224, 227, 228, 231, 232, 233, 236
Raymond-Barker, Private C.L., 120
Reddick, George, 260
Rees, Private J.T., 120
Rees, R.F.W., 162
Reeve, Ada, 87
Regimental Club, 53, 65, 66, 161
Regimental Roll of Honour, 120, 162, 180, 217, 220, 313, 320, 325
Regulation of the Forces Act (1871), xxi
Reigersburgh, 169
Reynolds, Sir Joshua, 17, 18, 19, 20, 31, 35, 37, 47
Rhodes, Cecil, 5, 67, 68, 76, 77, 196
Ribbentrop, Joachim von, 292
Ricardo, Captain, 103
Rice, E.B. Howard, 236
Richborough, 290
Richmond, William Blake, 3, 8, 9, 10, 24, 27, 29, 43, 309, 325
Rickwood, John Edgell, 204
Ridge, Captain Lacey, 13
Rifle Brigade, 229, 232, 233, 240, 242, 253, 258, 259, 261, 271
Rifle Volunteer Act (1863), 13, 51, 52, 94
Rifle Volunteer Movement (1871), xviii
Rivers, Captain W.H.R., 135
Riviere, Briton, 27, 29
Robb, Captain Tom, 277
Roberts, Lord, 80, 83, 84, 85, 86, 91
Roberts, Thomas, 309
Robins, Lance Corporal W.P., 162, 163, 165, 262, 309
Robinson, Padre, 180
Robinson, T.W.C., 237, 251
Robotham, Ralph, 284, 289, 298
Rochincourt, 168, 174
Rogers, J.E., 309
Rogers, N., 298
Romer, General Sir Cecil, 117, 161, 215, 239
Rosa, Salvator, 12, 322
Ross, Robert, 136
Rossetti, Christina, 4
Rossetti, Dante Gabriel, 3, 4, 5, 6, 9, 22, 307, 309
Rossetti, William Michael, 22, 23
Rotger, B.A., 237, 241
Rought, Private C.G., 120

Royal Academy, 2, 3, 7, 16-48, 73, 125, 174, 201, 202, 209, 229, 289
Royal Academy Guard, 228, 239, 250, 254, 257, 261
Royal Academy Schools, 1, 2, 4, 21, 24, 27, 29, 35, 36, 70
Royal Artillery Memorial, 202
Royal Garrison Artillery, 203
Royal Review of Volunteers, 15
Royal Scot, 237
Royal Scot type locomotives, 237
Royal Tournament, 14, 67, 228, 231, 239, 250, 257, 265, 272
Royds, Captain A.F., 169, 215
Royds, Private, 268
Ruskin, John, 3, 4, 6, 7, 8, 23, 306, 307, 309, 363
Russell, 268
Russell, F.T., 298
Russell, Lord John, xvi, 23

Sadler, Dendy, 50
Saint, 49
Salisbury, Lieutenant, 173
Salisbury, Lord, 8, 143
Sambourne, Linley, 50
Sampson, Private H.F., 120
Samson, A.J., 293
Samson, H.J., 293
Sandby, Paul, 18
Sandby, Thomas, 18
Sanders, Private, 268
Sanderson, Eric E., 260
Sant, James, 22, 30
Sargent, John Singer, 30
Sartoris, Adelaide, 42
Sassoon, Siegfried, 136, 137, 209
Saunders, Corporal N.E., 245
Sawtell, Miss A., 189
School of Arms, xxii, 14, 15, 53, 63, 65, 66, 196, 200, 217, 228, 236, 239, 242, 252, 265, 293, 319
Scotcher, H.G., 293
Scrutton, A.E., 206, 293
Scrutton, Lieutenant John, 206
Scrymgeour-Wedderburn H.J., 261
Selfe, Miss O.M., 189
Serres, Dominic, 18
Severn, Arthur, 309
Severn, Walter, 309
Seymour, Katie, 87
Shanks, Edward, 205
Sharpe, Private E., 164
Shaw, Lieutenant E. St. L., 160, 178

Shaw, Richard Norman, 22
Shearer, Lance Sergeant G.H., 242
Shee, Martin Archer, 21, 24
Sheehan, Lance Corporal F.G.E., 145
Shepherd, Lewis H., 3
Shepherd, Private W.S., 120
Sherriff, R.C., 209, 210
Shilling, Ivy, 216
Shirley, Lieutenant Colonel H.J., 124, 215, 217, 218, 219, 224, 268
Shirley, Lieutenant Colonel W., 123, 124, 160, 161, 162, 165, 178, 219, 290
Shirley, Mrs Herbert, 189
Shorncliffe, xx, 218, 219, 281
Short, Sir Frank, 30, 32
Sieveking, Lance, 263
Silcock, Lieutenant A., 120, 213
Simmons, Private, 268
Simple, Peter, 205
Sims, Charles, 33
Sitwell, Osbert, 136
Skeats, Leonard F., 309
Skinner, Lieutenant, 172, 173
Smalley, Bill, 236
Smirke, Sydney, 25
Smith, Second Lieutenant Ernest Kennedy, 146, 147, 152
Smith, A.R., 293
Smith, Arnold, 216
Smith, Private E. Findlay, 163, 164
Smith, Corporal G.W., 242
Smith, Ian, 282
Smith, Captain Quartermaster J.A. 'Jacko', 142, 198, 199
Smith, Corporal Montague, 165
Smith, M. Pollock, 272
Smith, Sergeant, 127
Smith, RQMS H.R. 'Smithy', 241, 242, 247, 251, 268, 290, 292, 293
Smith, Private W., 268
Smith-Dorrien, General Horace, 84
Smoking concerts, 50, 63, 67, 69, 73, 90, 104, 126, 142, 146, 193, 208, 222, 259, 263
Smyly, Cecil, 246
Smyly, C.F., 216, 236, 251
Smyth, Montague, 165, 166, 309
Soldier's Pocket Book, 103, 105, 118
Solomon, H., 236
Solomon, S.J., 50
Somerset House, 19, 20, 21, 244
Somme, Battle of, 135, 154, 159, 172, 206
Speaight, Robert, 209

Special Reserve, 93, 94, 95
Spencer, Douglas, 162
Spencer, Earl, xxiii
St Ghislain, 185
St John's Wood Clique, 7, 14, 102, 305, 306, 312
St Mary's Bay holiday camp, 277, 279, 281
St Omer, 115, 117, 131, 142, 143, 144, 145, 146, 155, 163, 190, 195
St Pol, 167, 184
Stacey, Colonel, 49
Städelsches Kunstinstitut, 41
Staley, David C., 310
Stallard, Dr. Henry, 264, 268
Standing, Herbert, 51
Standring, Sergeant B.A., 120
Stanhope, Spencer, 3, 8
Star Shells, 126, 208
Stathcona, Lord, 260
Statute of Westminster, xiii
Steinle, Jacob Eduard von, 41, 42
Stephenson, Peter, 277
Sterling Club, 1
Sterling, Edward C., 1, 2, 3, 7, 310
Sterndale-Bennett, Thomas C., 209, 216
Stevens, F.G., 22
Stewart, Private J.R., 120
Stirling, A.M.W., 325
Stirling, Antoinette, 51
Stirling, Lieutenant Colonel David, 297
Stocken, F.A., 243, 252
Stocks, Arthur, 49, 310
Stokes, Adrian, 310
Stokes, Captain Walter, 172
Stone, Marcus, 29, 49
Store, R.F., 236
Stothard, Thomas, 21
Strang, William, 30
Strathcona, Lord, 260, 267, 296
Stratton, Eugene, 50
Strawson, Private F.M., 120
Street, G.E., 6
Stromberg, 79
Strube, Sidney C., 162, 201, 310
Suffragettes, 30
Sugden, Harold D., 262
Sullivan, Sir Arthur, 49, 242
Sweet, L.K., 236
Swinburne, Algernon, 3, 8, 102
Swing Riots, xvi

Talfourd, Field, 2, 310
Tank, 159, 160

Tanner, Lieutenant, 267, 268
Taylor, Chevallier, 50
Taylor, Private, 268
Taylor, Sergeant, 245
Tenniel, 50
Tennyson, Alfred Lord, xviii, 1, 5, 23
Territorial and Reserve Forces Bill, 94
Territorial Force (TF), 90, 92, 94, 95, 96, 97
Terry, Edward, 51
Terry, Ellen, 5
Tetley, J.C.D., 264
Thackeray, Lance Corporal Lance, 164, 165, 310
Thackeray, William Makepeace, 8, 42
Thackwell, Private H., 251
The Artistics, 126, 208
The Badminton Club, 73
The Baggage Guard, 16, 89, 90, 103
The Boyhood of Raleigh, 3, 27
The Garden of the Hesperides, 46
The Germ, 23
The Green Book, xx
The Grey Book, 53, 54, 105
The Hydra, 136
The Light of the World, 4
The Monarch of the Glen, 24
The Reformers, 76
The War, xix
The Young Men of the Tribe of Benjamin Seizing their Brides, 22
They All Love Jack, 12, 81
Thomas, Bert, 162, 201, 311
Thomas, Brandon, 50, 51, 68, 69, 70, 87, 106, 155
Thomas, Edward, 202, 203, 204
Thomas, Percy, 262
Thomas, Captain W.H., 155
Thompson, Captain, 123
Thorne, Major General A.F.A.N., 276
Thornycroft, Hamo, 27, 49, 311
Thorpe, James, 163, 164
Thorpe, J.N., 207
Thwaites, Major General Sir William, 222, 223
Toms, Peter, 18
Toole, J.L., 49
Toutencourt Woods, 179, 191
Tower of London, 110, 114, 123, 199, 214
Trained Bands, xiv, xv
Transvaal, 68, 75, 76, 77, 78, 83, 85
Travers, Lance Sergeant H.C., 64
Treaty of Vereeniging, 86

Trebelli, 51
Tree, Beerbohm, 87
Trigwell & Co., 64
Trollope, Anthony, 7
Tubbs, Carrie, 208
Tucker, Lieutenant, 268
Tucker, W.E., 264
Tupper, Martin, xix, 23
Turnbull, Captain R.F., 193, 194, 215, 235
Turner, General, 87
Turner, Sergeant H., 64
Turner, J.M.W., 22, 35
Turner, John B., 2
Turner, Joseph, 24
Turton, Miss W., 189
Tyer, Captain Austin A., 200, 236

Uitlanders, 68, 76, 78
Underdown, Robert L.L., 3
United Arts Force, 31
United Arts Rifles, 209
Urquart, Major General R.E., 296

Van Maurik, Private E.H., 268, 273, 277
Vann, Lieutenant Bernard W., 316
Vasari, Georgio, 23
Venables, Lance Corporal A.L., 207
Venables, Janet, 189
Veterans' Company, 227, 252, 266, 292
Victory March (1919), 213
Vimy Ridge, 174
Volunteer Act, 1863, xxi
Volunteer forces, xv
Volunteers, xviii
Voortrekkers, 75
Voyle, Gladys, 216

Waetzig, John G., 3
Wagg, Arthur, 72, 215
Wagg, Edward, 72
Wale, Samuel, 18
Walker, Frederick, 311
Wallace, Private J.R., 120
Waller, 50
Wallis, Sir Barnes, 125, 290, 303
Wallis, Charles F., 163
Walters, Glyn, 213
Walters, Lance Corporal Ivor, 207
Walwyk, Captain E. Van, 217, 219, 227, 232, 235, 243, 251, 258, 259
Ware, Samuel, 26
Waterhouse John William, 311
Waterlow, Sir Ernest, 311

Watts, George Frederick, 2, 4, 5, 10, 11, 27, 29, 30, 311
Watts, I, 213
Way, Thomas R., 311
Webb, Sir Aston, 32, 311
Webb, Philip, 6
Webber, Captain T.J.B., 224, 227
Webber, Major, 244
Webber, P., 298
Wellington, Duke of, xvi, xviii, 31
Wells, Private Denys G., 164, 166
Wells, H.G., 136
Welsh Ridge, 172, 175
West London School of Art, 2
West, Benjamin, 18, 20, 21, 32
West, Private F., 120
West, Captain W.G., 215
Westminster, Duke of, xxiii
Whall, Christopher W., 311
Wheatley, John, 163, 164, 311
Wheeler, Charles, 37
When did you last see your father?, 27
Whistler, James, 8, 39, 45, 50
White, A. Charles, 3
White, Sir Bruce, 290, 291
White, Sir George, 79
White, Private L.S., 120
White, Major, 155
White, R.G.J., 246, 251
Whittingham, Private, 268
Widdop, A.N., 207
Wigan, Alfred, 2
Wild Oats, 228
Wild Oats (Second Crop), 228
Wildash, John, 311
Wilhelm II, Kaiser, 91
Wilkins, William, 21
Wilkinson, Revd. A.E., 294, 295
Wilkinson, C.T.A., 207
Wilkinson, Lieutenant Colonel H.G., 178
Willans, H.J., 247
Willans, Lieutenant Colonel Harry, 120, 223, 224, 228, 232, 233, 234, 235, 239, 240, 244, 246, 247, 250, 251, 252, 264, 267, 291
William IV, 12, 21, 22
Williams, 171
Williams, E.F., 236
Williams, Captain Gordon, 170

Williams, Hubert, 261, 311
Williams, Private R., 207
Williams, Private T., 207
Williamson, Miss H., 269
Willis, Captain, 160
Willis, Private, 268
Willis, Private S.G.E., 242
Wilson, Miss M., 189
Wilton, Joseph, 18, 20
Winters, Private J.W., 120
Wirgman, Theodore B., 312
Wisques, 146
Witheries, 184
Wollen, W.B., 32, 312
Wolseley, General Viscount, 47, 49, 53, 103, 105, 107, 118
Wood, Wilfred, 312
Woods, Henry, 32, 312
Woolner, Thomas, 22
Wornum, Private T.H., 120
Wyler, 180
Wyllie, W.L., 24, 32
Wynfield, Captain D.W., 14, 102, 103, 312
Wyon, Alfred B., 312
Wyon, F.W., 2, 12
Wyon, J.W., 12
Wyon, William, 21

Ye Crooked Crusader, 228
Yeames, W.F., 49, 312
Yeo, Richard, 18
Yeomanry, xvi
Yeomanry and Volunteer Consolidation Act of 1804, the, xix
Yewdall, Private Mark, 171
Yockney, Colour Sergeant H.C., 64
Young, Captain, 184
Young, Corporal, 268
Young, Fergus, 182
Young, H.H., 145
Young, R.H., 251
Youth Will be Served, 228
Ypres, 32, 117, 152, 164, 167, 169, 171, 177
Ypres Salient, 117
Ytres-Bus-le-Transloy, 179
Yvrench, 160